John Henry Ne[wman]

A Very English Saint

Oriel Portrait by George Richmond

John Henry Newman

A Very English Saint

Peter M. Chisnall

GRACEWING

A version of this book first published 2001 by St Paul Publications

This new revised edition published 2010

Gracewing
2 Southern Avenue
Leominster
Herefordshire HR6 0QF

ISBN 978 0 85244 683 6

Typeset by Action Publishing Technology Ltd, Gloucester GL1 5SR

Contents

Preface   vii
Foreword   xi
Acknowledgements   xiii
List of Illustrations   xiv

Chapter 1: Newman – The Early Years   1
Chapter 2: The Oxford Movement   16
Chapter 3: Littlemore and Conversion   63
Chapter 4: Oratorianism comes to England   92
Chapter 5: 'The Cultivation of the Mind'   132
Chapter 6: The Challenge of Controversy   185
Chapter 7: 'Champion of the Laity'   235
Chapter 8: Newman – The Later Years   256
Chapter 9: Sainthood   286

Bibliography   298
Index   308

The Letters and Diaries of John Henry Newman are identified as follows: LD. Volume No. Page No. Date of Letter.

Preface

Several excellent and extensive biographies of John Henry Newman have been written and are listed in the bibliography. The aim of this book is to focus on specific aspects of Newman's life, during which he fearlessly challenged traditional beliefs and attitudes in both the Church of England and, later, the Roman Catholic Church, of which he became a member when almost halfway through his long life, spanning virtually the whole of the Victorian era.

Throughout the succeeding chapters, this strong historical base is maintained, enriched by dedicated study of the thirty-one volumes of Newman's *Letters and Diaries*, now fully published, and amplified by selective study of the secondary data.

Chapter 1 discusses Newman's family background, early education, spiritual crises and illnesses, from which emerged a conviction that his life was destined to be dedicated to serving God. In the next chapter, Newman is seen to have sought to reinvigorate the Church of England, notably through the development of what became known as the Oxford Movement, with publication of the historic *Tracts*, of which he contributed the majority, as well as giving the influential series of *University Sermons* in St Mary's, Oxford. After deep deliberation, Newman retired to Littlemore and to dedicated prayer. As noted in Chapter 3, he finally decided to become a Roman Catholic. Cardinal Wiseman was a significant influence on Newman's eventually taking the path to Rome, and to the founding of an Oratory in Birmingham.

Chapter 4 shows how Newman, now nearly fifty years of age, a Catholic priest and Oratorian, tackled the challenges of founding and leading a new religious venture in Protestant England. His problems were made more stressful by some members of his community, including Fr Frederick Faber and his group of 'Wilfridians'. Even in such testing times, Newman maintained his regular flow of spiritual discourses to 'mixed congregations'. Further anxieties resulted from Faber's plans to found an Oratory in London, and led to a distressing series of misunderstandings.

Notable among Newman's achievements was the founding of a Catholic University in Ireland, to benefit Catholics who were virtually cut off from higher education because Rome had forbidden them to study at Trinity College or at the 'Queen's Colleges'. Archbishop Paul Cullen had invited Newman to head this new venture, which was to prove to be an almost unsupportable burden. Newman's short-lived involvement in Ireland resulted, however, in three notable activities in Dublin which are now part of its cultural heritage: University College (UCD), the University Church in St Stephen's Green, and the seminal series of *Dublin Discourses* given at the Rotunda in 1852, from which the celebrated *The Idea of a University* originated.

As seen in Chapter 6, Newman, almost throughout his adult life, was engaged in controversial issues, some of which – like the notorious Achilli case, and the unexpected controversy with Charles Kingsley – caused him considerable concern. However, the latter dispute motivated Newman to write the acclaimed *Apologia pro Vita Sua*.

In Chapter 7: 'Champion of the Laity', Newman's long-standing of the vital role of an educated laity in the Church is emphasised. In higher education, spiritual values should be recognized. The supremacy of conscience was declared to be of paramount importance. Newman perceived the Oratorian way of life as appealing to educated men, enabling them to develop their combined talents in their priestly vocations.

Newman conducted a remarkable correspondence with an exceptionally wide variety of people: prelates, politicians, old Anglican friends, etc. He regarded the writing of letters as an important part of his pastoral duties. His *Letters and Diaries* reveal his aptitude to express the same ideas to different correspondents.

Only towards the end of his life was Newman made a cardinal by Pope Leo XIII, who declared: 'I always had a cult for him.' Newman died on Monday, 11 August, 1890; he had chosen for his memorial tablet in Birmingham Oratory this inscription: *Ex umbris et imaginibus in veritatem* (Out of shadows and images into truth).

The final chapters reveal Newman's willingness to challenge

conventional views on some aspects of sainthood, and also the cult of saints in public worship over the centuries. Newman's Cause was opened in Birmingham in 1958, and, in 1991, he was declared 'Venerable' by Pope John Paul II, who had stated his long-held and dedicated interest in Cardinal Newman. After extended scrutiny of the medical evidence of a 'miraculous cure', presented by the Procurator of the Cause, the 'positive findings' of the Roman panel were placed before Pope Benedict XVI, who, in July 2009, signed a formal declaration conferring the title of 'Blessed' on Cardinal Newman.

Peter M. Chisnall

Foreword

John Henry Newman has not lacked biographers and commentators and sometimes one thinks that the market for publications on Newman may have reached 'saturation point'. Yet crowded as the field of Newman scholarship has become, the interest and demand for books and information on Newman has increased, is increasing, and seems bound to increase, given the current expectations raised as to his impending beatification and possible future canonization. Therefore, the need for a popular introduction and work of synthesis to Newman scholarship for the non-specialist was never greater than it is today. Professor Chisnall has provided just such a work. While it is not primarily a study of Newman as a thinker or writer, he has produced an admirably balanced and exhaustive biographical survey of Newman's long life and religious journey, with all its drama and vicissitudes. Chisnall does full justice to Newman the controversialist and champion of the laity, as well as to his reputation as preacher, theologian, hymn writer, and educationalist. Full weight is given to Newman's formative Oxford and Anglican years, of which his Catholic life and Oratorian ministry (which forms the major component of this study) was in so many ways a fulfilment.

Professor Chisnall's study is underpinned by a very secure analysis of the extant printed sources, notably the large and now (almost) complete run of the series of Newman's *Letters and Diaries*, the originals of which are largely (though by no means completely) to be found in the Newman archives at the Birmingham Oratory. The great strength of Chisnall's work is his mastery of, and extensive citations from, the vast *corpus* of Newman's extant letters. Newman himself would have fully approved of this approach, being convinced that 'a

man's life lies in his letters'. Some commentators on Newman hardly
let him 'speak', so anxious are they to parade their own interpretations
and to make Newman 'relevant' (such as being an apparent precursor
of Vatican II). In happy contrast to this approach, Professor Chisnall
through a full, though judicious, use of quotation from Newman's
letters, allows the reader to catch something of Newman's authentic
voice during the many controversies in which he was involved during
his long and sometimes painful religious journey. Newman's was
indeed a pilgrim life. Chisnall's study chronicles that pilgrimage at
every twist and turn in the road.

Peter Nockles
October 2009

Acknowledgements

I am indebted to those who have given me advice and encouragement during my research and writing activities, and I recall with special gratitude the late Gerard Tracey, who for many years was the highly regarded archivist of the Birmingham Oratory, and whose deep knowledge of Cardinal John Henry Newman was generously available to all who sought his expertise. I am also grateful to the Fathers of the Birmingham Oratory for permission to publish the illustrations in this book, and to Dr Francis J. M. McGrath, Editor of the *Letters and Diaries of John Henry Newman*, who kindly arranged for this co-operation. I also thank, in particular, Dr Peter Nockles, of the John Rylands Library, in the University of Manchester; David Sheehy, Archivist, Archdiocese of Dublin, and Father Liam Rigney, Archdiocese of Dublin, also Mr Peter Jennings. I should also like to thank the editorial and publishing staff of my publishers, and Mrs Lynn Dalton, whose computer skills were so helpfully given.

List of Illustrations

p. ii   Oriel Portrait by George Richmond
p. 55   Bust of Newman by Sir Richard Westmacott
p. 77   Newman and Ambrose St John in Rome, 1847
p. 104   The house at Litttlemore: Newman's rural retreat
p. 126   View across the Hagley Road of the Oratory House,
            Birmingham.
p. 295   Pope Leo XIII

*All illustrations are reproduced by kind permission of the Fathers of
the Birmingham Oratory*

Chapter 1

Newman – The Early Years

John Henry Newman was born on 21 February 1801 in the City of London, and was to be the eldest of six children. He had two brothers: Charles Robert (born 1802) and Francis William (born 1805), and also three sisters: Harriett (born 1803), Jemima (born 1808) and Mary (born 1809). His mother Jemima, née Fourdrinier, was the daughter of a French Huguenot family of paper manufacturers who had settled in England after the revocation of the Edict of Nantes (1685) by Louis IV of France in 1585.[1] Newman's father John, whose family came from Cambridgeshire, had married when he was thirty-three and his bride was twenty-eight. 'They were a well-matched pair and devoted to each other.'[2] He became a partner in the London-based bank of Ramsbottom, Newman and Ramsbottom of 72 Lombard Street, one of the many private banks that were busily engaged in meeting the growing demand for financial services from governments, industry, commerce and consumers both at home and abroad.

In those prosperous years the Newman family lived in some style, with a house in Bloomsbury and a country retreat near Richmond. But this serene existence was shattered in early March 1816 when the bank ceased trading, a fate shared by many other banks during the difficult trading period following the Napoleonic wars. However, all the Newman's bank depositors were paid so bankruptcy was avoided; this settlement clearly remained in Newman's mind all his life, as reflected in a letter, dated 9 June 1882, to Thomas Mozley: 'My father's bank never failed. It stopped – but paid by the end of the month its creditors in full.'[3] In his private diary, Newman noted that the bank had 'paid its creditors in full, but the effort involved his father personally in difficulties which ended in his premature decay and death'.[4] (The

widely spread banking crash had also affected the bank of William
Manning – the father of Henry Edward, the future Cardinal – and
resulted in bankruptcy.)

The former banking partners of Newman's father also had extensive
brewery interests, and they introduced him to one of their friends who
owned a brewery in Alton, Hampshire. He was given charge of this
enterprise but, lacking business skills, was not successful in his unac-
customed occupation and, in late 1819, he moved his family back to
London. In Meriol Trevor's words: 'he lost confidence in life and was
never again to succeed in any undertaking'.[5] Sadly, after another
unsuccessful venture, he was declared bankrupt on 1 November 1821,
and all the family possessions had to be sold. Throughout these tribulations, the family, although shattered, maintained their constancy and
Newman's father kept a strong interest in his eldest son's early
schooling at Ealing where he came under the benign 'influence of the
Reverend Walter Mayers of Pembroke College, Oxford, one of the
classical masters from whom he received deep religious impressions,
at the time Calvinist in character, which were to him the beginning of
a new life'.[6] So, these formative years of Newman's education,
between the ages of seven and fifteen, were virtually completed before
the calamitous series of events which followed from the bank failure.

In December 1816 – two months off his sixteenth birthday –
Newman was entered as a commoner at Trinity College. However, he
did not take up residence until the following June and, in May 1818,
he gained a Trinity scholarship and was elected a scholar for nine
years at £60 per annum. During these early years at Trinity, Newman
met John William Bowden, with whom he developed a warm friendship through their academic studies and, later, with the Oxford Movement. He confided to his mother: 'Bowden is certainly an excellent
man to study with.'[7] His family correspondence and private journal
indicate his diligence and the 'high expectations' of his tutors, as well
as reflecting that he was becoming 'half conscious of some mental or
moral change' within himself.[8]

As late as November 1820, Newman assured his father that, despite
the 'anxious declaration' of his mother, he was not 'very anxious'
although he would 'not deny' that he had moments of terror', otherwise he was 'cool and in spirits', and thought he might 'attain a first
class in Mathematics and a second in Classics'.[9]

He was, however, reassured by his friend Bowden, who had already
passed well in mathematics, that he also, would do well in his exam-

inations. In only a few days, these optimistic expectations were to be shattered; Newman failed in Mathematics and achieved 'merely an "under-the-line" or second in Classics'. On 1 December 1820, Newman wrote to his father: 'It is all over; and I have not succeeded. The pain it gives me to inform you and my mother of it I cannot express.' He confessed that although he had worked excessively hard at his studies, his nerves 'quite forsook me and I failed'.[10] By return, Mrs Newman replied supportively that she and his father sent their 'warmest affection', and that he should not think that they were 'disappointed or vexed'; they were 'more than satisfied' with his 'laudable efforts'. With tender maternal insights, she assured him: 'Everybody who knows you, knows your merit; and your very failure will increase the interest they feel for you.'[11]

Newman also informed the Reverend Walter Mayers, his evangelical school tutor, of his disappointing academic results: 'My failure was most remarkable. I will grant I was unwell, low-spirited, and very imperfect in my books; yet in the Schools, so great a depression came upon me, that I would do nothing. I was nervous in the extreme, a thing I had never before experienced, and did not expect, – my memory was gone, my mind altogether confused.' He concluded this honest account by reflecting that: 'I am not only enabled to believe failure to be best for me, but God had given me to see and to know it ... God is leading me through life in the way best adapted for His glory and my own salvation ...yet I have great fears of backsliding.'[12] (Seven years later Newman was to experience again severe reactions from academic overwork and also personal bereavement.)

On 5 December 1820, Newman took his BA degree: 'Of course I got a common pass, but of honours nothing; only the record that I had tried and got them not', he recorded in his private journal.[13] However, the Trinity Scholarship he had been awarded in 1818 was still open; this enabled him to continue his academic career and secure a Fellowship at Oriel College at the early age of twenty-one, despite the misgivings felt by some of his Trinity friends, who feared that he would experience yet another academic disappointment. Oriel, however, had adopted a new approach in its elections, and candidates were not assessed exclusively on their academic strengths but also on religious, ethical and social considerations, as determined by Oriel's ancient statutes. This enlightened assessment became apparent to Newman as he made tentative enquiries about his chances of securing a fellowship, when 'every barrier seems swept away'.[14]

Over the next few weeks, during which time he had bouts of depression and illness, Newman concentrated on preparing intensively for the Oriel qualifying examination, which commenced on 6 April 1822. In his journal he noted that he was 'uncommonly tired with the continual exertion of between eight and nine hours of composition', and his entry for Monday 8 April stated that he felt 'so ill' that he 'could do nothing and was obliged to walk up and down the Oriel hall'.[15] But his journal entry for Friday 12 April was of a very different tone; 'I have been elected Fellow of Oriel: Thank God, thank God.'[16] In his own triumphant words, obtaining the fellowship 'raised him from obscurity and need to competency and reputation'.[17]

A diverting insight into Newman's complex character is given by an entry in his diary which records that, following tradition, the news of his Oriel Fellowship was made personally to him by the 'Provost's Butler' who called at his lodgings in Broad Street, and was 'disconcerted' to find Newman playing his violin, which was thought rather inappropriate for a candidate for the Oriel Common Room. His 'perplexity increased' when Newman responded to the customary formal announcement of his success and 'required immediate presence' at Oriel, by merely saying '"very well" and went on fiddling', as he judged the formal language as 'savouring of impertinence'. This unexpected reaction confused the Oriel messenger who asked Newman if he had come to the wrong person, 'to which Mr Newman replied that (it) was all right'. Immediately the puzzled man had left, Newman 'flung down his instrument and dashed down stairs with all speed to Oriel College'.[18]

With obvious delight, Newman wrote to his father: 'I was *installed* (literally) Fellow of Oriel on Friday last, and have dined there ever since . . . For the first year there is no dividend – for during that time, a Fellow is only a Probationer, but his dinner (and I fancy his breakfast) is found for him.' He added that 'pupils will be great in abundance'.[19]

During this time of jubilation, Newman was also endeavouring to secure a place for his brother Francis at Oriel. In his diary entry for 24 January 1822, Newman noted that there were 'three things' for which he had been praying lately, and 'all three Thou has granted me – that I might be in the Church, that Francis might come to Oxford, and that I might have another pupil'.[20] Towards the end of the year he was able to tell his parents that Francis had 'his name put down on the Worcester books' and there was no need for them to be anxious: 'every thing will, I see it will, be very right, if only you will let me manage'.[21]

In a diary entry for 16 May 1824, Newman recorded 'that he had come to a most important determination'.[22] St Clement's Church in Oxford was to be rebuilt, and the ageing rector sought a curate to help him in the fast-growing parish 'which was likely to give much trouble'. After reflecting for several days, Newman accepted the curacy, and he was ordained an Anglican minister on Sunday 13 June 1824.[23] His parents were 'much gratified' to learn of his curacy and he assured his father that he was 'convinced it was necessary to get used to parochial duty early, and that a Fellow of a College after ten years residence in Oxford feels very awkward among poor and ignorant people'.[24] Newman tackled his parochial duties vigorously and systematically, as a letter to his father, dated 9 August 1824, reveals: 'I am more convinced than ever of the necessity of frequent visiting the poorer classes – they seem so gratified at it and praise it. Nor do I visit the poor only – I mean to go all through the parish; and have already visited the shopkeepers and principal people.'[25] Two weeks later, Newman confided to his sister Harriett: 'My parish has given little *trouble* at present, though I must *expect* much. I have gone through from house to house.' However, he admitted that: 'Two sermons [a week] are rather a drain upon my head – but time (I trust) will accustom me to it.'[26]

For some time, Newman's father had been ailing: he never seemed to have recovered from the shock of losing his assured position as a banking partner, and his subsequent inability to develop an alternative career. On 17 September 1824, Mrs Newman wrote to tell her son that his father's 'indisposition had increased' and that she felt 'it would be no longer kind to keep' him 'in ignorance of this sad illness'.[27] In his diary for 19 September, Newman wrote: 'Alas, my Father is very ill ... Francis says he fancies he shall never get better.'[28] On 25 September, Newman 'went to town by the night coach' to see his father who was now gravely ill. During that week, the rest of the Newman family came to pray and say their sad farewells. On Wednesday 29 September 1824, Newman recorded: 'at a quarter-to-ten last night my dear Father ceased to breath';[29] and on 6 October, his diary entry mournfully recorded: 'Performed the last sad duties to my dear Father. When I die, shall I be followed to the grave by my children? My Mother said the other day she hoped to live to see me married, but *I* think that I shall either die within a College walls or as a missionary in a foreign land – no matter where, so that I die in Christ.'[30] But, as Meriol Trevor acutely observed: 'and when Mr Newman died, not yet sixty, leaving John the only earning member of the family, the prospect of dying a Missionary in a foreign land became extremely unlikely'.[31]

On the death of his father, Newman, as the eldest son, took over the responsibilities of head of the family, a role which he fulfilled with marked commitment. The Oriel Fellowship, which he had secured in 1822, together with the coaching fees from private pupils, had enabled him to finance Francis, who was to be awarded a double-first degree in 1826, to be followed by election to a Fellowship at Balliol College. But their brother Charles proved to be a continual source of anxiety. After their father's death, he abandoned Christianity, resigned from a position in the Bank of England – which his brother John had been able to secure for him – and became dependent on the generosity of John and Francis. Despite continuous fraternal support, this 'unrepentant prodigal'[32] displayed distressingly erratic and ungrateful behaviour, mostly towards his relations. On his death in 1884, his eldest brother paid for his tomb.[33]

Newman's three sisters: Harriett, Jemima and Mary, together with his widowed mother, were constantly in his thoughts, as his *Letters and Diaries* show. As well as providing regular financial help, he took a strong interest in the intellectual development of his sisters, as his correspondence discloses. But Newman's tribulations were to be tragically increased by the unexpected death, on 5 January 1828, of his youngest sister Mary, just after her nineteenth birthday.[34] Almost fifty years later, he was to write: 'October 23rd 1887, I have vivid feelings of love, tenderness and sorrow, when I think of dear Mary, as ever I had since her death.' He had always held her in 'great affection', and had a presentiment for some time that she would not live long. 'I thought I loved her too well, and hardly ever dared to take my full swing of enjoyment in her dear company.'[35]

After Mary's premature death, Mrs Newman and her remaining two daughters moved to Iffley, where they lived from 1830 to 1836. Though Newman cared deeply for his mother and sisters, he began to feel that having them so close to him at Oxford was 'a mistake', and it made him 'realize more acutely his intellectual and spiritual estrangement from them'.[36] His university and pastoral work was 'engrossing' and, inevitably, also restricted the time he could spend with them.

But this 'close intimacy' with his family was to be broken in 1836 with the marriage of Jemima, his second sister, to John Mozley, a prosperous printer and banker in Derby, on 28 April, a union warmly approved by Mrs Newman. Sadly, she was to collapse suddenly and die on 17 May. After a few months – 27 September – Harriett married Thomas Mozley, the elder brother of John Mozley, who had become Newman's pupil at Oriel. With Newman's support, Thomas had secured the living of Chalderton in Wiltshire, although earlier Mrs Newman had disapproved of the prospective marriage, presumably because a parson's stipend compared unfavourably with that of a successful businessman.

Unlike Jemima, Harriett tended to lack sympathetic understanding of her eldest brother's complex religious developments, including the Tractarian Movement. Her strong feelings were, sadly, increased when, to her deep concern, Tom Mozley became involved with Tractarianism, and succeeded Newman as editor of the *British Critic* in 1841. Harriett was further irritated because of Newman's counselling of her husband when he faced the dilemma of possibly resigning his rectorship and converting to Roman Catholicism. What she termed her husband's attack of 'Roman fever'[37] seems to have been at the root of her decision to break off all fraternal relationships with her brother. However, Tom Mozley's 'fever' did not persist and he remained in the Church of England. Harriett died, unreconciled to her brother, in 1879. Many years later – 1890 – and in the last year of Newman's life, Grace Mozley, the only child of Harriett and Tom Mozley, called on Newman at the Birmingham Oratory. The last time they had met was in 1843, when she was a four-year-old child. Jemima, who died in 1879, remained on friendly terms with her brother John throughout her life.[38]

Spiritual Crises and Illnesses

From an early age, spiritual crises and illnesses were closely connected in Newman's life; they marked turning-points in his spiritual and intellectual progression.

In his *Autobiographical Writings*, he records that he had 'three great illnesses' in his life. 'the first keen, terrible one, when I was a boy of fifteen, and it made me a Christian ... My second, not painful, but tedious and shattering was that I had, in 1827, when I was one of the Examining Masters, and it too broke me off from

an incipient liberalism – and determined my religious course'. The
third illness 'was in 1883, when I was in Sicily, before the
commencement of the Oxford Movement'.[39]

His first illness and 'the experience before and after, awful and
known only to God', were, as Newman described later, the beginning
of a new life.[40] He denied, however, that his was a typical Evangelical conversion and, by January 1817, he was challenging some traditional Calvinist doctrines. He regarded Calvinist predestination as a
'detestable doctrine'. But the religious truths which he had imbibed
from this early evangelical teaching proved to be indelible influences
throughout his life.

Gilley has declared that: 'The Calvinist experience of conversion
was the beginning of Newman's mature devotional life; the dogmas of
Calvinism were the beginning of his intellectual life'.[41]

An entry in Newman's private diary for June/July 1821, records:

> I speak of [the process of] conversion with great diffidence, being obliged
> to adopt the language of books. For my own feelings, as far as I can
> remember, were so different from any account I have ever read, that I
> dare not go by what *may* be an individual case.[42]

Five years later, Newman was to return to the issue of conversion by
stating that, in his case, his 'feelings were not *violent*, but a returning
to, a renewing of, principles, under the *power* of the Holy Spirit,
which I had *already* felt, and in a measure acted on, when young'.[43]

But, as Avery Dulles has stressed, this does not mean that 'even in
Newman's case' conversion did not involve 'the renunciation of
certain beliefs he had once held'. Such beliefs would have been
regarded as expendable: 'they could not have been certitudes' which
by their nature are irreversible.[44]

During this first experience of religious conversion, Newman
confirmed his 'mistrust of the reality of material phenomena': he
'rested' in the 'thought of two and two only absolute and luminously
self-evident beings, myself and my creator'. Another 'deep imagination' possessed him in the autumn of 1816: 'that it would be the will
of God that I should lead a single life'. He felt that his vocation in life
'would require such a sacrifice as celibacy'.[45] Trevor comments that
'this element in his conversion was anathema to the Protestant Evangelicals of the day'.[46]

In the *Apologia*, Newman stated that he had formed no religious
convictions until he reached the age of fifteen, although he had a

'perfect knowledge of the Catechism'. But a 'great change of thought' the occurred and he fell under the influence of a definite creed as the result of conversations and sermons of the Reverend Walter Mayers at his Ealing school. This 'excellent man' put into Newman's hands 'all the school of Calvin' and was, Newman declared, 'the human means of this beginning of divine faith' in him. In particular he noted the doctrine of final perseverance which led to his 'inward conversion'.[47] Later, in the *Apologia*, Newman stressed that 'From the age of fifteen, dogma had been the fundamental principle of my religion; I know no other religion; I cannot enter into the idea of any sort of religion; religion, as a mere sentiment, is to me a dream and a mockery.'[48]

The second 'great illness' referred to by Newman resulted from severe overwork and also personal bereavement. As a tutor at Oriel, to which post he had been appointed at the early age of twenty-one, he had undertaken an onerous load of academic duties. He collapsed when acting as a Public Examiner and, on his doctor's advice, was leeched on his temples. Following this stringent traditional treatment, Robert Wilberforce, second son of William Wilberforce the philanthropist, and a close friend of Newman, took him away for a short holiday.[49]

Further medical consultation determined that Newman was suffering from 'overexertion of the brain, with a disordered stomach', as he recorded in his private journal.[50] He was obliged to extend his enforced absence from Oxford and in early December returned home. Newman's stressful condition was to be poignantly deepened by the sudden death of his youngest sister, Mary.

The third significant illness – which was almost fatal – occurred when Newman was travelling in Sicily. In December 1832, he accompanied Richard Hurrell Froude (who was to make a major contribution to the Oxford Movement) and his father, Archdeacon Froude, on a tour of the Mediterranean which, it was hoped, would improve Hurrell's health. The voyage was 'entirely uneventful';[51] Newman's thoughts were fixed on England and what was happening there. In company with the Froudes he had visited Wiseman at the English College in Rome on 9 April 1833 and, when the latter had suggested that they might visit Rome again, Newman 'with great gravity' replied: 'We have work to do in England.'[52] While on his travels he pondered deeply over the direction which his life should take.

However, his views on the 'Romanist system' remained unchanged. 'A union with Rome, which is what it is, is impossible: it is a dream.

As to the individual members of the cruel church, who can have but love and feeling for them? There is so much amiableness and gentleness, so much Oxonianism, (so to say) such as an amusing and interesting demureness, and such simplicity of look and speech, that I feel for those indeed who are bound with an iron chain, which cripples their energies and (one would think) makes their devotion languid.'[53] In a long letter to his sister Jemima, Newman again expressed the distressful perceptions he held of the Catholic Church: 'Oh that Rome were not Rome; but I seem to see as clear as day that a union with her is *impossible*. She is the cruel Church – asking of us impossibilities, excommunicating us for disobedience, and now watching and exulting over our approaching overthrow.'[54]

Newman parted company with the Froudes on 9 April 1883 and sailed for 'Naples with Sicily as his objective'.[55] His ambitious travels were to end in an appalling sequence of illnesses, including typhoid fever, from which he almost died. To everyone's surprise he survived and his health greatly improved. He came to regard this prolonged period as a 'purifying illness, preparing him for his mission in England'.[56] On his return journey to England, Newman's ship was becalmed in the Straits of Bonifacio, during which time he wrote 'the lines "Lead, Kindly Light" which have since become well known'.[57] These entreating words form the opening lines of the poem 'The Pillar of the Cloud', which has been widely adopted as a hymn.

Until virtually the end of his life, Newman's correspondence contained references to 'Lead, Kindly Light', and publishers asked for permission to include it in a collection of hymns.[58] Yet Newman agreed with the publisher Edward Bickersteth 'that these verses are not a Hymn, nor are they suitable for singing, and it is that which at once surprises and gratifies me, and makes me thankful that in spite of their having no claim to be used as a hymn, they have made their way into so many collections'.[59]

When, many years later, a Hastings doctor, who had once been one of Newman's churchwardens at St Mary's, Oxford, inquired about the exact meaning of the last two lines of 'Lead, Kindly Light' (*And with the morn those angel faces smile/which I have loved long since, and lost awhile*), Newman pleaded that after nearly fifty years he was 'not bound to *remember* my own meaning. Anyhow there must be a statute of limitations for writers of Verse' who should not be expected to give a detailed account of the 'transient thoughts' which came to them 'when homesick or seasick or in any other way sensitive or excited'.[60]

But to an 'Unknown Correspondent', Newman confided that 'one of the pregnant meanings of "Lead, Kindly Light" is 'contained in the words *One step enough for me*. Beyond that step is the province simply of Faith'.[61] Newman never tires, as Ker says, of repeating the biblical injunction for 'unreserved obedience' to God's Will.[62]

Vocational Commitments

During his first influential illness Newman felt that God was calling him to dedicate himself to serving Him, and that this should entail a celibate vocation. The belief that he should 'lead a single life' was held firmly, as he says in the *Apologia*, except for very brief periods up to 1829, but after this he never wavered. He noted that this calling 'strengthened my feeling of separation from the visible world'.[63] In Maisie Ward's opinion, Newman was 'by nature a bachelor, by grace a celibate'. She adds, however, that his 'attitude upon celibacy in general was misunderstood by some of his most intimate friends'.[64]

In a letter to Jemima, he assured her that:

> I am full of work as usual ... I am not more lonely than I have been in a long while. God intends me to be lonely. He has so framed my mind that I am in great measure beyond the sympathies of other people and thrown upon Himself ... God, I trust in supporting me in following whither He leads.[65]

Ian Ker has observed that celibacy was considered by Newman to be 'a spiritual ideal as opposed to a pragmatic convenience' which provided freedom from marital responsibilities. It impelled the celibate towards total commitment to God's service.[66] Gilley also notes that Newman's commitment to celibacy was an intrinsic part of his personal dedication to God, but he concedes that Newman was for a time under the influence of Hurrell Froude and sometimes seemed to have disparaged marriage, although there is no proof that he was a misogynist.[67] He had, in fact, a circle of women – including his mother and sisters – with whom he kept up a regular correspondence concerned with a wide range of topics apart from family news. He frequently discussed, at considerable length, sophisticated concepts of religious dogma and observance with them.

Newman's willingness to discuss the appropriateness of celibacy for Anglican clerics is evident in correspondence with George Ryder, son of the Bishop of Lichfield and who had been one of Froude's students.

He sought Newman's assurances that he could marry and also pursue a vocation in the Church of England. Newman's reply was both positive and pragmatic:

> It is quite absurd to suppose that you are not at *liberty* both to marry and go into the Church – indeed I think that country parsons ought, as a general rule, to be married – celibate is a high state of life, to which the multitude of men cannot aspire – I do not say, that they who adopt it are necessarily better than others, though the noblest ethos is situated in that state.

But Newman gave his opinion that he thought Ryder too young too marry and was 'most likely to make a bad choice'.[68] About four years later, Newman confided to his close friend Frederic Rogers: 'parsons' wives ... are useful in a parish, and that in a way no *man* can rival them'.[69]

In an entry in his private journal, date 25 March 1840, Newman reflected on who might conceivably be interested in reading accounts of his illnesses and experiences in Sicily: 'Whom have I, whom can I have, who would take an intrest in it?' He thought that perhaps Henry Wilberforce might, but he wondered when he should ever see him. He mused:

> This is the sort of interest which a wife takes and none but she – it is a woman's interest – and that interest, so be it, shall never be taken in me. Never, so be it, will I be other than God has found me. All my habits for years, my tendencies are towards celibacy. I could not take that interest in this world – and, above all, call it what one will, I have a repugnance to a clergyman's marrying. I do not say it is not lawful – I cannot deny the right – but, whether a prejudice or not, it shocks me.

Newman concluded his thoughts: 'and therefore I willingly give up the possession of that sympathy, which I feel is not, cannot, be granted to me'.[70]

As far back as 1829, Newman had regularly shared confidence with Jemima, and he told her that he was 'more than ever imprest with the importance of staying in Oxford for many years', and that he felt 'more strongly than ever the necessity of their being men in the Church, like the R. Catholic friars, free from all obstacles to their devoting themselves to its defence'.[71] In the same year, Newman's mother, when discussing possible places to live had, with maternal insights into her son's feelings, told him: 'I should vote for a nice little cottage with a garden *near you*, as you seem to intend to be a sort of "Monk" for some time.'[72] This intimate perception of Newman's leanings was echoed by her daughter Harriett the following year, when she wrote to her brother: 'I wish you had someone with you, poor fellow – but a monk deserves no compassion.'[73]

Newman, whose spiritual development commenced in his early years of schooling and academic life had, through prayer, personal suffering and bereavement, discovered and clarified his vocation in life. Now, still a young man whose intellectual endowments had attracted wide attention, he was about to face new challenges and conflicts in pursuit of his vocational aspirations.

The following chapters will show how readily Newman faced up to the many challenges he encountered in both the Church of England and then, virtually halfway through his long life, in the Catholic Church, which was regenerating itself after centuries of penal subjection. He relished argument; controversy fired his intellect and emotions and resulted in a wealth of writings which still stimulate discussion today. Above all else, Newman was truly a man of God, who, from his earliest years, responded to the call to dedicate himself to the service of his Creator.

Notes
 1. Newman, 1956, p. 12.
 2. Trevor, 1962, *Newman: the pillar of the cloud*, p. 7.
 3. LDXXX.94, Thomas Mozley, 9 June 1882.
 4. Newman, 1956, p. 10.
 5. Trevor, 1962, *Newman: the pillar of the cloud*, p. 15.
 6. Newman, 1956, pp. 29–30.
 7. LDI.56, 19 October 1818.
 8. Newman, 1956, pp. 46–50.
 9. LDI.92, 12 November 1820.
10. LDI.94, 1 December 1820.
11. LDI.95, 2 December 1820.
12. LDI.99, January 1821.
13. Newman, 1956, p. 52.
14. Newman, 1956, pp. 57–8.
15. Newman, 1956, p. 185.
16. Newman, 1956, p. 186.

17. Newman, 1956, p. 163; LDI.127, footnote 2.
18. Newman, 1956, p. 62.
19. LDI.134, 16 April 1822.
20. Newman, 1956, p. 198.
21. LDI.156, 5 December 1822.
22. Newman, 1956, p. 198.
23. Newman, 1956, p. 200.
24. LDI.174, 5 May 1824.
25. LDI.184, 9 August 1824.
26. LDI.186, 26 August 1824.
27. LDI.192, 17 September 1824.
28. Newman, 1956, p. 202.
29. LDI.193, 25 September 1824.
30. Newman, 1956, p. 203.
31. Trevor, 1962: *Newman: the pillar of the cloud*, p. 55.
32. Gilley, 1990, p. 56.
33. LDI.38
34. LDII.47, footnote.
35. Newman, 1956, p. 213.
36. Tristram, 1933, pp. 48–9.
37. Ker, 1988, p. 279.
38. Tristram, 1933, p. 48.
39. Newman, 1956, p. 268.
40. Newman, 1956, pp. 119–20.
41. Gilley, 1990, p. 24.
42. Newman, 1956, p. 166.
43. Newman, 1956, p. 172.
44. Ker (ed), 1997, p. 22.
45. Newman, 1993, p. 92.
46. Trevor, 1996, p. 8.
47. Newman, 1993, p. 89.
48. Newman, 1993, p. 123.
49. LDII.37, Edward Hawkins, 26 November 1827.
50. Newman, 1956, p. 212.
51. Newman, 1956, pp. 111–20.
52. Dessain, 1980, p. 33.
53. LDIII.277, J. F. Christie, 6 April 1833.
54. LDIII.284, 11 April 1833.
55. Newman, 1956, p. 111.
56. Dessain, 1980, pp. 33–4.
57. Newman, 1956, p. 119.
58. LDXXIX.363, 13 April 1881; LDXXVIII.399, 28 August 1878;
    LDXXIX.351, 25 March 1881; LDXXXV.425, 1 November 1871.
59. LDXXVII.80, 20 June 1874.
60. LDXXIX. Dr W. A. Greenhill, 18 January 1879.
61. LDXXXI.277, 30 August 1887.
62. Ker, 1991, p. 138.

63. Newman, 1993, p. 92.
64. Maisie Ward, 1948, p. 272.
65. LDV.313, 26 June 1836.
66. Ker, 1990, p. 132.
67. Gilley, 1990, pp. 19–25.
68. LDIII.70, 22 July 1832.
69. LDV.346, 30 August 1836.
70. Newman, 1956, pp. 137–8.
71. LDII.132-4, 17 March 1829.
72. LDII.177, 11 December 1829.
73. LDII.254, 16 July 1830.

Chapter 2

The Oxford Movement

One of Newman's perceptive biographers, Wilfrid Ward – whose daughter Maisie also wrote an outstanding life of Newman – declared that:

> John Henry Newman is indeed himself a remarkable instance of one of his most characteristic contentions, that the same object may be seen by different onlookers under aspects so various and partial as to make their views, from their inadequacy, appear occasionally even contradictory.[1]

There are so many facets to Newman's character. He was a dedicated scholar, an eloquent preacher, a highly talented writer, a religious poet of unusual merit, an ecclesiastical activist, a visionary and also a remarkably powerful protagonist and controversialist. One scholar who has studied Newman concludes that the mind of Newman 'is characterised not by contradictions but by supplementary strengths, so that he may be called, without inconsistency, both conservative and liberal, progressive and traditional, cautious and radical, dogmatic yet pragmatic, idealistic but realistic'.[2] The Oxford Movement, in which he played a leading and enthusiastic role, showed him to be a man of action, whose self-declared mission was 'to save the Church of England from the perils that encompassed her'.[3]

It is not surprising, therefore, to find that a man so richly endowed stirred the hearts and minds of many and thus exercised considerable influence over those who, like himself, were deeply disturbed about the position and responsibilities of the Church of England in a society which was experiencing challenges from 'liberalism' and from unrest emanating from revolutionary France. It has been noted that

In the 1830s, the Church of England was still closely enmeshed with the nation and its rulers; the great majority of English people were Christian in the sense of never having thought they were anything else.[4]

Religious faith has often been considered to have been behind the moral intensity that was a distinctive mark of the Victorian era; while church-going varied among the social classes, 'Christian values were the central values and all deep individual problems were related to Christian morals'.[5] Of course, personal moral standards were not immune from other influences, and religious beliefs tended to be uncertain in dogma. Disbelief was becoming evident and, indeed, prevalent, among intellectuals.

Newman recognized the emergence of these trends before the Church of England experienced the resurgence that became known as the 'Oxford Movement' or 'Tractarianism'. In 'coming forward as the champion of Revealed Religion', he realized fully that his real battle was with "liberalism"'[6] as 'thinking established notions worth nothing – in this system of opinions a disregard of religion is included'.[7] In an *Essay on the Development of Christian Doctrine,* Newman stressed that 'The search for truth is not the gratification of curiosity; that liberalism holds truth and falsehood in religion is merely a matter of opinion; that one doctrine is as good as another . . . that there is no truth . . . that it is enough if we sincerely hold what we profess.'[8] As Trevor puts it: 'By the term Liberalism Newman did not mean the idea of political freedom, but the notion that "one opinion is as good as another" and that there can be no objective truth in religion.'[9] When, in his advanced years, Newman came to Rome to be raised to the rank of cardinal, he made a formal speech of acceptance of the high honour in which he declared that for 'thirty, forty, fifty years I have resisted to the best of my powers the spirit of Liberalism in religion. Never did Holy Church need champions against it more sorely than now'.[10]

But religious concerns were not alone in motivating the Movement; other factors intervened, involving political and constitutional matters, as Nockles has emphasized.[11] For almost two decades Sir Robert Peel, in line with Tory policy, had stoutly opposed the principle of Roman Catholic emancipation, but later, in 1828, as Home Secretary, he changed his views in order to avert the imminent danger of civil strife in Ireland following the election of Daniel O'Connell to the Clare constituency. After this *volte-face*, Peel

formally tendered his resignation as the MP for Oxford University
stating that 'I consider myself bound to surrender to the University
without delay the trust they have confided in me.'[12] However, he
also offered himself for re-election. This led to a sharp difference
of opinion between the Provost of Oriel, Edward Hawkins, who
supported him, and the four Tutors of the College who viewed his
re-election as 'far more a question of politics and political expedi-
ency; it was a moral, and academical, an ecclesiastical nay a
religious question; not least it grew to be such with them'.[13] In a
long letter to Samuel Rickards, dated 6 February 1829, Newman
told him that the previous year the Convocation of the University
of Oxford had increased its majority from 3:1 to 2:1 against granting Roman Catholic emancipation; this is 'manly and I like it ...
It is not *pro dignatate nostra*, to have a Rat as a member'.[14]
Newman's objection, which provoked such strongly worded sentiments, lay in the fact that Peel had suddenly switched his views
on Catholic emancipation for political advantage, not because of any
convictions on the religious issues involved. To his sister Jemima
he confided that while, as she knew, he had 'no opinion about the
Catholic Question', he was concerned that the way in which it was
settled signified the 'encroachments of philosphism and indifferen-
tism on the Church'.[15]

On Peel's defeat by Sir Robert Inglis by a majority of 146 in the by-
election of 28 February, Newman exulted openly. In a letter to his
mother he declared; 'We have achieved a glorious Victory ... We
have proved the independence of the Church and of Oxford.'[16] As
Gilley comments: 'Newman's fierceness was that of a young man who
with his friends have found a cause.'[17] It seems as though there was an
almost over-eagerness by Newman and his friends to seize the opportunity offered, unintentionally, by Peel, to take a stand against those
who would seek to challenge the dominance of the Established
Church. Indeed, Nockles holds that Peel's repudiation by the University 'deserves to be regarded as an even more appropriate date for the
rise of the Oxford Movement than was Keble's Assize Sermon'.[18]

In a postscript to a letter to Samuel Rickards, Newman stated 'I
believe indeed in the doctrine of the *Genius loci*.'[19] It may have been
that this indomitable belief in the essential and unique quality of
Oxford intellectual life caused, as Maisie Ward remarked, early
writers on the Oxford Movement to see a 'special strength in the
narrowness of its scene ... like a Greek republic or an Italian city

state of the Middle Ages'. But this, she continues, 'is only partly true'. While Oxford had an 'intensive life of its own', it was 'also the intellectual centre of England; in a sense the spiritual centre. The Movement gained from Oxford its historical basis, but Oxford was not isolated'.[20] From the fertile soil of Oxonian intellectualism, enriched by profound religious commitments, grew the Movement which, according to Nockles, was to 'form a chapter in the intellectual history of nineteenth-century Europe, and was in tune with such deep cultural currents as Romanticism'.[21]

Walgrave states that Newman's convictions about the uniqueness of the Church's position in society and of the importance of its independence in fulfilling its sacred mission, derived from the influence of Dr Richard Whately, later Protestant Archbishop of Dublin, whose 'anti-Erastian views (opposing the subordination of the Church to the State) deeply coloured this thought'.[22] This seminal influence was recorded by Newman in his journal:

> On looking back, he found that one momentous truth of Revelation he had learned from Dr Whately, and that was the idea of the Christian Church as a divine appointment, and as a substantive visible body, independent of the State, and endowed with rights, prerogatives and powers of its own.[23]

From this point of view, the inviolability of the Christian Church was seen as of paramount importance in Church-State relationships. Erastianism, whose roots lay in attempts to impose State control in ecclesiastical affairs, was utterly repugnant to Newman and his associates. They recognized that, from time to time, the Church of England had suffered from what they considered to be this abuse and were determined to do all they could to rid it of this interference. Nockles has thus described the Oxford Movement as 'an anti-Erastian, moral protest against the apparently unpopular notion that the Church of England was but a human establishment, subservient to the material and secular interests of the State'.[24]

Following his third illness, and after exhausting travel, Newman eventually arrived back in England on 9 July 1833 and entered into the fast-erupting controversy over the Irish Church Temporalities Act of 1833. In a letter dated 21 February 1833, Harriett and Jemima had warned their brother of the 'strange things, public and private' which had been happening in his absence, namely 'the mad scheme of Government, and the despoiling of the poor Irish Church'.[25] The 1833

Act was introduced by the Whig Government in an attempt to rationalize the situation of the Established Church of Ireland. Two of the four archbishoprics were abolished as well as eight bishoprics: these were amalgamated with neighbouring dioceses, their stipends removed and revenues of the two wealthiest sees, Armagh and Derry, were reduced; church cess, the tax paid by Roman Catholic families as well as the Protestant minority, was abolished. Owen Chadwick records that these proposals were received in the House of Commons in a 'chilly silence'.[26] Such unwelcome legislation was viewed by many High Churchmen as rank Erastianism, which should not be tolerated. It directly challenged the traditional status and authority of an established Church; the freedom of the clergy to preach the Word of God was being imperilled. In uninhibited letters to his friends, Newman showed clearly that he was outraged by the Temporalities Act. He confessed to Thomas Morley that it had made him 'hate the Whigs . . . more bitterly than ever', and he referred to the legislation as 'the atrocious high sacrilege bill'.[27] Of Henry Wilberforce, he requested news of 'what various individuals in England think of this cursed Irish spoliation bill'.[28] In similar vein, he asked George Ryder's opinion of the 'accursed Whig spoliation bill'.[29]

It is widely admitted that the Church of Ireland in the early 1800s was in need of some fairly radical reorganization: pluralism was rife, absenteeism was common, great endowments were enjoyed by a Church which had relatively few adherents, probably just over ten per cent of the population. Although the majority of the population were Roman Catholics they had to pay local taxes to support the Established Church, which they viewed as an instrument of British colonialism. Some attempts were made to improve the administration and pastoral standards of the Church of Ireland, but these internal initiatives were inadequate on the whole and more stringent measures were deemed necessary. These were to be imposed by the 1833 Act and under the supervision of the Ecclesiastical Commission of 1835.

The furore caused by the 1833 Act was brought to a head in July 1833 by a celebrated sermon by John Keble, one of the Fellows of Oriel College, whose discussions on ecclesiastical affairs had already attracted wide attention across the University. This elite circle also included John Henry Newman, Edward Bouverie Pusey and Richard Hurrell Froude. Keble, Professor of Poetry at Oxford, was invited to preach the annual assize sermon before the University. His theme was 'National Apostasy', which he perceived as aptly describing the sacrilegious intervention by the State in the ecclesiastical concerns of the Church of Ireland. His forthright sermon on the text 'I will teach you the good and the right way', though not intended to be a call to arms was, nevertheless, a publicly declared expression of the fears felt by High Churchmen over the Whig Government's proposals for reform for the Church of Ireland.[30] Gilley, however, describes Keble's sermon as 'couched in generalities' and suggests that its use of analogies from the Old Testament would have 'delighted a Scottish Covenanter'.[31]

But Gilley also described Keble as 'the most brilliant student of his generation' who had 'resigned his Oriel tutorship in 1823 to become his father's curate at Fairford'.[32] In 1835 he became vicar of Hursley, Hampshire where he lived for thirty years. In the *Apologia*, Newman wrote touchingly of this remarkably gifted cleric, who was 'young in years, when he became a University celebrity, and younger in mind. He had the purity and simplicity of a child ... He instinctively shut up before literary display, and pomp and donnishness of manner, faults which always will beset academical notabilities'.[33]

The precise date on which the Oxford Movement was born has been the subject of debate among historians of that Movement and among Newman scholars. In his journal, Newman records that he heard the Assize Sermon on 14 July 1833 and that 'I have ever considered and kept the day as the start of the religious movement of 1833'.[34] However, Fr Henry Tristram, a leading Oratorian scholar, adds an editorial comment that Newman 'without a thought of self, assigned the credit to another. But others have assigned an earlier date as the birthday of the Movement: 22 January 1832, the day on which, in his turn as Select Preacher, he delivered the sermon *Personal Influence, the means of Propagating the Truth*. These two views are not irreconcilable with each other; Newman's sermon was an appeal for volunteers in the spiritual combat; Keble's a call to action in the political crisis that seemed to menace the Church of England.[35] Only after the Whig Government's 1833 Act did the Movement move from expressed concern to organized action.

Although Nockles considers that Peel's repudiation by the University in 1829 could be considered to mark the start of the Oxford Movement even more appropriately that Keble's sermon four years later, Vargish traces the causes of the Movement even earlier and states that 'in a large measure it was a reaction against what its leaders regarded as the corruptions of the eighteenth century'.[36]

Hurrell Froude and William Palmer – 'a dry and learned Irishman from Trinity College, Dublin'[37] – returned to Oxford after enlisting the support of Hugh James Rose, the editor of the *British Magazine*. With Newman and Keble, they drew up some guiding principles for their new movement, but not without some conflicting notions about the desirable objectives. 'Both Keble and Newman wanted the campaign to be more religious and less political than the others did.'[38] This is reflected in correspondence between Newman and his close associates.[39] Their concern was to reassert the independence of the Church and to emphasize that its authority is derived from the Apostles; these aims reflect Newman's feelings of personal responsibility and were expressed in a letter to Henry Wilberforce.[40] Fr Henry Tristram, as editor of Newman's *Autobiographical Writings*, commented on these feelings as follows:

> When he left England in December 1832, he was in a state of perplexity about his future course; when he returned in July 1833, he appeared as a man charged with a mission – a mission to save the Church of England from the perils that encompassed her.[41]

In animated correspondence with his former pupil Charles Portales Golightly, who was to foment anti-Newman feelings in connection with *Tract 90*, Newman declared: 'We have everything against us but our cause.'[42] In a later letter he disclosed that:

> We have formed a society here for the purpose of rousing the clergy ... we have decided to keep most of our views in the background at present ... to stir up our brethren to consider the state of the Church, and especially to the practical belief of preaching of the Apostolical Succession.[43]

The earliest Tracts, Owen Chadwick observes, were 'anonymous and ephemeral sheets of a few pages, privately circulated'. Newman conceived them 'not as regular troops but as sharpshooters'.[44] They have also been described as 'short clarion calls in defence of the Church's independence'.[45] The urgency of the situation spurred Newman to write the first Tract, *The Ministerial Commission*, which was an imperative call to the clergy to recognize and assert the spiritual basis of their authority, and so fulfil their own God-given role. This stirring opening to the 'Tracts for the Times' was published anonymously but its authorship was soon recognized. Newman's fiery words stressed their spiritual vocation and the Church of England's inheritance from the earliest days of Christianity, that is, from the time of the Apostles.

It was a radical assessment of the Church's position that was to force out into the open, and intensify, internal strifes which had afflicted it for many years. High Churchmen and Tractarians professed the Catholic traditions of the Church of England; Low Churchmen and Evangelicals stressed the significance of the Reformation period and its ecclesiastical implications. In only a few years' time the Oxford Movement itself was to experience similar internal discord and the departure of Newman with some other leading Anglo-Catholics to Rome.

The writing and dissemination of the Tracts continued apace. By the end of 1833 twenty had been published, of which Newman had written eleven. Another major contributor was John William Bowden, Newman's close friend, who wrote six tracts between 1833 and 1835. His premature and deeply mourned death in 1844 deprived Newman of one of his most loyal and active supporters. In addition to writing many of the Tracts, Newman had been very active in distributing parcels of them throughout the district.

In his *Instructions for Propagandists*, Newman stated categorically:

> We have no concern with politics. We have nothing to do with maintaining the temporalities of the Church, much as we deprecate any undue interference with them on external authority.[46]

Clearly, however, the origins of the Oxford Movement are too often overlooked. In many ways, Tractarianism represented a revolt of Oxford Toryism at the reforming measures which the Grey ministry brought into Parliament in the early 1830s. Yet historians, taking their cue from Tractarian historiography, have tended to regard the Movement as always unconcerned with constitutional and political questions. Pusey himself had encouraged this misunderstanding.[47] Not for the first time in English history, political and religious motivations were so meshed and interactive that it becomes virtually impossible to isolate their individual influences. 'Old fashioned Churchmen were Tories. They loved the Church, but that love was bound up with hatred of Whiggery, and they had no necessary sympathy with the new Oxford theology.'[48] There was always, of course, the fact that both the Church of England and the Church of Ireland were established by law and that this conferred on them privilege, special status, exclusive rights to university education, entry to the professions and, until the repeal of the Test and Corporations Acts of 1828 and the Catholic Relief Act of 1829, certain civil and religious freedoms.

Disestablishment of the Church of Ireland was still over twenty-five years away, while the prospects of the Church of England being forced to accept the same fate seemed a remote, faintly rumbling threat. When the Ecclesiastical Commission was set up by Sir Robert Peel in response to demands for reform of the administration of the Church of England, the 'threat of disestablishment evaporated just before the Commission was first created'.[49]

In October 1833 Newman felt able to tell Frederic Rogers, an old Oxford intimate, that 'We are getting on famously with our Society, and are so prudent and temperate that Froude writes up to me we have made a hash of it, which I account to be praise.'[50] Towards the end of 1833, the Tractarians' efforts were significantly strengthened by Pusey, who wrote *Thoughts on the Benefits of the System enjoyed by our Church* (Tract 18), and appended his initials, EBP, to indicate his tentative association with the other Tractarians. As Dessian suggests, this ruse, however, had an effect 'contrary to his intention and gave the movement the prestige of his name ... The Tracts soon changed their form and developed into small treatises'.[51] From being 'airy missiles' they evolved, as Trevor puts it, into a 'heavy bombardment of scholarly tomes' reflecting the growing maturity of the Movement.[52] 'Newman himself, however, declined the name of "Newmanites" as referring to himself and his ardent band of followers ... yet a party they certainly were ... He must have enjoyed using his powers of leadership.'[53]

In William Oddie's opinion, Newman was the Movement's strongest intellectual influence through 'the Tracts, his sermons and his *Lectures of the Prophetical Office of the Church* (1837)'.[54] Gilley also judges that Newman's voice was the dominant one in the Tracts although, of course, he had many helpers.[55] Nockles claims that at this time, Newman can be regarded 'both as a political conservative and a spiritual revolutionary'. He shared with radical Evangelicals 'a belief that political events had necessarily to be interpreted theologically'.[56]

With the valuable addition of Pusey to the Tractarian team, a third way of describing these religious zealots came into use: 'Puseyites'. This term, however, was not in common use until after Newman's secession in 1845, whereas 'Tractarianism' had been a widely adopted alternative for Oxfordism since the early 1840s. The term Oxford Movement was, however, seldom used without inverted commas until the 1880s.[57] The predilection for labelling specific religious affiliations has been noted by Gilley:

> It was in the 1830s that Newman and his friends gave a novel currency to the terms 'Anglicanism' and 'Anglo-Catholicism'; it was the first time that the Church of England was to be known as an 'ism' describing its identity as a third way between Protestantism and Rome.[58]

Whatever appellation was attached to them and their dedicated activities, the important thing to note is that the Tractarians asserted the spiritual independence of the Church from the State, emphasized its apostolicity, and attempted to revive the piety and authority which had supposedly been inculcated by the Fathers of the early Church.[59]

In time, and among themselves, Newman and Froude designated their supporters 'Apostolicals' or 'Ys', whereas 'Zs' referred to ultra Protestants, 'Peculiars' or Evangelicals, 'of whom there were at first a fair sprinkling in the Associations'.[60]

Hurrell Froude's health began to give rise to further anxiety and in October 1833, as Newman notes, he 'left for good' to travel to Barbados.[61] Newman had then taken on full responsibility for the Tracts. Froude had contributed significantly to Newman's doctrinal insights, such as those concerning the Eucharistic Real Presence and devotion to the Blessed Virgin. These themes came to be reflected in his sermons.[62] Froude had also played a key role in the early stages of developing the notion of writing Tracts, both in giving advice and in his animated views on how the Movement should progress. Newman himself relied heavily on Froude for advice on his projected publications.[63]

In 1834, the first volume of Newman's *Parochial and Plain Sermons* appeared. This eight-volume series covered sermons preached to congregations at Oxford and Littlemore between 1835 and 1841. Following conventional Anglican practice, the sermons were read; hence they were meticulously and sensitively structured. Trevor has noted that if the *Tracts* were the 'fighting front' of the Movement, the sermons were the 'spiritual power' and were 'the real strength of Newman's leadership. She also observed that few of his sermons could be regarded as controversial; rather they were 'psychologically penetrating' with wide appeal to 'Christians of every tradition'.[64]

These *Parochial and Plain Sermons* were the first of Newman's Anglican works to be republished in 1878. Then, at his request, the volumes were edited by W. J. Copeland, who had been his curate at Littlemore. In a letter to Copeland, Newman expressed his gratitude:

> You have been of the greatest use to me in the matter of the Sermons . . . Unless you had broken the ice, I could have republished nothing which I wrote before 1845–6. The English public would not have borne any alterations and my own people would have been much scandalised had I made none. They murmured a good deal at the new edition of the sermons, as it was – but since you, not I, published them, nothing could be said about it.[65]

In a draft of the 'Advertisement' for the Sermons which, in 1877, he sent to Copeland for clearance, Newman stated: 'The author has been careful to follow faithfully the text as it stands in Mr Copeland's edition of them. At the same time he is glad to be able to state that they do not contain a word which, as a Catholic, he would wish to alter.'[66]

In a lengthy letter to Hugh James Rose, editor of the *British Magazine*, Newman gave his reasons for supporting the continued imposition of subscription to the Thirty-Nine Articles demanded of entrants to Oxford University.[67] He signed the 'Oxford Declaration against the Admission of Dissenters', which was enthusiastically championed by eighty-seven university dons.[68] When the bill to admit dissenters was defeated, he openly rejoiced. But the protest by university teachers was challenged by Renn Dickson Hampden, Principal of St Mary's Hall, who published a pamphlet, *Observations of Religious Dissent*, in which he advocated strongly the total abolition of religious tests. Newman expostulated strongly to Hampden: 'While I respect the tone of piety which the pamphlet displays, I dare not trust myself to put on paper my feelings about the principles contained in it, tending as they do in my opinion altogether to make a shipwreck of Christmas faith.'[69] Newman received from Hampden a courteous dismissal: 'I think the same candour and good motives should induce to you wait rather for a full discussion of a question, and a fair hearing of parties on both sides.' He would be 'quite ready' to hear any arguments that may be brought.[70] Newman's reaction to Hampden may have been partly influenced by the fact that when Dr Hawkins, Provost of Oriel, took from Newman his tutorship, it had been given to Hampden. In his journal, Newman admits that 'ever since [he] had unfriendly feelings towards Hampden'.[71]

Newman entered in his private journal that the matter of his Oriel tutorship . . . 'is too important an event in his history to pass over it',[72] so a brief account of this troublesome episode will be given. In Hawkins' view – which was held by others – the duty of tutors should be confined to lecturing and he disliked intensely some of the changes which had been introduced without properly consulting him. Newman, with his co-tutors Froude and Wilberforce, had earlier submitted a plan to Dorford, the Dean and Senior Tutor, but the Provost had not been explicitly informed. In a subsequent letter to Hawkins, Newman explained that 'their lecture system is founded on the principles that Tutors have full authority to arrange their lectures without consulting the Provost', and that 'each Tutor is especially responsible for the instruction for the Pupils committed to him on entrance'.[73] An extended and rather acerbic correspondence resulted during 1830–1, both sides holding stubbornly to their differing perceptions of the role of tutorship at Oriel.[74] The crux of Newman's argument is contained in a letter to Hawkins in which he states that his 'chief private objection' to the Provost's tutoring proposals is that 'mere lecturing . . . would be incompatible with due attention to that more private instruction, which has been imparted to the office of Tutor the importance of a clerical occupation'.[75] He considered that it was essential for tutors to be able to exercise pastoral care in addition to their lecturing responsibilities.

The impasse was resolved by Hawkins, who informed Newman, Froude and Wilberforce that he intended 'to stop their supply of pupils, as he had a right to do, thus gradually depriving them of their office, according as their existing pupils took their degrees and left the University'.[76] Newman accepted this radical decision: 'I am now ready to submit to it at once and cheerfully at your bidding', he wrote to Hawkins on 15 June 1830. But he also told the Provost: 'I cannot alter my views.'[77] He informed his mother that 'The matter with the Provost was at length settled.' Wilberforce, Froude and himself would 'die off gradually with our existing pupils. This to me is a delightful arrangement . . . but for the College, I think it is a miserable determination'.[78] The following week he wrote again to tell his mother that he was . . . 'full of projects . . . the Fathers rise up again before me'.[79]

Newman's antipathy towards Hampden was to be further aggravated when he was unsuccessful in securing the Chair of Moral Philosophy, which was awarded to Hampden who had been 'put up' by Hawkins 'at the last moment'.[80] Hostile feelings were rekindled when, in 1836,

Lord Melbourne appointed Hampden Regius Professor of Divinity, to
the disgust and alarm of the High Churchmen. Protests were made
without avail and Convocation had to be content with passing a public
vote of no confidence in the allegedly 'unorthodox' appointment.[81]
Newman considered that the way things turned out 'was a lesson for
both Church and State ... Erastianism dies a natural death ... the
State casts us off. The Clergy will be forced back upon the truth by
the pressure of circumstances'.[82]

Meanwhile, the Oxford Movement was steadily growing and
Newman's reputation had been enhanced by the *Parochial Sermons*
and by *The Arians* 'which has caused a stir among the learned of the
University'.[83] Newman reflected in his journal: 'Humanly speaking,
the [Oxford] Movement never would have been if he had not been
deprived of his tutorship, or had Keble, not Hawkins, been
Provost'...[84] In the *Apologia*, Newman declares that he 'saw clearly in
the history of Arianism, that the pure Arians were the Protestants, the
semi Arians were the Anglicans, and that Rome now was what it was
then'.[85] Maisie Ward says that Newman undertook writing *The Arians
of the Fourth Century* in the spirit of Traditional Anglicanism – the
defence of the Council of Nicaea, the return to early Christianity.[86]
(The Arians of the fourth century denied the full divinity of Christ as
being co-eternal with God the Father. The heresy was named after its
originator, Arius *c*.250–*c*.336.)

The *Arians* has been described as 'a young man's book, written with
enthusiasm but without the rhetorical grace and effortless flow of
Newman's later books'.[87] Newman himself referred to it critically:

> As to *The Arians*, except that the matter of it is true, I have long
> thought of it the most imperfect work that was ever composed ... I
> once asked Froude, if it was not pompous, thinking that a sin of it,
> but he said decidedly no.[88]

Some forty years later, Newman told a correspondent that his book on
the Arians should not be referred to as '"great", it is not even little. It
was to have been in Mr Rose's intention, the beginning of a Manual
on the Councils, and the gun went off in quite another direction,
hitting no mark at all'. He explained that he had to finish it by 'a fixed
day' and had to hurry through the last pages especially, 'till I knocked
myself up'.[89] In his eighties, Newman mused that considering that *The
Arians* was his first book, 'that my reading up to then had not got as

far as the Nicene Council and that I had but a year to do it in, and that
I was in weak health, I do wonder that it was not worse ... Yet with
all its defects I think it has some good points in it, and in parts some
originality'.[90] In Ker's opinion, although *The Arians* was 'far from
being a history of the principal Councils ... there was no question,
however, about the distinction of the work'.[91]

The principle of reserve or 'economy' was identified by Newman as
important in communicating religious knowledge in terms that are
comprehensible to the receiver. According to Selby,

> Since we are at a distance from truth and can only apprehend it by means
> of economical representations, words themselves are economies ...Words
> do not transmit the essence, but afford a partial insight into truth; they
> demand the participation of the reader.[92]

Ker notes that Newman's treatment of the principle of economy 'is
perhaps the most interesting aspect of the book [*The Arians*]'.[93] A
similar point is made by Nockles: 'Reserve became a distinctive
element of the Tractarian spiritual ethos.'[94]

In December 1835, Newman wrote to Bowden:

> We have determined to commence a series *against Popery* ie to devote
> next year at length to the subject. Many advantages will follow from this.
> Two years since the cry was against the Dissenters this helped us – now
> Popery is the popular alarm.[95]

He also wrote in similar vein to Henry Wilberforce[96] and to H. E.
Manning.[97] His motives in the decision to attach Rome seem to have
been mixed. In a long letter to Mrs William Wilberforce [but marked
'not sent' in his papers], Newman disclosed that 'The more I examine
into the RC system, the less sound it appears to me to be; and the less
safely could I in conscience profess to receive it.' He listed his objections; they were to the doctrine of Transubstantiation, to the 'polythe-
ism' associated with 'saint-worship'; to the 'praying to images', and
to the 'frightful doctrine of Purgatory'. He ended his letter in a rather
more relaxed manner:

> Surely we shall be judged according to our conscience, and if we have a
> clear sight of what is wrong with Rome, we must follow our inclinations,
> because Rome has what is attractive in some part of her devotions.[98]

At the same time, Newman was becoming increasingly aware of the charge that his views and actions could be perceived as indicating that he was drifting towards Rome. Bowden warned him: 'the world accuses you of popery'.[99] This so shocked Newman that he decided to devote three Tracts (38, 40 and 71) to the 'Roman question'. However, Maisie Ward maintains that the need to clear his reputation was not a major motive; rather, he considered that it was necessary to attack Rome 'because the *via media* could not be justified unless Rome were shown to be wrong'.[100] To this task Newman applied himself with characteristic commitment and enthusiasm. He affirmed that the 'glory of the English Church' lay in having taken a *via media* 'between the so called Reformers and Romanists', but it had 'fallen away from its principles and is in need of a second reformation'.[101] Two of these Tracts consist of a dialogue between 'Laicus' and 'Clericus'.

Earlier it was briefly mentioned that, to clarify his thoughts, Newman gave a series of lectures in St Mary's, Oxford during 1834–6; from these weekly talks, *Lectures on the Prophetical Office of the Church, viewed relatively to Romanism and Protestantism,* was published in 1837, and was to form the first volume of the *Via Media* in which he expounded the distinctive character of the Church of England as a *via media*: 'Anglican theology against Liberalism and Protestantism on the one side and popery on the other'.[102] In the *Apologia*, Newman refers to the careful consideration and comparison of the principal Anglican divines of the seventeenth century on which the *Lectures* were based, and to the 'considerable retrenchments and additions which were made before publication'.[103]

The *Lectures* had largely originated from controversies over 1834–6 with Abbé Jean Nicholas Jager, who had developed a strong interest in the theological aspects of the Tracts. Abbé Jager had a varied career as a schoolmaster, army chaplain and then professor of ecclesiastical history in the University of Paris. One of Newman's younger friends, Benjamin Harrison, a brilliant Hebrew scholar and contributor to the Tracts had, on a visit to Paris in 1834, become involved in a controversy. Apparently, Harrison had hoped to persuade Newman to support him but this was not possible immediately because Newman was away from Oxford. Eventually, however, Newman took over the controversy, which occurred at an interesting moment in his life. He had been a fellow of Oriel for more than a decade and vicar of St Mary's since 1828. His first book, *The Arians of the Fourth Century,* was finished in July 1832 and, on 9 July, he returned home from Sicily convinced that God had preserved him for some great work. On 9 September 1833 the first of the Tracts was issued, anonymously.[104] With his customary appetite for controversy, Newman then became embroiled in a lengthy, time-consuming and, at times, discursive correspondence with Jager. However, the time and effort was well spent since Newman was able to develop his thoughts on the *via media* and to deliver a series of lectures. During these, he confided to Bowden: 'The Abbé has replied to me – and the controversy is getting interesting. He is so weak that so far it is not fun. But it is an object to make known our opinions.'[105] But, over ten years later Newman revealed to Henry Wilberforce that his belief in the 'theory of the *Via Media* was so strong in the year 1834 or 1835' that he feared his arguments might have unsettled Abbé Jager. He also confessed that the arguments were

> not, in fact, his own but were evolved from works by Laud, Stillingfleet and others. I do not think I had that unhesitating belief in it in 1836–7 when I published my *Prophetical Office*, or rather I should say that *zeal* for it for I believed it fully or at least was not conscious that I did not. It is difficult to say whether or not a flagging zeal involves an incipient doubt.[106]

The influence of the Fathers of the Church on Newman's mind was apparent from his early years; his extended study of them led to his finding the *Via Media* less and less satisfactory and he eventually abandoned it altogether. Walgrave comments that this concentrated study of Newman's, which included the great heresies and schisms of early Church history, gradually led him to views about 'the ancient Church as it really was and the positions taken by both sides in the controversies of the patristic era'.[107]

Newman's strong interest in studying the early Fathers of the Church is clearly evident in a letter to his sister Jemima, dated 1 May 1826, in which he mentions 'an undertaking I have in mind, viz. to trace the sources from which the corruptions of the Church, principally the Romish, have been derived. It would consequently involve a reading of all the Fathers 200 volumes at least'.[108] His ambitious plan earned Jemima's observation that 'it took Archbishop Usher 18 years to accomplish the same task, which he began at the age of 20'.[109] Undaunted, Newman asked Pusey to send him, from Germany, various volumes which duly arrived in 1827. In the *Apolo-*

gia, Newman recorded: 'In proportion as I moved out of the shadow
of the Liberalism which had hung over my course, my early devotion to the Fathers returned; and in the Long Vacation of 1828 I
set about to read them chronologically.'[110] His dedication to Patristic study was further encouraged by being presented, in 1831, with
thirty-six volumes of the Fathers by 'many of my friends and pupils'
to mark the close of his Oriel tutorship. He told his mother that
his difficulty now was 'where to put my acquisition they are too
deep for my study bookcases, I mean no pun on the word'.[111]
Newman's determined reading of the Fathers during his Oxford
years resulted, according to Boekraad and Tristram, in valuable
theological works, 'and influenced him to readjust his theological
opinions'.[112] In 1871 Newman assured an enquirer that 'my condemnation of the Anglican Church arose *not* out of despair, but, when
everything was hopeful, out of *my study of the Fathers* ... It was
not that I despaired of the Anglican Church, but that their opposition *confirmed* the interpretation which I had put upon the Fathers,
that they *who loved the Fathers, could have no place in the Church
of England*'.[113] In the *Apologia* Newman admitted that the *via media*
'was an impossible idea; it is what I have called "standing on one
leg", and it was necessary, if my old issue of the controversy was
to be retained, to go further either one way or the other'.[114] According to Gilley, the *via media* was an attempt by Newman to justify
the existence of the Established Church as a separ-ate Christian
Communion besides the Churches of the Reformation and Rome.[115]
In 1887 Newman produced a new edition of the *Via Media*.

Newman had already indicated something of his increasing spiritual
anguish in a long letter to Hugh James Rose in May 1836, in which he
confessed that: 'You have spoken the truth, I do *not* love the "Church
of England".' Rather, he loved

> the old Church of 1200 or 1600 years ... I cannot love the 'Church of
> England'commonly so designated – its very title is an offence ... for it
> implies that it holds, not of the Church Catholic but of the State ...
> Viewed *internally*, it is the battlefield of two opposite principles: Socian-
> ism and Catholicism – Socianism fighting for the most part by Puritans its
> unconscious ally ... Luckily, none of the Articles are positively Calvinis-
> tic ... what is wanting in one is supplied in another ... but there are grave
> omissions ... My heart *is* with Rome, *but not* as Rome, but as, and so far
> as, she is the faithful retainer of what we have practically thrown aside.[116]

Despite his worries, Newman was able to assure Jemima, in April 1837, that his *Prophetical Office* was selling very well: 'It only shows how deep the absurd notion was in men's minds that I was a Papist; and how they are agreeably surprised.'[117] Nockles notes:

> Up until 1839, as he later confessed, Newman remained secure and confident in his Anglicanism ... yet, even in the *Via Media* phase ... one can sense that Newman's concept of Anglicanism was nebulous and somewhat theoretical ... Viewed in retrospect, Newman's *Via Media* phase seems but a temporary staging post in his religious odyssey, but, at the same time it was held and propounded with a conviction, passion and fierceness which could not have been excelled.[118]

In 1835 the future Cardinal Nicholas Wiseman delivered a series of public addresses on his visits to some of the principal centres of Roman Catholicism in England. These attracted considerable attention and were 'the first public presentation of Catholic doctrines in England'.[119] Wiseman harnessed his considerable intellectual and dialectical skills in co-founding with Daniel O'Connell, in 1836, a journal, the *Dublin Review*, for which he wrote many articles including one on the *Schism of the Donatists* which was published in August 1839 and was to have a major influence on Newman. In it Wiseman made 'his famous comparison between the Anglicans and the Donatists' which, according to Newman 'absolutely pulverised the Anglican theory of the *via media*'.[120] According to Wilfrid Ward, 'Newman never really recovered from the blow inflicted by Wiseman's article ... The isolation of the English Church from the rest of the Church Catholic – a commonplace of the controversy – had suddenly got hold of him ... He never returned to the old *Via Media*'.[121] The Donatist schism had been condemned by St Augustine in the celebrated utterance; *securus judicat orbis terrarum*. Wiseman had been following closely the development of the Oxford Movement, respecting and sympathising with Newman and his associates but, according to Gwynn, his appeal to the voice of ancient authority 'threw a bombshell into their camp by pointing out the analogy between the claims of the Donatists and what the Tractarians were now attempting ... In each case, a local church asserted the Roman Catholic Church was in error, while it alone retained the title to be called Catholic'.[122] The famous dictum of St Augustine 'pricked Newman's mind ... because suddenly he wondered about his national church, the Church of England, i.e. its differences from an

international Church. *Securus judicat orbis terrarum* might be interpreted either to indicate that if everyone agrees, the verdict must be
right, or it 'could be stretched to give a very authoritarian meaning –
the international Church is the see of Rome, now to its solitary edict
... it was this second meaning that was present in Newman's
mind'.[123] Ker states that Newman's own free translation runs: 'The
universal Church is in its own judgements secure of truth.'[124] Over
thirty years later, Newman informed one of his correspondents that
Securus judicat ... means 'The Christian world judges with security;
that is, "when all Christians agree together in judgement, that is a sure
warrant that its judgement is right" ... This saying of St Augustine's
is in the teeth of the Anglican maxim, "Nothing is true but what is to
be found in the Antenicene Church".'[125]

Mrs Helbert, a married lady with four children, felt strongly drawn
to Catholicism but had been persuaded by Newman to remain an
Anglican. Writing to correct her remarks on Wiseman's article in the
Donatists, Newman emphasized that what had struck him was not the
article itself – because he had 'known about it for years' – but the
passage from St Augustine 'which had contained a maxim going far
beyond the purposes of the controversy – *securus judicat orbis
terrarum*. That is the maxim (As I also feel now), on which it all
depends'.[126] Before her death on 8 March 1874, Mrs Helbert became
a Catholic and, later, her husband wrote gratefully to Newman.
Newman's letter typifies his strong commitment to the pastoral aspects
of his private correspondence.

In the *Apologia*, Newman admitted that the 'palmary words of St
Augustine had escaped his observation'.[127] During a walk with Henry
Wilberforce in October 1839, Newman told him that for the first time
since he began the study of theology, 'a vista had opened up before
me, to the end of which I do not see'.[128] Newman confided to his
friends the intensity of his shock at reading Wiseman's hard-hitting
article:

> I have had the first real hit from Romanism which has happened to me ...
> I must confess it has given me a stomach-ache ... I seriously think this is
> a most uncomfortable article on every count ... How are we to keep
> hotheads from going over?[129]

He was, however, increasingly reluctant to 'attack the Roman Church
as a sister Church'[130] and wrote an article for the *British Critic*, of

which he became editor in 1838, entitled *The Catholicity of the Anglican Church*, in an effort to console himself and his friends. But, as Owen Chadwick observes, 'He was not quite the same. He said later that he had seen the shadow of a hand on the wall . . . He discovered in himself a growing dislike of speaking against the Church of Rome.'[131] Newman notes in the *Apologia* that he was editor from July 1838 to July 1841, and that the journal covered a wide variety of subjects as well as theological . . . 'and upon the Movement none are to be found which do not keep quite clear of advocating the cause of Rome. So I went on for years, up to 1841. It was, in a human point of view, the happiest time of my life. I was truly at home'.[132] The journal had been founded in 1793 as a conservative monthly and changed to a quarterly when it was acquired by a group of High Churchmen. Since then it had had a precarious existence and had been subject to a series of disputes over editorial policy. When Newman assumed editorship he imposed a Tractarian agenda.[133] Before long he found his editorial role burdensome, particularly because contributors failed to produce articles on time. He complained to Jemima that he had to produce 'five sheets of the Review' himself.[134] His duties continued to be irksome and he told Tom Mozley that he had made what may seem to be 'a sudden resolution, but it is not' – to 'relinquish editorship of the *British Critic* after the April issue', and asked if he would take over the journal for him.[135]

Newman was still engrossed in delivering lectures and in developing these into published works. His *Lectures on the Doctrine of Justification* were given in the Adam de Brome Chapel in St Mary's during 1837 and published the following year. In 1837 Newman had become engaged in a debate with Samuel Wilks, the editor of the *Christian Observer*, over the subject of Justification and he seized this opportunity to explore the topic in his lectures at St Mary's, Oxford. He told Jemima that he was 'quite worn out with correcting' the book he was writing on Justification. Despite numerous re-writings – 'I literally fill the page with corrections' – seven of the fifteen lectures 'are in the printer's hands'.[136] Newman wrote in the *Apologia* that the *Essay on Justification* was 'aimed at the Lutheran dictum that justification by faith only was the cardinal doctrine of Christianity. I considered that this doctrine was either a paradox or a truism – a paradox in Luther's mouth, a truism in Melanchthon's'. He believed that the Anglican Church followed the latter, consequently 'between Rome and Anglicanism, between the high Church and low Church, there was no real intellectual difference on the point'.[137] The outcome of his endeavours were lectures which, Ker has noted, 'some would claim' to be 'his most acute and theological work'.[138] Maisie Ward has described these lectures as 'a marvelous treatment of the doctrine of divine grace', adding that Newman 'found it hard to keep in these lectures any kind of *via media*'.[139] As Nockles points out, Newman's position was seen by 'Protestant controversialists' to be 'much closer to the Roman than to the Reformed position'.[140] Newman's views on Justification clearly aroused indignation, misunderstanding and even suspicion among High Churchmen as well as Evangelicals. He exchanged several extended letters with George Stanley Faber (an uncle of Frederick Faber) trying to clarify their differing views on Justification. In the end, they left the matter unresolved.[141]

The lectures were dedicated to Bishop Bagot of Oxford – the only time that Newman made a dedication to an Anglican bishop – but, unexpectedly and to his dismay, he had to face a charge from the bishop concerning the Tracts. In characteristically gentle but firm words, Bagot warned him that some of the language used in these publications 'might lead people into error'.[142] Newman, ever mindful of the sacredness of the episcopacy, was perplexed, although willing to withdraw any Tract that was judged to be offensive or even to suppress all of them, as he indicated to his friends.[143] He stressed to Bowden that what Bagot said 'was very slight indeed, but a Bishop's lightest word *ex Cathedra* is heavy'. As it happened, the bishop himself was much disturbed by the intensity of Newman's reaction. According to Trevor 'he was alarmed by such apostolical submission'[144] and the issue was quietly set to rest. But the matter clearly rankled with Newman as may be judged from a letter to F. W. Faber in which he commented that people 'will always lag a little behind in order to be safe and moderate, and to have the satisfaction of abusing you'.[145] (However, this problem with the Tracts tended to persist, as later discussed.)

In 1838 another troublesome matter involved Newman: Hurrell Froude, his closest friend since undergraduate days, had died on 28 February 1836 leaving Newman stricken with grief, as he intimated to Bowden, another close friend.[146] Hurrell Froude's father, the Archdeacon of Totnes, sent to Newman the many articles, sermons, manuscripts, a few private letters and, more dramatically as it was to prove, the remnants of his private journal. The Archdeacon told Newman and his associates that they had the freedom to publish whatever they wished. This fragmentary assortment of papers – known as the *Remains* – contained material that was to cause Newman and Keble, who were somewhat reluctantly acting as literary executors, far more trouble than they ever anticipated. They circulated the papers among their friends and sought their advice on how to deal with some of the highly sensitive issues involved. Newman told Frederic Rogers that 'Keble, Pusey, Williams, Copeland, Wood and you are for publication of F's papers'.[147] At the end of the month, apparently still wavering for a time, he then wrote to Keble stating clearly why publication should go ahead.[148] It was not until 31 August, however, that Newman was able to tell Rogers[149] that he had just received from Archdeacon Froude Hurrell's private journal (1826–7), of which he was not previously aware. The entries included details of fastings, faults and temptations over that period. These intimate spiritual revelations, together with details of Hurrell's private and personal views on aspects of religious belief and practice, began to make Newman nervous. He wrote to Keble: 'I do wish *you* would seriously think of the objection which will be made to dear Hurrell's papers, which the Journal I shall send you on Tuesday will confirm.'[150]

Newman's anxieties persisted, as may be seen from a letter to Bowden the following January: 'Anxious I have been, and am very, about several things. Froude's volumes will open upon me a flood of criticism, and from all quarters.'[151] His fears were to be fulfilled when the papers were eventually published and he was beset on all sides by Evangelicals, Low Churchmen and moderate Anglicans who fiercely attacked the views of Froude now made public. Froude had written, for instance, 'I am becoming less and less a son of the Reformation',[152] and 'The Reformation was a limb badly set; it must be broken again and righted.'[153] Such sentiments were presumably not intended by Froude for publication but they provoked furious feelings and added to the strong suspicion that Tractarianism was full of 'Romanist tendencies'.[154] Owen Chadwick comments that 'The repudiation of Protestants appeared before the public in a new and shocking light. Newman's Tracts disliked the word Protestant, Froude disliked Protestants, Froude seemed to want to destroy the Reformation.'[155] In addition to inflaming the opinions of many High Churchmen, the *Remains* disconcerted some Tractarians; Newman and Keble might perhaps have exercised more discretion in their responsibilities as literary executors. 'The controversial publication ... represented a landmark and a turning point in the history of the Oxford Movement

... it brought into the open the first rumblings of official disapproval of the Movement.'[156]

In spite of the earlier uncertainties about publishing Froude's papers that were expressed to his confidante, Newman seems almost to have shrugged off the belligerence of his critics. This is reflected, for instance, in a letter to Edward Churton, a High Churchman who was sympathetic to the Oxford Movement:

> As to the passages in the *Remains* you speak of, I never have repented publishing them one single moment, and though I cannot imitate your language and say 'I *never* shall regret', yet I have no reason to suppose I ever shall.[157]

He declared that he fully believed that Keble and he had 'acted on the truest and wisest view of what is *expedient*'. Maisie Ward feels that he did not doubt that 'Froude, Keble, Pusey and himself were Catholics, and that the Protestant attack on the *Remains* had been a furious attack on its Catholicism'.[158] While, however, Newman, Keble and many other Tractarians upheld the principles of antiquity, Pusey himself retained his respect for the English reformers even thought he gradually took a more critical view of the Reformation.[159]

It was popularly believed that publication of the *Remains* caused Golightly to ferment the anti-Tractarian feelings which resulted in the erection in Oxford, by public subscription, of the Martyrs' Memorial to the memory of Cranmer, Latimer and Ridley. Although, at first, Pusey seemed to favour such a monument, he eventually decided not have anything to do with it. In a letter to the Bishop of Oxford, he said that he was concerned that this proposal might well 'tend to increase the vulgar impression that we were a new Church at the Reformation, instead of the old one purified', and he suggested that 'the testimonial would be termed "a commemoration of the blessings of the Reformation", thus hoping to make it possible for Newman and others to join in'.[160] But the bishop countered this proposal by suggesting that 'the Tractarians should give an unequivocal declaration of their principles'.[161]

Almost fifty years later, Newman, replying to Canon Liddon, Pusey's biographer, stated:

> The 'Memorial' was Golightly's work but from the first I would have nothing to do with it. I entreated Pusey not to be swayed by me but to act upon his own view. But I cannot be sure that there was some compromise between me and Pusey though I cannot recollect it at all, that is I cannot

fancy that I came into the plan of building a church to the Reformation . . .
Down to this day I have not thought of it as a great event; I think rather
that I despised it.[162]

According to Gerard Tracey, 'The testimonial was certainly seen as a
test for Newman and Pusey, and suspicions increased when they did
not subscribe.'[163] Newsome notes that apart from wanting to demon-
strate against Froude's *Remains*, the 'notorious skirmisher' Golightly
had schemed 'to split the Oxford Movement by this project from the
"Martyrs' Memorial" and he had enjoyed some measure of
success'.[164] Tractarianism was, however, strengthened in 1839 when
William George Ward joined it. His book *The Ideal of a Christian
Church* was condemned by the Convocation of Oxford University in
1845 because of its perceived 'Romish' doctrines. With Frederick
Oakeley, a former Fellow of Balliol, Ward infused new life into Tractarianism. The Wardites, who also included J. D. Dalgairns and F.
W. Faber, discarded the historical rhetoric and preoccupation of early
Tractarianism, enthusiastically prompting a 'Romanising' of the
liturgy and introducing other pious practices. As Nockles puts it, 'An
ideological watershed had been reached in the Movement.'[165]

In January 1840 Newman told Rogers that he had received a visit
from 'Mr Spencer, the RC priest'. Originally, he had refused to meet
him because he was in *loco apostatae*, but later he was persuaded to
see him. Newman wrote that he found this aristocratic convert to
Roman Catholicism to be a 'gentlemanlike, mild, pleasing man, but
sadly smooth. I wonder whether it is their habit of internal discipline,
the necessity of confession, etc., which makes them so'.[166] Although
Newman had declined an invitation to meet Spencer over dinner, he
met him privately when they discussed the desirability of praying for
unity among the Churches. While the proposal appealed to Newman,
it was received suspiciously by Manning and Pusey.[167] Spencer's visit
and his own apparent distinctly reserved response to the suggestion of
some form of mutual prayer for church unity, clearly lay on
Newman's mind. A few weeks later he put forward the rationale of his
views to Spencer in a long and courteous letter.[168] Newman and
Spencer exchanged letters again in August 1841, when they discussed
their mutual interest in the restoration of unity in the Church.
Newman assured the Catholic missioner that he would with pleasure
comment on the various papers which Spencer had contributed to
Catholic journals. He also expressed 'great satisfaction' at the 'kind

spirit in which many persons of your communion have displayed during the past year towards the English Church'. He added: 'Meekness and sincerity must subdue the most prejudiced among us.'[169] This pleasant exchange seems to have led to some misapprehension about Newman's intentions and he hastened to inform Wiseman at Oscott College that W. G. Ward had misled him into thinking that he, Newman, and others were anticipating joining the Church of Rome. Newman stated that what he meant to say was that

> Whatever became of us, the English Church will remain as it is, till Roman Catholics change their behaviour towards it. We may remain it, or we may leave it, but in either case the effect upon it of our writings would be the same, viz. not to conciliate it to you, but to strengthen it in itself. We cannot conciliate it to you; you alone can do this, and that by a kinder line of conduct towards it.[170]

These adamantine views were, however, not transmitted directly to Wiseman; Newman comments in his diary: 'Not sent nor any instead, because I do not like to commit myself again and Ward said that he would correct the misapprenhension.'[171] W. G. Ward had just returned from a second visit to Wiseman at Oscott, and he appears to have clarified the position. However, Newman's draft letter certainly reflects some of his stressful feelings about the relative positions of the Churches in Britain and his personal commitments.

The Honourable and Reverend George Spencer (1799–1864) was one of the notable Cambridge men – including Ambrose Phillips de Lisle and Kenelm Henry Digby – who became Catholics over the period 1825–30. He was the youngest child of the second Earl Spencer and, for a few years, was rector of Great Brington, Northamptonshire, where his father was patron of the living. After his conversion, he resigned the living, studied at the English College in Rome, of which Wiseman was rector, and was ordained a Catholic priest in 1832. He returned to England as a missionary and, in 1847, entered the Passionist monastery at Aston-by-Stone, Staffordshire and was known as Fr Ignatius. He was a zealous colleague of Fr Dominic Barberi, who was to play an historic role in Newman's life.

Newman felt that he needed some peace and quiet. He advised Henry Wilberforce that he would be 'going up to Littlemore on Saturday week to stay there till Easter Eve, – and wish to have as little to do as I can'.[172] During this time he would, as customary, impose on himself a very strict regime of fasting and penance.[173] He also completed writing the account of his illness in Sicily, recovery from which had been a turning point in his life.[174] Newman's preoccupation with religious problems and his despondency at this time about the Church of England can be seen in a letter to Jemima: 'I begin to have serious apprehensions lest any religious body is strong enough to withstand the league of evil, but the Roman Church.'[175]

When Newman was appointed vicar of St Mary's, Oxford, his pastoral duties also extended to Littlemore. He then wrote in his private journal: 'I am just entering upon St Mary's as vicar; thus I am taken from literary work to Parochial.'[176] However, as events were to show, he had a remarkably active and successful decade or so in which he produced a series of notable lectures and sermons. He also took on his pastoral duties with his customary diligence. During this time Newman had reflected on developing Littlemore as a rural retreat where he and some of his close friends could share a communal life of prayer, meditation and study. He drafted one of his customary memoranda setting out reasons for founding such a centre: He would need a library and might set up a '*Monastic* house' which 'could *train up* men for the "great towns"'. He would not give up the university and could continue his Sunday afternoon duties at St Mary's. It might be possible to be considered a 'head of hall offspring and in a way dependent upon Oriel as in old times at St Mary's Hall'.[177] He also told Pusey and S. F. Wood of these aspirations.[178]

During May 1840, Newman wrote to tell Harriett that a nine-acre field had been purchased in Littlemore where it was 'planned to build a retreat'.[179] Newman asked Harriett's husband, Thomas Mozley, to give him 'some hint about building' and specified the accommodation needed.[180] Committing himself still further, he wrote to the Provost of Oriel, Edward Hawkins, enquiring whether 'the college would be likely to consent to my resigning from St Mary's and keeping Littlemore'.[181] To Keble, Newman wrote an extended explanation of why he was considering resigning from St Mary's. His reasons included the impossibility of creating a truly pastoral ministry, the influence he knew he exerted on young Oxford students who were not his responsibility, and the fact that his sermons were considered to be 'disposing his hearer towards Rome'.[182] Keble replied that it would be virtually impossible for Newman to avoid such problems in 'any other place' where his 'net was cast'. In his opinion, the Heads of Houses 'did not have the smallest authority over you as Vicar of St Mary's'. They might forbid undergraduates to attend but Newman was free to preach.

He could not see how giving up St Mary's would help in the least.[183] Newman willingly accepted this down-to-earth advice and, in thanking his friend, commented that 'fair trial' had not yet been made 'of how much the English Church must be able to tolerate 'infusions of Catholic truth'.[184] About three weeks later he wrote to another confidant, Frederic Rogers, of his discussions with Keble regarding St Mary's:

> The upshot is, whether I continue so or not, that I am much more comfortable than I have been. I do not fear at all any number of persons as likely to go to Rome, if I am secure about myself. If I can trust myself, I can trust others. We have so many things on our side, that a good conscience is all that one wants.[185]

Over this eventful period of his life, Newman's correspondence reveals his growing resolution to develop in Littlemore a monastic way of life. He told H. A. Woodgate, an Anglican clergyman with whom he had been friendly since 1825, and to whose eldest daughter he was godfather: 'You forget that I am an incipient monk, in my noviciate at least. I am preparing a monastery at Littlemore and shall shortly retire from the world.'[186] Traces of Newman's developing attraction to some form of Christian brotherhood are to be seen in a lengthy letter to Woodgate, some eight years earlier, which Newman wrote from Naples on 17 April 1883.[187] Newman's preoccupation with the notion of founding a monastic institution is also reflected in a letter, dated 3 January 1842, to another friend, James Robert Hope, who had been a regular source of advice to him over the years:

> I am almost in despair of keeping men together. The only possible way is a monastery. Men want an outlet for their devotional and penitential feelings and if we do not grant it, to a dead certainty they will go where they can find it ...Yet the clamour is so great, and will be so much greater, that, if I persist, I expect though I am not speaking from anything that has *occurred* that I shall be stopped. Not that I have any intention of doing more at present than laying the foundation of what might be.[188]

However, in only about three months' time, Newman felt able to reassure Bishop Bagot that Littlemore was in no way a 'so-called Anglo-Catholic monastery', an explanation which was fully accepted.[189] The bishop was not the first to be reassured that Newman had no intention of founding a monastery at Littlemore. In a postscript to a letter to Pusey, dated 3 August 1841, Newman told him that 'he had given up the notion of a monastic body at present, lest talk should be made'. He had space for books and himself, as well as a number of spare cottages for any visitors who may wish to spend time at Littlemore.[190] Referring directly to the bishop's letter of 12 April 1842, Newman declared that there was 'no monastery in process of erection ... no chapel, no refectory, hardly a dining room or parlour'. The alleged cloisters were merely 'a shed connecting the cottages'. Further, he could 'repeat your Lordship's words that I am not attempting a revival of the Monastic orders, in anything approaching the Romanist sense of the term'.[191] Such emphatic denials were clearly based on Bagot's specific charges – which had been derived from the popular secular journal *John Bull* – although Newman's earlier private correspondence with some of his intimate friends suggests that a monastic ethos permeated his Littlemore aspirations and activities. Less than a fortnight after his letter of reassurance to his bishop, Newman write to Henry Wilberforce in committed terms: 'We are a small household here, small indeed – but we have begun the Breviary Service here this morning.' He requested that Wilberforce 'should not tell anyone what they were doing because it was sure to be misinterpreted'.[192] Newman and his associates followed an ascetic life which, although not formally monastic, was certainly strict and abstemious, as his private journal reveals in some detail.

Newman returned to vigorous controversy in seven spirited letters, signed 'Catholicus', in *The Times*, The last of these appeared on 27 February 1841 and the collection was published later as *The Tamworth Reading Room*. In these letters Newman attacked Sir Robert Peel who had made a speech at the opening of the new library and reading room at Tamworth. The speech had attracted considerable attention on account of its decidedly utilitarian emphasis. Newman was alerted to the speech and seized the opportunity to strike against a politician for whom he had slight regard. According to Ker, 'Apart from their political and social interest and the ways in which they anticipate the *Idea of a University*, the letters constitute the one sustained work of satire that Newman wrote as an Anglican.'[193] Trevor comments, however, that education makes people better morally, 'He did it with ridicule and was set at the top of his form.'[194] On the same day as the last of his letters to *The Times* appeared – 27 February 1841 – *Tract 90* was published under the unchallenging title of *Remarks on Certain Passages in the Thirty-nine Articles*. As usual, it was anonymous but its authorship was an open secret. Newman, who was experiencing a personal religious crisis, argued with singular skill that although the Thirty-Nine Articles were drawn up for the establishment of Protestantism, they may also be interpreted as compatible with Catholicism.

> While our Prayer Book is acknowledged on all hands to be of Catholic origin our Articles also the offspring of an uncatholic age, are, through God's good providence, to say least, not uncatholic, and may be subscribed by those who aim at being Catholic in heart and doctrine.[195]

Latitude of interpretation was held to be a vital characteristic of the Thirty-Nine Articles; Newman argued that while the Articles were intentionally written to establish Protestantism, 'they are not framed on the principles of excluding those who prefer the theology of the early ages to that of the Reformation'. The framers so worded them that those who did not go so far in Protestantism themselves might be able to subscribe to them:

> The Protestant Confession was drawn up with the purpose of including Catholics; and Catholics now will not be excluded. What was an economy in the reformers, is a protection to us. What would have been a perplexity to us then, is a perplexity to Protestants. We could not then have found fault with their words; they cannot now repudiate our meaning.[196]

Newman's reference to 'Catholics', never 'Roman Catholics', reflects his care to avoid associating the term 'Catholic' exclusively with the Roman Catholic Church. It was, rather, an attempt by the Tractarians to emphasize the inherent Catholicity of the Church of England, and to make the claim that Anglo-Catholics are indeed some of the people which the framers of the Articles had in mind. Newman, a theologically conservative Anglican, believed that the articles were intended to include various parties within the Church of England. Dessain comments that *Tract 90* propounded two main arguments for this Catholic interpretation:

1. the historical point that the Articles were drawn up 'early in the reign of Elizabeth I in such as way as to induce Roman Catholics to subscribe to them', and
2. that 'since the Anglican Church was a branch of the Catholic, its formularies must admit of being interpreted in accordance with what the Church Catholic had held from primitive times.

Further, Dessain states that there was an 'underlying irenical purpose in Tract 90'.[197] However, the reaction to the Tract was decidedly different, although Trevor had described it as a 'short treatise, not a polemic'.[198] It was subtly argued and some might have considered it to smack of sophistry. But Gilley comments that Newman discussed only fourteen of the Articles, and shocked his readers by extracting from a number of these 'a sense which contradicted their obvious literal meaning'.[199] Newman's hopes that it would be an instrument of reconciliation were dashed. In a letter dated 14 March 1841, R. W. Church told Frederic Rogers of the furore caused by *Tract 90*:

> He [Newman] did not think it would be more attacked than others, nor did Keble or H. Wilberforce. Ward, however, prophesied from the first that it would be hotly received, and so it proved.[200]

On 12 March 1841, Newman admitted to Harriett; 'I fear that I am clean dished. The Heads of the House are at this very moment concocting a manifesto against me.'[201] On the following day he told Bowden that he expected 'the very worst, that is, a condemnation will be passed in Convocation upon the Tracts as a whole'.[202] Meanwhile *Tract 90* was being widely read – 2,500 copies were sold within a fortnight. The ever-active Golightly, in attempting to discredit Newman, had disseminated copies of the Tract, and sent it to all the bishops.[203] Newman, however, had suspected Golightly would make mischief for him and called him 'Tony-fire-the-faggot of the resulting agitation'.[204] With Golightly's connivance, four senior tutors had been scrutinizing *Tract 90* and, on 8 March 1841, they wrote to the editor of the *Tracts for the Times* that *Tract 90* opened the door to the teaching of Roman Catholicism in the University.[205] In the meantime, Newman had been producing a pamphlet; he also told Jemima, in a letter dated 15 March 1841, 'What will be done I know not. I try to prepare myself for the worst.'[206] On the same day he wrote to Bowden saying that he believed the Heads had 'just done a violent act; they have said that my interpretation of the Articles is an *evasion*'. But he assured his reader, 'Do not think that this will pain me – no *doctrine* is censured, and my shoulders will bear the charge.'[207] The Heads' decision had overtaken his pamphlet which, in the custom of the time, was in the form of a *Letter addressed to the Rev J. H. Jelf*, who was a Canon of Christ Church and an old and impartial friend of Pusey's. The

Letter was largely made redundant by the Heads' action but it gives
an insight into Newman's defensive posture.[208]

On 16 March 1841, Newman advised the Vice-Chancellor of
Oxford that he was the sole author 'of the Tract on which the Hebdo-
madal Board has just expressed an opinion', and that his own opinion
of 'the truth and honesty of the principle maintained in the Tract'
remained unchanged.[209] Writing to Keble on 25 March 1841, Newman
said that Bishop Bagot wished him to write a letter saying that 'at his
bidding, I will suppress *Tract 90*. I have no difficulty in saying and
doing so if he tells me, but my difficulty is as to my *then* position'.[210]
He felt, as Trevor puts it, that he was 'being driven into a corner
where he must either defy his Bishop or deny his principles, for to
suppress the *Tract* would imply its censure'.[211] His predicament was
made even worse because episcopal condemnation was virtually unanimous. What crippled Newman, as David Newsome points out, was 'a
broadside from the Bench of Bishops – a succession of hostile
charges, which threw him into a position from which not even his
most skilful casuistry could rescue him'.[212] In the end, his consistent
exaltation of Episcopal authority compelled Newman to retract what
he had written. In Nockles' view, Newman had misconceived the
Episcopal response and, never slow to sense a personal affront, in
human terms he found the Episcopal disowning' of *Tract XC* 'a humiliation'.[213] Eventually, Newman agreed with the compromise offered
by the kindly and troubled Bishop Bagot, distasteful though it was to
have to write of Roman corruptions in his letter to the bishop.
Newman's formal letter ran to around a dozen pages in which he put
forward some remarks of his own on the issues raised by the critics of
Tract 90 and, in particular, the expressed wishes of the bishop that the
Tracts should be discontinued. After assuring Bagot that he would
'most readily and cheerfully obey' him, he then proceeded to offer
skilful and elaborate explanations of the principles underlying the
Tracts, and regretted that some misunderstandings had risen about
their nature and purpose. In *Tract 90*, he declared, he had been 'very
unwilling to commit the view of the Articles which I was taking to any
precise statement of the ultimate approaches to the Roman system
allowed by our own'. In his final paragraph, Newman admitted that he
had 'nothing to be sorry for, except having made your Lordship
anxious, and others whom I am bound to revere'.[214] This settlement
was mentioned in a letter to his devoted sister Jemima:

The Tract affair is settled on these terms, which others may think a disappointment, but to me is a very fair bargain. I am now publishing a letter to the Bishop at his wish stating that he wishes the Tracts to be discontinued, and he thinks No.90 objectionable as tending to disturb the Church. I am quite satisfied with the bargain I have got, if this is all as I suppose it will be.[215]

Newman wrote on 4 April to Bowden: 'The bishop sent me a message that my Letter had his unqualified approbation.' As for himself, he declared that he had 'not one misgiving throughout and he trusted that what had happened will be overlooked to subserve the great cause we all have at heart'.[216] Bagot's letter of acceptance had closed with the typically benign observation that Newman's response was 'once calculated to soften and silence opponents, as also to attach and to regulate friends, whilst the tone and temper of mind with which it is written must please and gratify all who read it'.[217] Newman records in a memorandum in his private journal, dated 26 October 1863:

In September, 1833, I began the series *Tracts for the Times*. In 1838 I became editor of the *British Critic*. In 1841, on occasion of the publication of No.90 of the Tracts, the Board of Heads of Houses brought out a censure of the doctrine contained in it as an evasive interpretation of the Thirty-nine articles, and at the wish of Dr Bagot, Bishop of Oxford, I brought the series to an end. At the same time, I retired from Oxford to Littlemore.[218]

Yet, despite all the anguished undertakings given by Newman, Nockles asserts that *Tract 90* to the Bishop of Oxford's surprise continued to be re-printed, and Newman was 'disingenuous in making it appear that Bishop Bagot had, or could have, tied the hands of his fellow Bishops. It was simply not in the Bishop of Oxford's power to have done this'.[219]

Later, Newman was to write to an 'unknown correspondent':

If conversions to Rome take place in consequence of the *Tracts for the Times*, I do not impute blame to them, but to those who, instead of acknowledging such Anglican principles of theology and ecclesiastical polity as they contain, set themselves to oppose them. Whatever may be the influence of the *Tracts*, great or small, they may become just as powerful for Rome, if our Church refuses them, as they would be for our Church if she accepted them.

He concluded that there would not be one or two but many secessions to Rome.[220] Newman, as Owen Chadwick observes, had 'courageously

essayed to treat the catholicity of the Articles in *Tract 90*,[221] but he had
been forced to retract and sought consolation in his beloved Littlemore.
He had abandoned the *via media*; he was now on the *via cruces*, on his
pilgrimage towards Rome.

In 1843, another prominent Tractarian – E. B. Pusey – was also to
undergo a distressing experience as the result of a sermon he had
preached on 'The Holy Eucharist as a comfort to the Penitent'. In the
sermon he spoke with marked fervour about the Real Presence. His
sermon was delated to the Vice-Chancellor as being heretical; a
university court was set up and found against Pusey, who was
suspended from preaching within the precincts of the University for
two years. Newman worried about the effect that this would have on
his friend, who was still suffering from the death of his wife a few
years earlier. In a letter of 24 May 1843, to Jemima, he expressed this
concern: 'Do you know that the Vice-chancellor has taken to a sermon
of Pusey's preached last Sunday at Christ Church, and that six doctors
(of divinity) are about to sit on it? . . . I am not without anxiety as to
the effects on him personally.[222] Pusey, however, bore his suspension
stoically and, as Gilley notes: 'His faith was untroubled by the
disgrace, and it was as Puseyites, not Newmanites, that the Anglo
Catholics were to remain within the Church of England.'[223]

Newman continued his largely reclusive life at Littlemore, 'for
some days, quite alone, without a friend or servant',[224] studying the
Fathers, praying and meditating intensely, and reflecting on the possibility of 'having to join the Church of Rome'.[225] His mind was
wracked with conflicting thoughts: should he stay in the Church of
England, to which he was intimately attached and continue to enjoy its
protective environment and the opportunities for a preferment, or
should he join the Church of Rome and experience a chaotic upheaval
of his whole life, with all the uncertainties that this would involve.

Newman's University Sermons, briefly mentioned earlier, were
influential and inspiring not only to those who heard them but, over
the years, they have attracted much wider attention for the insights
they gave to his personal intellectual and spiritual progression. On 29
December 1842, Newman wrote to Bowden; 'I am publishing my
University Sermons, which will be thought sad, dull affairs; but
having got through a subject, I wish to get rid of it.'[226] He also told
Jemima, on 23 January 1843, that his University Sermons 'are not
theological or ecclesiastical though they bear immediately upon the
most intimate and practical religious questions'.[227] Newman's preach-

ing attracted hundreds mainly because of 'the depth of his spiritual insight and freshness of his ideas, and his plain-spoken eloquence'.[228] For example, in his first sermon: 'The Philosophical Temper first enjoined by the Gospel', Newman tells his listeners; 'The philosopher might speculate, but the theologian must submit to learn', and, later ... 'it is obvious to be in earnest in seeking the truth is an indispensable requisite for finding it'. He warns that men may too often be led astray in their scientific researches; 'they have inferred much from slender premises, and conjectured when they could not prove'. On the other hand, 'the philosopher has only to confess that he is liable to be deceived by false appearances ... he is humble because he knows himself to be fallible, docile, because he really desires to learn'.[229]

In the *Apologia*, Newman stated that in 1826 he preached his first University Sermon, and that the following year he was one of the Public Examiners for the BA degree, when he suffered his second 'great illness'. A year later, he was appointed the vicar of St Mary's; this was a happy transition: 'It was to me like the feeling of spring weather after winter; and, if I may so speak, I came out of my shell; I remained out of it until 1841.'[230] He clearly experienced an exhilarating sense of release – although temporary – from earlier anxieties about his path in life. The earlier sermons belong, as Maisie Ward shrewdly observed, 'to the young Newman, still partly an Evangelical, still influenced by Whately but passing gradually under the influence of Keble and Hurrell Froude'. His later sermons reflect 'the profound developments in his personality' as well as his already noted dedicated study of Patristic literature. The promise shown in his earlier years, when, as Maisie Ward states, 'the later ones take us to the verge of his full Catholic development'.[231] On 7 March 1843 Newman told the Revd S. Rickards that his University Sermons, 'which have been published little more than a fortnight, have come to a second edition. I cannot think that they have been bought for their contents'.[232] These fifteen sermons of Newman's Anglican ministry, preached in the University Church from 1826 to 1843, were occasionally described by Newman as Discourses. He never repudiated them. To W. G. Ward, grandfather of Maisie, the 'sermons brought a renewal of faith; forty years later he gave them to his son to save him from doubt'.[233] Newman noted in the *Apologia* that his 'last sermon was in September, 1843', after which he was 'at Littlemore in quiet for two years'.[234]

In a memorandum of 26 October 1863, Newman recorded succinctly the major events in his life, including his eventual retirement from

active involvement in the Oxford Movement. He also noted that in
1843, he 'published a retraction of the strong charges I had made
against the Church of Rome'.[235] This retraction, although appearing
anonymously, was published in the *Conservative Journal* on 28
January 1843, and he confided to J. R. Hope, on 25 January 1843, that
his conscience had goaded him to 'eat a few dirty words of mine'.[236]

Newman consulted Keble again about his possible retirement from
St Mary's and was assured that, provided he could continue his
ministry at Littlemore, the decision could be taken.[237] Newman then
confessed that his feelings for Rome had been getting stronger, where-
upon Keble urged him to retain his active ministry, otherwise he
would be exposed to the dangers of secession from the Church of
England. Apparently Newman was now experiencing a stressful
conflict of loyalties to the Church of England, to the Oxford Movement in which he was so closely involved, and now to the pressing
needs of his conscience that he should abandon these treasured affilia-
tions and become a Roman Catholic. In a revealing letter to James
Mozley, dated 1 September 1843, Newman conceded: 'The truth is, I
am not a good enough son of the Church of England to feel that I can
in conscience hold preferment under her. I love the Church of Rome
too well.'[238] Throughout his life Newman 'insisted on the supremacy
of conscience' and stated that every man 'experienced an authoritative
moral dictate within him, which praised, blamed and issued
commands ...The more a man listens to and obeys it the clearer it
becomes, until it produces an intimate perception of the one true
God'.[239] After long and deliberate reflection, Newman eventually
decided that he would have to leave the Anglican Church for the
Church of Rome and, on 7 September 1843, he sent his resignation to
the bishop, assuring him that his decision 'is already no secret to
friends and others', while also thanking him heartily for all the past
'acts of friendship and favour' received from him.[240]

Following his resignation, Newman exchanged several letters with
Archdeacon Manning and also Gladstone. He set out firmly his views
to the former:

> I must tell you then frankly, unless I combat arguments which to me are,
> alas, shadows, that it is from no disappointment, or, impatience, that I
> have, whether rightly or wrongly, resigned St Mary's but because I think
> the Church of Rome the Catholic Church, and ours not a part of the
> Catholic Church, because not in communion with Rome, and I felt I could
> not honestly be a teacher in it any longer.[241]

Such clearly stated convictions thoroughly alarmed Manning who, despite his warm feelings of friendship towards Newman, felt compelled to deliver his relentless *No-Popery* sermon on Guy Fawkes Day, 1843, in Oxford.[242] On the following day, Manning called on Newman at Littlemore who refused to see him. As Gilley notes:

> It was Manning's first experience of Newman's inability to separate persons and principles, and of his unforgiving strain, when as a rival cardinal, he came to embody the alternative to Manning's unbending Ultramontanism.[243]

On the other hand, it would seem that Manning displayed some degree of insensitivity in attempting to see Newman after preaching an anti-Catholic sermon. However, deeply shocked, Manning returned to Oxford but in just five years he, himself, was destined to tread the path to Rome. But even forty years later this matter was to re-surface and in a Memorandum: *Manning's Call at Littlemore*, Newman referred to a review of 'Dr James Mozley's Letters' which had appeared in the November 1884 issue of the *Spectator*. This related to Manning's frustrated call at Littlemore in 1843, immediately after delivering a sermon in the 'University pulpit in favour of the puritan party, etc.'.[244] Newman asked his old and trusted friend, Dean Church, for help in dealing with the comments in the *Spectator*, adding that he could recollect nothing about it and 'if I did give such a message [of refusal], I don't think I should have given a young door-keeper my real reason'.[245] Church replied that he had seen the reviewer (Charles Kegan Paul), who had first published the account in the previous year in another journal. Newman's response reveals his bewilderment over the whole reported affair, especially because he said that he had sent Manning, 'just before Guy Faux day 1843, three successive and most free letters'. Newman speculated that there was only 'one hypothesis for my refusing to see him, *if I did* ... my fear of being pumped on and on by Manning' who 'of all the men I know down to this day there is no one so merciless and successful as a pumper'. Newman concluded by observing it was 'odd that the account has been bottled up until now'.[246] Following Church's enquiries, Newman was obviously unimpressed with the further account given by the journalist; 'as the statement does not come from him [Manning], I do not think much of it'. He alluded to the same journalist's biographical article in the *Century Illustrated Monthly*

Magazine of June 1882, following a call made on him at Littlemore.
Newman thanked him for his article

> But a friend in this house said to me afterwards: 'Do you see what you
> have done? You have let pass an unjustifiable, unfounded, offensive impu-
> tation on yourself and the Oratory ... He takes occasion to say that you
> showed your scorn of moral theology (casuistry) by keeping silence on one
> of the questions proposed at table for discussion'.[247]

Newman's loyal friend Richard Church informed him, on 7 January
1885: 'Of course I have not told Paul [the journalist] about your note.
I only said that as the story did not come from Cardinal Manning, you
did not trouble yourself more about it.'[248] Accounts of this curiously
misunderstood episode reappeared, however, after Newman's death.

On the seventh anniversary of the consecration of the Littlemore
church – 25 September 1843 – Newman preached his last sermon: *The
Parting of Friends*. His text was *Man goeth forth to his work and
labour until the evening*. In Maisie Ward's poignant words; 'Like the
singing of the Reproaches, or the Lamentations of Holy Week, the
little church was filled with the clear voice making audible every word
of Christ's lament over the holy city that had rejected Him.'[249]

Newman now immersed himself in the task of preparing a philosophical treatise: *Essay on the Development of Christian Doctrine*, and
which, according to Trevor 'was germinating all through the painful
year that followed his resignation'.[250] He wrote in the *Apologia*:

> During the last half of that tenth year 1844 I was engaged in writing a
> book *Essay on Development* in favour of the Roman Church and indirectly
> against the English; but even then, till it was finished, I had not absolutely
> intended to publish it, wishing to reserve to myself the chance of changing
> my mind when the argumentative views which were activating me had
> been distinctly brought out before me in writing.[251]

For many years, Newman had been gathering thoughts on this topic,
i.e. that the doctrine of the Church had been gradually defined. The
idea had been first aired publicly in his last University sermon, given
on the Feast of the Purification of the Blessed Virgin in 1843. This
hagiographic discourse Ker describes as 'the most brilliant of the
University Sermons and one of the most original and penetrating of his
writings'.[252] Newman postulated that a principle of development could
be discerned by which the Christian Church from its early days was

able to define its doctrines by 'making explicit that which had been implicit'.[253] As Dessain points out, Newman's *Essay on Development of Christian Doctrine* was published fourteen years before Darwin's *Origin of Species* appeared, and Newman experienced no problem in accepting the idea of evolution 'as long as it was theistic'.[254] Nearly thirty years later, Newman assured a biologist correspondent that he 'must not suppose I have personally any great dislike or dread of his [Darwin's] theory, but many good people are much troubled at it – and at all events . . . it is well to show that Catholics may be better reasoners than philosophers'.[255] Newman's correspondent – St George Mivart – was to dedicate his *Lessons from Nature* to Newman in 1875. To Dr Brown, Professor and, later, Principal of the Free Church College, Aberdeen, Newman wrote: 'I see nothing in the theory of evolution inconsistent with an Almighty God and Protector.'[256]

Not unexpectedly, Newman's theory of the development of religious doctrine attracted sharp criticism from various quarters, but it was to become accepted and applied in the historical study of the development of ideas and institutions. His essay was essentially an exploration in which he involved himself deeply and through which he clarified his own thoughts about where his future lay. On 8 June 1844, in a letter to Keble, Newman made a long statement about his state of mind and conscience from his boyhood years down to the present time. He referred to Keble's stirring sermon 'National Apostasy' – which was to be so influential in opening the Oxford Movement – and to his own growing feelings that the 'Roman Communion is the only true Church', a process of study of the Fathers, as well as from his attempts 'to resist such urgent and imperative thoughts by his writings and great efforts to keep others from moving in the direction of Rome also'. But, he confessed, the time for argument was past; 'I have been in one settled conviction for so long a time, which every new thought seems to strengthen.'[257]

From this period of intense recollection and study of his religious beliefs and experiences, from boyhood to middle age, and, virtually, as it turned out, half way through his long life, Newman recorded in the *Apologia*:

So, at the end of 1844, I came to the resolution of writing an Essay on Doctrinal Development; and then, if, at the end of it, my convictions in favour of the Roman Church were not weaker, of taking the necessary steps for admission into her fold. I acted upon this resolution in the beginning of 1845, and worked at my Essay steadily into the autumn.[258]

As he advanced in writing the Essay he admitted that his view had 'so cleared that instead of speaking any more of the "Roman Catholics", boldly called them "Catholics"'.[259] By September 1845, Newman had still not finished the Essay, and he then realized that he had to make a decision which would change the whole direction of his life;

> He decided not to wait any longer but to seek admission to the Roman Catholic Church. The unfinished book was sent to the printers in late September and published before the end of the year.[260]

A second printing was published in 1846 and, in 1878, a new edition appeared, but Newman declared that he had made ... 'no substantial alterations in it, but nearly turned it inside out, as far as arrangement goes'.[261]

On 31 October 1874, Newman told John Finlayson, a member of the Free Church of Scotland, that he had 'never read' his *Essay on the Development of Doctrine* since he had written it: 'I never either have read the criticisms on it.'[262]

Ker has pointed out that the Essay 'is not only the starting point for the study of doctrinal development, but so far as Catholic theology is concerned, it is still the last word on the subject'. He states that 'no other theologian has yet attempted anything on the scale or of similar scope', and declares that 'even if the *Essay* was not one of the great theological classics', it would still be of lasting interest. He gives two reasons for this claim; the first is that 'it is one of the key intellectual documents of the nineteenth century' comparable to Darwin's *Origin of Species* – which 'it predates by over a decade', and, secondly, its rhetorical art and style 'surely place Newman among the masters of English prose'.[263]

On 11 July 1845, Newman wrote to Richard Westmacott (1799–1872), an acclaimed sculptor and friend since their early schooling days at Ealing: 'I suppose I may now tell you, it is morally certain that I shall join the RC Church ... It has been the conviction of six years – from which I have never receded, and (for which) I have waited patiently a long time.' He explained that his conviction was founded on the study of early church history, and that he had come to the conclusion that the Church of Rome (was) in every respect the continuation of the early Church. 'I think she is the early Church in these

Bust of Newman by Sir Richard Westmacott, a school fellow and life long friend

times. They differ in doctrine and discipline as child and grown man, not otherwise.'[264] In this remarkable and explanatory letter, the influence of Newman's theory of doctrinal development is evident; in only a few months he would be making his historic decision, but 'it was with no anticipation of human happiness that Newman approached his journey's end'.[265]

Westmacott's reaction to Newman's stirring message was forthright: 'Although I may not agree with you I am bound to respect your taking the step you contemplate under the conscientious belief that you are doing right.' He regretted that Newman had taken six years and had 'allowed [his] friends and admirers to believe all this time that [he] had been, what was so wanted, a reforming Anglican'.[266] In 1840, Richard Westmacott – who was appointed professor of sculpture at the Royal Academy in 1857 – had taken a plaster cast of Newman with a view to making a full marble bust, although Newman was not told this at the time. The sculpture was completed in the following year and, for many years, it was owned by the Mozley family, who presented it to the Birmingham Oratory in 1974.[267]

Notes
  1. Wilfrid Ward, 1913, p. 2.
  2. Ker, 1990, p. viii.
  3. Newman, 1956, p. 120.
  4. Trevor, 1996, p. 46.
  5. Briggs, 1990, p. 71.
  6. Dessain, 1980, p. 71.
  7. LDII.264, Simon Lloyd Pope, 15 August 1830.
  8. Newman, 1989, p. 357.
  9. Trevor, 1996, p. 26.
 10. Ward, 1913, II, p. 460.
 11. Nockles, 1997, p. 67.
 12. LDII.117, footnote.
 13. Newman, 1956, p. 97.
 14. LDII.118.
 15. LDII.120, 8 February 1829.
 16. LDII.125, 1 March 1829.
 17. Gilley, 1990, p. 73.
 18. Nockles, 1997, p. 69.
 19. LDII.372, 30 October 1831.
 20. Maisie Ward, 1948, p. 224.

21. Nockles, 1997, p. 324.
22. Walgrave, 1960, p. 31.
23. Newman, 1956, p. 69.
24. Nockles, 1997, p. 53.
25. LDIII.186.
26. Chadwick, 1971, p. 56.
27. LDIII.242, 11 March 1833.
28. LDIII.247, 9 March 1833.
29. LDIII.249, 14 March 1833.
30. cf Newsome, 1993, p. 163.
31. Gilley, 1990, p. 111.
32. Gilley, 1990, p. 63.
33. Newman, 1993, p. 388.
34. Newman, 1956, p. 119.
35. Newman, 1956, p. 120.
36. Vargish, 1970, p. 91.
37. Chadwick, 1971, p. 70.
38. Chadwick, 1971, p. 72.
39. LDIV.20-22, 25 August 1833.
40. LDIV.9, 16 July 1833.
41. Newman, 1956, p. 120.
42. LDIV.13-14, 30 July 1833.
43. LDIV.28-29, 11 August 1833.
44. Chadwick, 1971, pp. 74–5.
45. Dessain, 1980, p. 35.
46. LDIV.78, autumn 1833.
47. Nockles, 1977, p. 57.
48. Gilley, 1990, p. 119.
49. Chadwick, 1971, p. 126.
50. LDIV.56, 2 December 1833.
51. Dessain, 1980, p. 37.
52. Trevor, 1996, p. 52.
53. Maisie Ward, 1948, p. 315.
54. Cf Oddie, 1993, p. vii.
55. Cf Gilley, 1990, p. 130.
56. Nockles, 1996, p. 100.
57. cf Nockles, 1997, p. 38.
58. Gilley, 1996, p. 65.
59. Vargish, 1970, p. 97.
60. Maisie Ward, 1948, p. 242.
61. LDIV.72, 26 October 1833.
62. Dessain, 1980, pp. 26–9.
63. LDIV.38-40, 2 September 1833; LDIV.47–9, 9 September 1833.
64. Trevor, 1996, p. 51.
65. LDXXVI.293-94, 20 April 1873.
66. LDXXVIII.190, 7 April 1877.
67. LDIV.249-50, 7 May 1834.

68. LDIV.239, 25 April 1834.
69. LDIV.371, 28 November 1834.
70. LDIV.372, 28 November 1834.
71. Newman, 1956, p. 98.
72. Newman, 1956, p. 86.
73. LDII.208, 28 April 1830.
74. LDII.208–361.
75. LDII.233, 8 June 1830.
76. Newman, 1956, p. 93.
77. LDII.242, 15 June 1830.
78. LDII.244, 18 June 1830.
79. LDII.245, 25 June 1830.
80. Trevor, 1996, p. 98.
81. LDV.265, 'Declaration', Oxford, 10 March 1836.
82. LDV.xiv.
83. Maisie Ward, 1948, p. 255.
84. Newman, 1956, p. 96.
85. Newman, 1993, p. 193.
86. Maisie Ward, 1948, p. 345.
87. Gilley, 1990, p. 89.
88. LDV.399, Henry Wilberforce, 29 December 1836.
89. LDXXVIII.172, Robert Charles Jenkins, 27 February 1877
90. LDXXX.240, William Bright, 25 July 1883.
91. Ker, 1990, p. 48.
92. Selby, 1975, p. 67.
93. Ker, 1990, p. 49.
94. Nockles, 1997, p. 198.
95. LDV.142, 11 September 1835.
96. LDV.142, 9 September 1835.
97. LDV.136, 8 September 1835.
98. LDIV.367–9, 17 November 1834.
99. Dessain, 1980, p. 38.
100. Maisie Ward, 1948, p. 258.
101. Dessain, 1980, p. 39.
102. Wilfrid Ward, 1913, p. 59.
103. Newman, 1993, p. 134.
104. Allen, 1975, pp. 10–11.
105. LDV.25, 5 February 1835.
106. LDXI.100-1, 27 January 1846.
107. Walgrave, 1960, p. 38.
108. LDI.285, 1 May 1826.
109. LDI.286.
110. Newman, 1993, p. 105.
111. LDII.369, 24 October 1831.
112. Boekraad & Tristram, 1961, p. 22.
113. LDXXV.352–3, 3 July 1871.
114. Newman, 1993, p. 203.

115. Gilley, 1990, p. 156.
116. LDV.303–5, 23 May 1836.
117. LDVI.61, 25 April 1837.
118. Nockles, 1991, pp. 38–9.
119. Norman, 1985, p. 123.
120. Norman, 1985, p. 148.
121. Wilfrid Ward, 1913, p. 69.
122. Gwynn, 1929, p. 330.
123. Chadwick, 1990, p. 43.
124. Ker, 1990, p. 35.
125. LDXXV.215, Miss M. R. Giberne, 15 October 1870.
126. LDXXIV.354–6, 20 October 1869.
127. Newman, 1993, p. 174.
128. Bacchus, 1913, p. 14.
129. LDVII.154, Frederic Rogers, 22 September 1839.
130. Gilley, 1990, p. 184.
131. Chadwick, 1971, p. 180.
132. Newman, 1993, pp. 142–3.
133. Nockles, 1997, p. 279.
134. LDVII.138, 8 September 1839.
135. LDVII.411, 21 October 1840.
136. LDVI.192–3, 29 January 1838.
137. Newman, 1993, pp. 140–1.
138. Ker, 1991, p. 140.
139. Maisie Ward, 1948, p. 306.
140. Nockles, 1997, p. 262.
141. LDVI.229–31, 241–3.
142. LDVI.285–6, 14 August 1838.
143. LDVI.286–8, John Keble, 14 August 1838; & LDVI.292, J. W.
     Bowden, 17 August 1838.
144. Trevor, 1996, p. 64.
145. LDVI.320, 25 September 1838.
146. LDV.249–50, 2 March 1836.
147. LDVI.76, 1 June 1837.
148. LDVI.96–7, 30 June 1837.
149. LDVI.120–1.
150. LDVI.118, 27 August 1837.
151. LDVI.188, 17 January 1838.
152. *Remains*, VI.336.
153. *Remains*, VI.433.
154. Wilfrid Ward, 1913, p. 60.
155. Chadwick, 1971, p. 175.
156. Nockles, 1991, pp. 35–6.
157. LDVI.325, 3 October 1838.
158. Maisie Ward, 1948, p. 337.
159. cf Nockles, 1997, pp. 126–7.
160. LDVI.332, footnote.

161. LDVII.xv.
162. LDXXXI.246, 22 July 1888.
163. LDVI.xviii.
164. Newsome, 1993, p. 284.
165. Nockles, 1997, p. 143.
166. LDVII.205-6, Frederic Rogers, 8 January 1840.
167. LDVII.214-5, H. E. Manning, 15 January 1840.
168. LDVII.233-5, 9 February 1840.
169. LDVIII.251, 19 August 1841.
170. LDVIII.297, 14 October 1841.
171. LDVIII.297, footnote.
172. LDVII.246, 27 February 1840.
173. Newman, 1956, pp. 217-8.
174. Newman, 1956, pp. 121-38.
175. LDVII.245, 25 February 1840.
176. Newman, 1956, p. 213.
177. LDVII.263, 'Memorandum'.
178. LDVII.264, E. B. Pusey, 17 March 1840 & LDVII.267, S. F. Wood, 17 March 1840.
179. LDVII.328, 20 May 1840.
180. LDVII.328, Thomas Mozley, 20 May 1840.
181. LDVII.409, 20 October 1840.
182. LDVII.416-8, 26 October 1840.
183. LDVII.431-2, from John Keble, 3 November 1840.
184. LDVII.433, 6 November 1840.
185. LDVII.448-51, 5 November 1840.
186. LDVIII.276-8, 22 September 1841.
187. LDIII.297-300.
188. LDVIII.409-10.
189. LDVIII.504-7, 14 April 1842.
190. LDVIII.237-8.
191. LDVIII.507.
192. LDVIII.512-3, 25 April 1842.
193. Ker, 1990, p. 206.
194. Trevor, 1996, p. 72.
195. 'Introduction': Tract 90, Newman, 1841, pp. 4-5.
196. Tract 90: 'Conclusions', Newman, 1841, pp. 83-7.
197. Dessain, 1980, p. 74.
198. Trevor, 1996, p. 74.
199. Cf. Gilley, 1990, p. 199.
200. Mozley, 1891, p. 327.
201. Mozley, 1891, p. 326; LDVIII.61, 12 March 1841.
202. Mozley, 1891, pp. 326-7; LDVIII.70, J. W. Bowden, 13 March 1841.
203. Mozley, 1891, p. 329; Trevor, 1996, p. 74.
204. Mozley, 1891, p. 330.
205. Ker, 1990, p. 218.

206. Mozley, 1891, p. 235; LDVIII.90.
207. Mozley, 1891, pp. 235–6; LDVIII.77.
208. LDVIII.78–88, 13 March 1841.
209. LDVIII.93.
210. Mozley, 1891, pp. 338; LDVIII.120.
211. Trevor, 1996, p. 76.
212. Newsome, 1993, p. 284.
213. Nockles, 1997, p. 295.
214. LDVIII.125–44, 2 April 1841.
215. Mozley, 1891, p. 341; LDVIII.145.
216. Mozley, 1891, p. 344; LDVIII.154–5.
217. LDVIII.144, 1 April 1841.
218. Newman, 1956, p. 12.
219. Nockles, 1997, p. 57.
220. LDVIII.303, 23 October 1841.
221. Chadwick, 1971, p. 183.
222. Mozley, 1891, p. 183; LDIX.356.
223. Gilley, 1990, p. 218.
224. Wilfrid Ward, 1913, p. 75.
225. Maisie Ward, 1948, p. 132.
226. Mozley, 1891, pp. 405–6; LDIX.188–9.
227. Mozley, 1891, p. 406; LDIX.213–4.
228. Tillman, 1997, p. viii.
229. Tillman, 1997, pp. 8, 9, 12.
230. Oddie, 1993, p. 98.
231. Maisie Ward, 1948, p. 132.
232. Mozley, 1891, p. 409; LDIX.270–1.
233. Maisie Ward, 1948, p. 351.
234. Oddie, 1993, p. 230.
235. Newman, 1956, p. 12.
236. Mozley, 1891, p. 406; LDIX.215.
237. Mozley, 1891, pp. 422–31; LDIX.494–5.
238. Mozley, 1891, p. 423; LDIX.493–4.
239. Cf. Dessain, 1980, p. 145.
240. Bacchus, 1917, pp. 262–3; LDIX.514–5.
241. Bacchus, 1917, pp. 276; LDIX.585–6.
242. Bacchus, 1917, pp. 280; LDIX.599.
243. Gilley, 1990, p. 221; LDX.9, footnote.
244. LDXXX.437–8, 18 November 1884.
245. LDXXX.446, 21 December 1884.
246. LDXXX.448–9, 23 December 1884.
247. LDXXXI.4–5, 4 January 1885.
248. LDXXXI.5, footnote 4.
249. Maisie Ward, 1948, p. 402.
250. Trevor, 1996, p. 94.
251. Oddie, 1993, p. 231.
252. Ker, 1989, p. xix; LDX.264–8.

253. Griffin, 1993, p. 6.
254. Dessain, 1980, p. 81.
255. LDXXV.446, 9 December 1871.
256. LDXXVII.43–4, 4 April 1874.
257. Bacchus, 1917, pp. 313–8; LDX.259–63; LDX.412–3; LDX.416–7; LDX.426–7.
258. Oddie, 1993, pp. 263–4; LDX.603, footnote.
259. Oddie, 1993, p. 269.
260. Ker, 1990, p. 301.
261. LDXXVIII.288–9, 23 December 1877; LDX.780–1, footnote.
262. LDXXVII.146.
263. Newman, 1989, p. xxv.
264. Sugg, 1983, p. 70; LDX.729; LDX.84, footnote.
265. Maisie Ward, 1948, p. 448.
266. LDX.732, 16 July 1845.
267. LDXXIX.385, footnote.

Chapter 3

Littlemore and Conversion

On 6 September 1843 Newman, as mentioned in the preceding chapter, had resigned as vicar of St Mary's, the University Church, a post to which, in 1828, he had been 'presented by Mr Hawkins, Provost of Oriel'.[1] After resigning he lived in seclusion at Littlemore, immersed in writing and battling against growing convictions that would eventually lead him to take the further step of severing his official links with the University. But he was able to reassure his old friend, R. W. Church, in a letter dated 3 April 1845, that 'I have never for an instant had even the temptation of repenting my leaving Oxford ... How could I remain at St Mary's, a hypocrite?'[2]

He had secured on 12 April 1822 – at the early age of twenty-one – a Fellowship at Oriel College, 'then at the height of its literary fame'.[3] The young Newman described this conspicuous achievement 'as a turning-point and most memorable event', declaring that he never wished for anything in life 'better or higher than to live and die a Fellow of Oriel'.[4] Such youthful elation is understandable; so also can his distress be realized when, some twenty-three years later, he became aware that he would have to resign his post in the College, to which he was so deeply attached. It was at Oriel that Newman had benefited greatly, according to Chadwick, from 'intellectual osmosis', the most important influence being exercised by 'the sweet-natured, godly pastor and poet John Keble'.[5]

At Oriel, the young Newman also came into close contact with the Noetics, an intellectual coterie which included Copleston, Hawkins, Whately, Hampden and Thomas Arnold. These distinguished and disputatious Fellows were always ready to explore virtually any topic, including religion. Whately, for example, held distinctly anti-Erastian

views and was ready to challenge any attempts to impose state control
in ecclesiastical affairs. (See Chapter 2: Oxford Movement, and the
hardening of attitudes following the Irish Temporalities Act 1833.)

In the *Apologia*, Newman confessed that he owed Whately 'a great
deal', and described him as 'a man of generous and warm heart: all
his geese were swans'. Newman's mind was, 'emphatically opened';
Whately 'taught me to think and use my reason'.[6] Whately also
encouraged Newman to develop his knowledge of logic and, in 1822,
asked for his assistance in preparing an article on Logic for the *Ency-
clopaedia Metropolitana*.

Newman's linkages with Whately increased when he was appointed
Vice-Principal at Alban Hall, which was headed by Whately. Newman
relinquished this office on taking up a tutorship at Oriel, and he
recorded that from then Whately's 'hold upon me gradually relaxed.
He had done his work towards me or nearly so, when he taught me to
see with my own eyes and to walk with my own feet'.[7]

As he matured, Newman began increasingly to recognize that
Whately's mind was 'too different from his own for them to remain
long in one line'.[8] He was also aware that the Noetics' influence had
caused him to drift into a form of incipient Liberalism, as noted in
Chapter 1. At the same time, Newman acknowledged his debt to
Whately, who was so influential in his early years as a young
academic but whose influence, 'after a few years had passed ... had
not been satisfactory'. However, Whately's strong views on Erastianism were to be reflected in and become 'one of the most prominent
features of the Tractarian Movement'.[9]

Newman's association with Oriel must be 'considered a potent
factor in the shaping of his mind, there is imbibed a good deal of
philosophy which was formally Aristotelian'. It is said that while
'again and again in his works there is mention of Aristotle', it seems
that any other explicit reference to that philosopher or his doctrines is
limited to poetry'.[10]

During his earlier years at Oriel, Newman, though proud of his
college was, in his own words, 'not quite at home there' – he was
'very much alone' although he treasured the company of his 'dear
and true friend Dr Pusey' who, however, left Oriel just as Newman
'was getting to know him well'.[11] Newman was left without an intimate friendship but, with the Oriel tutorship and the appointment
as vicar of St Mary's, Newman's life became more settled, as he
noted in the *Apologia*, 'It was to me the feeling of spring weather

after winter; and, if I may so speak, I came out of my shell; I remained out of it until 1841.' At the beginning of 1829, Newman also noted that there occurred a 'formal break between Dr Whately and me', resulting from 'Mr Peel's re-attempted election', as mentioned in Chapter 2.[12]

On 21 November 1844 Newman, in a lengthy letter, confided that 'I scarcely was every present at a Roman service even abroad. I knew no Roman Catholics. I have no sympathies towards them as an existing body... I am setting my face absolutely towards the wilderness.'[13] Three days later he wrote almost identically to his sister Jemima, adding 'I am not conscious of any resentment, disgust or the like, to repel me from my present position: and I have no dreams whatever – far from it indeed. I seem to be throwing myself away.'[14] He viewed with some trepidation the prospect of abandoning the assured and comfortable life of an Anglican cleric and Oxford academic in order to associate himself with those who professed a religion which largely lacked acceptance in the polite society of the period and, of whose members he knew virtually none.

In a moving letter to his sister Jemima, dated 15 March 1845, Newman confided his inner thoughts about what he believed he was 'called to do ... I am making myself an outcast, and that at my age ... I may be wrong, but He that judgeth is the Lord'.[15] In her reply of 21 March, Jemima wrote firmly but tenderly, 'but yet I have no bias towards Rome, nor see any compensation in Rome to make up for the defects of our Church'. She also assures her brother that 'I am not conscious of a bitter feeling towards Rome; we seem to have enough to do with sorrow and humiliation at home without quarrelling with other Churches.'[16] She shared his confidences while remaining a member of the Church of England, even though she was aware of her brother's likely influence over her religious convictions.[17]

In a letter of 20 April 1845, Newman alerted James Mozley that 'By November I expect to have resigned my Fellowship.' He added: 'I don't mind your telling this in confidence to anyone you please.' Not surprisingly, the news soon circulated, as Newman no doubt expected it would.[18]

Just over six months later, on 3 October 1845, Newman wrote officially to Hawkins, the Provost of Oriel, resigning his Fellowship. He received a cold, formal acknowledgement, with the hope expressed that Newman would be spared some of the worse errors of Rome. He informed Newman, officially, that 'The form of Resignation is quite

correct; and if I hear nothing further from you to the contrary, I must
of course comply with your desire and withdraw your name from our
books on my return to Oriel.' He added that the tone of Newman's
letter seemed 'strong confirmation of the rumours that he intended to
join the Church of Rome ... which I cannot but regard as a very
serious error'.[19] Newman retained, however, an affectionate memory
of Dr Hawkins, as reflected in the *Apologia*:

> I can say with a full heart that I love him, and have never ceased to love
> him; and I thus preface what otherwise might sound rude, that in the
> course of many years in which we were together afterwards, he provoked
> me much from time to time, though I am perfectly certain that I have
> provoked him a great deal more ... He was the first who taught me to
> weigh my words, and to be cautious in my statements ... He is a man of
> most exact mind himself, and he used to snub me severely, on reading,
> and other compositions which I was engaged upon.[20]

Many years later, Newman wrote to Mrs Hawkins on the death of her
husband, and in sending condolences, assured her; 'your dear husband
had never been out of my mind of late years' and he recalled their
early years and 'the kindness and benefits done to me by him close
upon 60 years ago'.[21]

On 6 December 1845, Jemima (Mrs J. Mozley) wrote to her sister-
in-law Anne Mozley (who was to edit Newman's correspondence
during his life in the Anglican Church)[22] that 'I have had a letter
which I have been expecting and half dreading to receive, this week
from JHN to say that he has written to the Provost to resign his
Fellowship. He adds that now anything may be expected any day.'[23] In
fact the resignation from Oriel was the necessary step towards finaliz-
ing his long-maturing plans to submit to Rome. This action had
already been taken, in September 1845, by W. G. Ward, a member of
the Oxford Movement since 1839. Ward, as noted in Chapter 2, had
incurred the wrath of the University because of alleged 'Romish
doctrines' in his work *The Ideal of a Christian Church*, and it was
proposed to penalize him heavily. Newman had written to James
Mozley on 5 January 1845, protesting against the harsh treatment
given to Ward, particularly when 'atrocious heresies' had been
published elsewhere without apparent censure.[24] At the same time as
Ward's case was being considered, the Convocation of the University
had a proposal before it to censure Newman's *Tract 90*. Such an ill-
conceived measure was robustly denounced by Charles Marriott,

Fellow and Dean of Oriel, and a close friend of Newman. He asked 'If the tract was to be condemned by the University, ought it not to have been condemned in 1841' instead of four years later and 'thus called for a fresh and gratuitous infliction of pain when no single fresh act on the author's part has occurred to warrant such repetition?'[25]

The proposal aroused Newman's friends and they rallied to his aid, determined to veto the censure on him. At a meeting of Convocation on 13 February 1845 to hear the cases against Ward and Newman, the former was deprived of his degrees by only a narrow majority, while the censure on Newman's *Tract 90* was vetoed by the Proctors. Ironically, in a few months' time both these leading members of the Oxford Movement would be received into the Roman Catholic Church.

J. D. Dalgairns, one of the early Tractarians, who had joined the Littlemore community in 1847, visited Fr Dominic Barberi in September 1845, and was received into the Church. In 1847, Dalgairns was to join Newman in Rome at the Oratorian noviciate. Ambrose St John, a former curate of Henry Wilberforce, and who was to become Newman's closest friend during his Oratorian years, was also received into the Church at the Catholic College of Prior Park on 30 September. Dalgairns' visit to Barberi seems to have motivated Newman to invite the missioner to break his journey, en route for Belgium, to attend a meeting of his congregation and stay overnight at Littlemore. In the *Apologia*, Newman recorded that as he 'was in some perplexity what steps to take for being received myself' he 'assented to the proposition made to me that the good priest should take Littlemore in his way, with a view to his doing for me the same charitable service as he had done to my friend'.[26] Newman confided to Henry Wilberforce that Fr Dominic Barberi 'does not know of my intentions but I shall keep this all back till it is all over'. He added that the missioner 'is a simple quaint man, an Italian; but a very sharp clever man too in his way'. Newman also mentioned that he had seem him once, 'for a few minutes on St John the Baptist's Day last year', when he had 'called at Littlemore to see the chapel'.[27] In another letter to Wilberforce, written later on the same day, Newman – as always busy, even on the eve of his historic conversion – told him that 'meanwhile, my book drags through the Press to my disappointment. The printers have hitherto been very slow – only 128 pages are in type of about 400. It is an *Essay on the Development of Christian Doctrine*'.[28]

To Jemima, on 8 October 1845, Newman had written a brief letter: 'I must tell you what will pain you greatly . . . This night Dr Dominic, the Passionist, sleeps here. He does not know of my intention, but I shall ask him to receive me in what I believe to be the One Fold of the Redeemer.[29] This letter, as Newman told his sister in a further letter dated 9 October, (with a time entered of 5? am),[30] was written before he had received a letter from her dated 6 October, in which she expressed concern, apparently, that her brother intended to remain at Littlemore after his impending conversion.[31] In reply Newman defended his 'position' sturdily: 'The Apostles, when converted, were told to begin with Jerusalem, not to quit it', while 'St Paul preached first to them of Damascus, Jerusalem and Judea'. He continued: 'I think I have found those who fear me and wish me away, think I ought to go – and those who really wish me to stay, have no such thoughts. All depends on their own view of the general question.'[32] In a further letter, responding to another one from his sister, [33] Newman assured her that he had 'no distinct views about remaining at Littlemore, but to *move* would be to *decide* one way. *While* I am undecided, I *remain*. So far as being a sacrifice to go, as you suppose, it is a great trial to remain – to remain in the midst of known faces, perplexed, and whose perplexity I cannot possibly relieve ...'[34]

After an exhausting journey of over four hours from his monastery at Aston-by-Stone, Staffordshire, Barberi eventually arrived at Littlemore on the evening of 8 October 1845. He had endured the considerable discomfort of being seated on the top of a horse-drawn coach in torrential rain. Newman recorded : 'Father Dominic came at night, I began my confession.'[35] He completed his confession the next day and, with two other members of the Littlemore community, Frederic Bowles and Richard Stanton, was received into the Roman Catholic Church. The Passionist missionary left Littlemore the following day and reported to his superiors that Newman was 'one of the most humble and lovable men I have met in my life'.[36]

From 8 October onwards, Newman wrote about thirty letters to his many friends announcing his conversion. He told Mrs J. W. Bowden, the widow of his old college friend,

> Father Dominic the Passionist ... was a poor boy, who (I believe) kept sheep near Rome and from his youth his thoughts have been singularly and distinctly turned to the conversion of England. He is a shrewd clever man, but as unaffected and simple as a child; and was most singularly kind in his thoughts of religious persons in our communion ... I believe him to be a very holy man.[37]

(In 1846 Mrs Bowden became a Catholic, and her conversion was followed by that of several members of her family.) Also among Newman's correspondents was Archdeacon H. E. Manning who, in 1851, was to follow him into the Church.

Subsequently, Newman was always reluctant to discuss his reasons for becoming a Catholic.[38] Some time later, he told James Spencer Northcote, a friends of his and also of Pusey's, that: 'Catholicism is a deep matter – you cannot take it up in a teacup.'[39] Northcote's wife – and three sisters – became Catholics in 1845, as he did the next year. After his wife's death in 1853, Northcote, who had been an Anglican curate, joined the Birmingham Oratory, where he studied under Newman for the priesthood, and was ordained after two years. From 1866 he was President of Oscott College and Provost of the Birmingham Chapter from 1885.

In the *Apologia*, Newman wrote of his determination to serve faithfully:

> When at length in 1845, I had written to Bishop Wiseman, in whose Vicariate I found myself, to announce my conversion, I could find nothing better to say to him, than that I would obey the Pope as I had obeyed my own Bishop in the Anglican Church.[40]

Dessain observes that a 'considerable number' had preceded Newman into the Church and that over the next few years 'several hundred University and educated men followed his example'.[41]

Among Newman's regular correspondents was Father Charles Russell, Professor of Ecclesiastical History at Maynooth College, Co. Kildare, and co-editor with Wiseman of the *Dublin Review*. They had exchanged letters since 1841 and Russell had also sent Newman a number of books which he thought might be helpful in his spiritual odyssey. Russell had read *Tract 90* and was deeply disturbed by the reference in article XXVIII to Transubstantiation, which reflected misunderstandings of this important Roman Catholic doctrine. After much hesitation – he was a comparatively young seminary professor, under thirty years of age – he wrote to Newman on 8 April 1841, giving a scholarly account of this 'precious doctrine' and 'most earnestly remonstrated' against the treatment given to 'our belief of the Eucharist'. With great respect, Russell intimated that Newman had 'completely misconceived us'.[42] In an urbane reply, Newman assured Russell:

> I do *not* accuse your Communion of holding Transubstantiation in the
> shocking sense we both repudiate, but I impute that the idea of it to our
> Articles which, I conceive, condemn a certain view of it which some
> persons or party in your Church have put forward against the sense of the
> sounder part.[43]

With his letter, Russell had sent Newman a text used in seminaries
'giving a brief summary of Catholic teaching'.[44] On 21 April 1841
Russell wrote at length, saying that Newman's letter had 'completely
reassured' him. 'I find that I have not erred in the estimate which your
writings led me to form of you'. He added, zealously, 'our other
doctrines, and the practices which flow from them, will bear the same
rigid examination'.[45] The correspondence continued with Newman's
letter of 26 April 1841 in which he reflected on the position of the
Anglican Church, stating that he 'did not look so despairingly as you
do' on it. He believed that

> It never could be, that so large a portion of Christendom should have split
> off from the Communion of Rome, and kept up a protest for 300 years for
> nothing. I think I never shall believe that so much piety and earnestness
> would be found among Protestants, if there were not some very grave
> errors on the side of Rome. To suppose the contrary is most unreal, and
> violates all one's own notions of moral probabilities.[46]

After this declaration, Newman felt he should, perhaps, reassure
Russell that he was in no way advocating Protestantism. His present
position was concerned with seeking an acceptable *via media*.
Newman's frankly expressed views drew from Russell another letter,
although he explained that he had no intention of prolonging a correspondence except to express how heartily he associated with
Newman's views for reconciliation between the Churches. At the
same time, Russell agreed that there had been 'grievous corruptions
and abuses in the Church at the period of the Reformation';[47] he was
'almost certain that they had come down to us in a very exaggerated
form'. He also commented that 'Protestantism, in its origins, may
have, and probably was, a witness against those existing abuses', but
he felt that Newman would acknowledge that Protestantism 'soon
outstepped, and therefore forfeited its commission; and it outlived its
time by refusing to submit to the voice of Catholic truth in Trent'.
Newman's reply was both courteous and firm. Russell and his friends
should dismiss 'any lurking suspicion that persons who think with me

are likely by the growth of their present views to find it imperative on them to pass over to your communion'. Furthermore, 'people must be well acquainted with what he had written': he did not deny that his 'sympathies had grown towards the religion of Rome, but it will be difficult perhaps to prove that his *reasons* for *shunning* her communion had lessened or altered'. He ended by emphasizing that he wished 'to go by reason not by feeling'.[48] To this honest expression of the views held by Newman and his close friends, Russell responded, on 8 May 1841, by saying that he looked forward in due time 'not to individual movements' or for a 'few individuals, however distinguished, leaving the communion of their Church', but to see that Church itself 'coming into communion with ours'.[49] For the time being, this correspondence closed with an exchange of volumes and warm feelings. Newman sent Russell a volume of his sermons and Russell gave Newman a collection of books.

In the *Apologia* Newman testified to Russell's solicitous interest in him over the years: 'He sent me at different times several letters; he was always gentle, mild, unobtrusive, uncontroversial. He left me alone. He also gave me one or two books.'[50] Russell's influence was also acknowledged in these remarkable words: 'He had, perhaps, more to do with my conversion than any one else.'[51] Newman's journal records that on 1 August 1843, he had received a visit from 'Mr Russell'.[52] According to Gilley, Russell's friendship with Newman 'is notable as Newman's sole warm connection with a Roman Catholic before he became one'.[53] Russell wrote congratulating him on his conversion and sent him a translation he had made of *The Moral Tale* written by Canon Carl von Schmid, for which Newman thanked him for his kind present.[54] When Newman was writing a revised edition of the *Apologia*, Russell, who had noticed in an advertisement for this publication, got in touch with him in 1865, saying that it was 'exceedingly important' to ensure that Newman expressed clearly his 'position towards the Roman Church while still an Anglican'. Newman assured him that he had 'altered some things ... but only with the purpose of expressing my own meaning more exactly'.[55]

From Keble, Newman received a reply on 3 October 1845, typical of his gentle and gracious friend. He told Newman that he had been a 'kind and helpful friend in a way scarce anyone else could have been, and you are so mixed up in my mind with old and dear and sacred thoughts that I cannot well bear to part with you ... I must cling to the belief that you are not really parted: you have taught me so, and I scare think you can unteach me'. He sent Newman his blessings and hoped he 'would have peace when you are gone'.[56] In correspondence with Fr Henry James Coleridge, SJ, Newman strongly repudiated comments that he was reported to have made about Keble; '... the report you speak of is a simple-that-is-not. What I have ever said is this – that Keble had from youth a great drawing to Catholicism, and that Pusey never had, as far as I can see, any such drawing.'[57] To another correspondent, Newman disclosed that he 'was prepared for dear Mr Keble's death, from knowing how frail he was and how his wife's illness tried him ... The one doctrine dear Keble did not receive was that communion with the Holy See was necessary for being in the Church'.[58] Condolences over Keble's death – in 1866 – were sent to Newman by Archbishop Manning:

> I have just heard of dear Keble's death; and I feel as if it had put me back half my life to the days when we used to look to him and his *Christian Year* as the service of our happiest thoughts. Nobody can understand this as you, and I write to you almost instinctively.[59]

Ten years later, Newman was asked by a writer who was preparing a publication for Keble's *Occasional Papers and Reviews* to give his opinion. In a lengthy letter, Newman wished it were easier for him to give a judgement on Keble's literary merits, although it 'would not be any great effort to descant in a general way on his various endowments'. He stressed that Keble 'had as little aim at literary success in what he wrote, as most authors have a thirst for attaining it', yet 'nothing he wrote could really be a failure'. Newman declared that he was 'unfitted to pass a literary judgement on Mr Keble' because he was unable to 'discriminate what is of intellectual origin in his writings from what is of ethical'. However, Newman concluded that 'it was the latter qualities – keen religious instincts, unworldly spirit, delicacy of mind, tenderness of others, playfulness, loyalty to the Holy Fathers, and his Toryism in politics' – which influenced his writings and gave them a distinctive character or, as Newman termed, a 'personality'.[60] Friendships were always cherished by Newman. Throughout the various vicissitudes of his long life, and the lives of his intimate friends, Keble had exercised a pervasive influence, particularly in founding Tractarianism.

Before his own conversion, Newman had expressed strong feelings about those who converted to Catholicism, such as William Lockhart, who had joined the Littlemore community in July 1842 and, realizing that Newman had doubts about exercising his sacramental powers of confession, had promised that he would, nevertheless, remain for three years. Later, however, he felt unable to stay and, in just over a year, visited Fr Gentili, the Italian Rosminian missioner, at Loughborough and became a Roman Catholic. This defection clearly upset Newman and appears to have accelerated his decision to resign the living of St Mary's. In a letter to Keble about Lockhart's abrupt departure he stated that 'You must fancy how sick it makes one.'[61] He also told his sister Jemima that Lockhart's departure 'will very likely fix the time of my resigning St Mary's'.[62] Following this correspondence, Newman had sent Bishop Bagot his resignation on 6 September, as noted in the preceding chapter.

Not everyone was as kind to Newman as his old friends Pusey and Keble; the latter's gentle reaction has already been noted. Pusey had expected Newman's conversion, preparing himself and others for the blow, and had benignly developed a theory that Newman was responding to a divine call – 'a mysterious dispensation', as he described it in correspondence with Keble and Woodgate.[63] Pusey thought that Newman would be working in 'another part of the vineyard' of Christianity. Newman, however, had argued, particularly in *Tract 90*, that 'there was a Catholicism that was not Roman'. Therefore, when he seceded to Rome, many of his former associates treated him as a traitor. He was regarded 'as a crypto-Romanist' while he was in the Church of England and, on his conversion, he was also thought of as 'a crypto-Protestant' by many.[64]

Suspicions about the 'new arrivals' tended to persist among Roman Catholics, particularly among many of the 'old Catholics'. Also, Chadwick observes that when Newman left the Church of England, he thought himself repudiated by that Church; prejudices about 'Romanists' lingered; historical associations with the Marian Martyrs, the Armada, Jacobitism and 'Popish plots' tended to flavour popular perceptions and attitudes. The eminent philosophers and historians of the nineteenth century 'resented Newman's departure and tried to forget him'.[65] His conversion had 'sent a *frisson* of alarm through English Protestantism, leading some to suppose that the Church of England really was liable to disintegration'.[66]

Newman's dominant influence in the University was no longer felt. Trevelyan puts it that 'as if a spell had been snapped, Oxford swung round to more secular interests and more liberal thought ... what had been the Oxford Movement went out into the world and became a pan Anglican movement . . . to penetrate the general body of the clergy'.[67]

The Oxford Movement regrouped after Newman's secession: 'Pusey assisted by Keble and Marriott, took over the mantle of leadership.'[68] This new era of the Movement was, as noted already, characterized by a diffusion of its ethos and activities by parochial clergy inspired by its principles and practices. From its intellectual and religious roots, via Littlemore, a second generation Tractarianism spread its influence far beyond the pulpit of St Mary's or the 'monasticism' of Newman's haven at Littlemore, into the East End of London and the industrial cities and towns. Finding themselves generally disbarred from established areas of church activities, these second-generation Tractarians moved out into the suburbs. As a result, the Church of England tended to become 'polarised into two rather uncommunicative groups': High Churchmen who looked longingly, though not submissively, to Rome as the acknowledged leader of Catholic Christendom, and Low Churchmen who continued to stress the 'serious Roman aberrations from fundamental beliefs'.[69] This grassroots tendency was, perhaps, developed through force of circumstances, but it certainly echoed Newman's own devotion to ministering for the spiritual needs of not just Oxford intellectuals but also for those who lived on a less exalted level in the hamlet of Littlemore.

On the morning of 31 October 1845 Newman, accompanied by Ambrose St John and Walker, went to Oscott at Wiseman's invitation to receive the sacrament of confirmation on All Saints Day. It was only the second occasion that Newman had met Wiseman who, since 1840, had been President of Oscott College and also Coadjutor to the Vicar Apostolic of the Midland District. The first time they met was in Rome in 1833 when, as Anglican clerics, Newman and Hurrell Froude called on Wiseman, then rector of the English College in that city. They were told forthrightly by Wiseman 'that not one step could be gained without swallowing the Council of Trent as a whole'.[70]

Wiseman's stipulation that his Anglican visitors should be prepared to accept in full the doctrines of the Church as defined by the Council of Trent (1545–1563) doubtless led to Newman's eventual renouncement of the 'notion' that the 'Church of Rome was bound up with the cause of Antichrist by the Council of Trent', which, as mentioned in the *Apologia*, he had held in 1832–33.[71] Wiseman's uncompromising utterance did not, however, discourage Newman, who responded that he was sure 'God had some work for me to do in England.'[72]

On meeting as Oscott twelve years later, Newman offered Wiseman a draft copy of his book on the *Development of Christian Doctrine* which Wiseman 'had the breadth of mind to insist it should be published as it stood; Newman, therefore, brought it out on his own responsibility'.[73] Wiseman's toleration of the book was remarked on approvingly by Newman in a letter to James Hope, written from Oscott on 2 November 1845.[74]

At one stage in his life, after leaving St Mary's, Newman, as mentioned already, passed through a period of wracking uncertainty about his religious faith and also about what to do with his life. He speculated whether he should live as a layman but Wiseman, who had great insight into Newman's troubled mind, persuaded him that he should enter the Roman Catholic priesthood. Newman demurred at first because, as Trevor puts it, he 'had so long been a teacher in a Church he now felt to be in schism'. This initial concern was soon cleared, however, as also was the question of second ordination, which 'was customary if there was any doubt of authenticity'.[75]

During his stay at Oscott, Newman was shown a building by Wiseman, which was in use as a boys' school and owned by Oscott: it had been a centre of Catholic activities since the seventeenth century. 'Bring your friends here', he was told by Wiseman, 'and carry out your studies for the priesthood with the help of our professors from Oscott.'[76] Newman accepted the offered accommodation which he was to call Maryvale in place of its existing title of Old Oscott College. Part of Wiseman's strategy was to keep the Roman Catholic converts from Littlemore together under his protective care and, eventually, he planned to nurture the development of a new infusion of Roman Catholic life into England through the establishment of an Oratory of St Philip Neri in England. (This plan is discussed in the next chapter.)

Newman wrote to Dalgairns telling him of Wiseman's offer and shrewdly assessed its suitability for the Littlemore community. He thought it was impossible for them to remain in their present accommodation 'unless we are simply to be literary laymen ... Fr Dominic wishes us to be a congregation ... It grows on me more and more that I must go to Rome, even if I move first to Oscott'. He reflected astutely that if he 'ultimately went into orders ... there would be decided advantages for going to Rome, to avoid an individual bishop [e.g. at Oscott] appropriating me'.[77] He secured the agreement of his associates at Littlemore for this move.

In response to many invitations, Newman paid visits to Catholic centres in Ware, Stonyhurst, Prior Park, London and elsewhere during the next few months and was most hospitably received. Gilley suggests that 'Newman's treatment by his new co-religionists was at first one of pride'.[78] From London he wrote to Ambrose St John, reporting that he had an hour's talk with Dr Griffiths, the Vicar Apostolic of the London District 'who is a very amiable taking person – not at all what I expected'.[79] Newman also told St John of his visit to St Edmund's College, Ware, where he had discussions with Dr Edward Cox, the President and found him 'a very pleasing man'.[80] On the same day Newman wrote to Frederick Faber, who had earlier intimated that he was bringing forward the date of his reception into the Roman Catholic Church, that 'I have just returned from St Edmund's,

where my news about you ... caused great joy.' He hoped that they would meet before Faber's intended overseas trip.[81]

In between his visits, Newman wrote to Wiseman, thanking him profusely for all the kindness and help he was giving the Littlemore community in offering them a new base at Old Oscott – 'Littlemore continued'. However, he expressed some concern about taking steps which would 'implicate others besides myself ... They are so different from each other, and their calling so uncertain that I should be very loth to do anything to commit them absolutely to a particular course in a particular place, any more than myself, though I have every wish to bring them for their own sake under your Lordship's influence'.[82] Newman's letter reflects his cautious approach to the idea of moving to Oscott although, as he conceded in a letter to Fr Dominic Barberi, 'There are a great many difficulties in the way of our remaining here ... and besides this and other things, I suppose the Bishop's wishing it is a strong reason for moving.'[83] Wiseman had followed Newman's activities closely over some time, and the planned move of the Oxford Movement converts to his district was all part of his scheme.

That Newman had an informal and growing friendship with Fr Dominic may be seen from a letter to him about an impending visit to the Passionists at Aston Hall: 'But as to my speaking to your people, please put that out of your thoughts. It is not in my line. Nor would it be becoming. And I come to enjoy your society, not to have any work put on me.'[84]

On Christmas Eve 1845, Newman wrote to tell Henry Wilberforce that

Yesterday we came to the conclusion of leaving this place and availing ourselves of an offer which has been made to us under the highest sanction... It is a sad thing to leave poor Littlemore – but one has no function, position, or occupation there – and one cannot stand all the day idle.[85]

Early in 1846 Newman wrote a *Memorandum* of discussions he had with Dr John Briggs, Vicar Apostolic in Yorkshire, on whom he had called during his travels around the country, about the imminent move to Old Oscott: 'Dr Briggs seemed quite prepared for what I had to say, nay he went on to tell me it was an old plan of Dr Wiseman's, which he did not see his way to follow.' He stressed that such 'local institutions' (as the proposed community at Old Oscott) 'must be subject to the Bishop of the district'; every one should be 'either under the Bishop of his birthplace, or of his domicile – he would have us at once get formal leave of our respective Bishops to go to Old Oscott'.[86]

Newman and Ambrose St John in Rome, 1847

In a letter dated 13 January 1846, written from Ushaw, where Newman had met Bishops Mostyn and Riddle – 'who are young men' who received him 'very kindly' – he next visited Dr Newsham of Ushaw, described by him as 'a warm-hearted and ready-made friend'. At Durham, Newman also met Fr Gentili, the noted Italian missionary priest who had received William Lockhart into the Church. As mentioned earlier, Lockhart had left Littlemore in 1842 – to Newman's annoyance and that of his community. In due course, he joined the Order of Charity (Rosminians) to which Gentili belonged. Newman's travels were over in a week or two, and he stated that he and his associates 'would be going to Old Oscott, or Mary vale (Sta Maria in valle) as it is to be called'.[87]

A letter to Faber – who was about to go abroad – gives a revealing insight into Newman's evolving and marked interest at this time in the Oratorian way of life. He writes: 'I have long felt special admiration for the character of St Philip Neri ... I wish we could all become good Oratorians, but that, I suppose, is impossible.'[88] An editorial footnote by Fr Charles Dessain states that 'The plan of joining the Oratory, hinted at by Dr Wiseman, was discussed at Littlemore, and Newman produced a copy of the Rule of St Philip, published in 1687.'[89] Wiseman's influence had encouraged Newman's own growing interest in Oratorianism, and he was quietly considering with his Littlemore associates its essential nature and suitability for their future way of life in the Catholic Church.

In February 1846, members of the Littlemore community departed for Old Oscott, leaving Newman, as he told Ambrose St John '*Solus cum solo*'.[90] He advised Mrs Bowden that his new postal address would be 'Mary Vale, Oscott, Birmingham', and confided that the plan of quitting this place was eased by the 'pleasant memory which attaches to it ... it has been the happiest time of my life, because so quiet. Perhaps I shall never have such quiet again ... I shall have a great many anxieties of various kinds to come'. He ended his letter, 'I must go over to the poor house before the fly comes.'[91] Maisie Ward remarks on Newman's 'real clinging to Littlemore village as well as the parish', seeing his solicitude as part of the same tender affection show to his family, to memories of his childhood home, and to Oriel.[92] Some of the villagers of Littlemore recalled his kindness in visiting them and comforting them in their times of distress, even though he himself experienced many trials.[93]

Newman stayed the night of 22 February with an old friend, Manuel

Johnson, observer at the Radcliffe Observatory, where several old friends, including Pusey, came to say farewell.[94] He left Littlemore on the following morning, in the company of Bowles, and full of melancholic memories; he was not to be in Oxford again for over thirty years.[95]

Newman told James Hope – who was to change his name to Hope-Scott following his marriage in 1847 to the granddaughter of Sir Walter Scott – that he was 'to go to Rome at the end of June, and become a student at the Propaganda'. (The College of Propaganda was concerned with preparing students from across the world for the priesthood.)

> As you may suppose, it is simply my own act. I first mentioned to Dr Wiseman my wish for a regular education – and when he opened the subject today, he asked if I was of the same mind as before ... He is going on business to Rome ... and will introduce and settle me.[96]

Wiseman's continued commitment in helping to smooth Newman's path as he entered a new phase of his life is reflected in this correspondence.

While at Maryvale, Newman kept up his regular correspondence with his wide circle of friends, among whom was W. J. Copeland, who, as mentioned in Chapter 2, had been his curate at Littlemore and had stayed on after Newman's departure. Newman wrote,

> As you suppose, it was, of course, a very trying thing for me to quit Littlemore – I quite tore myself away ... I have been most happy there, though in a state of suspense ... I cannot help thinking I shall one day see Littlemore again; including yourself.[97]

But they were not to meet for about sixteen years when, in a London street, they had a chance encounter.[98]

In a diary entry for 6 June 1846, Newman recorded that he, Ambrose St John and others received the tonsure and minor orders at Oscott.[99] Another interesting diary entry[100] notes that Newman, in company with St John and Bowles, went to Coventry for Dr Ullathorne's consecration as Vicar Apostolic of the Western District. Ullathorne was transferred to the Central District in 1848 and made the first Bishop of Birmingham two years later when the Catholic hierarchy was restored in England and Wales. Ullathorne was to be Newman's bishop for many years after the Oratory was established in

Birmingham. Their destinies, as will be discussed in the next chapter, were to become closely linked in their care for the spiritual welfare of Roman Catholics in this rapidly expanding industrial centre.

From a long and frank letter to Dalgairns, it can be gathered that Newman and St John found life at Oscott quite trying at times. To some extent this was due to its mixed function. It was both a boys' school and a seminary. They felt that the two student bodies should be separated, Oscott being a boys' school and Maryvale for clerics. The former is a 'bustling place – divines require something more strict, more monastic ... all is disorder at Oscott ... consequently the clerical "slip away" to other places such as Stonyhurst'. Newman concedes that Dr Wiseman 'is a punctual precise man ... but Oscott is a bustling thoroughfare'.[101] After the serenity and privacy of Littlemore, the hectic environment of Oscott was obviously unwelcome to Newman and his group.

Newman's feelings are revealed in this plaintive entry in his journal:

> How dreary my first year at Maryvale...when I was the gaze of so many at Oscott, as if some wild incomprehensible beast, caught by the hunter, and a spectacle for Dr Wiseman to exhibit to strangers, as himself being the hunter who captures it! ... I was made a humiliation at my minor orders and at the examination for them; and I had to stand at Dr Wiseman's door waiting for Confession amid the Oscott boys. I did not realise these as indignities at the time, though, as I have said, I felt their dreariness.[102]

For Newman it was, as Meriol Trevor puts it, 'a difficult time, for Oscott was the show-place of English Catholics and the illustrious convert the showpiece'.[103]

On the lighter side, Newman was invited by the 16th Earl of Shrewsbury to visit his ancestral seat, Alton Towers, for the consecration of the new Roman Catholic church in Cheadle, Staffordshire, on 1 September 1846. This invitation was 'gladly accepted'.[104] Newman was overwhelmed by the new church:

> The most splendid building I ever saw ... coloured inside every inch in the most sumptuous way ... the windows are all beautifully stained. The Chapel of the Blessed Sacrament is, on entering, a blaze of light – and I could not help saying to myself; *Porta Coeli*.[105]

John Talbot, the 16th Earl, a devout and munificent benefactor, spent a substantial part of his wealth patronizing the highly talented Gothic-revivalist architect, Augustus Welby Pugin, who considered Cheadle church to be his ecclesiastical masterpiece. Together with Ambrose Phillips de Lisle, a Catholic landowner in Leicestershire, this triumvirate made a conspicuous contribution to the Roman Catholic parishes of Victorian England. For instance, they fostered the missionary work of Luigi Gentili, the Italian Rosminian priest, who became chaplain to Ambrose Phillips' household. Phillips had also donated land from his estate for the foundation of the first post-Reformation Cistercian abbey in England; the Passionist priest, Dominic Barberi, received hospitality and encouragement in his ardent missionary activities. Pugin worked frenetically in designing Catholic churches and chapels, with the liberal financial support of the Earl of Shrewsbury and the collaboration of Ambrose Phillips. Newman was drawn into this potent fellowship, and later on negotiated with the 16th Earl in connection with the Oratorian foundation. (This will be discussed in the next chapter.) Some time before, Phillips had written to Newman congratulating him on becoming a Catholic and invited him to his Leicestershire home. Newman thanked him, but regretted that pressure of work precluded him from accepting the invitation.[106] About four years before this date, Newman was composing *Tract 90*, and Phillips had 'written enthusiastically to his friends about the impending revolution of religious attitudes'.[107]

Newman had seen some of this correspondence, in particular a letter to Mr Bloxam, in which Phillips had urged those who agreed with his opinions to 'commence a movement in behalf of a union between the Churches'. He strongly disassociated himself from such sentiments: 'I have uniformly said that I did not expect the union of the Churches in our time, and have discouraged the notion of all sudden proceeding with a view to it.' He continued by maintaining that:

> If there is any one thing calculated more than any other to extinguish all hope of a better understanding between Rome and England ... it would be the conversion by you or some of your members. If your friends wish to put a gulf between themselves and us, let them make converts, but not else.[108]

In these intervening years, much had happened in Newman's life affecting his religious opinions, beliefs and practices, as already discussed. His religious odyssey was over, as he noted in Chapter V

of the *Apologia*; 'From the time I became a Catholic of course I have
no further history of my religious opinions to narrate.' He added that
did not 'mean to say that his mind had been idle' or that he had 'given
up thinking on theological subjects'. Rather, he had 'no variations to
record', and 'no anxiety of hear whatever. I have been in perfect
peace and contentment; I never have had one doubt'.[109]

Just before leaving Maryvale for Rome, Newman told one of his
friends:

> Dr W (Wiseman) wishes us to join some body such as the Oratorians. The
> objection to them is that they have only to do with towns, and that a
> country house like ours would have no definite meaning. Else the name of
> St Philip Neri is great, and there is no one whose patronage I would
> sooner be under... But I can have no view about any thing till I get to
> Rome.[110]

It was not until September 1846 that Newman and Ambrose St John
left Maryvale to study theology at the College of Propaganda; they
stayed there for just over a year. As they travelled to Rome, Newman
and St John received warm welcomes and generous hospitality. On
arrival they found that the College did not have their rooms ready for
occupation so they were accommodated in a nearby hotel. Eventually,
in early November 1846, their rooms were available. 'They are
certainly very nice rooms, and everyone is very kind', Newman wrote
in a long letter to Richard Stanton, who had been received into the
Catholic Church by Fr Barberi at the same time as himself. He added
that he had contacted the Jesuits at the Collegio Romano and went on
to say that 'There is no doubt the Jesuits are the real men in Rome . . .
We hope to hear something of the Oratorians – but at present I see
nothing except seculars and Jesuits – the Oratorians may prove a
middle point between them.'[111] In a letter to Dalgairns a week or so
later, Newman again refers to Jesuits: 'with no persons do we get on
so well. Not that I mean to be a Jesuit or to persuade you – but I really
think we should leave ourselves open to everything'.[112]

To Dalgairns, he had also mentioned that criticism of his theory of
development were being made. 'The Theologians of the Roman
College, who are said to sway the theology of Rome, are introducing
bits (without having seen the whole book) of my Essay into their
lectures to dissent from.' He had complained but had been assured
that the professors were 'not speaking against my book'.[113] However,

he felt that he had finally been able to convince the chief theologian at Rome, Fr Giovanni Perrone, Professor of Dogmatic Theology, of the soundness of his beliefs.

In November Newman and St John had a private, informal interview with the Pope. Newman reported that 'He is a vigorous man, with a very pleasant countenance and was most kind.'[114]

Towards the end of the year Newman felt able to tell Henry Wilberforce: 'I was happy at Oriel, happier at Littlemore, as happy or happier still at Maryvale – and happiest here' in the College of Propaganda at Rome.[115] In a rather self-deprecating aside, Newman said he was little known in Rome 'both because I am so slow at the languages and because I am so bashful and silent in general society . . . Rickards has apparently said of me, that when my mouth was shut, it seems as if it would never open and when open as if it would never shut. So that I don't expect people will know me'.[116]

Some aspects of Roman life disconcerted him. He was, for instance, appalled to discover, during a conversation with a Jesuit priest, the low level of studies in philosophy and theology at the College; 'Aristotle and Aquinas are out of favour'. When Newman voiced his astonishment that the Pope had not intervened to put right this serious omission, his informant 'shrugged his shoulders and said that the Pope could do nothing if people would not obey him . . . the Romans were a giddy people, not like the English'.[117] While, however, the education at the College failed to impress Newman, the range of nationalities certainly did: thirty-two languages were spoken there.

In another lengthy letter to Dalgairns, Newman wrote about Roman life and the possibilities of various religious Orders, for example, the Dominicans, the Jesuits and the Redemptorists. The latter 'are said to be like the Jesuits, only less military, at least so I understand it'. He described a visit that St John and he had paid to the Chiesa Nuova – St Philip's Church:

> If I wished to follow my bent, I should join them, if I joined any – They have a good library, and handsome sets of rooms apparently. It is like a College with hardly any rule. They keep their own property, and furnish their own rooms. It is what Dr Wiseman actually wishes, and really I should wonder, if at last I felt strongly inclined to it, for I must own I feel the notion of giving up property [would] try my faith very much.[118]

Wiseman's pervasive interest and Newman's reluctance to abandon some degree of personal freedom, are factors which seem to have influenced the type of religious vocation chosen by Newman and his associates.

As Dessain states,

> The Oratorians were free subjects, who had few rules and must learn to live together by means of tact, self knowledge and the knowledge of others. Each had his own work and was to rely on personal influence rather than discipline in pursuing it. This was Newman's way, and the fact that he and his companions had learned to live together at Littlemore and Old Oscott meant that their work of preparation was already half done.[119]

Writing to Dalgairns in January 1847, Newman put forward 'an idea' on which he wanted an opinion:

> The more we see, the more we seem to think that our choice lies between being Jesuits and being seculars ... The Oratorian Rule seems a sort of *Deus e Machina* here; and so Dr Wiseman wished it to be. Well then, we have said to ourselves, let us see what the Oratorians are like.

He proceeded to a fairly detailed analysis of the Oratorian life and duties, which he believed, would need some alteration 'in order to adapt it to the state of England, and this would be in favour of study'.[120]

Newman's views on his religious vocation were beginning to clarify, and after a prolonged period of introspection and uncertainty, it seemed to him that the way in which he and his companions could best serve the Church was becoming evident. He had studied the Rule of St Philip diligently and, according to Ffinch, 'in many ways, St Philip reminded him of Keble'.[121] When still at Littlemore, Newman had, as noted earlier, secured a copy of the Rule of St Philip and discussed it with his friends.

On 17 January 1847, Newman wrote to Wiseman that 'it is curious and very pleasant that after all the thoughts we can give the matter, we come round to your Lordship's original idea, and feel we cannot do better than be Oratorians'.[122] In a further letter to Dalgairns, Newman intimated that the Oratorian Rule 'was almost in all its parts perfectly unsuited to a country of heretics and Saxons'. However, he was having discreet enquiries made about what, if any, alterations might be tolerated to enable an English Oratory to be founded.[123] Later Newman wrote again, and at some length, to Wiseman about developments in Rome related to the Oratorian concept. He confessed difficulty in communicating at a distance of 1400 miles, particularly when so much change was taking place, but he hoped that matters would, in the end, allow them to proceed with 'your written sanction than only in the belief that we have it'.[124] In discussions in Rome Newman's patience and diplomatic skills were well tested but he was soon to reap the reward. Just over a week later, he was able to inform Wiseman that the Pope had 'taken up' the proposed plan for an English Oratory with a Rule adapted to suit that environment. The Holy Father wished more aspiring Oratorians to come to Rome at once and he would provide a noviciate. (This extended letter was added to by Ambrose St John, in Newman's absence on a visit to Rome for further negotiations.) St John himself stressed that the Pope had 'at once expressed his approbation for an adaptation of St Philip's rule'.[125]

Newman gratefully acknowledged Wiseman's influence in leading him and his followers to the Oratorian life in a dedication to the *Discourses addressed to Mixed Congregations*, published in 1871, as follows: 'It is to you principally that I owe it under God, that I am a client and a subject ... of St Philip, of whom I had so often heard you speak before I left England, and whose bright and beautiful character had won my devotion, even when I was a Protestant.'[126]

Writing to Mrs Bowden from Rome, Newman was able to report enthusiastically that 'There is a great stir here for the Catholic Church in England ...The Pope will not rest till he has put Catholic affairs on a better footing, but it is very difficult to make changes without the thorough good will of English Catholics, through whom they are to be carried out.'[127] To the priest who received him into the Church, Newman was delighted to tell him, 'We are to be Oratorians. The Pope has been very kind to us.'[128] In thanking Faber for his congratulations, Newman reassured him that there was 'not a chance of your and our interfering with each other. England is large enough'.[129] In retrospect, this was a rather over-optimistic opinion of the way in which their relationship would develop.

Newman told his former Anglican curate, whom he held in warmest regard, that 'one very prominent reason' for founding an Oratory in England 'has been that it admits of *so many different sorts of minds*'.[130] Newman also remarked to Mrs Bowden that

The more I understand it, the more the Oratory seems the proper thing for England at this moment ... the object of St Philip was to educate a higher class of priests for parish work – most of his followers were highly

educated men, corresponding precisely to the fellows of English universities. There is an abundance of piety and zeal in the English priests at
present, but they want education.[131]

To another correspondent, Newman pronounced:

> We [the Oratorians] are the Athenians, the Jesuits Spartans. Ours is in one
> respect more anxious and difficult – we have no vows, we have fewer rules
> – yet we must keep together – we require a knowledge of each other, which
> the Jesuits do not require. A Jesuit is like a soldier in the phalanx – an Orato-
> rian like a legionary – he fights by himself by *carita* [sic] – which means tact,
> self-knowledge, knowledge of others. This requires a specific training.[132]

This classically inspired statement of the distinctive nature of Oratorianism summarized, imaginatively, the essential appeals he had
discerned in his new vocation. The recipient of this letter became, in
due course, Fr Francis Knox of the London Oratory.

On the feast of St Philip Neri, 26 May 1847, Newman and Ambrose
St John were ordained sub-deacons by Cardinal Fransoni and, on the
following Saturday at St John the Lateran, the cathedral church of the
Pope as Bishop of Rome, they were ordained deacons. On Trinity
Sunday, 30 May 1847, they were raised to the priesthood in the Prop-
aganda Church.[133]

In the retreat he made at St Eusebio, the Jesuit Retreat House,
before ordination, Newman declared that he had in his mind a 'wound
or cancer' that prevented him from being a good Oratorian. He
reflected earnestly and deeply on his life and admitted that for some
years he had 'had many things to oppress him'. 'In the Church of
England I had many detractors; a mass of calumny was hurled at me;
my services towards the Church were misrepresented by almost everyone in authority in it.' He shared with certain of his friends an exile
'but not even in that retreat was I safe from those who pursued me
with their curiosity'. He felt oppressed and lost hope, and the cheerfulness he used to have almost vanished. He felt acutely that he was
no longer young – he was then forty-six – and that his best years were
spent: 'I see myself to be fit for nothing, a useless log.' When he
became a Catholic, he 'lost not a few friends', and death claimed
others most dear to him. Religious observances were faithfully
followed in his 'retreat' at Littlemore, but now he felt a reaction
against such practices. 'I am always languid in the contemplation of
divine things, like a man walking with his feet bound together.'[134]

Such self-analysis reveals something of the inner torment which, over the years, had afflicted Newman. His feelings of rejection and persecution, and his declarations of uselessness arose from a period of intense reflection on his life so far – and yet, if he had but known, he had just passed the halfway mark in his long life, and was still to make his historic and unique contributions to the regeneration of the Roman Catholic Church in England, through his pervasive intellectual, theological and spiritual leadership.

After ordination, Newman and members of the Maryvale community spent five months in the Oratorian noviciate for English students at Santa Croce, Rome. Before the College of Propaganda, Newman had communicated to the rector the 'general discontent among English-speaking students'.[135] They were not allowed outside visits, their reading was greatly restricted and mature students like Newman and his group felt keenly the lack of opportunities for philosophical and theological discussions. To his sister Jemima, Newman confided his concern about the 'conservatism' which seemed to stifle intellectual progress at the College of Propaganda:

> It is astonishing, with my recollections of Oxford, 16 or 17 years ago, how exactly they resemble the Kebles, Perceval, etc., etc., and Froude before his eyes were opened to see through the hollowness of the then so called Toryism ... There is a deep suspicion of *change*, with a perfect incapacity to create anything *positive* for the wants of the times.[136]

Newman found such an intellectual environment directly antipathetical to his own restless, searching spirit and committed belief in intellectual and religious development. (Newman's pre-eminent contributions to the theories of university education are discussed in Chapter 5.)

While in Rome, Newman had the opportunity for discussions with Wiseman, as he noted, for example, in his diary for 11 and 31 July, and 17 August 1847.[137] On 9 October Newman wrote from Rome to Wiseman, saying he had hoped to tell him that they had been given a brief to found an English Oratory but this was delayed 'until after the Congregations meet again in November'. But he was able to report that the Pope had appointed him to be 'first Superior', with powers to choose the 'four Deputies'.[138] Wiseman sent a 'long reply' in which he mentioned that although he had 'considered Maryvale in every respect the proper place for Noviciate, House of study and retreats, and central house', Newman might bear in mind the opportunities by 'having a house in London'.[139] Among Newman's diary entries is one recording that on 1 December 1847, he 'called on Manning and walked with him'.[140] The latter was still a senior Anglican cleric and it was not until 1851 that, like Newman, he entered the Roman Catholic Church and later became a Catholic priest, eventually being created Cardinal Archbishop of Westminster.

On 6 December 1847 Newman, with St John, began the journey back to England and thence to Maryvale. They went via Loretto, where both said Mass at the Holy House.[141] As they travelled, Newman managed to keep up the flow of his correspondence, including a letter to his sister Jemima telling her that, 'We had one or two very nice interviews with him [the Pope] before parting . . . There is every appearance of his being as firm as he is kind.'[142] The weary travellers at last reached London on Christmas Eve and stayed there over Christmas, visiting various friends and also having lunch with Wiseman. On Friday 31 December, they travelled on to Maryvale where they were greeted as Catholic priests and Oratorians.

Notes
   1. Newman, 1956, p. 86.
   2. Mozley, 1981, p. 465; LDX.613, 3 April 1845.
   3. Newman, 1956, p. 10.
   4. Newman, 1956, p. 14.
   5. Chadwick, 1990, p. 14.
   6. Newman, 1993, p. 94.
   7. Newman, 1993, pp. 94–5.
   8. Newman, 1993, p. 95.
   9. Newman, 1993, p. 95.
  10. Boekraad, 1961, p. 17.
  11. Newman, 1993, p. 98.
  12. Newman, 1993, pp. 97–8.
  13. Bacchus, 1917, p. 351; LDX.426, 21 November 1844.
  14. Mozley, 1891, p. 445; LDX.435 24 November 1844.
  15. Mozley, 1891, pp. 459–61; LDX.595–7, 15 March 1845.
  16. Mozley, 1891, pp. 461–2; LDX.605–6, 21 March 1845.
  17. Maisie Ward, 1948, p. 438.
  18. Mozley, 1891, p. 464; LDX.612–3, 2 April 1845.
  19. Bacchus, 1917, p. 387; LDX771, 3 October 1845; LDX.782, 6 October 1845.
  20. Newman, 1993, pp. 92–3.
  21. LDXXX.152, 21 November 1882.

22. Mozley, LDX.734, 17 July 1845.
23. Mozley, 1891, p. 467; LDX.782, footnote.
24. Mozley, 1891, p. 453; LDX.480, 5 January 1845; LDX.501; 506; 556.
25. Mozley, 1891, p. 454; LDX.524–5, 5 February 1845; LDX.511–2; LDX.520.
26. Newman, 1993, p. 269.; LDX.566, footnote; LDX.598.
27. LDXI.3, 7 October 1845.
28. LDXI.4.
29. LDXI.8, 8 October 1845.
30. LDXI.8-9, Mrs John Mozley.
31. LDXI.13-5, Mrs John Mozley.
32. LDXI.13, footnote.
33. LDXI.14, Mrs John Mozley.
34. LDXI.16–17, Mrs John Mozley.
35. Newman, 1956, p. 12; LDX.562, footnote.
36. Trevor, 1996, p. 101.
37. LDXI.5, 8 October 1845.
38. cf Dessain, 1980, p. 84.
39. LDXI.110, J Spencer Northcote, 8 February 1846.
40. Newman, 1993, p. 124.
41. Dessain, 1980, p. 88–9.
42. LDVIII.172–3.
43. LDVIII.174.
44. LDVIII.172, footnote.
45. LDVIII.180.
46. LDVIII.182.
47. LDVIII.186.
48. LDVIII.187.
49. LDVIII.188, footnote.
50. Newman, 1993, pp. 237–8; LDX.110.
51. LDXI.9, footnote; Newman, 1993, p. 237.
52. Newman, 1956, p. 242.
53. Gilley, 1990, p. 206.
54. LDXI.53, 7 December 1845.
55. LDXXI.447, 19 April 1865; LDXXI.459, 5 May 1865; LDX.774–5, 3 October 1845.
56. Mozley, 1891, pp. 471–3.
57. LDXXII.202, 3 April 1866.
58. LDXXII.208, Miss Charlotte Wood, 8 April 1866.
59. LDXXII.198, 31 March 1866.
60. LDXXVII.372–3, Miss Maria Tench, 29 October 1875.
61. Mozley, 1891, p. 417; LDIX.472, 25 August 1843.
62. Mozley, 1891, pp. 417–8; LDIX.479, 28 August 1843.
63. Maisie Ward, 1948, p. 454; LDX.586, footnote.
64. Trevor, 1996, p. 47.
65. Chadwick, 1990, pp. 76–7.

66. Norman, 1986, p. 209.
67. Trevelyan, 1948, p. 280.
68. Nockles, 1997, p. 302.
69. Pawley, 1974, p. 136.
70. Newman, 1993, p. 124.
71. Newman, 1993, p. 125.
72. Newman, 1956, p. 136.
73. Trevor, 1996, p. 102.
74. LDXI.23.
75. Trevor, 1996, p. 102.
76. Meynell, 1890, p. 51.
77. LDXI.29–31, 9 November 1845.
78. Gilley, 1990, p. 245.
79. LDXI.38, 22 November 1845.
80. LDXI.39, 22 November 1845.
81. LDXI.38–9, 22 November 1845.
82. LDXI.53–4, 8 December 1845.
83. LDXI.61–2, 14 December 1845.
84. LDXI.77, 23 December 1845.
85. LDXI.79, Xmas Eve 1845.
86. LDXI.89–90, 10 January 1846.
87. LDXI.92–3, T. F. Knox, 13 January 1846.
88. LDXI.105, 1 February 1846.
89. LDXI.105, Dessain, footnote.
90. LDXI.124, 21 February 1846.
91. LDXI.125–6, 22 February 1846.
92. Maisie Ward, 1948, p. 426.
93. Trevor, 1996, p. 104.
94. LDXI.125, 21 February 1846.
95. LDXI.126, footnote 1.
96. LDXI.152, 18 April 1846.
97. LDXI.132–3, 10 March 1846.
98. Newman, 1956, p. 261.
99. LDXI.173.
100. LDXI.179.
101. LDXI.193–6, 6 July 1846.
102. Newman, 1956, p. 255.
103. Trevor, 1996, p. 104.
104. LDXI.225, 18 August 1846.
105. LDXI.209–10, Mrs J Bowden.
106. LDXI.19, 19 October 1845.
107. Norman, 1985, p. 209.
108. LDVIII.213–4, A. L. Phillips, 28 June 1841.
109. Newman, 1993, p. 273.
110. LDXI.226–7, T. F. Knox, 20 August 1846.
111. LDXI.267–70, 6 November 1846.
112. LDXI.275, 15 November 1846.

113. LDXI.281, Feast of St Cecilia, 1846.
114. LDXI.285, F. S. Bowles, 26 November 1846.
115. LDXI.294, 13 December 1846.
116. LDXI.295, 13 December 1846.
117. LDXI.279, J. D. Dalgairns, Feast of St Cecilia, 1846.
118. LDXI.303-7, 31 December 1846.
119. Dessain, 1980, p. 92.
120. LDXII.16, 15 January 1847.
121. Ffinch, 1992, p. 146.
122. LDXII.19-20, 17 January 1847.
123. LDXII.22, 22 January 1847.
124. LDXII.43-4, 14 February 1847.
125. LDXII.50-4, 23 February 1847.
126. LDXII.20, footnote.
127. LDXII.59, 7 March 1847.
128. LDXII.62, Fr Dominic Barberi, 14 March 1847.
129. LDXII.66, 31 March 1847.
130. LDXII.69, 23 April 1847.
131. LDXII.101, 21 July 1847.
132. LDXII.113, T. F. Knox, 10 September 1847.
133. LDXII.84-5, Mrs J. W. Bowden, 30 May 1847.
134. Newman, 1956, pp. 245-8.
135. Ker, 1990, p. 331.
136. LDXII.102-4, 28 July 1847.
137. LDXII.92; 106; 108, footnotes.
138. LDXII.124-7, 9 October 1847.
139. LDXII.126, 29 October 1847.
140. LDXII.131, footnote 1, 3 October 1847; footnote 2, 1 December 1847.
141. LDXII.131, footnote, 10 December 1847.
142. LDXII.136-7, 21 December 1847.

Chapter 4

Oratorianism comes to England

The seed of Oratorianism had lain in Newman's mind for some time; he had shown his Littlemore group of close friends a copy of St Philip Neri's Rule, as noted in the preceding chapter. His mind had been further stimulated by Wiseman's sympathetic interest in the Oxford Movement and by his readiness to offer practical help when Newman and several of his close associates seceded from Anglicanism and became Roman Catholics.[1] At this critical convergence of events, Wiseman offered accommodation and opportunities for the converts to continue to share fellowship, to reflect on their future lives, and to discuss ways in which they might pursue an active ministry in their new environment. From discussions at Littlemore, they had become familiar with the general nature of the Oratorian way of life and had reflected on its relevance to their religious aspirations and experiences.

In his perceptive appraisal *Newman and His Friends*, Tristram observed that Newman gave two reasons influencing their deliberations: 'that whereas the tastes of all of us are different, the Oratory allowed greater scope for them than any other institution; and again it seemed more adapted than any other for Oxford and Cambridge men'. Tristram also comments that Ambrose St John fulfilled his role as a trusted counsellor when he 'fixed Newman's destiny by saying to him, "We really ought to go to St Philip", recalling a suggestion thrown out by Dr Wiseman, but forgotten by Newman'.[2]

This process of evaluation and assimilation of Oratorianism continued in Rome until Newman himself had become convinced that the Rule of St Philip Neri was the one most likely to give him and his associates the best opportunities for developing their religious vocations. In the autumn of 1847 he wrote from Rome saying that the Brief for setting up the English Oratory had been effected; it was 'made out for Birmingham – and Maryvale will be the mother house of the whole kingdom'. This historic and welcome news was given in a letter to Mrs J. W. Bowden, an old family friend. Newman added, perceptively, that 'It is certain, important changes are about to take place in the state of Catholicism in England, and we must in some way or other be brought nearer to London, even if my home continues to be Maryvale.'[3]

Now, with papal authority, Newman and his associates were back in England, after ordination in Rome, with the mission of opening an Oratorian House. For the time being they would, once again, be living at Maryvale where, on 2 February 1848, the Feast of the Purification, Newman formally established the first English Oratory, of which he was the Superior. According to Ward, Newman chose that day deliberately. It was the Foundation Day at Oriel. He also wished his new Oratory to benefit from the blessings of this special feast day of the Blessed Virgin Mary.[4]

Newman's long-held devotion to Our Lady is reflected in a postscript to Dr Ullathorne on Easter day 1866, when he described how he had 'set up the English Oratory on the feast of the Purification, and next year, the Birmingham Oratory also on the Purification'. The Oratory in Hagley Road, Edgbaston was founded under the 'Invocation of the Immaculate Conception and an Altarino and Image of Our Lady was placed in entrance hall'. When he went to Ireland, Newman 'at once placed the new University under Mary as *Sedes Sapientiae*, and the University Church . . . under Saints Peter and Paul'.[5]

On 3 February 1848 Newman, writing from Maryvale, was clearly delighted to tell Mrs J. W. Bowden:

> We are at last a Congregation, I admitted nine after Vespers of the Purification. We are six Fathers, one novice, three lay brothers . . . We are very busy getting ourselves and house in order, and when it will be as it should be, I cannot prophesy.[6]

Dessain stresses the importance of the Oratory for Newman:

> It was his chosen vocation; to found it in England was the first commission he received from the Catholic authorities; it was the framework for the rest of his long life, and, as has so often been the case with founders, through it some of his cruellest trials came.[7]

In his Anglican years, Newman had experienced many tribulations but these were by no means over when, approaching fifty years of age, he became a Catholic priest and a member of the Congregation of the Oratory. Some of the turbulence and trials which Newman endured arose from his publishing and polemical activities, others from challenging educational aspirations, while several involved clashes of personality and arose from differences of perception of what should be done. Newman's early years as an Oratorian Superior were, unfortunately, made stressful by members of his own community, in particular Frederick Faber. Newman had, in fact, been told by Wiseman, when they met in London over Christmas 1847 as Newman was returning from Rome, that Faber and his community of 'Wilfridians' wished to join the Oratory. Newman at once wrote to Faber that

> You may fancy the joy with which St John and I heard the news that you proposed we should be one . . . I cannot say more till I know your precise wishes and intentions - I will but say that, from the very wish I have that we may come to an understanding, I am anxious you should try if you have fully mastered *what* Oratorianism is. In many important aspects it differs from what you are at present. It is not poetical it is very devotional.[8]

Newman's welcoming words were thus tempered by his concerns about Faber's realization of the essential nature of Oratorianism. In a letter to Dalgairns in Rome, Newman informed him that

> Faber has offered himself and his to me, simply and absolutely – his house, his money, his all. The proposal came through Dr Wiseman – but, as I wanted his own words, he has written to me this morning on the subject . . . I need counsel. The sooner you can come the better.[9]

On the same day, Newman wrote to Faber, inviting him to visit and talk over the whole matter.[10] In a diary entry for 6 January 1848, Newman recorded that Faber and two of his community visited Maryvale and stayed until Saturday 8 January.[11] The visit 'went off very well', as Newman was able to tell Richard Stanton. It was agreed that the entire Wilfridian community should be received as Oratorians.[12] On 14 February, Newman travelled to Cheadle and fulfilled this agreement. But he was soon to discover that he had taken on 'more than the responsibilities for Faber and seventeen young men'.[13]

These enthusiastic young converts, led by the mercurial Faber, were to cause Newman many heartaches. As he confided to Ambrose St John,

> My great trouble is some of the giovani [Newman's habitual way of describing the members of this young community] – not that any thing new has occurred, but they have so repelled any thing between us but what is external, shown so little confidence, as to throw me back upon myself – and now I quite dread the fortnightly chapter.[14]

As an undergraduate, Faber had heard Newman preaching at St Mary's, Oxford and, like so many of his generation, had been enthralled, so much so that he became known as 'Newman's acolyte'. His university career was not remarkable, although he became a Fellow of University College living as rector of Elton in Huntingdonshire. Almost immediately, with letters of introduction from Wiseman, he then visited Italy, paid homage at the shrine of St Philip Neri, and had a private audience with the Pope. On return to England in 1845, Faber – who was a bachelor – transformed his household of men servants, together with some of the village boys, into a quasi-monastic community. Very soon after Newman's conversion to Roman Catholicism in 1845, Faber, six boys and one woman from his parish were also received into the Roman Catholic Church. His next move was to set up his community in Birmingham and later, at Cotton Hall, Cheadle, Staffordshire, where the devout and generous 16th Earl of Shrewsbury was their patron. Here Faber established the community of the 'Brothers of the Will of God', or 'Wilfridians' as they came to be called.

It has been said that Newman, while welcoming Faber and his Wilfridians as Oratorians, stressed that their earlier aspirations to monasticism would no longer be relevant if they were to adopt the Rule of St Philip Neri. While still at Littlemore, Newman had been approached by Faber, suggesting that the two 'communities' might be merged, but he had firmly discouraged the proposal. He suggested that should Faber's plan fail, then he might prolong his stay in Rome and 'give some further months to the discipline of some seminary'. Further, he shrewdly observed that 'I shall not be surprised, even though you join us . . . you would find yourself ultimately called elsewhere. I cannot help thinking you should be a distinct centre of operation and collect people about you.'[15]

Just over a year later Newman was to write again to Faber, who had sent his congratulations on 'the news of your becoming an Oratorian', and commenting that his own community had been discouraged by Wiseman from 'making an Oratory'. Newman's response was cordial but carefully worded.

> Do not for an instant fancy our plans will clash, there is no chance of it. You have your own ways and powers, which no one can rival, of working out your object, even if our object were precisely the same, which is not the case. At the same time I am surprised to find our general plans are more the same that I thought at first.[16]

However, on Christmas Day 1847, Newman wrote in his diary that 'There is great difference at present between us, that he (Faber) is much more *poetical* in the largest sense of the word than the Oratorians. In devotions, in asceticism, on obedience, in dress, in names, etc.'[17] These views were enlarged in a letter to Faber quoted on page 137.[18] Newman was becoming more and more aware that although he and Faber shared much in common in that they were both Oxford men who had changed their religious affiliation to the rather suspect Roman Catholicism and had attracted others to follow them in a life of profound religious dedication, nevertheless there were distinct differences in their personalities which affected the ways in which they developed their Oratorian vocations. These markedly divergent developments were almost constant sources of irritation between them. Newman disliked Faber's enthusiastic adoption of Italianate forms of devotion, of sermons laced with miraculous legends, and of fervent religiosity that fitted uneasily into contemporary England. He specifically advised Antony Hutchinson, who had joined Faber in 1848, to 'avoid everything extreme'. Stories introduced into sermons should be relevant and edifying, 'not such as are likely to surprise or offend people, as some miraculous accounts would do'.[19] Newman's dislike of religious 'excesses' epitomized his own essentially restrained, reflective approach to his pastoral activities in the expansion of Roman Catholicism in Victorian England. Faber's exaggerated pious practices, his predilection for ornate vestments, exuberant 'Roman' church architecture, and Ultramontanism tended to alienate the 'old Catholics', who were more comfortable with Newman because of his 'Englishness' which was in direct contrast to the Italianate religion of the Ultramontanes. It seems that they sensed in him views and practices which fitted in happily with the more moderate way in which they and their forbears had, particularly in penal times, observed their

Faith. Newman's published opinions on the position of the laity in the Church must also have influenced their perceptions of him.[20]

While Faber played an important role in the growth of Oratorianism in England he had made no contribution at all to the initial stages of developing its Brief in Rome of the choice made by Newman and his close companions or the Oratorian vocation.[21] When, in the end, Faber followed the path taken by these early 'pioneers', his behaviour oscillated between deep affection and reverence for Newman, and a nearly non-stop flow of criticisms and complaints about various aspects of Oratorian life and other matters. After a noviciate of only one month, Newman had appointed Faber to be novice master. Trevor remarks that this 'was a great mistake... Faber and his novices had nothing to do except worry Newman and blame him for everything they did not like'.[22] Friction between them became so unbearable that, later on, separate communities had to be established in Birmingham and in London.

This, however, was in the unseen future. For the present time Newman was trying to solve the problems which had been brought about by Faber's ardent and sudden desire to join the new English Oratory. The Oratorians were now split between two sites – one in Birmingham, the other in a remote part of rural Staffordshire; added to this was the obligation to continue to provide pastoral care for Catholics living within the vicinity of Cotton Hall which, together with the Church of St Wilfrid, largely donated by the Earl of Shrewsbury, had been the original centre of Faber's Wilfridian community.

To Newman's dismay he discovered from Faber that St Wilfrid's was in financial difficulties,[23] and he asked him to consider alternative ways of ridding themselves of this 'so little an Oratorian place'; he also requested Faber to provide an account of the expenses incurred in living there.[24] Lord Shrewsbury's chaplain was assured that they would 'take into our best considerations the views expressed about Cotton Hall' which, although well placed as a missionary centre 'is not quite the place for an *Oratorian*'. Newman explained that 'Our brief speaks expressly of *urbes ampliores* [large towns]'.[25] Extended correspondence arose from attempts to satisfy the expectations of the Earl of Shrewsbury regarding continuation of Catholic pastoral care in the neighbourhood of his estate, and his view that abandonment of the monastery he had provided for Faber's Wilfridians would be a breach of contract.[26]

Newman had already told Lord Shrewsbury of the conflicting pressures he was experiencing: 'We see our way so little at present, that I am not able to speak about Cheadle. Certainly the wish at Rome was that we should place ourselves in large towns, such as Birmingham, London and Manchester'.[27] Two weeks later, he firmly re-stated 'the case . . . as we view it:- We come to England Oratorians; the Oratorians are notoriously, even more than Jesuits, inhabitants of cities; the community of St Wilfrid's proposes to join us, and . . . I am expressly told that [their application] has your Lordship's sanction'. He repeated that the Oratorian Brief 'expressly destines us for *urbes ampliores* and for the *nobilor splendidior, doctior* class of society' [the more educated and wealthy upper classes].[28] The unsuitability of the rural location was again emphasized in another letter to the Earl: 'We do not think Cheadle is a place which would answer the purpose of an Oratorian Mission.'[29]

From time to time misunderstandings and a note of exasperation creep into both sides of this extensive correspondence, to which Newman was a harassed and rather reluctant contributor. A viable solution still seemed to be remote; Newman's time and energy were being exhausted and costs were rising. As a result, in the autumn of 1848, all the English Oratorians became centred at Cotton Hall and it was agreed to maintain pastoral care in the district, as requested by the Earl of Shrewsbury.

In a memorandum dated 18 September 1848, Newman recorded that he had been informed by Dr Ullathorne, Vicar Apostolic of the Central District, that he wished the Oratorians to be in Birmingham, and he hoped to find premises suitable for a chapel and accommodation for a small community in a short while.[30] On 29 September Newman wrote another short memorandum: 'We decided by vote to leave this place [Maryvale] for Birmingham, the residue going to St Wilfrid's. This is the only way in which by the Brief we could give up this House.'[31] He also wrote to Ullathorne confirming their conversation and the agreement to move to Birmingham, provided suitable accommodation for 'as many of our community as shall live there would be available'.[32]

Meanwhile the Oratorians were clustered at Cotton Hall, in a community numbering around forty, which Newman considered far too large for the Rule of St Philip Neri to be followed faithfully. An authentic Oratorian community was comparatively small – perhaps no more than ten – where a small group of secular priests and lay brothers'learned to live together by means of tact, self-knowledge and the knowledge of others' and relied 'on personal influence rather than discipline in pursuing their specific duties'.[33] The situation at Cotton Hall put the whole ethos of an Oratory at risk, apart from the fact that the rural location was directly contrary to the traditions of Oratorianism and to the special Brief which Newman had received from Rome. To find himself and the English Oratory in such an unacceptable situation, and at so early a stage in their development, may be presumed to have been very worrying. Ullathorne's intervention was, therefore, timely as well as challenging, and it gave Newman an opportunity of disentangling himself, to some extent from the immediate problems of the Cotton Hall community. In following Ullathorne's request, Newman doubtless realized that he would, in fact, be conforming to the papal brief, which specifically referred to a Birmingham Oratory.

But Faber – known as Fr Wilfrid in the Oratorian community – was to be, once again, a source of anxiety to Newman. Worries arose over the translations of Italian, French and Spanish *Lives of the Saints* which Faber had been working on since 1847. With typical care for his community, Newman warned Faber

> There is a row blowing up. Now, if we are advocates of doctrines, however true, with no *authority* to back us, it is the story of the Oxford Tracts over again – we shall be in a false position, and the harm and scandal done to religion, and the mischief to the Oratory, will be incalculable.[34]

A row certainly did blow up and lasted for two months. Some 'old Catholics' were affronted by Faber's vivid account of miracles and austerities, as well as revelations about ecclesiastical scandals in some Continental countries, and they sharply criticized his publications. When Faber joined the Oratorians in February 1848, it had been agreed to defer for a year the decision as to whether the Oratory should take over the Series but Newman hesitated about informing the publishers of the possible suspension. The September issue of *Dolman's Magazine* contained a ferocious review by Fr Edward Price, a London priest, of Faber's translation of the *Life of St Rose*, accusing him of promoting 'gross, palpable idolatry'.[35] Newman quickly realized the perilous position and told Faber that 'the question of the *Lives of the Saints* had been submitted to the Bishops assembled at Ushaw' as 'it would be unfair to the Oratory, ungrateful to the Pope, to plunge the Oratory on its commencement here into a controversy, where dogmatic correctness was on the side of its opponents'.[36] In the post-script to a further letter four days later, Newman added, with typical subtlety, that for a long time they should limit themselves to publishing 'such *Lives* as have no startling forms of worship, etc., in them – or if this cannot be, then the *Lives* not of *contemplatives* but of those who have *done some work* in their life-time: St Vincent of Paul, St Francis de Sales, St Vincent Ferrer, etc., etc.'.[37] Newman also wrote to Wiseman, Newsham and Ullathorne seeking their support and defending the heavily criticized *Life of St Rose*. However, Ullathorne ordered publication of the Series to be stopped forthwith. Newman told Faber that the decision 'took me quite by surprise' but, he assured him 'I will stand by you, and no reproach shall fall on you, which does not fall on me.'[38] Two days later he advised Faber that, after consulting the Fathers of the Oratory, it had been unanimously concluded that the Series should be suspended at present since 'We are given to understand that the Lives of foreign saints, however edifying in their respective countries, are unsuited to England, and unacceptable to Protestants.'[39]

In the lengthy correspondence over this contentious and irritating matter, Ullathorne had, as Newman readily remarked, been 'very kind and easy in his manner', but also very firm in his views about the possible disservice such publications might do to the Roman Catholic Church in England.[40] Newman was not, however, content to let the bluff Yorkshire prelate's remarks pass without comment:

> I conjecture that you would not dislike, or rather would wish, to hear of my opinion on the subject. I fear then, I must say, with deference to your Lordship, that my own experience as a Protestant leads me to an opposite conclusion to that which your Lordship has so clearly expressed. Protestants are converted by high views, not low ones... Having been one of a party who were led on to the Catholic Church by her stronger doctrines, and who despised half measures and uncertain statements, of course I am justified in speaking for that party, though I may not be a fair representative of other sets of Protestants.[41]

Ullathorne replied by return, thanking Newman for the 'straightforward expression of your sentiments which is always so satisfactory'. But he warned that 'we must guard against mistaking each other'. He suspected their viewpoints tended to be different. *The Lives of the Saints* had been one of the 'principal enjoyments' of his life and he reflected on how 'hard and toilsome and full of pain are the unseen labours of a Bishop in a country like this' where, for twenty years, he has had to deal with the virtues and vices of laymen and clergy. From this long pastoral experience, he confessed that whenever he committed a blunder exercising his ministry, it had arisen 'from assuming the existence of a higher degree of the habit of the cardinal virtues in individuals than they possessed'.[42]

This frank and intimate exchange of views between two of the leading Roman Catholic churchmen of the period presaged the close relationship that developed over the next four decades or so, as both Newman and Ullathorne grew increasingly to respect, value and, eventually, to hold each other in affectionate regard.

To his confidante, Mrs J. W. Bowden, Newman wrote forcefully that

> There is an old timid party among the Catholics who fear them [*The Lives of the Saints*] – and we are determined that if they are to go on, they shall go on without the carpings and criticisms of men who do, or can do, little more *than* carp . . . no one ever began a good work without ten thousand oppositions and trials, as the *Lives of the Saints* abundantly show.[43]

Newman stuck like a limpet to the hard core of the criticism made of Faber's translation as 'gross, palpable idolatry'. This serious charge against a priest of his Oratory had not, he informed Wiseman, been condemned outright by his vicar apostolic.[44] A few days later, Ullathorne conceded that 'though negative in form, the disapproval [of the reference to Faber] is very positive in substance. And the words of a Catholic Bishop, spoken publicly, in direct censure of a particular act, even mildly expressed, fall on the public ear with great weight'. He took the opportunity to state that he was 'pained to witness the acute sensitiveness which several little matters have been viewed of late . . . this cannot be without a hidden ingredient of self-love a most subtle spirit, and the object of the fears and combats of the humble saints of God'. After this gentle rebuke, Ullathorne expressed a hidden concern:

> I have often in my secret heart regretted that the course of events has tended [sic] to isolate the fathers of the Oratory from the body of Old Catholics in this country. I am not solitary in that feeling which is a most kind one.

He closed his lengthy personal letter by reflecting sensitively:

I know that your lives have been lives of warfare and contest, and that you have had painfully to controvert the authorities under which you were brought up. We have not had that fierce trial. Habits still cling in hidden ways and will come back unknown to us in this poor restless nature of ours.[45]

The next day Ullathorne was able to send Newman 'an apology from Mr Price to Mr Faber ... written at the intimation of his bishop' i.e. Wiseman.[46] This was a welcome end to the long-drawn, frustrating matter into which, once more, Newman had become involved so personally, although Dessain notes that 'Ullathorne seemed not to allow for Newman's being the Superior of a religious community, with the obligation of protecting those under him.'[47] Newman warmly thanked Fr Edward Price for his 'kind and generous letter to Mr Faber, which was most touching', and invited him to call at St Wilfrid's 'to allow us to show... the love and respect we feel for you'.[48] *The Lives of the Saints* resumed publication in January 1849.

Early in 1848 Newman had been involved in another commitment which he had found troublesome, as he recorded, idiosyncratically, in his journal:

To please Dr Wiseman, I made the wretched throw off in London, against my will, of the Oratorian Lent-preaching 1848 at Passiontide – a blunder and failure, which even now I cannot think of without a raw sensitiveness.[49]

Few attended the sermons given by Newman and his fellow Oratorians: according to Ward 'it was a fortnight of complete failure'.[50] Newman had, in fact, told Lord Adare, who was later to become a Catholic, that 'It is a great trouble to me to preach at all, and this kind of preaching does not suit me. I can preach to people I know, but any thing like a display is quite out of my line ... Others of my party will preach much better.'[51] Newman left London dejected. His next task was to be setting up an Oratory in Birmingham, which was the wish of Ullathorne, as mentioned already.

The search for suitable premises in Birmingham was underway. A disused gin distillery in Alcester Street, in a run-down working class district was discovered. Newman commented that it would suit them 'very well' as it had space sufficient for a chapel, library and living accommodation. He declared that 'We shall throw ourselves on the piety of the Catholics of Birmingham for all our expenses ... [although] there is hardly a Catholic, and hardly a wealthy person.'[52] About three weeks later, Newman reported to R. A. Coffin, rector at Cotton Hall,

As to the gin shop they grant us a lease for those three year but it is doubtful whether they can promise a renewal, if we want it. This is a difficulty,
but I suppose not a serious one ... It is magnificent, but *will take a mint of
money to get into it*, at least a £200 touch.[53]

Towards the end of the year Newman asked Ullathorne to 'mark
down the streets which we consider to be our boundaries'. But he
pointed out:

An Oratory in its proper idea is not a *Mission*, and ought not to have any
district attached to it. Its work is simply within its own homestead for
those who choose to come, whether for the sermons, for Confession, or
for its Exercises; but in the *present* state of Birmingham, we wish, as
mentioned to your Lordship, with your permission, to undertake a
mission, leaving the future to take care of itself.[54]

When the matter of the renewal of the faculties of the Oratorians
arose, i.e. episcopal authority to fulfill specific priestly offices in a
diocese or defined area, Ullathorne requested 'certain information ...
needed for my guidance'.[55] Newman responded at once and confirmed
that they always considered the faculties for hearing confession *within
the Community* to be derived from the bishop, but they also claimed
certain exemptions in accordance with their rule and as bestowed in
the papal brief to the English Oratorians, which privileges are enjoyed
by all Oratories.[56] This information satisfied Ullathorne who declared
that 'I have no other object in view simply to understand the precise
relations which canonically exist between the English Oratory and the
Vicar apostolic.'[57] This correspondence typifies the directness with
which Ullathorne and Newman dealt with each other in setting
Newman's spheres of influence. At the same time, Newman was
aware of the sensitivities of the situation, as shown in a letter to Mrs
Bowden, in which he states:

There has always been a rivalry and opposition between regulars and seculars and though we are not regulars quite, and our Bishop *is* (strange to
say) a regular . . . [Ullathorne belonged to the Benedictine Order] . . . it
is showing itself in the mutual intercourse of him and ourselves. However,
we have so kind a patron in the Pope himself, and so strong a Brief that
we are not *very* anxious – though all disputes are anxious.[58]

On a more mundane level, Newman was able to tell Ullathorne at the
end of December 1848 that 'the house in Alcester Street is at last

made over to us, and we have sent whitewashers and char-women in forthwith. It is still uncertain when it will be tenable, for workmen are not very quick in their operations in an empty house'. He reminded Ullathorne that they proposed 'simply to set up an Oratory... not to undertake a Mission or formally to commit ourselves to its duties'. The three parts of an Oratorian's day were: prayer, sacraments, and preaching: 'where by prayer are meant our peculiar exercises, and by sacraments those of the Holy Eucharist and Penance. Our confessionals, where there is need of it, could be open a good part of the day'.[59]

In his diary for Friday 26 January 1849, Newman wrote, 'set off for Birmingham [Alcester Street] for good with Fr Frederic' and on the next day, 'An altar was set up for Mass.'[60]

Formal opening of the new Oratory was on 2 February, the Feast of the Purification, on which same feast day the Oratorians had been first

The house at Littlemore: Newman's rural retreat

established in England at Maryvale in 1848. At this opening ceremony, Newman preached a sermon, *The Salvation of the Hearer the Motive of the Preacher*; this was to become Discourse I of his collection of twenty-eight *Discourses addressed to Mixed Congregations*, which was his principal publication during 1849 while he was immersed in ministering to the poor who came in hundreds to Alcester Street.

These *Discourses* were the first of Newman's publications as a Catholic; the 'ambiguous title implied that his audience was made up of all classes and conditions of men'.[61] Later he admitted that these sermons were 'more rhetorical' than his earlier ones.[62] Ian Ker considers their rhetoric to be 'often more Italianate than Newmanian', although he allows that Newman's 'characteristic genius is not altogether absent'.[63] In these sermons dedicated to Wiseman, Newman deliberately chose to speak in terms that would be intelligible and appeal to his 'mixed' congregation, largely made up of poor, working-class people. With them he shared his thoughts about the divine mysteries of the Catholic faith. According to Ffinch, 'Even Benjamin Jowett, that great bulwark of Broad Church Anglicanism, admitted that "Romanism had never been so glorified before".'[64] Dessain observes that these sermons of Newman's were 'much more elaborate and ornate than the Anglican sermons, and contain many passages of eloquent beauty, although there is nothing above the head of his mixed audience. They are genuine Newman, but not typical'.[65] The reception given to Newman's Birmingham sermons was certainly very different from that of those he had delivered in London the previous year. His listeners were by no means the educated upper classes – the *nobilior splendidior, doctior ordo* of the papal brief – but they thronged to hear Newman's 'discourses', as he preferred to call these sermons. Such activities reflect the ways in which Roman Catholicism was being spread in an industrial city by an Oxford intellectual and convert, whose natural inclinations seemed more inclined towards scholarship than a pastoral apostolate. He was not indifferent to the pressing material problems of the poor but he regarded social conditions as of less immediate hazard than the spiritual needs of the people around him. Norman states that, 'as a matter of ordinary Christian duty, of course, he offered succour to the afflicted if he could', and it is said that he used to pay the medical bills of the poor living in the neighbourhood of the Oratory.[66]

Many years later, Newman was told by a Dublin-based correspondent that the *Discourses to Mixed Congregations* had 'broken up the hard Protestant soil of his heart', adding that Newman's name was held in veneration by priests throughout Ireland.[67]

Wiseman was still wanting the Oratorians to open a House in London, but Newman reported to him in January 1849, that his brethren had unanimously agreed that 'we must set going the Birmingham House well before we think of London'.[68] Wiseman wrote on 19 January 1849 accepting the postponement of a London Oratory.[69] Newman told Mrs Bowden:

> We are trying to put our house to rights, but what weary work that is – I have had a clearing out from Oriel, a clearing out from Littlemore – a getting into Maryvale, a getting in and out at Rome, a getting in to St Wilfrid's, and now a getting in to Birmingham. I intend to be here for good – but what can one promise oneself? [70]

His weariness was aggravated by Faber's complaints, including a long letter about an alleged 'gap' between the novices at Cheadle and Newman, their dislike of Ambrose St John, and Faber's impatience about the opening of a London Oratory.[71] Newman dealt patiently with the novices' perceptions, allowing that particular friendships had, apparently, existed between some of the Apostles, and suggesting that separate congregations might be the solution.[72] He agreed that 'Fr Ambrose had great influence with me, but it is in *certain* things, and I give as full influence to others in other certain things.'[73]

As Newman continued his correspondence with Faber, he put forward the proposal that some members of the Birmingham Oratory could go to London and, after five or ten years, might be constituted as a separate London House. Until then, however, they would remain members of the Birmingham Oratory and he would remain their Father Superior.[74] He rejected outright Faber's argument that the founding in Birmingham of the first English Oratory was accidental: the plan had been carefully worked out during his noviciate in Rome, 'after a minute study of the origins of the Oratory'.[75] In another letter, Newman reminded Faber that 'since mutual *carita* [sic] is the basis of St Philip's Rule, an Oratory must necessarily be of a size that would encourage the development of a family ethos'.

Newman viewed the Oratory 'as a family – six children form a fair fireside – I would allow 11 including novices – which makes 12 with the Padre. More than that is, I think simple evil – and, if I could, I would not have as many as 12 – but the number of offices seems to require it... we are at least too many by half for one Oratory.'[76]

As Dom Placid Murray puts it, 'Newman never wavered in his preference for a small Oratory, feeling that one cannot really love (intimately) a large number of persons with the supernaturalized but still human affection traditional in the Oratory.'[77]

Newman also found it necessary to reject other misconceptions about Oratorian life. Finally Faber assured him that 'all was now plain and every one seems to understand how matters are',[78] but he was unhappy at the prospect of leaving Newman's immediate charge. Newman even considered, briefly, the possibility of himself going to London to avoid such problems of separation.[79] But he put aside the idea of being based in London. He would have to leave his library behind and it would be 'impossible to read or write in London'. The choice lay between the 'exclusively missionary [London] and the partly theological [Birmingham]'. London was at the centre of political and cultural life where many of the upper and educated classes could be reached, whereas Birmingham was a grim manufacturing town with distinctly limited cultural interests. He was, however, also mindful of his responsibilities to the Pope for developing the Birmingham House, which was expanding despite all the problems of being virtually in a slum area. An evening school of 100 children was being run and other missionary activities were planned. Newman had been able to get the lease extended to fifteen years, which enabled certain alterations and repairs to be undertaken. Nevertheless, in the midst of all these activities, Newman's thoughts were never far from his Oxford days: 'It is this day 27 years that I was elected Fellow of Oriel – what a changed state of affairs I find myself in.'[80]

The decision to open a London House was taken; Newman divided the Oratory into two teams, as recorded in the Decree Book of the Birmingham Oratory for 28 May 1849.[81] Faber was to be rector of the new community; Newman was to be the overall Father Superior of the Birmingham and London Houses. Premises in King William Street (later called King William IV Street), off the Strand, in London, were obtained. Like the Birmingham House, the London one was to start in 'another gin shop' – not a distillery, however, 'but a place of entertainment'.[82] Once again Newman was embroiled in battles with builders and also the owner of the property who was refusing to let it to the Roman Catholics on the grounds that the 'organ would be a great nuisance', and that a Roman Catholic chapel attracts the 'lower classes' and 'beggars'.[83] These difficulties were overcome and the building was made suitable for Oratorian

use. It was opened on 31 May 1849, when Newman preached on
Prospects of the Catholic Mission (Discourse XII of *Discourse to
Mixed Congregations*). Faber was in his element in London society,
preaching and converting all whom he could reach and persuade.
Newman was anxious, however, about Faber's flamboyancy, particularly in view of his erratic behaviour at Cheadle and over the
Lives of the Saints. Faber was a prolific and talented writer of
devotional treatises and hymns, some of which achieved ready
acceptance by Catholics and Protestants alike. These frequently
displayed sentimentality and emotional appeals which, although influential at that time, often seem over-exuberant today. But, as Norman
expresses it, 'his writings were of quite outstanding importance',
redolent of Italianate poetry and particularly related to Marian devotions.[84] Faber was to receive a Doctorate in Divinity from Pope
Pius IX in 1854. By this time his health, never sound, was in
serious decline and led later to his extended absences from the
London Oratory.

As was his custom, Newman drew up a memorandum on the 'Birmingham and London Communities' in which he recorded the pension
arrangements and financial contributions to be made by the members
of the two houses.[85] This detailed attention to pecuniary matters
reflects Newman's conscientious approach to all issues – spiritual and
mundane alike. It may even have been imbibed from his early years
when his father was a banker.

Gilley points out that Newman's mind was still pre-occupied with
'the encumbrance of St Wilfrid's, which brought him into conflict
with both Ullathorne and Shrewsbury'.[86] He had to tell the Earl of
Shrewsbury that, after Ullathorne had checked with Propaganda about
having some Oratorian priests at St Wilfrid's, it had been stipulated
that they should 'keep to our Rule *exactissime*'.[87] In a later letter,
Newman stated that since keeping an Oratorian community at St
Wilfrid's was against their Rule, he 'regretted that any further
approach to the Sacred Congregation would be very undesirable in the
case of so young a body as we are'.[88] To Ullathorne, Newman wrote
on the same day informing him that he 'did not at present mean to
make a second application'.[89]

He had to remonstrate sharply with Faber [90] about the irresponsible
attitudes that he had displayed and that had caused great offence to
these leading Catholics as well as to 'old Catholics'; Newman felt that
he had been left to sort out a problem that, largely, was not of his own

making. Faber and the London Oratorians showed little interest and gave virtually no help to Newman in this frustrating task.

In his diary for 17 December 1849, Newman entered a 'Memorandum for Fr Faber', in which he summarized the problems attached to St Wilfrid's and into which he had, reluctantly, been led by Faber. With mordant wit, he introduced the problems by recalling: "There is the famous story of the man who bought an Elephant, and was too poor to keep, and too merciful to kill it, and was unable to persuade anyone to accept it". He perceived that they were 'in somewhat of the same case' with St Wilfrid's.[91] After protracted negotiations, it was reluctantly agreed that the Oratorians should 'place two Fathers there i.e. at St Wilfrid's in Staffordshire, one from Birmingham, the other from the London House, with the provision that each of the other Fathers should be bound to reside there as much as a month each year. Moreover, that in addition to the Mission, a College should be established there, the age of the youths received being for the present undetermined'.[92] In an earlier letter to Miss Giberne, Newman had mentioned that 'We want to form a little school of possible Oratorians there (Cheadle) but can't find the boys. Our married friends will not turn Catholic.'[93] For the time being, however, the burden of St Wilfrid's had been lessened, although it was not until the summer of 1850 that 'Newman succeeded in handing over St Wilfrid's to the diocese'.[94]

On 18 January 1850, Newman listed the various responsibilities of the members of the London Oratory. These would be in force until the Feast of the Purification, 1851 'at which time, I suppose, I cease to be superior, and my authority is at an end'.[95] The position of Father Superior relates to a specific Oratory and its Congregation and, as noted earlier, Newman had fulfilled this responsibility at both establishments. On the London Oratory's achieving independence from Birmingham, Newman would then relinquish the post of Superior at both Oratories.

Newman's persistent financial worries were significantly reduced by a liberal endowment brought by Edward Caswall when he joined the Birmingham Oratory. He was a former Anglican clergyman who had been influenced by Newman's *Development of Doctrine*. After the death of his wife from cholera, he had studied in Rome. Following ordination as a Catholic priest and having no family, he became an Oratorian.

Newman acknowledged Caswall's great generosity (£4,000) with warmth:

You have indeed done us the greatest benefit that could be done to us in external matters. At the moment, we do not want any great thing, but the power to make a great many beginnings ... You have answered all these purposes at once.[96]

His donated wealth enabled Newman to buy, for £1,800 in May 1850, the site in Edgbaston on which the present Oratory was built.[97]

During May 1850 Newman delivered a series of lectures at the London Oratory. These were published as *Certain Difficulties felt by Anglicans in Catholic Teaching*, and together with *Sermons to Mixed Congregations* have been described as belonging to the 'honeymoon period' of his Catholic life, having a 'tone of exultant optimism which we find at no other moment of his life either as an Anglican or as a Catholic'.[98] He had been persuaded by Wiseman to involve himself but did so with marked reluctance, not wishing to rake up old fires and possibly offend some of his old Anglican friends. At the same time, he realized that it would be extremely hard not to do so if he were to talk openly about the undeniable differences between the adherents of these faiths. He did so with devastating irony. In the end – and in Owen Chadwick's opinion to his discredit – Newman wrote the only one of his books 'which many Anglicans found it impossible to forgive'.[99]

Ker states that '*Difficulties of Anglicans* was intended by Newman to persuade Anglo-Catholics to follow him into the Roman Catholic Church' and that 'he describes the difference between the faith of Protestants and that of Catholics by arguing that the former hold religious opinions, while for the latter the objects of belief are simply facts'.[100]

Jaki, however, has observed that 'Undoubtedly, the *Lectures on Anglican Difficulties* bring home most painful difficulties to Anglican Newmanists such as Chadwick'.[101] Certainly, Newman's reference to the Church of England as 'so much the prisoner of a largely agnostic Parliament' was likely to offend Anglican susceptibilities to the charge of Erastianism. Even Newman's benign biographer, Wilfrid Ward, described the first seven lectures as the 'only instances among his writings of what might be called aggressive controversy... they are an attack ... addressed to the Tractarians who remained in the Anglican Church – the friends he had left behind him'. But he added that Newman had expressly stated that it was not his wish 'to weaken the hold of the Anglican Church on the many, but only on those who he believed ought to join the Church of Rome'.[102] Newman himself confessed that in preparing the lectures, he had never written before 'so intellectually against the grain'.[103]

However, Jaki takes a rather different view of the feelings that Newman experienced when writing *Anglican Difficulties*, and he asserts that the last Lecture refutes the suggestion that Newman was not writing according to his deepest convictions, intellectual and moral.[104] The true meaning of that often misunderstood remark is in a letter to R. H. Hutton, in which Newman disclosed that the writings of books 'has been to me, in point of pain, a mental child-bearing'.[105] Some years back, he had expressed some concern about the Lectures in a letter to Charles Russell: 'I am conscious that they are a mere ephemeral publication, and I shall be far more than satisfied, if, as you think, they will do good at the moment'.[106]

Dessain says that Newman always insisted that in writing these lectures 'he was not acting in direct hostility to the Anglican Church as such, but merely carrying the Oxford Movement to its legitimate conclusion'.[107]

The lectures were planned to coincide with the trial of the Reverend George Gorham, an outspoken Low Churchman who had been presented to a living by the Crown in the diocese of the High Church Bishop Henry Phillpotts of Exeter. After exhaustive enquiries, Phillpotts alleged that Gorham regarded baptism merely as a *symbol* of regeneration and refused to institute him to the living. On appeal the ecclesiastical Court of Arches' judgement against Gorham was set aside by the Judicial Committee of the Privy Council. Thus a secular court of appeal overruled a Church court: a civil court had asserted its supremacy in spiritual affairs, namely those to do with doctrine. The decision evoked considerable debate in certain quarters and resulted in several defections from the Church of England to the Roman Catholic Church; they included H. E. Manning. The Gorham Case (1850) revealed, according to Newman, 'that Erastianism held sway in the Church of England'. Newman had followed the trial and its outcome influenced his decision to focus in these lectures on the Oxford Movement in the hope of attracting the remaining 'Puseyites' to Roman Catholicism.[108]

Anglican Difficulties gave insights into Newman's own spiritual odyssey which, as Jaki suggests, could be taken as a pattern for Anglo-Catholics. 'Thus, a decade and a half before the *Apologia*', Newman outlined his reasons for becoming a Roman Catholic. He referred to the last of the Lectures (XII *Ecclesiastical History No Prejudice and the Apostolicity of the Church*) in a letter dated 15 October 1862: 'I certainly did not become a Catholic, as others have, on the ground *Ubi Petrus, ibi Ecclesia.*'[109] Instead, he strongly stressed the logic of his conversion, as he sketched out his spiritual progression from boyhood years onwards. In this remarkable Lecture, he set down firmly his reasons for eventually rejecting the *Via Media* approach. He described the *Via Media* of the Anglican Church as 'an interposition or arbitration between the extreme doctrines of Protestantism on the one hand and the faith of Rome which Protestantism contradicts on the other'.[110] Towards the end of this Lecture Newman, after a wide-scanning historical survey of the development of Christianity, summed up the *Via Media* as having a 'tendency in theory towards latitudinarianism; its position historically is one of heresy; in the National Church it has fulfilled both its theoretical tendency and its historical position. As this simple truth was brought home to me, I felt that, if continuance on the National Church was defensible, it must be on other grounds than those of the *Via Media*'.[111]

In response to Mgr George Talbot, who 'was on his way to becoming a close adviser to Pius IX and eventually a nemesis to Newman, [112] Newman rejected the idea of having the Lectures translated into Italian:

> As to my lectures, I very much doubt if they will do to translate. They are addressed solely to Puseyites, about whom the good Monsignori and Padre of Rome are about as ignorant as Protestants are of them. They are based upon principles and arguments, of which they never heard – and will not feel interest in – or may misunderstand.[113]

In the same year, and soon after the publication of Newman's *Difficulties of Anglicans*, the newly appointed Cardinal Archbishop of Westminster – Dr Wiseman – issued a tactless pastoral letter announcing the restoration of the Catholic hierarchy. This resulted in violent 'No-Popery' agitation against what became known as the 'Papal Aggression'. Anti-Catholic feelings were fanned by *The Times, Punch* and other journals. The latent anti-Catholicism which had last raised its head during the notorious Gordon Riots again became very visible, and resulted in some mob demonstrations and damage to Catholic chapels by a few fanatics. Newman was spurred to writing once more and, from the Birmingham Oratory, produced what some twenty years later he 'ever considered' to be his 'best book'.[114] In *Lectures on the*

Present Position of Catholics in England, he sought to refute with energy and irony the misrepresentations of Catholicism deliberately fostered by some fanatical Protestants. In a letter to Canon Estcourt, Newman commented that 'In my lectures on Catholicism in England I oppose, not the Anglican Church, but National Protestantism, and Anglicans only so far as they belong to it.'[115] Throughout his life, Newman never lost affection for the Anglican Church, but he maintained that these lectures were aimed at 'the misconceptions concerning Catholicism which generally occupy the English mind'.[116]

The nine lectures which constitute *The Present Position of Catholics in England* were delivered at the Corn Exchange in High Street, Birmingham, to packed audiences in 1851, a year in which the Ecclesiastical Titles Bill was passed to re-impose prohibitions on the use of ecclesiastical territorial titles by Roman Catholic bishops which duplicated those used by the Established Church (see Prologue). Each lecture was printed and made available in the week following its delivery. Chadwick puts it that in his lectures Newman 'intended to expose the more ludicrous and revolting forms of anti-popish prejudice. He mocked the number of the Beast, and John Bullism, and tried to expose "Maria Monk" and the ex-priest Achilli'.[117] The last of these targets, however, resulted in Newman being involved in a long and unpleasant libel action, which was brought about by Achilli with the support of the Evangelical Alliance (see Chapter 6).

Newman's Birmingham lectures were not solely for the purpose of dismissing popular myths about Catholicism: he also called his Catholic listeners to accept that they had a duty to live their lives in such a way that their Protestant critics would see with their own eyes what Catholicism really meant. He stressed the importance of the laity, i.e. themselves, in becoming well informed about their religion so that they, in turn, would be able to give insights to enquirers about the nature and practices of their faith. He declared that 'Catholics ought to know Catholicism better than other men.'[118] In these lectures Newman deplored that 'more use was not made of married converts, like clergymen, who, I have said and truly, viewed together have an amount of talent, which the unmarried clergy converted have not'. He went on to suggest to J. Spencer Northcote, an old Oxford friend and Catholic convert, that 'One most interesting series of lectures would be, if every one of you gave his *own* ground of conversion' and he reminded him that 'many of the early apologists were lay men'.[119] Dessain notes that one of the weaknesses of the Church was its clericalization and the consequent inferior position of the laity, and claims that Newman was 'keenly aware that the Church was not merely the clergy but all who had received the Holy Spirit'.[120] Newman, in fact, formally 'addressed' the Corn Exchange lectures, when they were published, to the 'Brothers of the Oratory' who were a confraternity of laymen attached to an Oratory. He viewed the *Orat. Parv.* (Little Oratory) as 'more important than anything else', for without it the Oratory itself 'would have failed'.[121]

Newman's attachment to the Little Oratory lasted over his life; in 1880 he stated that he wished to see it formally restored and, after Pontifical First Vespers of Candlemas on Sunday 1 February 1880, he enrolled new brothers.[122]

Tristram notes that the *Lectures on the Present Position of Catholics* were open to the public, and the Brothers represented a very small proportion of the audience.[123] Newman fully intended that his words should influence the minds and hearts of 'educated men' in the outside world, so that prejudices against Catholics would be removed.[124] Wilfrid Ward asserts that Newman's Birmingham lectures 'not only set right with great rhetorical effect the actual slanders and misrepresentations against the Church ... but owe their subtler and greater qualities to his wonderful analysis of British prejudice, of the actual workings of the mind of the prejudiced man'. In so doing, Newman brought 'into play his deeper qualities as a psychological analyst; it was largely due to the outspoken and independent admiration of Richard Holt Hutton, editor of the *Spectator*,[125] that Newman's outspoken words were to reach far and wide. Hutton, a former Unitarian who had converted to Anglicanism, was a man of wide interests and many friendships, including notable Catholics. He was later to espouse Newman's cause in his controversy with Charles Kingsley, which was to inspire the *Apologia* (see Chapter 6). Hutton wrote a perceptive biographical study of Newman in which he described the Birmingham lectures as representing 'very effectively the forces of "Protestant tradition" as it was in 1851, though what was truly enough said then, now enormously exaggerates the fore of that tradition, the difference being largely due to Newman's personal influence, exerted partly through the publication of these lectures, though in a far greater degree through the publication of his religious autobiography thirteen years later'. While the Lectures 'depicted very powerfully the nonsensical and fanatical side of Protestantism', Hutton considered that they also contained passages which 'pass the limits of irony, and approach the region of something like controversial force, yet force of no common order'. He also reflected that 'probably the most important of the immediate results of this course of lectures was the action for libel brought by Dr Achilli against Newman'.[126] (Refer to Chapter 6.)

Newman had distinct reservations about the need at that time for the restoration of the Catholic hierarchy. He stated that 'We want seminaries far more than sees. We want education, *view*, combination, organization.' There should be a concerted effort to encourage young Catholics to band together to go out and tell the people about their faith, and to start up journals for this purpose.[127]

In a further letter to the editor of the *Rambler*, Newman expressed his support of his activities in organizing lectures in London and other cities, given by laymen in defence of Catholicism.[128] However, a few weeks later one such layman, J. M. Capes, was warned by Newman that 'our bishop [Ullathorne] is a cautious man' and he doubted whether Capes' lectures would be liked by Ullathorne 'in his heart'.[129] The bishop had a strong aversion to laymen involving themselves in some kind of 'lay preaching'. Capes was advised to avoid misapprehensions of his activities; he should make clear that there was no intention that these lay efforts should be regarded as preaching with authority, which remained the exclusive province of priests. But Newman reassured Capes that 'I am sure that they [laymen] may be made in this day the strength of the Church'.[130]

In the summer of 1850 Newman declined an invitation from Archbishop Cullen to preach at the dedication of a church in his diocese of Armagh, pointing out that the Fathers of the Oratory 'do not commonly preach out of their own church, and the Father Superior in particular does not quit the town where he is situated during the period of his office'. He likewise declined requests from other prelates and religious organizations'.[131] In his journal, Newman records that 'I first knew Dr Cullen at Rome in 1847, when he was very civil to me ... When the University was to be founded for Catholics in Oreland he wrote to consult me on this subject'.[132] (In the next chapter, extended discussion of Cullen's negotiations with Newman over the University occurs.)

Ullathorne sent Newman the Rescripts by which Pius IX had conferred on him a Doctorate of Divinity; Newman acknowledged them with a 'hasty line' expressing his 'extreme gratification'. He was already attracting admiration in Rome through his responses to the Gorham affair.[133] It was, therefore, perceptive of Ullathorne to choose

Newman to give the sermon in St Chad's Cathedral on the occasion of
his, Ullathorne's, installation as the first Bishop of Birmingham, for
Newman was (and remained), as Norman observes 'an isolated figure,
yet always at the centre of men's perception of English Catholicism
but at the periphery of the institutional Church'.[134]

According to Ian Ker, Newman's celebrated sermon *Christ upon the
Waters*, delivered on 27 October 1850, 'contained all the elements of
his satirical genius, not least the kind of imagery typical of this period
of his writings'.[135] Newman pilloried the materialism of a provincial
society which had no sense of moral purpose and had shown disregard
of moral values. In flowing phrases he glorified the regeneration of
the Roman Catholic Church in England,

> Coming out of prison as collected in her teaching, as precise in her action,
> as when she went into it ... she seeks, she desires no temporal power, no
> secular station; she meddles not with Caesar; she obeys him in his place,
> but she is independent of him. Her strength is in her God; her rule is over
> the souls of men; her glory is in their willing subjection and loving
> loyalty.[136]

Of course *The Times* and other publications took up their customary
carping attitude towards Catholic events and Newman's rhetoric was
picked at gleefully. It was even said publicly that he deserved to be
'kicked out' of the country – for which offensiveness an apology was
later made.[137] Newman told Philip Howard, a Catholic MP, who
reported a speech by the Reverend A. C. Tait, Dean of Carlisle
(formerly one of the Tutors who had denounced *Tract 90*), and who
now denounced his sermon *Christ upon the Waters*, that for seventeen
years he had been the subject of so much daily misrepresentation, in
the public prints and at public meetings, that 'I never think at all about
whatever is said against me in the one or at the other'.[138]

When, as noted already, a site in Edgbaston had been bought
through Fr Edward Caswell's generosity, it was decided in May 1850
to build a house for the community and to collect funds for the erection of a church. (Early in the twentieth century, a widespread appeal
would be made to build the present Oratory church as a memorial to
Newman.) The Oratorians then vacated Alcester Street and moved to
their new home in Hagley Road, Edgbaston on Low Sunday 1852.[139]

Apart from being preoccupied with appealing for funds and in writing
lectures and sermons, Newman had continuous worries about the
London Oratory and particularly about their joint responsibilities for the

mission at St Wilfrid's, Cheadle. In a long letter to Faber he 'unbur-
dened' himself and urged him to 'put his should to the wheel' and to
provide 'some plan' to clarify the position.[140] Faber's response was not
helpful: 'I have relinquished the task as hopeless . . . As to what we are
to do now, I cannot at all see; and as superior we must look to you to
propose something.'[141] Newman was thus left to negotiate with the Early
of Shrewsbury to find an acceptable solution.[142] After protracted discussions, which also involved the Redemptorists, the Passionists eventually
took over St Wilfrid's from the Oratorians.[143]

This tedious business being settled at last, Newman gave his attention once more to the relative positions of the two Oratories. He told
Faber that he was 'decided on their separation . . . it was impossible to
be a non-resident Superior, or to govern an absent House'. He also
dismissed rumours that he would be made a bishop: 'no one can seriously wish it, who is loyal to St Philip; and there are no limits to
which I would go to prevent it'.[144] Matters now moved quickly to a
head and on 9 October 1850 a Decree was issued formally setting up
a London Congregation of the Oratory.[145] On 12 October, Faber was
elected the first independent Superior of the London Oratory.[146]

These events had virtually coincided with the restoration of the
Catholic hierarchy, and Newman felt worried about possible repercussions in society at large. According to Trevor, 'the London Oratorians
were in the thick of it . . . Birmingham too was not without its excitement'.[147]

As already noted, there were marked differences in personality and
temperament between Newman and Faber. The result was a degree of
incompatibility that led to mutual frustration and misunderstanding.
The separation of the two houses resulted in these differences being
reflected in the ways in which their communities developed and
reacted to one another. Faber tended to be erratic and unreliable;
Newman was cautious and disciplined, yet in his scholarly approach
he was also capable of challenging beliefs and behaviour if an issue of
importance sufficiently aroused him. Both men tended to suffer bouts
of illness. Newman, apart from his near fatal illness in Sicily during
1833, was particularly prone to colds and toothache, although he must
presumably have had a remarkably strong constitution since, until a
venerable age, he kept up an exacting routine. Faber, on the other
hand, suffered at a relatively early age from a degenerative disease
that brought on his early death at the age of forty-nine years. Nevertheless, despite their psychological and physiological differences, the

two men also displayed from time to time, fraternal feelings of touching concern for one another. These spasmodic occasions seemed, however, insufficient to temper their habitual reactions to each other.

Faber's failing health and extended periods of convalescence and Newman's prolonged absences in Dublin during the time he was connected with the Catholic university, also contributed to some degree of instability within their communities.

In October 1850 when the London House formally became independent of the Birmingham House, Faber had proposed that Newman should keep up some measure of supervision over them. Newman declined this proposal but did agree that he should be consulted on important matters for a period of three years. Both Houses had become well-established by 1855; the Birmingham House had moved in 1852 from a slum area of the city to the attractive environment of Edgbaston and, the following year, the London House migrated from their insalubrious building off the Strand to fashionable Brompton.

Relationships between the Houses reached a crisis point in 1855 when the London Oratory applied to Rome for relaxation from the Oratorian Rule that forbade the hearing of nuns' confessions. This prohibition dated back to the time of the founder, St Philip Neri, who considered that Oratorians should not be diverted from their principal duties by undertaking the spiritual direction of nuns. When Newman had made certain modifications to St Philip's Rule so that an Oratory could be effective in the conditions of Victorian England, he had retained the original ban on Oratorians becoming involved in giving spiritual direction to nuns.

The origins of the problem in 1855 arose from a request by Wiseman to the London Oratorians to take charge of the spiritual care and direction of nuns. After doing this for some time, they decided to ask Rome 'for an interpretation or suspension of the particular rule which forbade it'.[148] This was done by Faber without consulting Newman. The Congregation of Propaganda in Rome assumed that Newman would have been consulted and, after conferring with the bishops in Birmingham and London, prepared to issue the necessary dispensation. Newman first became aware of this matter when Ullathorne told him that he was glad to hear 'a rescript from Rome was coming to dispense them [the Oratorians] from this provision of the Rule: Dalgairns [at Birmingham Oratory] had undertaken similar work for the nuns at Stone, which they had felt some qualms about, but which the bishop encouraged'.[149] In his journal Newman noted, perhaps a little unfairly, that 'All that sad quarrel with the London House was owing to Fr Dalgairns thinking he might do what he pleased in my absence.'[150] Newman and the Birmingham community were deeply shocked to discover that London, unilaterally, had decided to seek Rome's permission to change the Rule without the knowledge or consent of the other English House. The special nature of the Oratorian vocation was governed by their Rule; independent attempts to alter it threatened the whole way of life by which they had chosen to serve God. In their judgement, the London Oratorians' action was not merely a matter or legalistic niceties: it had profoundly disturbing implications which could strike at the heart of Oratorianism.

From Dublin Newman wrote to Ambrose St John as Father Rector. He set out at considerable length the problems arising from London's independent action. He warned the Birmingham community that 'If one part of our Rule is suspended, while we sleep, so may another. We may wake in the morning, and find that the Fathers at Brompton have demanded a virtually *new* Rule, and impose it, through Propaganda, upon us.'[151]

Newman decided that he should visit Rome and present personally to Propaganda his concerns about the misunderstandings that had arisen as a result of Faber's arbitrary action. In a diary entry for 26 December 1855, he records that Ambrose St John and himself 'set off for Rome'. He told Mrs Bowden that, as he passed through London, he would 'tell the Cardinal who is for some one of the Birmingham House going to Rome – but not me'.[152] In fact, Newman sent a letter, dated 27 December, to Wiseman to inform him of his visit and his plans to 'lay before Mgr Barnabo and others the real state of the difficulty about the Oratory, which will be greater, I am sure, as time goes on'. He also requested Wiseman's opinion of two resolutions which he had sent to him earlier: namely, that any decision by Propaganda for one House should apply solely to that one; and that any request to come for an interpretation of the Rule should be submitted to the other Houses for their opinion.[153] Newman's statement thus indicated that his aim was to preserve the future independence of his own House, not to oppose the granting of permissions to London Oratory.[154]

Newman's letter was immediately sent to Faber by Wiseman, who explained that he had received a letter from Cardinal Fransoni intimating that Propaganda 'could not imagine' that Faber had not consulted Newman before making his original application. The London Oratory at once circulated the Italian Oratories and also Propaganda giving their account of the breach with Newman, and accusing him of wanting to exercise a '*generalate* over the whole Congregation'.[155]

On 12 January 1856, Newman and Ambrose St John arrived in Rome. On the way they had had discussions with various Oratories, among which were Verona, Turin and Florence, about their respective ways of observing the Rule of St Philip Neri, particularly as related to the spiritual direction of nuns. In an interview with Mgr Barnabo on 17 January, Newman thought he 'seemed defensive', appeared to have 'some idea of other of me, which we could not get to the bottom of'. But Newman added that 'a long interview with the Pope was most satisfactory'.[156]

Newman and Ambrose St John had their interview with the Pope on 25 January. According to Newman,

> He wished to *hear our side*, having heard the other. I suppose he got part of his information from the Bishop [Ullathorne], but the greater part came from the London House ... Then he went on to speak *in extenso* of various things, as if to put us on our ease.

After some time, Newman stated, the Pope referred to the letter from the London House, and St John gave a clear account of the trouble which had arisen because London had made an application for a faculty to hear the confessions of nuns without Birmingham's knowledge which, if granted, 'would make the Oratory seem to be one order'. A few days later Barnabo recommended to Newman not to pursue his official supplication that

> Nothing done by the Holy See by one Oratory might affect another ... because the grant of it would *diminish* my power, inasmuch as I was *Deputato Apostolico* for setting up the Oratory in any part of England. (He said that our brief was to be extended by Rescript to Ireland, where I suppose I should have the same office.)

Newman confessed that he was puzzled by Barnabo's information and could only suppose that 'Propaganda overrides Canon Law'; it seems, he thought, 'that, in setting up a House, I may make *conditions*, if not inconsistent with the Brief and Rule. And this seems to be Barnabo's meaning ... that for the Pope to rule any thing about the existing independent *action* of Oratories, is to limit my existing powers'.[157]

Trevor suggests that the original Brief Newman had been given by the Pope conferred on him powers greater than he had realized.[158] This opinion presumably rests on the fact that Newman, as noted, had the status of *Deputato Apostolico*. Birmingham would not, therefore, be compelled to follow London's lead in the matter in question. This was reassuring and some reward to Newman and his loyal community. Partial success was better than downright failure; but it did little to reduce the friction between the two Houses.

Newman now thought the time was right to recapitulate the essential nature of an Oratory and the Oratorian vocation. He did so in seven letters written from Dublin to Birmingham in March 1856. They were later published as *Remarks on the Oratorian Vocation*.[159] Each of these seven letters focuses on one particular point and the argument is then taken forward through the succeeding letters as follows: Letter I: The Oratory is not a religious body, and yet is like one; its members aim at perfection, yet at a perfection different in its circumstances and peculiarities from that of regulars; Letter II: Certain qualifications attaching historically to Fathers of the Oratory, by which they are distinguished from ordinary secular priests, that is, the breeding of a gentleman, the mental elevation and culture which learning gives, the accomplishments of literature, the fine arts and similar studies; Letter III: The literary qualifications and liberal knowledge traditional in the Italian Oratory; Letter IV: Various characteristics of a Father of the Oratory, both in how he differs from the ordinary run of secular priests, and how he differs from the type of a regular; various counsels (of perfection) he does not pursue; Letter V: The precise instrument of Oratorian perfection, is that he is 'a secular priest'; but not only so, but a secular priest 'living in a community'; Letter VI: The duty of obedience to the Rule; Letter VII: Obedience to the Superiors. According to Murray, 'The kernel of the whole matter is Letter V on community living as the precise instrument of Oratorian perfection.'[160]

Newman's afflictions were added to by a rather tactless letter from Wiseman in June 1856 saying that he proposed to write a dedication to Newman and Faber jointly in his 'poor panegyric of St Philip' that was to be published under the auspices of the London Oratory. Newman responded that he 'rejoiced to hear' about the publication that 'his name was included with those of the Birmingham Fathers'.[161] Wiseman showed Newman's letter to Faber, and through him to various persons, and commented on it 'in most disrespectful terms ... and, without a word of explanation to me, immediately proceeded to publish the Dedication to Fr Faber and myself'.[162] Some time earlier, Newman had commented to his old friend Henry Wilberforce that 'The Cardinal has a thousand good points, but you must never *trust* him.'[163]

Two years later Newman was to repeat virtually the same views of Wiseman to one of his friends:

> There is no difference at all between the Cardinal and me. I think of his as *you* do. He has ten thousand good points – but, as an individual, you cannot *trust* him; not from any moral fault, but from his character... It often happens that one finds one cannot *trust* people. *We* cannot trust *them*, as one cannot trust the *Cardinal*.[164]

In June 1856 Newman wrote from Dublin to his community in Birmingham a lengthy and formal account of the 'painful controversy' which had been taking place with the London Oratory. He ended his letter by admonishing his brethren that in dealing with those of the London Oratory they should 'be kind to them individually; pray for the welfare of their Congregation; but keep clear of them. St Philip is not the Saint of far-spreading associations; but of isolated bodies, working severally in their own spheres'.[165]

Throughout 1856 correspondence flowed between Newman and Faber on the highly sensitive issue of London's independent application to Rome, which had caused Newman so much concern because of the implications that it seemed to him to have for the Oratorian vocation itself. Perceptions clearly differed considerably regarding the seriousness of the alleged breach of the founding Brief which Newman had drawn up from St Philip Neri's Rule and amended it to fit conditions in England. Faber's letters show an almost over-eager willingness to seek forgiveness for anything done to cause so much distress to Newman. But at the same time, Faber seemed to lack – or deliberately avoid – any understanding of the real issue involved.[166] Newman 'professed very great satisfaction' in hearing from Faber again, and regretted to learn of 'his continued indisposition'. Sadly, the gap between them seemed unbridgeable; also, Faber, on his admission, was still far from well.[167]

Further correspondence resulted in apparent frustration on both sides. Newman declared that if it was to go on, he would recognize no one but the Secretary of the Congregation as the person to write to about the matter in question.[168] Yet another letter of deep regret and profuse apology came from London, signed formally by the Provost (Faber) and the Secretary.[169]

In a lengthy and formal reply, Newman reiterated that 'Our rule is our Vocation ... To touch a Rule is to unsettle vocations.' Any attempts to meddle with the Rule 'by some of its members' which is 'unknown to the rest', stirs 'deeply a religious body'. London without consultation, had applied to Rome for 'an interpretation of a Decree' and when he had expostulated, they had put 'aside his expostulation'. He had felt sure they would now realize they had caused him 'the deepest pain'. He stated that 'the substance of his complaint remains', and so far, 'they had done nothing to remedy matters'.[170]

Newman's concerns about London's unilateral application to Rome were again expressed in two more letters to Faber.[171]A formal letter from the London Oratory indicated that they did not regard their application to Rome 'in the serious light you do'. They trusted that 'no fresh act of their Congregation would ever suggest that they were unmindful of their obligations owed to Newman and his relationship as founder of their House'.[172] The next letter Newman sent to Faber – from Dublin – was a cordial invitation for him to 'take our University Sermon on Sunday, 20th July'. Faber at first accepted this, but then declined.[173]

Newman then sent to Wiseman 'as a melancholy memorial of the past', a detailed account of the correspondence which had passed between the two Houses. In it he referred to 'Three Propositions', the agreed basis on which the London House should be constituted.[174] A copy of this letter was also sent to the London Congregation and it was circulated to the Birmingham Congregation.

Fr Bernard Dalgairns, who had caused Newman considerable annoyance during this troublesome period, had decided to leave the Birmingham Oratory. This was recorded in the Decree Book on 2 September 1856:

> Fr Bernard Dalgairns, having written to the Father to say that he has not the spirit of the Oratory, and therefore no Vocation for it, and that he asks in consequence to be released from his allegiance to us, is pronounced to be no longer one of our members.[175]

Fr Dalgairns then rejoined the London Oratory.

Gilley reports that feelings between the two Oratories had been further aggravated in 1856 when London requested Rome for a separate Brief and the Pope demanded that Newman should be consulted; but Barnabo, now Cardinal Prefect of Propaganda, stated that Newman himself had suggested separate Briefs for the two Houses and that he had written to Rome in support of London's application.[176]

In Newman's judgement 'the harm done to him by the London Oratory letter to Propaganda was lasting'[177] and his reputation in

England was damaged by the unedifying quarrel. Committing his innermost thoughts to paper, he wrote in his journal:

> First in 1853, came my mistake in asking for Dalgairns from the London House; then my going to Ireland, in order to impinge upon Dr Cullen, while Dalgairns intrigued at home in my absence. Then the great plot of him, Faber, etc., - my going to Rome – and the treatment I met at Propaganda. Then the thousand whisperings against me at the London Oratory, which have succeeded in prejudicing the Catholic body to a great extent against me ... all sorts of suspicions and calumnies have attended my name.[178]

In November 1860, Newman wrote a confidential comment to one of his old and intimate friends, James Hope-Scott: 'As you love me, do not get me into a fresh correspondence about Fr Faber. I wish he would consent to leave us alone. To you I will speak frankly, and as I have done *to no one else*.' From long experience, Newman confessed that he had a 'profound and intense distrust' of Faber. Although he admitted that Faber 'had a thousand attractive points', he also had a 'restless spirit of intrigue which nothing can quench'. Newman felt sincerely that Faber was 'doing so much good in his important position, that it would be a great scandal if his name were touched'. He reflected:

> It is now years since the separation, 1855 [of the Oratories]; we quite desire to be at peace ... but the first step is for them to *say* that the two Oratories have ever been at peace (not to speak of a *reconciliation*), which would be making matters worse, but that the Oratories have ever been friends, and *to cease to talk*.[179]

Newman acknowledged a letter from Wiseman, on 14 July 1863, advising him that Faber was gravely ill: 'I am perfectly aware of the hopeless stated in which Fr Faber lies. Your Eminence will be glad to know that Fr Faber has already been informed by me, not only of my wish to see him, but of the precise time when I hope to have that sad satisfaction.'[180]

On Faber's death in September 1863, Newman assisted at his Requiem at London Oratory. From correspondence it is evident that Newman's memories of the problems he had with Faber and the London Oratory rankled. 'I know no more about them [London Oratory] than you do, nor am likely. They absolutely and intentionally threw me off eight years ago just.'[181]

More than two decades later, Newman was to be reminded of the distressful relationship that had developed between Faber and himself over the status of the two Oratories – see earlier discussion. Through the Duke of Norfolk, Newman learned that Fr William Gordon, who had succeeded Faber as Superior of the London Oratory, wished to invite him to the opening of their new church in Brompton. As a close personal friend of the new cardinal, the Duke had endeavoured to persuade Newman to accept the invitation:

> It will be a most bitter disappointment to them if you are not able to come ... It would be a terrible blow not only to the Fathers but to all of us who have any right to call St Philip our Father if you were not present at the opening and able to crown the work you set on foot.[182]

Newman wrote directly to Gordon in words that expressed clearly his distress and annoyance: 'Why could you not have sounded me, before you let the Duke write to me? Why did you do so little consult for me as not to hinder his making a request to me, which I am obliged for so many reasons not to entertain?' He reminded the London Superior that three years earlier he 'was the first to move towards you' so that 'we might end well with act of grace on both sides ... Thus things seemed well settled; now all is reversed'. Newman pointed out that he was being 'asked to take part in an act, which concerns intimately and solely the London Oratory. Thus shall we end in a recognized disruption'.[183] From the further correspondence with the Duke of Norfolk, it is evident that Newman felt that he had, perhaps, been misunderstood and regretted any annoyance and trouble he may have caused the Duke, although he maintained that the London Superior 'would have had such a vivid and delicate sense of the indelible relations which had been created years ago between the London Oratory and me, as would have warned him against an act which could only bring trouble to me and to him'.[184]

Gordon wrote to Newman that he 'can only express my great sorrow at having most unintentionally displeased your Eminence' by having spoken to the Duke before writing to him.[185] This sincere apology was accepted by Newman who, in turn, withdrew anything he had said which 'was unnecessary and inconsiderate to you'. He also stated that, as far as he knew, no one at Birmingham had 'any thought of my being asked to the opening of your Church (so no harm is done)'.[186]

In a follow-up letter, Newman advised Gordon that he 'supposed some of our party here will be going up to the opening of your new

Church. I want your Fathers to accept from me an offering for one of
its altars of devotions, which I should send up to you with a letter by
them'.[187]

Newman confided to the Duke of Norfolk: 'Alas, alas, why did I not
confine myself to the true and sufficient reason that I was too old, too
infirm, too worn in mind to leave home? That, my dear Duke, would
have been my proper answer to you and there would have been an end
of it...' Instead, he became 'involved . . . in a correspondence which I
cannot carry through; for the weariness, which unfits me for going to
London, unfits me for letter writing'. He reminded his lòyal friend that:
'Oratories were never meant to be intimate.' He had 'done what I could'
and would be sending a gift with a kind letter to Fr Gordon.[188]

On 25 April 1884, Newman informed John Hungerford Pollen, one
of his long-standing friends and the architect of the University Church

View across the Hagley Road of the Oratory House, Birmingham.

in Dublin, that three of the Birmingham Oratorians attended the opening of the new Church of the London Oratory, and were bearers of Newman's gift – a chalice.[189] Newman's gift was received with great appreciation by the Fathers of London Oratory: it was a symbol of the commitment which Newman, now in his ninth decade, continued to have for his Oratorian vocation.

Notes

1. LDXII.19–20, 19 January 1847.
2. Tristram, Henry, 1933, pp. 212–32.
3. LDXII.114, Mrs J. W. Bowden, 15 September 1847.
4. Ward, 1913, p. 199.
5. LDXXII.199.
6. LDXII.165.
7. Dessain, 1980, p. 93.
8. LDXII.140, 31 December 1847.
9. LDXII.143, 2 January 1848.
10. LDXII.144, January 1848.
11. LDXII.145.
12. LDXII.148, 11 January 1848.
13. Trevor, 1996, p. 117.
14. LDXII.243, 12 July 1848.
15. LDXI.105, 1 February 1846.
16. LDXII.66, 31 March 1847.
17. LDXII.137.
18. LDXII.140, 31 December 1847.
19. LDXII.197, 2 April 1848.
20. cf Norman, 1985, p. 317.
21. Murray, 1980, p. 95.
22. Trevor, 1996, p. 120.
23. LDXII.162, footnote.
24. LDXII.162–3, 26 January 1848.
25. LDXII.162, 26 January 1848.
26. LDXII.184–5, 17 March 1848.
27. LDXII.169, 11 February 1848.
28. LDXII.172, 25 February 1848.
29. LDXII.184–5, 17 March 1848.
30. LDXII.264, footnote.
31. LDXII.275, footnote.
32. LDXII.75, Michaelmas Day 1848.
33. Dessain, 1980, p. 92; also see Chapter 3 above.
34. LDXII.278, 4 October 1848.

35. LDXII.278, footnote.
36. LDXII.284-5, 10 October 1848.
37. LDXII.297, 14 October 1848.
38. LDXII.314, 28 October 1848.
39. LDXII.316, 30 October 1848.
40. LDXII.302, R. A. Coffin, 22 October 1848.
41. LDXII.319, Bishop Ullathorne, 2 November 1848.
42. LDXII.320, 3 November 1848.
43. LDXII.345, 24 November 1848.
44. LDXII.349, Bishop Wiseman, 26 November 1848.
45. LDXII.352-3, 29 November 1848.
46. LDXII.360, 30 November 1848.
47. LDXII.353, footnote.
48. LDXII.362, 3 December 1849.
49. Newman, 1956, p. 256.
50. Ward, 1913, p. 205.
51. LDXII.198, 6 April 1848.
52. LDXII.279-80, Mrs J. W. Bowden, 5 October 1848.
53. LDXII.302, 22 October 1848.
54. LDXII.302, 22 October 1848.
55. LDXII.368, footnote, 8 December 1848.
56. LDXII.368-70, 9 & 13 December 1848.
57. LDXII.369-70, 10 December 1848.
58. LDXII.374, Mrs J. W. Bowden, 17 December 1848.
59. LDXII.383, 30 December 1848.
60. LDXIII.16.
61. Tristram, Henry, 1933, p. 129.
62. LDXIII.335, F. W. Faber, 9 December 1949.
63. Ker, 1990, pp. 342-3.
64. Ffinch, 1992, p. 164.
65. Dessain, 1980, p. 94.
66. Norman, 1985, p. 317.
67. LDXXV.7, footnote, James Stewart, 6 January 1870.
68. LDXIII.8-9, 15 January 1849.
69. LDXIII.14, footnote.
70. LDXIII.13 February 1849.
71. LDXIII.29-30, 5 February 1849.
72. LDXIII.30, F. W. Faber, 7 February 1849.
73. LDXIII.34, F. W. Faber, 9 January 1849.
74. LDXIII.44, F. W. Faber, 13 February 1849.
75. LDXIII.57, Dessain, footnote.
76. LDXIII.54-7, F. W. Faber, 17 February 1849.
77. Murray, 1980, p. 118.
78. LDXIII.76, footnote.
79. LDXIII.76, footnote.
80. LDXIII.108, Mrs J. W. Bowden, 12 April 1849.
81. Murray, 1980, p. 455.

82. Trevor, 1996, p. 124.
83. LDXIII.124–5, Faber, footnote.
84. Norman, 1986, p. 234.
85. LDXIII.165–7, 31 May 1849.
86. Gilley, 1990, p. 260.
87. LDXIII.321, 2 December 1849.
88. LDXIII.388, Lord Shrewsbury, 10 December 1849; Bishop Ullathorne, 10 December 1849.
89. LDXIII.338, 10 December 1849.
90. LDXIII.338, 14 December 1849.
91. LDXIII.342.
92. Decree Book of the Birmingham Oratory, 13 January 1850; Murray, 1980, p. 456.
93. LDXIII.238, 23 July 1849.
94. Trevor, 1996, p. 130.
95. LDXIII.390, F. W. Faber, 18 January 1850.
96. LDXIII.402, 3 February 1850.
97. LDXIII.439, Dessain, footnote.
98. Ward, 1913, p. 231.
99. Chadwick, 1971, p. 289.
100. Ker, Ian, (2003), p. 24.
101. Newman, 1995, p. xl.
102. Ward, 1913, pp. 232–3.
103. LDXIII.470, F. W. Faber, 2 May 1850.
104. Newman, 1995, p. xi.
105. LDXXI.69, 3 March 1864.
106. LDXIV.87, 2 October 1850.
107. Dessain, 1980, p. 97.
108. LDXIII.453, F. W. Faber, 31 March 1850.
109. LDXX.308, D. Radford, 13 October 1862.
110. Newman, 1995, p. 251.
111. Newman, 1995, p. 261.
112. Newman, 1995, p. xix.
113. LDXIV.35, 11 August 1850.
114. LDXXVI.115, R.W. Church, 16 June 1872.
115. LDXIX.360, 10 June 1860.
116. Preface to *Lectures*, p. x.
117. Chadwick, 1971, p. 306.
118. *Present Position of Catholics*, p. 329.
119. LDXIV.99, 10 October 1850.
120. Dessain, 1980, pp. 100–01.
121. LDXIV.274, 274, Richard Stanton, 3 May 1851.
122. LDXXIX.230, footnote.
123. Tristram, 1952, p. 215.
124. LDXIV.213, J. M. Capes, 18 February 1851.
125. Ward, Wilfrid, 1908, p. 256.
126. Hutton, 1891, pp. 213–14.

127. LDXIV.213, J. M. Capes, 18 February 1851.
128. LDXIV.216--18, J. M. Capes, 21 February 1851.
129. LDXIV.236, J. M. Capes, 12 March 1851.
130. LDXIV.250-2, J. M. Capes, 10 April 1851.
131. LDXIV.4, Archbishop Cullen, 7 July 1850.
132. Newman, 1956, p. 280.
133. LDXIV.32, Bishop Ullathorne, 6 August 1850.
134. Norman, 1986, p. 313.
135. Ker, 1990, p. 360.
136. Newman, 1874, p. 137.
137. Gilley, 1996, pp. 265-6.
138. LDXIV.140, 24 November 1850.
139. LDXIV.13, Dessain, footnote.
140. LDXIV.17-21, 22 July 1850.
141. LDXIV.21, 27 July 1850.
142. Cf. LDXIV.22, Mrs J. W. Bowden, 29 July 1850.
143. LDXIV.305, Dessain, footnote.
144. LDXIV.76, F. W. Faber, 22 September 1850.
145. Murray, 1980, p. 457.
146. LDXIV.102, Dessain, footnote.
147. Trevor, 1996, p. 132.
148. LDXVII.xiii, Dessain, footnote.
149. Trevor, 1996, p. 157.
150. Newman, 1956, p. 329.
151. LDXVII.44-51, 9 November 1853.
152. LDXVII.100, 23 December 1855.
153. LDXVII.103, Cardinal Wiseman, 27 December 1855.
154. LDXV.xiv, Dessain.
155. LDXVII.103, Dessain, footnote.
156. LDXVII.128-30, Edward Caswall, 20 January 1856.
157. LDXVII.135-8, Edward Caswall, 25 January 1856.
158. Trevor, 1996, p. 160.
159. Murray, 1980, pp. 298-346; Newman's Oratory Papers 24 & 25.
160. Murray, 1980, p. 145.
161. LDXVII.255, Cardinal Wiseman, 7 June 1856.
162. LDXIX.100-01, Robert Monteith, 5 April 1859.
163. LDXVIII.49, 27 May 1857.
164. LDXIX.112, Miss Holmes, 19 April 1859.
165. LDXVII.266-70, 14 June 1856.
166. LDXVII.234, from Faber, 8 May 1856.
167. LDXIV.235-6, F.W. Faber 1856, 9 May 1856; LDXIV.239-40, from Faber, 10 May 1856.
168. LDXVII.241, F.W. Faber, 13 May 1856.
169. LDXVII.246-7, from F.W. Faber & Richard Stanton, 22 May 1856.
170. LDXVII.248-9, Richard Stanton, 27 May 1856.
171. LDXVII.250, 31 May 1856; LDXVII.252, 3 June 1856.
172. LDXVII.254, from F. W. Faber & Richard Stanton, 5 June 1856.

173. LDXVII.257. from Faber, 9 June 1856.
174. LDXVII.259, 10 June 1856.
175. Murray, 1980, p. 462.
176. Cf Gilley, 1990, p. 287.
177. LDXVII.135, Dessain, footnote.
178. Newman, 1956, p. 256.
179. LDXIX.427–8, 28 November 1866.
180. LDXX.494.
181. LDXX.530, Miss M. R. Giberne, St Michael's Day, 1863.
182. LDXXX.329, footnote, 18 March 1884.
183. LDXXX.329, 19 March 1884.
184. LDXXX.336, 23 March 1884.
185. LDXXX.337, 25 March 1884.
186. LDXXX.341, 3 April 1884.
187. LDXXX.341, 3 April 1884.
188. LDXXX.347, 25 April 1884.
189. LDXXX.347 footnote.

Chapter 5

'The Cultivation of the Mind'

The history of the university in Ireland up to the middle of the nineteenth century has the 'merit of simplicity'. Only one university existed – the University of Dublin with its sole college that of Trinity College (TCD).[1] This ancient institution, founded in 1591 during the closing years of Elizabeth I's reign had imposed religious tests on students and staff from 1637 – Charles I's reign – which excluded Roman Catholics and Protestant Dissenters from membership of the college. Only practising members of the Established Church, who had sworn to uphold its supremacy, and had also taken oaths against fundamental Roman Catholic beliefs such as Transubstantiation, were admitted. This discrimination was theoretically eased by the Catholic Relief Act of 1793, by which Catholics were to have right of entry to any college of the University of Dublin which might be founded thereafter. More practical benefit was given by a Royal Letter of 1794 which partially abolished religious tests at TCD, although Roman Catholics were barred from scholarships or fellowships. 'A mere handful of the vast Catholic majority in the country availed themselves of the partial concession.'[2] However, the general ethos of TCD was 'deemed to be inimical and hostile to the Catholic faith'.[3]

For two and a half centuries, the only university in Ireland had, therefore, been virtually closed to the majority of its inhabitants, although many, admittedly, would not have been academically acceptable and others would have lacked aspirations of this kind. But it was clearly a source of substantial irritation to more liberally-minded politicians and other leaders of society that Roman Catholics and Protestant Dissenters had, for generations, suffered from a lack of equality with those of a minority, although established, Church in matters of higher education.

Following a conciliatory policy and to counter O'Connell's political agitation, Sir Robert Peel, in the spring of 1845, increased the grant to Maynooth Seminary and proposed the establishment of a non-sectarian system of higher education in Ireland, based on the Queen's Colleges in Belfast, Cork and Galway for those Roman Catholics and Protestant Dissenters who were unable or unwilling to attend TCD, where some degree of religious intolerance was still apparent.

> No religious tests were to be imposed either at entrance of admission to degrees, no religious instruction was to be given except what might be provided by the various religious bodies at their own expense, no religious topics were to be introduced into the classrooms, and no religious considerations were to weigh in the appointment or dismissal of officials.[4]

The explicitly secular and non-denominational nature of Peel's university proposals immediately aroused suspicions and downright hostility from the Roman Catholic bishops as well as leading politicians. Sir Robert Inglis, for example, anathematized the system as 'a gigantic scheme of godless education' and the epithet 'Godless Colleges' was popularly applied to the Queen's Colleges where so-called 'mixed education' was to be introduced into Ireland on 31 July 1845. ('Mixed education' referred to the mingling of pupils of various faiths, which was unusual in Ireland at that time.)

In England, non-sectarian higher education had become available in 1835, when London University received its charter. This secular institution, although distasteful to some Roman Catholics, conferred benefits to some Catholic schools and colleges, such as Ushaw, Stonyhurst, Oscott and St Edmunds, who sought affiliation and modified their curricula to make them compatible with the new, non-residential, degree courses. Apart from a few Catholics who had attended Oxford and Cambridge universities in the early part of the nineteenth century, and a small number who had entered TCD from the eighteenth century onwards, degree-level education had not generally been available to Roman Catholics.[5] Although the University Tests Act of 1871 opened up Oxford, Cambridge and Durham universities generally to men of any or no religion, Roman Catholic bishops, as a body, refused to permit Catholics to attend, although the prohibition tended to be disregarded by many upper-class Catholics. Catholic bishops – apart from the converts Manning, Coffin and Brownlow, who were Oxbridge graduates – had no direct experience of the ancient universities and so they 'feared what they imagined'. This lack of knowledge was even more pronounced at Propaganda in Rome.[6]

In Ireland the Roman Catholic hierarchy were not of one mind on the radical innovation on 'mixed education'. While some bishops vehemently opposed the concept of the Queen's Colleges, which were opened in 1849 at Belfast, Cork and Galway, a minority led by Archbishop Daniel Murray of Dublin and also the Primate, Dr Crolly, were prepared to give their support and see how the novel system worked out. At least it provided access for Roman Catholics to university education. But the majority, headed by the adamantine Dr MacHale of Tuam, rejected it outright and urged the Pope 'to take action against the Colleges'.[7] A papal rescript in October 1847 instructed the bishops to take no part in the colleges. Although this decision was not regarded as final, a second Rescript, in October 1848, confirmed the ban on co-operation. It is of particular interest to note that in this document 'occurred the first reference to the project of founding a Catholic University in Ireland'.[8] The papal pronouncements did not, however, inhibit the Government from going ahead with the Queen's Colleges scheme.

In April 1849 Dr Crolly died and, after rejecting three names submitted by the Irish hierarchy, Rome appointed as his successor, Dr Paul Cullen, rector of the Irish College in Rome. As young ecclesiastical students in Rome, Cullen and Wiseman had met and, some years later, were to be given the responsibility of leading the hierarchy and imposing Ultramontane disciplines respectively in Ireland and England. Cullen was influential in Rome, where he had lived since the age of seventeen years. Newman records that he first knew him in Rome in 1847 'when he was very civil to me, and took the trouble of being the official theological censor of my four Latin dissertations then and there published'.[9] Over the next few years, Newman was to become more deeply involved with this subtle prelate. Cullen was consecrated Archbishop of Armagh in February 1850, and came to Ireland with the added authority of Apostolic Delegate. One of his first tasks was to convoke and preside over the Synod of Thurles – the first national synod in Ireland since 1642. At it the bishops, following the papal rescripts, duly condemned the Queen's Colleges. A minority of them petitioned Rome for further discussion of the matter, but Pius IX replied firmly that the question had been settled. Cullen issued a pastoral letter on 9 September 1850; this was adopted by all the hierarchy. Cullen had thus stamped his authoritative leadership on the Irish Church very soon after setting up a Catholic University Committee of four archbishops and four bishops, to consider how the recommendations of the second papal rescript, mentioned earlier, should be made effective.

There was, as Owen Chadwick comments, 'no theoretical absurdity in attempting to create a Roman Catholic university'. Such universities existed in Catholic countries, as at Louvain in Belgium, and they could also exist elsewhere where there was a religious toleration. Admittedly, for such institutions to become 'reputable rivals of the ancient universities' adequate funding was vital.[10] But, as will be seen later, the concept of a Catholic university in Ireland, based on the Louvain model, was to be fraught with difficulties at almost every stage of its short life.

Meanwhile, Peel's ambitious – and well-meaning – scheme to open up opportunities of higher education for those who felt that TCD was an inhospitable environment, was severely affected by the decisions of the Holy See and of the Irish hierarchy. Further, the lack of an adequate secondary education system in Ireland meant that comparatively few pupils were able to attain university entry standards. These two factors resulted in a bleak existence for the Queen's Colleges during their first decade.[11] According to Wilfrid Ward, the new 'secularist education' was viewed suspiciously by the Irish hierarchy because of its results in England, as well as the fact that 'in countries like France and Belgium the undenominational universities were avowedly free thinking'. He adds that their fears were shared by 'some of the ablest and most religious men in the Church of England'.[12]

Newman advised his friend William Monsell, a rising politician who was seeking a compromise over the Queen's Colleges, that he had reflected on the problem of 'mixed education' but felt that the Pope had 'resolved on the Catholic University in Ireland . . . in opposition to certain Government Colleges'. He also considered that 'where professors and where students, are of distinct religions . . . there will be no *genius loci*, or at least not healthy *genius*'. Moreover, there was the problem of recruiting sufficient numbers of well-qualified academic staff for all four establishments. He also regarded it as 'disrespectful to the Holy See, for the State to ask it to *recognise* the State Colleges, while the State steadily persists in *ignoring* the Holy See's University'.[13]

To achieve the foundation of a Catholic university in Ireland, Cullen recognized that it was imperative to have someone of acknowledged intellectual eminence to head it, and for some time he had his eye of Newman. On 15 April 1851 he wrote to Newman telling him that the collection of funds for establishing a Catholic university had been very successful and that the next step would be to 'select a fit and proper superior'. Newman's advice was sought about this appointment and also those of a vice-president and professors. Cullen invited him to attend a meeting of the University Committee in Dublin. Further, if Newman could give 'a few lectures on education', he would be rendering good service to religion in Ireland.[14]

Newman responded that 'there is nothing at all which I can feel more interest in than the subject of Irish education' – but he excused himself from accepting Cullen's invitation to visit Dublin. He referred to 'one difficulty' in staffing the proposed University: 'that leading men must necessarily be priests . . . and England . . . has one to spare'. He suggested, however, that chairs in classics, history and maths need not be reserved to clerics.[15] About two weeks later he sent Cullen a list of 'persons who at present strike me as fit candidates for Professorships in the New University'.[16] Among the candidates was T. W. Allies to whom he wrote enthusiastically about the prospects of the new University, 'It will be the Catholic University of the English tongue for the whole world.'[17] Here Newman was echoing the papal rescript of October 1848, which urged the establishment of a Catholic university for students from the old and new worlds where English was spoken as a mother tongue. This message was also reflected in the appeal in 1851 by the University Committee to the clergy and laity of England, when it was declared that the new university was destined to benefit not merely the Catholics of Ireland but those of the empire as well.

On 8 July 1851, Newman entered in his diary that 'Dr Cullen came, and slept' (at the Birmingham Oratory).[18] No doubt they then discussed the projected new University. On his return from a London meeting, Newman records that Cullen, on 18 July, called again and that during conversation he proposed that he, Newman, should be President (rector) of the planned university. Newman responded that he felt 'it would be sufficient if I was Prefect of Studies', in view of his Oratorian duties.[19] Newman pursued this point in a later letter to Cullen but had to admit that 'Our Fathers here feel reluctant that I should be anything but rector'. He desired to do as much as possible for the university but with 'as little absence as possible' from the Oratory. 'This problem being satisfied, I do not care what you are pleased to make me'.[20] (The problem of having responsibilities in two locations and divided loyalties was never resolved; it was to prove the root cause of Newman's eventual severing of his connections with the Catholic University of Ireland.)

Dr Cullen generously, and no doubt diplomatically, sent Newman a donation to the Birmingham Oratory on 22 July 1851.[21] At a meeting of the University Committee on 12 August 1851, Newman was nominated rector of the Catholic university and he, together with Dr Leahy and Myles W. O'Reilly, were requested to draw up a scheme for the organization of the university.[22] Nevertheless, Newman noted that 'However, I did not at once pledge myself, either to be rector or Prefect of Studies; but became one of a subcommittee of three ... charged with the duty of reporting on the best mode of commencing, on the course of studies, etc., etc.'[23]

Newman reported to Cullen that although the subcommittee had sent letters of inquiry about university education to members of the consulting committee, no replies had been received. Regarding the archbishop's proposal for Newman to give a series of lectures, Newman 'most readily' acceded to it but felt that he 'ought to know... the state of public opinion and knowledge in Ireland on the subject of education', and also Cullen's own ideas on what the lectures should be about.[24] The Archbishop's reply reflected his distinctly narrow concept of education: 'What we want in Ireland is to persuade the people that education should be religious. The whole tendency of our new systems is to make it believed that education may be so conducted as to have nothing at all to do with religion'. He added a list of perceived, feasible topics.[25] Shortly before Newman delivered his first lectures in Dublin (which we will look at later) he wrote to one of his old friends: 'My subjects, I suppose, will be advertised next week, and will seem dry – but (in confidence) they were suggested by high authority...'[26] As Culler comments,

> Dr Cullen was the 'high authority', and if Newman's first few lectures do seem dry to some persons, once can only consider what they would have been if he had followed more closely the suggestions in this [Dr Cullen's] letter. Doubtless he foresaw the difficulty and so replied, rather vaguely, 'Thank you for the subjects you mention for Lectures: They are most important ones but will take a long time thinking out.'[27]

Newman sought advice from three old friends, English converts to Catholicism now living in Dublin: Frederick Lucas, Robert Ornsby and Henry Wilberforce. From discussions with them he built up 'a picture of Irish society, whether it was accurate or not, from which he worked in planning the rhetoric of his opening lectures'.[28] He gathered some diverting impressions; for instance, that nothing was more mixed about 'mixed education' than the question itself; that Dr Cullen was for an education that was religious before all; Dr MacHale for an education which was Irish before all; and Dr Murray for an education which could only be provided by a government that was neither Irish nor religious, while at the same time the bishops were alienated from more influential members of the laity.[29]

It dawned on Newman that he was being led by Cullen into highly dangerous territory, both in terms of nationalism and controversial points of view. 'The Irish were having a quarrel over education, and he, as a distinguished Englishman, was being called in to settle it.'[30] He sensed the delicate situation in which he was being placed and was decidedly unwilling to be treated like a puppet of the Irish prelate. 'If Dr Cullen had dirty work to do, he ought to do it himself or get an Irishman to do it; and, therefore, as the Archbishop continued to write to him reminding him of the lectures, Newman began to prepare himself for not finding them exactly what he had hoped.'[31] Newman's approach was, therefore, influenced by, but did not blindly follow, Cullen's expectations, as indicated in his letter to Ornsby quoted earlier. Cullen was not entirely satisfied but his criticism was constrained, and he reminded Newman that he should emphasize the need to unite religion with education, especially among those who had been 'educated in Trinity College and other Protestant establishments'.[32]

After a short visit to Ireland to discuss with his associates the development of plans for the new University, Newman wrote a long letter to Cullen in which he stated: 'It strikes me that the only right way of beginning the University is that which your Grace proposes, experimentally – the rector (with a constant subordination of course to a board – say the Archbishops) should be autocrat.'[33] To Mrs William Froude he confided:

> I suppose in a few days I shall know what is decided on in Ireland about the University. It is a most daring attempt but first it is a religious one, next it has the Pope's blessing on it, not in its members only but in its principles, methods, ways and arguments.[34]

McGrath states that it is undeniable that Newman embodied in the Catholic University of Ireland 'certain features of the great university to which he owed so much', notably college residence and the tutorial system. He was also inspired by the medieval model in which 'the lower faculty of arts led on to the higher faculties of theology, law and medicine, and so covered the whole field of human knowledge'. This model had, in fact, been adopted by the Catholic University of Louvain which, as noted already, had been projected as an appropriate prototype for the new Catholic University of Ireland.[35]

On 12 November 1851, Newman recorded that the University Committee passed a resolution that, subject to his acceptance, he should 'be named the first President of the Catholic University of Ireland'.[36] Newman's appointment was generally welcomed, although Dr Murray, Archbishop of Dublin, who had shown a liberal attitude towards the concept of the Queen's Colleges 'was still unenthusiastic, but his opposition was to the University rather than to its rector'.[37] This potential problem dissolved with the death of Dr Murray on 24 February 1852, and Dr Cullen's translation to Dublin meant that prospects for the new university had greatly improved.

Over the preceding few months, Newman had become aware of the threat of a libel action by the notorious ex-friar Achilli, and he duly advised the Archbishop of this impending case, which arose from the fifth lecture in the series, *Lectures on the Present Position of Catholics in England*, given in Birmingham in July 1851 (see Chapter 4). In this lecture, Newman had repeated some of the charges against the former Dominican friar which Wiseman had made in an article in the *Dublin Review*. Cullen reassured Newman – who had dedicated the published volume of the lectures to him – and advised him to contact Wiseman 'who had all the police reports on this unsavoury character'. He graciously accepted the dedication of the published collection and promised Newman assistance in his legal costs[38] (see Chapter 6 below for an extended discussion of this subject).

Newman had been busily preparing the lectures which Cullen had invited him to give in Dublin. They were not written without causing him 'infinite difficulty'.[39] He told Robert Ornsby,

> My lectures have taken me more trouble than anyone could by a stretch of the fancy conceive. I have written almost reams of paper, – finished, set aside – then taken them up again, and plucked them – and so on. The truth is, I have the utmost difficulty of writing to people I do not know, and I have commonly failed when I have addressed strangers.[40]

On Friday 7 May 1852, Newman travelled overnight to Dublin and delivered the first University lecture, or 'discourse', in the Exhibition Room of the Rotunda the following Monday. This venue was the scene of all the fashionable gatherings, musical entertainments and public meetings of Dublin in the eighteenth and nineteenth centuries.[41]
   The following day Newman wrote to Ambrose St John:

> The lecture . . . has been a hit; and now I am beginning to be anxious lest the others should not follow up the blow. The room 'being very small – holding about 400 – was nearly full . . . all the intellect, almost, of Dublin was there'.[42]

Newman's anxieties seem, however, to have been groundless, for he was to write to H. E Manning (who was to succeed Wiseman as Cardinal Archbishop of Westminster) at the close of the lectures,

> I have prospered here in my lectures beyond my most sanguine expectations, or rather beyond my most anxious efforts and pains – for I have had anxiety and work beyond belief in writing them, expectations none.[43]

But in his 'Memorandum on the Catholic University', dated 25 November 1870, Newman referred, rather dismissively, to his Dublin lectures – attended by Cullen – as a 'flash in the plan' – and the only public recognition given to him since he had been appointed rector.[44] However, Culler emphasizes that Newman's reference to the lectures should be read in context: he did not mean that the lectures were a failure, but that 'their effect, though brilliant at the time, was not lasting'.[45] In this, it might be said, that they shared the fate of oratorical deliveries although, of course, they were, as published later, to achieve lasting fame and influence. Newman, in fact, arranged for his lectures to be published in Dublin by the official publisher to Archbishop Cullen. Newman continued the series of lectures on the four Monday afternoons following his opening success on 10 May. These five discourses, completed on 7 June, were the only ones which Newman actually delivered. Exactly why he decided to deal with the remainder as 'closet lectures' is undetermined; perhaps pressure of work, disinclination, or because summer would be an inappropriate time for the lectures.[46] Whatever the explanation, he was clearly stressed by producing these remarkable discourses, a task which, on returning to the Birmingham Oratory in early June, had stretched through to almost the end of 1852, and had exhausted him. 'The

Discourses, now – thank God – all but finished', had been 'the most painful of all' his written works.[47] As Dessain puts it, the discourses, with 'certain alterations and omissions of ephemeral matter, now form the first part on *The Idea of a University*. All his Oxford life Newman had fought for the place of religion in education, so that in a certain sense he had a congenial theme'.[48]

There are two separate, and skilfully blended, themes in *The Idea of a University*:

1. the need to include religious teaching in any scheme of studies; and
2. the fact that 'the cultivation of the mind, rather than immediate preparation for professional occupations, is the primary end of a university.

The first theme was the focus of attention at the time Newman delivered his discourses; the second them, as McGrath points out, 'receives almost exclusive attention from writers on education today'.[49]

In the preface to *The Idea of a University*, dated 21 November 1852, Newman stated that the view taken in the discourses is that a university is a place of *teaching* universal knowledge; its object is, on the one hand, intellectual, not moral, and, on the other, it is concerned with the diffusions and extension of knowledge rather than with its advancement. While a university of such a type is essentially free and independent of the Church, it cannot fulfil its role and responsibilities – as discussed in the *Idea* – without assistance from the Church: in theological terms, the Church is necessary for its integrity. 'Such are the main principles the Discourses will follow.'[50] Newman profoundly believed that religion should have recognized place in a university, and that without this it could not rightfully claim this academic eminence. He also thought that religious teaching in a university should be controlled by the Church, as had been the practice for generations at Oxford and Cambridge. At Dublin, he argued, the Catholic Church should fulfil this function. But this did not mean that some form of censorship or repression of knowledge should be exercised in the name of religion; he always insisted that university was not a convent or a seminary – it was a place to fit a man for the world.[51]

In 'broad outline' the Discourses are as follows: 'In the first four and in part of the fifth, all knowledge is declared to be one, each division of which can only be studied adequately in relation to others.' Hence the omission of theology from any curriculum 'falsifies the

content of the other subjects contained in it'. The fifth to eight
Discourses enquire closely into the nature of knowledge which university studies are aimed to give. Pursuit of such knowledge may be for
intellectual cultivation or for 'some immediate utilitarian purpose'.
The former – culture of the mind – is 'a good in itself and is the
primary end of university education'. Subjects of study may be
broadly divided according to their relative powers of cultivating the
mind, so a university concerns itself primarily with those subjects
which tend to contribute most to intellectual culture. At the same time
– and secondarily – it provides for professional studies both directly
and mental cultivation – which is the best preparation for them. The
last two Discourses discuss in general terms the relationships between
mental culture and religion.[52]

Newman attempted to reconcile three factors in higher education in
his lectures:

1. the autonomy required by the intellect so that it can develop freely,
   without 'arbitrary and external constraint;
2. the rights and functions of theology 'within the economy' of a university; and
3. how far the Church has a right to exercise a pastoral authority within
   the university.

His approach is that the branches of knowledge form one whole (the
principle of unity is discussed more fully later), but he also invokes
the principle of limitation – which he calls *abstraction*, in the sense
that the mind cannot grasp an entire set of knowledge at once but, in
a kind of sequential progression, *abstracts* parts and eventually
achieves a state of more comprehensive knowledge. The limits within
each of the three factors specified by him may legitimately be exercised, and need to be defined, so that equilibrium of functions is
achieved which enables students to pursue their higher education.
Further, this desirable equilibrium should be applicable to the university itself.[53]

Newman stressed the qualities of liberal education which 'makes not
the Christian, not the Catholic, but the gentleman. It is well to be a
gentleman; it is well to have a cultivated intellect, a delicate taste, a
candid, equitable dispassionate mind, a noble and courteous bearing in
the conduct of life:- these are the connatural qualities of a large
knowledge; they are the objects of a University'.[54] In another passage
– from which the title of this chapter is taken – Newman says that

'Liberal education viewed in itself, is simply the cultivation of the intellect, as such, and its object is nothing more or less than intellectual excellence'.[55]

Newman's preoccupation with the relationship between liberal education and the fostering of gentlemanly qualities has prompted a modern biographer and critic to comment that he wanted the new university to be for gentlemen, and that in *Discourse VIII: Knowledge viewed in relation to religion*, 'he came very near to saying that gentlemanliness was next to godliness'.[56] This observation has the hallmarks of a politician's *bon mot*: it is a diverting but not necessarily reliable opinion.

Vargish points out that in his spirited response, some years earlier, to Peel's Tamworth Reading Room speech, Newman showed his deep concern for the moral principles which should underlie the education of the masses, who could not afford to buy books for private study, whereas in the Dublin *Discourses* he focused specifically on 'the education of gentlemen'. He excluded from his theory of university education the teaching of 'practical secular knowledge, or utilitarian training', and concentrated on the intellectual ideals which should animate the education of professional men, who were badly needed at that time in Ireland. As noted already, Roman Catholics had largely been excluded from higher education in Ireland, and so the professions were closed to them. However, Newman's preoccupation with this level of intellectual development attracted sharp criticism on the grounds that he wanted an education exclusively to produce gentlemen but for which 'money was collected from the peasants in order to pay for it'. In defence, however, it has been said that Newman was asked to help found a university, not a technical college to train skilled workers who could alleviate the distressing poverty of Ireland. It should be remembered that the bitter toll of the famine years of the 1840s was still evident, particularly in the west of Ireland.[57] The charge of educational elitism against Newman seems, therefore, hardly fair in the circumstances. Certainly, he was dedicated to scholarship and to the pursuit of academic excellence, but he had also experienced at first hand the pressing need for educational opportunities for the poor. In the first Birmingham Oratory in the slum district of Alcester Street, Newman had of course organized an evening school for the children of the needy families. Also, in his Anglican years at Littlemore he had organized an elementary school for the children of the village and he had visited regularly. Newman had a fine intellect and was a renowned scholar, but he also took a very practical role in the provision of education for children, particularly for those who otherwise would be likely to lack it. As his activities in Birmingham and Littlemore show, Newman viewed education as an intrinsic and inseparable part of pastoral care. Although his educational efforts in Dublin were primarily committed to the foundation of the Catholic University, he also organized evening classes open to the general public.

Tristram has described how, in the early part of 1858, certain professors of the CUI delivered courses of evening lectures to young Dublin men who 'were engaged in businesses during the day'. The number of enrolled part-time students 'soon rose to 179. They were allowed to matriculate and present themselves for the Scholar's Degree'.[58]

The projected university was not intended by the Holy See to be purely an Irish institution – although subsequent events suggest that the Irish hierarchy failed to appreciate this in their dealings with Newman. As Culler puts it, 'Properly considered, the university was not the Catholic University of Ireland but the Catholic University in Ireland, although Ireland, Newman believed, was the proper soil to produce it and Dublin was its natural seat.'[59] Some years after the founding of the CUI, Newman wrote that he had responded to Cullen's invitation because the Holy See had 'decided that Dublin was to be the place for Catholic education of the upper classes in these Islands'.[60]

It is interesting also to note that McGrath – who is widely accepted as an authoritative source of information on Newman's Dublin activities – has suggested that

> The concept of the University as one for English-speaking Catholics originated in the mind of Cullen, and was not improbably suggested to him by his conviction that Newman was the only man existing who could make the scheme a success.[61]

It was, in fact, the concept definitely put forward in all the public documents issued by the University Committee. The papal documents of 1852 and 1854 could at least be reconciled with it, and a good case could be made that they formally enunciated it. Since Cullen was influential in Rome, he doubtless persuaded Propaganda in this direction when the Rescript was being drafted.

Newman confessed that before becoming involved with the concept of a Catholic University, he knew little of Ireland:

> I was a poor innocent as regards the actual state of things in Ireland when I went there, and did not care to think about, for I relied on the word of the Pope, but from the event I am led to think it is not rash to say that I knew as much about Ireland as he did.[62]

While he was to become aware of the volatile nature of Irish nationalism, he avoided association with any political activists. He wrote, for example, to Bishop Grant,

> What is Ireland to me, except the University here is a University for England, as well as for Ireland? I wish to do good, of course, to all Catholics if I can, but to *English* Catholics, as is my duty, I have left England for a while, for what I conceive to be a great *English* interest.[63]

It seems, therefore, that Newman saw his educational 'mission' as a supra-national one in essence: Dublin was the arena – temporary as it turned out – for his involvement in higher education, but the philosophical base on which he built the Catholic University of Ireland was in no way restricted to that particular foundation. The Dublin *Discourses* were not parochial in content or chauvinistic in their orientation. From them came *The Idea of a University* which, according to McGrath, is 'considered by many to be Newman's greatest [work], is almost universally acknowledged as an English classic, and is remarkable that it is the only standard treatise on university education in that tongue. The ideas which it formulates had been germinating in Newman's mind during his thirty years at Oxford, but their final form was determined by events connected with ... Dublin [Catholic] University'.[64] In Chadwick's opinion, Newman's 'noble book' has remained the historic statement of an 'ideal of higher education which influenced Britain and through Britain the educational systems of many other countries'.[65]

The universality of Newman's treatise has influenced – and continues to influence – educationalists the world over. Unlike the Catholic University itself, his educational philosophies have survived and guided those who seek inspiration in developing their own educational efforts. In Nicholas Lash's opinion, Newman's *Discourses* 'still speak freshly to our so different situation [and] this is in no small measure due to the way in which, again and again, the values and assumptions

of the standard accounts of the nature and purposes of liberal education are bounded, corrected, checked, set in tension with the require-
ments of a very different vision'.[66] Newman himself observed to one
of his friends: 'My two most perfect works, artistically, are my two
last – the former of them [*The Present Position of Catholics in
England*] put me to less trouble then any I ever wrote – the latter
[*Discourses on University Education*] to the greatest of all.'[67]

Vargish has stated that Newman's mind, like Bacon's, was impelled
towards the concept of wholeness or the idea of unity, and that when
he used the word *idea* in *The Idea of a University* he wished it 'to
denote a vast often apparently heterogeneous complex'. Liberal education would provide the student with a key to unlock the treasure chest
of knowledge contained in the various sciences, so that his mind
'begins to reflect the unity of creation. He gains some insight into the
architecture of the universe, social and spiritual as well as physical'.[68]
Newman promoted the prime importance of the 'enlargement of the
mind' which would be the fruit of a liberal system of higher education, such as he advocated in the Dublin *Discourses*, and which he
believed to be vitally necessary for the development of an educated
laity. Each specialized branch of knowledge – the circle of sciences –
in his theory of higher education, 'provide an approach to the ultimate
unity of existence, enabling the mind to perceive truth in the only way
it can, through various aspects of the whole'.[69]

In the preface to *The Idea of a University*, Newman dismissed any
notion that his treatise was concerned with 'the true mode of educat-
ing' rather, the *Discourses* were 'directed simply to the consideration
of the *aims and principles* of Education'.[70] Culler takes up this point
when he declares that *The Idea of a University* deliberately omits any
consideration of means and concentrates exclusively upon ends and
that from this viewpoint it 'is not an educational work at all'. But his
qualified opinion is somewhat diluted when it is acknowledged that –
as Newman's own words have shown – the purpose of his work was
'concerned with constructing an intellectual and cultural ideal'.[71]
Essentially, Newman had no ambitions to write a manual of teaching
practice. Instead, he sought to show what should be at the hear of
higher education – a philosophical concept of learning that had roots
in Aquinas and Aristotle and which, in McGrath's judgement, he
presented with eloquence and erudition.[72] His occasional forays into
flamboyant rhetoric have sometimes attracted critical comment; but he
was writing at a time when such phraseology was more acceptable

than today, and was to be found in literature, political speeches, sermons and the like. Newman wrote with fervour – even vehemence – as well as with scholarly zeal, and the language he used reflected his own intellectual dedication.

After delivering these historic *Discourses* in Dublin – which attracted partisan criticism as well as general acclaim – Newman returned to the Oratory in Birmingham where he completed his writings on theories of higher education, and waited anxiously for Cullen to indicate what further progress had been made by the University Committee. Newman was not a member of this exclusively prelatic group which Cullen, as Apostolic Delegate as well as Archbishop of Dublin, increasingly dominated.

In his memorandum, Newman deliberated: 'universities are not brought into existence every day'; they tend to grow organically and without deliberate origination, whereas in Dublin 'private men' seek to 'dispense with time and circumstance, and to create in a day' and, apparently, without regard to the many problems and complications surrounding such a decision.[73] Newman listed the many, and mostly fruitless, negotiations about professorial appointments that had occurred and about suitable sites for the University. He says that this correspondence with Dr Cullen is 'illustrative of the fog through which I had to find my way ... [and] of the bearing which Dr Cullen, while really wishing to keep me, had thought most suitable to adopt in his dealings with me'. Newman did not know 'whom to trust and whom to choose'. As noted earlier, he had 'no seat on the University Committee which was composed of men of whom I knew nothing ... I was no party myself, and did not wish to be advised by party men, nor did I consider ecclesiastics were the best advisers in a great lay undertaking'.[74] In Newman's view, the purpose of the university was to provide the Catholic laity with an opportunity for higher education, so he sought the support of prominent laymen, as well as bishops and clergy, and encouraged them to become 'associates' of the university. In time, he hoped that such close links would lead to laymen being able to assume specific responsibilities in the development and administration of the institution. This new approach was, however, not acceptable to the hierarchy, and the university was to suffer from the lack of a strongly committed body of laymen who could have contributed significantly to its formation and development. Clearly, Cullen did not share Newman's views; he regarded clerical control of such a novel educational venture to be unquestionable. The Catholic

University had been ordered to be established by the Pope; it was not a lay initiative.

While Cullen had listened to Newman's *Discourses*, he did not fully share some of the philosophical aspects of higher education which had been presented. Like Wiseman, he was an Ultramontanist, steeped in Roman conventions – these often appeared to include deferment of decisions for unconscionable periods of time. Newman confided in his fellow Oratorian and close friend Ambrose St John,

> Why Dr Cullen should make such a mystery of his plans, and not talk with me like a friend, I cannot make out. I suppose he wishes to throw all responsibility on me, not to commit himself, and make me ask every point as it comes, as a favour from him.[75]

He thus found himself in 'a quagmire of Irish civil and ecclesiastical politics' from which he endeavoured to emerge and survive to pursue the development of the CUI. How well he actually understood the complexities of the situation is, however, open to some doubt.[76] After a protracted delay, Newman received a letter, dated 21 October 1853, from Dr James Taylor, secretary of the University Committee, summoning him to Dublin as soon as possible. Newman welcomed this news but, adding that he could not come until January, stated that 'I have no scruples in this delay, since for many months I have sacrificed all engagements to the prospect of being called over'.[77] He then discovered that only two prelates had been present at the University Committee meeting and that Dr Cullen was absent in Rome. Feeling dissatisfied, he wrote to Cullen in December: 'Should I not be publicly admitted or recognised as rector of the University, as soon as possible now?'[78] Through Dr Taylor he received a reply that 'nothing public could be done at present: that the Bishops were to be gained over first'.[79] This rebuff was followed by a letter postponing any immediate action, which led Newman to ask Hope-Scott for his advice on whether he should resign forthwith.[80] He was advised not to do so. It was not until 4 January 1854 that Cullen wrote, in rather oblique terms, and from this letter Newman deduced that he could now expect to receive some formal recognition of his role in Dublin.[81]

Two days earlier, Newman had written to Wiseman about the problems he was experiences in dealing with the Irish hierarchy. He conceded that 'Dr Cullen from first to last has given me the *most generous* support but he cannot do every thing he wishes at his mere will.'[82] This letter was translated and shown to the Pope by Wiseman during a private audience and acting in his role as a cardinal, who is 'bound to assist the Holy See ... on any matters proposed ... by it, without reference to country'.[83] At a private audience, the Holy Father agreed at once to a proposal that Newman should be created a Bishop *in partibus*. This would give 'the right to sit with the Bishops in all consultations'.[84] To Newman this news was stimulating: 'I really did think the Cardinal had hit the right nail on the head, and effected what would be a real remedy against the difficulties which lay in my way.'[85] Wiseman had told Newman to treat the news of his impending bishopric discreetly but Ullathorne, Newman's bishop at Birmingham, had got to hear the news and announced it at a public banquet. It soon became public knowledge and congratulations and gifts began to pour in. Newman now felt free to advise his friends of the papal decision.[86]

As the weeks went by and the honour failed to be confirmed, Newman suspected that something or someone had blocked his advancement. Exactly what had caused it was not readily discernible. Various speculations were rife, among which were the following: there was a certain degree of confusion about the Pope's actual intentions; Dr MacHale and other Irish bishops had placed some pressure on Cullen to oppose the proposed promotion; there were suspicions that the English hierarchy were seeking control of the new university, and so on.

Perhaps, as McGrath suggests, it is possible, as so often occurs in human events, that no one cause was the determining one.[87] Certainly, Cullen wrote to Rome on two occasions (23 January 1854 and 2 February 1854) urging that it would be better to defer for a while making Newman a bishop: 'It is better not to begin with too much fuss ... In Belgium the Rector Magnificus is not a bishop.' He even went so far as to suggest that jealousy would be aroused if the English Cardinal Wiseman were known to have intervened in the matter.[88] In his private journal Newman wrote resignedly,

> The Cardinal never wrote to me a single word, or sent any sort of message to me, in explanation of the change of intention about me, till the day of his death... Nor did Dr Cullen, nor Dr Grant, nor Dr Ullathorne, nor any one else, ever again say one single word on the subject; nor did they make any chance remark by which I have been able to form any idea why that elevation which was thought by Pope, Cardinal, and Archbishop so expedient for the University, or at least so settled a point, which was so publicly announced, was suddenly and silently reversed.[89]

In early 1854 Newman started a series of visits to the Irish bishops
and priests to seek support for the new university. He wrote that 'I am
received everywhere ... with the greatest cordiality and affection.'[90]
Among those on whom he called was Dr Charles Russell of Maynooth
who, some years earlier, had influenced his conversion to Catholicism
and who was not sanguine about prospects for the new university.[91]
His views were shared by others; some suspected that the new university was part of a sinister Anglicization, a perception which may have
been fostered by forceful clerics such as the Archbishop of Tuam.
According to McGrath, Dr MacHale's support for the university
became 'more and more grudging and his attitude towards Newman
more and more discourteous, whilst Dr Cullen, seeing the differences
growing greater as the University took shape, kept exasperating
Newman by his policy of silent procrastination'.[92] Between the two
prelates antipathy became so strong that the work of the University
Committee was virtually halted; eventually, Dr MacHale withdrew
from taking any active part in the proceedings.

    Newman also discovered that the prospect of a new university failed
to stir those who had suffered, and were still suffering, from the
effects of the devastating famine years. Looking back on his activities
at this time Newman later wrote,

> From what he had gathered about clerical and lay opinions of the prospec-
> tive University the Pope had been poorly served by his counsellors and he
> might well have taken a different approach to the Queen's Colleges or at
> least not decreed that a Catholic University should be set up in Ireland.[93]

However, the papal brief establishing the Catholic University of
Ireland was issued on 20 March 1854. This was the fourth formal act
on this topic taken by the Holy See. It is noted that two years had
elapsed since the previous brief yet so far the bishops had taken no
steps to advance the foundation of the university. They were thus
ordered to hold a synod, under the presidency of Dr Cullen, with a
view of opening the new institution without delay.[94] The Brief also
confirmed Newman as rector of the university 'in the most flattering
terms'.[95] Newman then wrote to Cullen offering to 'come to Dublin as
soon as convenient after Easter'.[96]

    The Synod opened in Dublin on 18 May, the statutes of the univer-
sity were approved and Newman was formally appointed as rector,
with Dr Leahy as sub-rector. Just before the meeting Newman had
asked Cullen to consider putting before the Synod a proposal that he

should be given the rank of vicar general, as he believed this was the custom at Louvain, as this would be helpful in the 'most arduous' task of developing the new University and assisting in his negotiations with the bishops.[97] Nothing resulted from Newman's request[98] and, like the rumours of a bishopric, the matter was never again raised by Newman. He achieved, however, some satisfaction from the Synod's endorsement of the *Memorandum* that he had submitted and which was to be the academic blueprint of the University. There were to be five faculties: theology, law, medicine, philosophy and letters, and science.[99]

Over the next few months Newman was busily engaged in the university building in Harcourt Street, Dublin, recruiting academic staff and students. He stressed that the reputation of the professors would be of paramount importance in the successful development of the Catholic University of Ireland, and he told Cullen that, if possible, he would prefer the majority of the professors to be Irishmen, provided they were up to his expectations.[100] Cullen, however, insisted on personally approving any such appointments and submitted Newman's list of candidates to the University Committee. This resulted in friction with the Archbishop of Tuam, Dr MacHale, who stated that 'with few exceptions' he was unable 'to express approval or disapprobation', and that he intended to raise the matter at the next meeting of the University Committee.[101] As McGrath points out, 'This letter was another unfortunate manifestation . . . of the obstructive attitude Dr MacHale was to maintain all through.' It seemed that the Archbishop could only give 'grudging' support because the university was so closely identified by him with Cullen.[102] Newman replied vigorously yet with traditional courtesy, that while the bishops had the power of veto over professional appointments, unless they exercised their powers with discretion, the commencement of the university would be at risk.[103] Newman sent copies of the correspondence to Cullen in Rome, and he proceeded to publish the list of professors and lecturers in the *University Gazette* of 19 October. 'The Lion of the West' – a popular soubriquet of the Archbishop of Tuam – had 'roared at me, and I have roared again', Newman commented to Ambrose St John.[104] The unfortunate tendency of Dr MacHale to frustrate matters related to the university then became apparent in Rome when he attempted to prevent confirmation of the university regulations. The Pope ignored his protests and ordered that the regulations should be approved for an initial period of five or six years. Cullen

told Newman that MacHale had declared that 'he would have nothing
to do with the University – so much the better – but I fear that he will
excite a storm against it'.[105]

In between his new duties as rector, Newman made several visits to
England to fulfil his responsibilities at the Birmingham Oratory. On
returning to Dublin, he was – at long last – formally installed as rector
on Whit Sunday, 4 June 1854, as he informed several of his close friends
and acquaintances.[106] One of Newman's 'sidelines' was the publication
of a University Gazette. This appeared weekly and contained official
university information and also papers by Newman on aspects of
academic life. It survived, as a monthly, until the end of 1856. Another
of Newman's ventures – mentioned earlier – was the introduction of
evening classes for young Dublin men who were working full-time.
'The Catholic University was a pioneer in University Extension
Lectures, which were not begun in England until 1873.'[107]

On 3 November 1854, the Catholic University of Ireland formally
opened its doors: Newman wrote to Henry Wilberforce that, 'We
number more than sixty – but not in residence or lecture; which is a
good beginning. Those actually in lecture at once are, of course, much
fewer'.[108] From Rome, Cullen sent his congratulations and assured
Newman that the Pope and cardinals were much interested in the
progress of the university.

In early December 1854, Newman asked Cullen permission to build
a church in Dublin, and this was granted.[109] Both hoped that an
Oratory could be established in Dublin in due course, but an Oratorian
foundation in that city never materialized. Newman was to allocate a
'sizable surplus' from a national appeal for funds towards the cost of
the Achilli trial to building the University Church in Dublin. After
considerable searching for a suitable site, Newman succeeding in
acquiring a site next to the main university premises in St Stephen's
Green. The University Church formed an essential part of Newman's
overall scheme of a Catholic ethos in higher education.

Newman's views on ecclesiastical architecture had been developing
for some time. On his way to Rome in 1846, Newman and Ambrose
St John visited Paris and Milan, and in the latter city they went to the
church of St Fidelis. This was once a Jesuit church before the suppres-
sion of the order, and was 'Grecian' or 'Palladian' in style. Newman
acknowledged that 'however, my reason may go Gothic, my heart has
ever gone with Grecian. I loved Trinity Chapel at Oxford more than
any other building. There is in the Italian style such a simplicity,

purity, elegance, beauty, brightness, which I suppose the word classical implies, that it seems to befit the notion of an Angel or Saint. The Gothic style does not seem to me to typify the sanctity or innocence of the Blessed Virgin, or St Gabriel, or the lightness, grace and sweet cheerfulness of the elect as the Grecian does'.[110]

In Discourse IV of *The Idea of a University*, Newman conceded that the Gothic style 'is endowed with a profound and commanding beauty, such as no other style possesses'. But he argued that the revival of the Gothic style 'which is at present taking place' may lead to the same kind of 'excesses' that followed the Renaissance in literature and art. He admitted that Pugin was 'a man of genius' and that Catholics owed him a great debt, but he 'is intolerant' of any other school of Christian art. 'Gothic is now like an old dress, which fitted a man well twenty years back but must be altered to fit him now'. Newman summed up by saying that for Oratorians, whose roots go back to the sixteenth century, 'to assume the architecture simply and unconditionally of the 13th, would be as absurd as their putting on them the cowl of the Dominicans or adopting the tonsure of the Carthusians ...'.[111]

Newman secured the services of a talented architect, John Hungerford Pollen who, at Newman's invitation, had become honorary professor of fine arts in the CUI towards the end of 1854. In accordance with Newman's distinct preferences, the basic design of the University Church was later described by the architect as 'a plain brick hall with an apsidal end, timber ceiling etc., somewhat in the manner of the earlier Roman basilicas'. He added that Newman 'felt a strong attachment to those ancient churches with rude exteriors, but solemn and impressive within, recalling the early history of the Church, as it gradually felt its way in the converted Empire, and took possession'.[112]

Newman involved himself closely with the design, decoration and furnishings of the church and he minutely checked the resulting costs. As an Oratorian, he took special interest in its suitability for music and preaching, and also for use as a lecture theatre and graduation hall. Building commenced in May 1855 and was completed in time for a ceremonial opening on Ascension Thursday, 1 May 1856. The day before, Newman had sent a cheque to Pollen, asking 'the kindness not to present it for some little while' because he was 'so hard up just now, having overdrawn both my private and the church accounts'.[113] Eventually, Newman arranged for the outstanding debt on the church to be cleared by a loan from the Birmingham Oratory.

Church architecture continued to interest Newman, as his correspondence shows. In January 1859 he informed the editor of *The
Tablet*: 'I have never set myself against the adoption of Gothic architecture in ecclesiastical structures.' For a while he had thought of
adopting it for the University Church in Dublin, but he stated that he
'would not approve of the intolerance of some of its admirers'. For
purposes of worship and devotion, he preferred a building 'which is
more cheerful in its interior, and which admits more naturally of rich
materials, of large pictures or mosaics, and of mural decoration'.[114]
To Miss Holmes, Newman confessed that until he went abroad in
1846, he had 'thought Gothic the only style for a Church – but seeing
so many beautiful Churches not Gothic, made me, not admire Gothic
less, but feel there were other things to admire besides it'. It was, he
declared, 'narrow-minded to make Gothic all in all, and tyrannical to
force others to do the like'.[115] Five years later, Newman wrote again
to Miss Holmes about her views, in particular, on church architecture:
'It is odd that you should ever be comparing Gothic with other styles.
I go into any Church, and can be happy there, whatever the style of
architecture is.'[116]

Sir Frederic Rogers, who had been tutored by Newman at Oriel and
was later a Fellow of Oriel from 1833 to 1845, sent Newman some
photographs of St Mark's, Venice. These led Newman to reflect on
the distinctive qualities of Byzantine architecture:

> Perhaps what I mean is this – that Byzantine cannot give an external –
> whereas I have long thought that Gothic excels far more in the outside
> than the inside. The beauty of an inside is that it should be broken up – but
> of an outside that it should be seen as a whole. Thus Byzantine admits of
> inside, not outside.[117]

To another old friend, H. R. Woodgate, Newman said he thought that
the Gothic architect Pugin 'was the worse of tyrants, but we never
employed him. Everyone thinks his own special art the Architectonic'.
In his opinion, however, the architectural design of 'ecclesiastical
structures should be subservient to devotion and theology. It is not
architectonic'.[118]

Newman believed that church architecture should be influenced by
its principal function: that of providing places where people could
assemble and worship according to the liturgy of the Church. As long
ago as 1848 he had listed what he perceived to be the liturgical inad-
equacies of Pugin's architecture:

In details Pugin is perfect but his altars are so small that you can't have a Pontifical High Mass at them, his tabernacles so low that you scarce had Exposition, his East windows so large that everything is hidden in the glare, and his screens so heavy that you might as well have the function in the Sacristy, for the seeing of it by the Congregation.[119]

More recently it has been stated that Pugin's 'zealous promotion of the Gothic was considered highly eccentric by most English Catholics . . . Catholics generally appear to have chose the style of their parish churches for reasons of economy and personal taste, quite oblivious to 'party' signficance.[120]

The launch of a medical faculty was to be the next step in expansion of the CUI. Newman had assessed the medical training facilities in Dublin and had found that 'Catholics were very inadequately represented in the existing schools of medicine.'[121] It was intolerable, Culler observes, that 'a profession whose duties were so intimately involved with religion, should be dominated by Protestants in the various hospitals and medical schools'.[122] As part of the medical faculty, Newman was determined to establish a first-rate Catholic school of medicine, whose graduates would be both Catholic and professional. Through an intermediary, he was able to acquire the fully equipped and privately-owned Cecilia Street Medical School. This School was recognized by the Royal College of Surgeons. It was up for sale because of the departure of two of its leading professors. To Mrs Bowden, Newman reported that,

We are getting on with the University as well as we possibly can. It is swimming against the tide to move at all; still we are in action. The great thing is to set up things. That we are doing. The Medical School will begin in October; the church is building; and an institution for Physical Science in course of formation. It will be years before the system takes root, but my work will be ended when I have made a beginning.[123]

The acquisition of Cecilia Street Medical School enabled Newman to develop a flourishing medical faculty which was to outlive the other faculties and become, in time, part of the National University.

In 1857, Newman responded to a letter from John Hungerford Pollen, architect of the University Church, who had expressed concern about future prospects in Ireland despite all Newman's efforts for the CUI, by reminding him that, for a time, London University had also relied on its Medical School as a 'sheet anchor'. In Ireland, he declared, 'We are prosperous in Medicine.'[124]

Newman continued doggedly to put into practice the theoretical ideas which he had so persuasively presented in his *Discourses*. At the same time, he began increasingly to feel the tide of events was against him; he was suspected by Cullen of nationalist sympathies, of being too lax with his students, and failing to keep adequate checks on expenditure. These irritating misconceptions were resented and added to the considerable anxieties which Newman endured concerning the recruitment of students and trying, desperately, to keep the university viable. From August 1854 to July 1855, Cullen was in Rome, taking part in the solemn definition of the dogma of the Immaculate Conception of the Blessed Virgin Mary. He was also 'defending his pro-government policy against Irish nationalists like Archbishop MacHale', and Cullen wrote to Newman to warn him to keep the university free of Young Irelandism. Newman's response was limited to an assurance that he had intended to exclude politics, but it fell short of a promise not to appoint Young Irelanders to the staff. As a result his further letters were left unanswered and he had no further contact with Cullen until the latter's return to Dublin.[125] Newman felt that his task was becoming intolerable because of Cullen's prolonged absence in Rome as well as because of his continued procrastination and secretiveness. This type of behaviour had become so habitual that no effective communication now existed between them and Newman felt that he was labouring in vain. In April 1856 he mentioned to Cullen that he wished to leave the university in July 1857 and, as he told Ambrose St John, although the Archbishop was 'at first startled or rather surprised, he quite acquiesced – and I consider I have gained a step'.[126]

In June, Newman was summoned to appear before a synod of the Irish bishops; before he attended, he circulated a long and detailed statement of the objectives and related expenditure plans of the university. A copy was sent to Cullen for distribution to the bishops.[127] Newman's document received overall approval, and he was reappointed for a period of three years. He noted, however, that while he was committed for three years, 'it ensured my getting away at the end of it'.[128]

In a letter to J. H. Pollen, the architect of the University Church, Newman alluded to the possibility of the Birmingham Oratorians opening a boys' school: 'a certain number of persons who are interested in a Catholic Eton should form themselves into a quasi-trust with a certain sum of money at their disposal'[129] – an early reference the eventual foundation of the Oratory School.

Meanwhile, Newman was experiencing the inevitable stresses arising from trying to work in two different places at the same time, and in two decidedly different institutions. His partial residence in Dublin had irritated Cullen who thought that he should relinquish his other duties. When the Birmingham Oratory Congregation indicated their unwillingness to approve Newman's continued stay in Dublin, Newman devised a 'middle plan', which would involve residence for a few weeks of each term; the proposal was agreed, but it was not really an effective solution. At the beginning of April 1857, Newman wrote to the Irish bishops, individually, stating his intention of resigning the rectorship in November; he felt that he could no longer leave his own Congregation without his regular guiding presence. As he commented in a letter to Ambrose St John, 'it seems to me that really I may be *wanted* in England, and that there may be a providential reason, over and above the compulsion of the Fathers at Birmingham, for me to return'.[130] On 6 May 1857, the Birmingham Congregation had made a 'formal recall of the Father Superior from Dublin',[131] to which Newman had to conform. He returned to Birmingham in November 1857 but agreed to remain in office as rector of the CUI until his successor and also a vice-rector had been appointed. The following November he left Dublin, never to return.

However, as he was to tell William Monsell in a few weeks' time, the 'Vice-Rector, who was *coming*, has vanished *in fumo*'.[132] In 1872, Newman commented:

Nothing can show more clearly how little chance Dr Cullen thought there was of my remaining, than the utter abstention the Archbishops observed all along from making me *au courant* with the search for a Vice-Rector. I was not only not consulted, but not informed of what was going on.[133]

Despite his many disappointments in Ireland, Newman was prepared to spend a few weeks each term in Dublin, but this 'compromise depended for its success on there being a resident vice-rector whom Newman could trust', and he proposed that one of the lay professors should be appointed. This was unacceptable to the Irish archbishops who stipulated that the post should be filled by a priest. So the compromise plan failed and it was not until the end of November 1858 that a vice-rector was appointed.[134]

During 1858 there had been some exploratory discussions about securing a charter for the CUI, and William Monsell wrote to Newman on 6 June: 'I have seen Disraeli about the charter. He entered into the question with interest, was extremely civil and agreeable but of course did no more than promise to take the matter into consideration.'[135] Newman drafted a formal letter petitioning for a charter for the CUI; after consultation with Monsell, this was left at Disraeli's house on 28 July by Aubrey de Vere. The document was 'merely acknowledged' by Disraeli, but a second application was made to him in January 1859 by Irish members of the House of Commons. Following this, Disraeli received a deputation in March 1859, and he promised to put the case before the Cabinet, but a general election resulted in a change of Government. In 1865–8, negotiations for a charter were resumed; these failed because the Irish bishops demanded a certain control over the professors, while the Government stipulated that the university, although denominational, must be independent and self-governing.[136]

It came to light that Cullen had earlier – without advising Newman – asked Monsell to apply for a charter for the CUI, when he wrote to Newman saying that he had heard that a petition had been made by him and the professors to the Government for a charter.[137] Newman assured Cullen that nothing was being done which would 'at all prejudice the prerogatives of the Bishops, or interfere with any movement of the Archbishops respecting it'. They were merely opening negotiations, and would 'not dream of proceeding further without referring to your Grace'.[138]

However all these negotiations were unsuccessful, as Newman seems to have anticipated: 'I don't much expect we shall succeed – but we shall certainly have done ourselves good.'[139] On 9 June 1859 Lord Derby, in the House of Lords, gave an assurance that the Government did not intend to grant a charter to the CUI.[140]

At the close of 1858, Newman had written to one of his oldest friends, Manuel Johnson of the Oxford Observatory:

> I have left Dublin for good, unless the Pope lugs me back, which he won't do, I know. We are in some excitement about the prospect of a Charter, which the Tory Minister is said to be intending for us. It will be a pleasant termination of my engagement – but, if the University does not get it now, it will get it from the Whigs, when they next come in; that is all.[141]

In September 1859, Newman received a letter from the Dean of the Faculty of Medicine at the CUI advising him – with due respect – that he and his colleagues would like to make a tentative proposal to the Irish bishops that Newman should be installed as Chancellor of the University, which they considered would be of the 'utmost value' to it.[142] Newman acknowledged the 'great kindness' of this proposal, which offered him the opportunity of keeping a connection with 'an Institution the success of which I have so much at heart, and which is ever in my prayers'. But he pleaded that his strength was 'not adequate to the undertaking'. Moreover, although he 'knew well what kind friends I have among the Archbishops and Bishops, I have felt very much certain difficulties in Dublin and out of it, which I cannot fancy have a chance of being removed'. So with 'real pain' he felt he had to 'decline the proposal'.[143] On 6 November, Ornsby informed Newman that 'Dr Cullen is Chancellor of the University, Dr MacHale, Vice-Chancellor (This, they say, to show the country that they are in accord').[144] Clearly, clerical influence in the Catholic University of Ireland was being maintained at the highest level, with the top posts being occupied by the two most prominent prelates, who had frequently clashed in the early days of Newman's appointment as Rector of the Catholic University of Ireland.

Newman was a distinguished man; he had taken on an almost unsupportable burden. Now he was fatigued, disillusioned and frustrated by his Irish experiences. Also, he felt let down by the English who 'had failed to rise to his vision of a University for the English-speaking world'.[145] He told Henry Wilberforce that 'We are at great disadvantage, abused in Ireland for being English, and neglected in England for being Irish.'[146] In his private journal, he elaborates on this theme:

It was (also) the fact, which by this time had become so plain, that English Catholics felt no interest at all in the University scheme and had no intention to make use of it, should it get into shape. I had gone to Ireland on the express understanding that it was an English as well as an Irish University, and the Irish had done all in their power to make it an Irish University and nothing else. And further, I say, the English Catholics had given up. It had begun a very little time ago, when Dr Ullathorne told me, as if a matter in which he acquiesced, that 'the English gentlemen would never send their sons to it'.[147]

After Newman had relinquished his formal association with the university, he continued to display an interest in its activities. Fairly

quickly, his feelings about his experiences in Ireland appear to have
mellowed. This is seen, for instance, in a letter to his friend Robert
Ornsby in which he stated,

> Don't fancy I feel annoyance at my plans being put aside ... The great
> thing is to *set up*, and then leave the direction of things to the currents
> which would determine it ... I could not have begun without a plan. I
> could not have begun with any other ... When I am gone, something may
> come of what I have done at Dublin. And since I hope I did what I did, not
> for the sake of men, not for the sake of the Irish University, not even for
> the Pope's praise, but for the sake of God's Church and God's glory, I
> have nothing to regret and nothing to desire, different from what it is.[148]

Dr Woodlock was appointed the next rector of the CUI in 1859. His
conception of the University was that it was a definitely Irish institution. Of 986 students registered during his rectorship, only thirty-
seven came from outside Ireland.[149] By 1873, the university had few
students or professors, limited finance and was still seeking legal
recognition for its degrees.

During 1868 Newman and Woodlock exchanged views on higher
education in Ireland. Newman declared that there was an 'abundance
of genius, and varied talent in Ireland to make it a very safe risk
indeed to accept the great venture of a real Catholic University'. But
he concluded that it was '*essential* that the Church should have a
living presence and control in the action of the University. But still,
till the Bishops leave the University to itself, till the University
governs itself, till it is able to act as a free being, it will be but a
sickly child, even though it has a charter and an endowment'.[150]

Woodlock wrote to Newman on 11 December 1873 to tell him that
Cullen and the bishops had invited three priests and three laymen to
assist in the general direction and the financial affairs of the CUI; this
radical move was what Newman had always advocated.[151] However,
the plan of having a mixed board of bishops and laymen 'came to
nothing', as Newman wrote in a letter to Ornsby, adding that from
what he had heard he concluded 'it was from the impracticality of Dr
MacHale who could neither find suitable laymen in Connaught nor
would take them from the Provinces'.[152]

Woodlock put forward a restructuring scheme but, despite his strenuous efforts, the institution's terminal decline seemed inevitable. In
1879 legislation resulted in the Royal University of Ireland being set
up. This was purely an examining body, which also provided a

number of Fellowships, evenly divided between Roman Catholics and Protestants. Although this step was generally regarded as academically regressive, it relieved the financial burdens of the CUI. In 1882, Newman's University House – St Patrick's – in St Stephen's Green, became, officially, University College. The hierarchy passed it over to the Jesuit Order for management. According to McGrath, 'This date may be said to mark the end of the Catholic University as a living educational institution, thought it continued to exist juridically in the group of institutions which had been named its constituent colleges.'[153]

In a letter to Bartholomew Woodlock, who had been consecrated Bishop of Ardagh in 1879, Newman summarised the collegiate arrangements of the new Royal University, as he perceived them, and commented that there may be some difficulty in working such a subtle system, which could only be 'resolved by the actual experiment'. However, as 'far as the original object of the Holy See and the Bishops is concerned, the scheme seems to be very satisfactory'.[154]

Some two years later, one of Newman's Oxford converts, Gerard Manley Hopkins, SJ, who had just been appointed Professor of Greek at the Royal University of Ireland, wrote affectionately to the ageing Cardinal on his birthday:

> I am writing from where I never thought to be, in a University for Catholic Ireland begun under your leadership, which has since those days indeed long and unhappily languished, but for which we now with God's help hope a continuation or restoration of success.

He reported that when the Jesuits took over the buildings they 'were a sort of wreck or ruin ... Only one things looks bright, and that no longer belongs to the College, the little Church of your building, the Byzantine style of which reminds me of the Oratory and bears your impress clearly enough'.[155] Newman sent Hopkins a short note of thanks for remembering his birthday and added that he was 'sorry you can speak of dilapidation'.[156]

Historians and others have deliberated at length about whether Newman's university should be judged as a success or failure. Clearly, the criteria used influence the opinions expressed. Was it more than a brave academic experiment that was before its time (in the sense that, for instance, it was founded when the Catholic Church in Ireland exerted a powerful influence over the lives of its members)? Or was it not merely an academic venture but one which was part of a

crusade for recognition of the rights of the majority of the Irish population, i.e. Catholics, to have access to higher education? Was it
doomed to die after a short, painful existence because political,
academic and religious motivations were inextricably mixed and
conflict was inevitable after a while?

There were certainly several identifiable factors which contributed
to the fate of the Catholic University of Ireland; together, these were
a potent and destructive mix which Sencourt, with acknowledgements
to McGrath, lists as:

1. the lack of a charter resulting in an inability to confer degrees (except
   in the medical faculty which was recognized by the Royal College of
   Surgeons as successor to the Cecilia Street Medical School);
2. inadequate financial resources (the CUI had no endowments and the
   Irish poor had to contribute to support it);
3. the lack of support from the Catholic laity – some preferred TCD or
   Queen's, or had not interest at all in higher education;
4. The Holy See. Both Cullen and Newman were mistaken in believing
   that support from the English Catholic community would be forthcom-
   ing, because the CUI had originally been projected for the English-
   speaking world;
5. the fact that the ideals of Cullen and Newman were in virtually continuous conflict.[157]

Of these multiple factors, the last was probably the one which had the
most serious effects, as has been shown by observations already made.
These two eminent clerics had distinctly different perceptions about
the essential nature of higher education, and also about the role of the
laity in developing and managing such an innovative institution as a
Catholic University in Ireland. Personality factors added to the
complexities and difficulties of communication between Cullen and
Newman: both were determined, driven men whose conflicting
temperaments and perceptions tended to cause both of them endless
frustration. Cullen suffered also from regular outbreaks of deliberate
harassment by senior ecclesiastics, such as the fiery Archbishop of
Tuam.

Although Newman's foundation itself may be judged by some to
have been a failure, he left a rich legacy of thought about higher
education which, as we have seen, has endured to this day. He once
remarked that to write effectively he needed a spur: Ireland was the

stimulus which brought to fruition 'the noble ideas which he sketched in immortal prose'.[158] Perhaps on that count alone, Newman's Irish higher educational venture should be judged successful. Coulson asserts that the validity of Newman's *Idea* 'is that of a university so organised, socially as well as academically, as to make possible a way of teaching by which the student is enabled to develop his powers of judgement and, thereby, to enlarge his mind'.[159]

After Ireland, Newman's next commitment to educational excellence was with the proposal to found an Oratory School for the sons of middle and upper-class Catholic families. This was to prove a more lasting enterprise than the Catholic University of Ireland. As Culler puts it, 'Newman's ambition was to provide an education that would be no less English, for being Catholic... He saw himself as raising up an educated elite, who would be the Catholic leadership of the coming generation'.[160]

In 1852, in the preface to *The Idea of a University*, Newman had stated that for centuries the 'Catholics of these Islands' had not been able to secure the type of education needed for the 'man of the world, the statesman, the landholder, or the opulent gentleman'. The time had come, he declared, when 'this moral disability must be removed'.[161] He was, of course, directly referring to the disabilities related to the lack of higher education suffered by Catholics in particular, although he became increasingly concerned about the poor standard of Catholic education in general, which impeded the progress of Catholics in the world at large. His anxieties were shared by several notable converts, who had approached him, seeking to attract his interest in their discussions on how to remedy the acknowledged inadequate provision for the education of their sons.

Wilfrid Ward alludes to 'the touch of mutual contempt occasionally visible' between 'old Catholics' and recent converts, many of whom were influenced by Newman or were his friends of longstanding. The converts regarded the typical 'old Catholics' 'as not having quite the education befitting a gentleman', while the 'old Catholics' tended to be 'slow to admit the newcomers to the intimacy which had for generations existed among the historical families belonging to the old faith' – among which, it may be added, a marked degree of inter-marriage took place.[162]

Dessain has commented that Newman had spent his early years as a Catholic founding first the English Oratory and then the Irish university at the request of the Pope. Now he would try 'to remedy some of the "miserable deficiencies" on the practical and apologetic level which were hindering the cause of the Church in her preaching of Revealed Religion in England'.[163] Among these 'deficiencies', appropriate education for middle and upper-class Catholic families was urgently needed.

Newman had already discerned the need for Catholics to be well educated at all levels, and he welcomed the opportunity to associate himself and the Oratory with those who were seeking to find a means of providing a typical English public school education with a Catholic ethos. According to Ker, he 'was ideally suited ... because, unlike some other converts ... he had not rejected his English past on becoming a Catholic'.[164]

In April 1857 Newman wrote to Sir John Simeon that 'having set the University off, which is all I proposed to do – I could be instrumental also, in setting up another great Catholic desideratum, a public school'. He thought that 'ultimately' a school of this nature should be in the country, but that while it was small, the neighbourhood of the Oratory – 'airy, high and covered with trees and gardens ... would not be inappropriate'.[165] Sir John replied that he had not yet seen a single 'old Catholic', priest or layman, whom he considered to be a 'well educated man'. It was his firm opinion that unless the education of 'our boys' improved, it would be 'impossible for the Catholic body in England to elevate themselves in intellectual equality with their fellow citizens'.[166]

On 28 January 1858 Newman reported to T. W. Allies that he had just discussed with 'our bishop the subject of the School', and discovered that Ullathorne had no objections; on the contrary, he encouraged the idea of 'a division of the lay from the ecclesiastical students'.[167] Three days later, Newman again wrote to Allies to tell him that 'Tomorrow I will look at several houses, and shall be able to say something about prices.'[168] Newman was losing no time in progressing his school project and, as ever, he quickly focused his mind and energies on this new task. Among the prominent Catholic laymen who became involved in this educational ambition was Sir John Acton (later, Lord Acton), a Shropshire landowner, politician and noted historian, who 'shared Newman's vision of an educated laity, devoted to intellectual free enquiry... Acton had ideas for a Catholic university in England to be linked with Newman's Edgbaston school and, as it would be near Oxford, to profit from Oxford's increasing liberality towards Catholicism'.[169]

Newman heard, in November 1857, from another of his Catholic friends, Serjeant Bellasis. This prominent lawyer told him that Hope-Scott and he were delighted that he was making a start with the concept of an Oratory School – of which Newman had sent a draft prospectus for their professional evaluation.[170] With legalistic precision, they had amended this document and returned it to Newman who noted that 'I am amused at your and Hope-Scott's lawyer-like caution, in cutting off every unnecessary word from my manifesto.'[171] He had written that the school was for 'the education of boys not for the ecclesiastical state' and not over twelve years of age on admission. 'He takes this step at the urgent instance of friends, and with the concurrence and countenance of a number of Catholic gentlemen whose names have been transmitted to him.'[172]

But, as usual, Newman was to encounter problems as he busied himself with developing his school plans and, at the same time, maintaining his commitments to the Catholic University in Dublin. He told J. S. Flanagan:

> The Cardinal has washed his hands of the school plan and has pointedly told our bishop that he will have the whole responsibility. Our Bishop (post propter, I know not) has advised us strongly against it because it is sure to be a failure, yet, when he gives reasons, they are so unintelligible, as to show they are not his real difficulty, whatever it is ...

Newman added that Bellasis and Acton had attempted to get the Bishop to clarify his views, but that they seemed to be experiencing considerable difficulties. However, the original plan would be reinstated and, 'as a trial, a house will be rented for two or three years to accommodate boys under 12 years of age'.[173]

Over the next few months, correspondence and meetings took place between Newman and his influential friends, as well as with Wiseman and Ullathorne. Serjeant Bellasis sent Newman a list of prominent Catholic laymen who supported the proposal for a new Catholic school; in thanking him for his efforts, Newman mentioned that there was 'one great difficulty'. This was because 'As far as I can see, children and boys take in religion principally through the eye. Either we ought to make a handsome chapel *in* or *close* to the school house, or we must alter and improve our own.' For both plans, he foresaw 'great difficulties'.[174]

On 21 April 1858, the Congregation of the Birmingham Oratory assented to the 'idea of a School', and Fr Nicholas Darnell was

appointed as Newman's representative in 'undertaking the establishment of a Public School'.[175] In a postscript to a letter to Ullathorne,
Newman mentioned that Bellasis had shown him the correspondence
which had passed between Ullathorne and himself about the proposed
school. From this correspondence and from conversations with the
bishop in February, Newman said he 'gathered ... that you approved
the object, and without directly forwarding did not disapprove of the
experiment'.[176]

The new Oratory School began in 1 May 1859 with seven boys, all
sons of converts.[177] Formal episcopal approval of the new school
appeared in a pastoral letter issued by Ullathorne on 21 November
1859, when he referred to the zealous pastoral work of the Oratorians,
which was 'all the more laudable, as at the very time the Fathers were
engaged in founding an important school for the education of the sons
of the higher classes'.[178]

Newman's involvement with the provision of suitable scholastic
accommodation was detailed, as a letter to Hope-Scott indicates.[179]
This letter had been preceded by a Memorandum dated 5 February, in
which Newman outlined his 'grand plan'. He reiterated that 'the one
object of the school ... is the education of the sons of gentlemen', so
the 'direct interest' in the school belongs to the parents'. But he
granted that the Oratorians had 'not inconsiderable interest' in the
school's prosperity. He added that Pius IX had 'sent us to the *nobil-
iores et honestiores*, and in Birmingham, they found 'no more direct
mode of fulfilling' their mission 'than that of keeping school'. He
pointed out that, despite their limited means, the Oratorians had 'made
an outlay of £7,000 upon the school', whereas parents – who had
direct interest in the undertaking, had 'subscribed only £550'. It was,
therefore, vital for the Oratory School's success that adequate funds
should be given or loaned 'by our friends' so that the plans for future
developments could be implemented.[180]

Towards the end of 1861 Newman, in correspondence with Edward
Bellasis, again referred to their 'pecuniary' problems with the school,
reflecting that parents had the 'whole of the advantage (except the
merit) and we the whole of the risk'. He recognized 'the great difficulty of raising money', and confessed that he 'was not a man of business'. But, typically, he commented that 'where there is a will',
business men are usually able to find a way to raise finance. He was
'quite willing' for gentlemen in London to have a 'hold over the
accounts, so as to have a claim to send a yearly auditor'.[181]

Fr Darnell, ambitious and keen to rival the public schools, 'never asked Newman for advice and ignored his suggestions'.[182] Newman was being deliberately isolated from the development of the school, and he was also subject to persistent rumours that he was no longer fit for responsibility. He was also concerned to hear criticism that the boys were not receiving religious instruction and that punishments were too severe. Added to these problems, according to Trevor, was an upheaval in the school caused by misunderstandings between the headmaster and the matron which resulted in her leaving the school.[183] Newman felt that he had ultimate responsibility for the school, and so he put to the Congregation of the Oratory the problem and requested their decision as to whether Darnell or he had this responsibility. The Congregation endorsed Newman's authority, and Darnell left precipitously, followed by most of the staff, whose resignations Newman had accepted.[184] By a Decree of the 1 April 1861, the Congregation assumed the liabilities of the school,[185] and on 18 July 1862, Fr Darnell's request for release from the Congregation of the Birmingham Oratory was granted.[186] Fr Ambrose St John became headmaster, a post he filled zealously until his death in 1876; Thomas Arnold, son of Dr Arnold of Rugby, was appointed senior master. The latter had been Professor of Literature at the Catholic University in Dublin but poor pay and prospects had forced him to look elsewhere for a suitable post. Newman himself undertook some teaching in the school and adapted Latin comedies for the boys to play in.

Regardless of the problems of the past months, Newman was able to tell J. H. Pollen, on 29 January 1862; 'We have met, without the loss of a single boy – and with the addition of several . . . So we must look forward not backward.'[187] In a private letter to Mother Mary Hallahan, he declared: 'Our storm has passed over us and is gone by. I never was in sharper distress and never was in shorter'.[188] Newman's returning optimism is to be seen in a letter to Dr Charles Russell of Maynooth:

> When we began, it was a simple *experiment*, and lookers-on seemed to be surprised when they found that we had in half a year a dozen – but at the end of our third year, we now have seventy, and though some will soon be going, yet more seem to be coming.[189]

In the first quarter of 1867 Newman was, once more, to experience anxieties related to the Oratory School which, it was alleged, had become involved in preparing youths for Oxford. Ullathorne alerted him to these imputations, which had caused Cardinal Barnabo, the Prefect of Propaganda, to write to Newman accusing him of disobedience. 'If I were in your place', Ullathorne advised Newman, 'I should go to Rome without delay . . . and there meet the statements that have been made.'[190] So Newman prepared a 'Memorandum on the Oratory School', to be presented by Fr Ambrose St John on behalf of the Oratory School.[191] In this document Newman described the origins and development of the School, and stated strongly that the misrepresentation . . . 'is one latest of a series of calumnies which have been persistently circulated against our School since its commencement':

> The latest form of slander has been to turn the very excellence of our teaching into an offence; and because we really ground well in Latin and Greek, and teach mathematics so successfully that some of our boys have succeeded in the difficult competitive examinations necessary for obtaining entrance into the Royal Military College, it has been 'spread abroad' that our system of education was 'formally and intentionally directed to the preparation of youths for the University of Oxford'.

Newman expressed 'just indignation' at these 'idle tales', and had sought the protection of the Cardinal Prefect. In fact, there had been no Roman instructions on the matter, and the English hierarchy had given their clergy the responsibility of deciding when it was permissible to send young men to Oxford. Not only had other schools prepared youths for Oxford but had also sent several there. Nevertheless, although Newman felt that the Oratory School had been the focus of unfair attention, he promised to conform to Barnabo's wishes.[192] This unfortunate episode probably influenced negotiations over the plans for an Oratorian presence in Oxford.

Newman scorned the idea that 'if a lot of knowledge is packed into young heads in schools', adult society would become more virtuous. As Chadwick puts it,

> The error lies in the belief that excellence comes from without, whereas it comes only from within. It cannot come if a child sits passive and receiving. It comes only through personal struggle and suffering. No one can be taught, no one can be interested, no one can be amused, into morality.[193]

Education, therefore, involves a moral mission; it was this responsibility which was recognized by Newman and it was at the heart of his strenuous efforts to found the Oratory School. During his lifetime the school remained small but successful. Dessain holds that 'its example and competition raised the standard of the other Catholic schools'.[194] In these ways Newman made distinguished contributions to the concept of education at both university and school levels.

During July 1864 Talbot called on Newman, who was away from the Oratory, so in a letter Talbot invited him 'to come to Rome for next Lent to preach at my Church in the Piazza del Populo, where you would have a more educated Audience of Protestants than could ever be the case in England, and where they are more open to Catholic influences'.[195] Newman was incensed at what he described as 'a pompous and insolent letter', and he sent a stinging, if rather undiplomatic, reply to Talbot: 'However, Birmingham people have souls; and I have neither taste nor talent for the sort of work, which you cut out for me: and I beg to decline your offer.'[196] He suspected that Manning, in fact, was instrumental in Talbot's approach to Newman to visit Rome.[197] Tristram has described Talbot as a 'mouthpiece for extremists in Rome', and who 'had the ear of Pius IX and never let slip an opportunity of belittling Newman and turning Roman opinion against him'.[198]

Between 1864 and 1871, Newman was yet again involved in the matter of higher education for Catholics, this time in England, and arising from plans to open an oratory in Oxford. In August 1864 Newman had bought, for £8,000, a five-acre site on which the old Oxford Workhouse stood – located behind St Giles. Newman recorded later that 'Ullathorne mentioned that he should like a Mission house and church there'. Newman replied that he feared their interests would clash, 'for we are looking out for ground for an Oratory'. The bishop answered 'I will give you the Mission.' Newman confessed that this took him utterly by surprise, 'for he had never meant to be involved in this way'.[199] But the bishop was going ahead and, as Newman told Hope-Scott, was 'collecting money for the Church and Priests' house. These would, *pro tempore*, become the Church and House of the Oratory, but no *college* would be set up – but the Priest, i.e. the Fathers of the Oratory would take lodgers'. But Newman was concerned about how he could 'without saying a word to any one, make the Oratory a Hall. I cannot tell. I don't see why I should not'. He reflected that the Oratory is 'confessedly out of the Bishop's jurisdiction', but that Propaganda would probably 'interfere'. He saw his 'only defence would be the support of the Catholic gentry'.[200]

In 1864, Newman's correspondence discloses that he was experiencing 'great misgiving' about the way in which the 'Oxford plan' seemed to be developing. His experiences in Ireland had, understandably, made him wary of becoming involved in higher educational ambitions associated with clerical control, although he recognized that there were marked differences between Irish and English Catholics, in that the latter 'are not of the lower classes'.[201]

Meanwhile, Newman devised an allocation of the five-acre site between the projected Oratory and the Mission, with sufficient land reserved for a prospective college.[202] He also started to raise funding from his wealthy friends, several of whom were keen that their sons should be able to study at Oxford, particularly if Newman founded a Catholic hall associated with the Oratory. He realized that to make the project viable in the long term – because there were only about 100 middle-class Catholics resident in Oxford – the Oratory's role would only be relevant if Catholic undergraduates were at Oxford. But Ullathorne was now emphasizing that while 'it was not impossible that there would be a Catholic University in England, there were great objections to a Catholic College in Oxford on point of principle and consequences, and that providing lodgings for young men was even worse'.[203] The bishop's views so disturbed Newman that he felt it necessary to write to Ullathorne setting out the reasons why he had 'contemplated an Oratory house at Oxford'. These were:

1. he thought that there would be a considerable danger to the souls of Catholic youth who go to Protestant Colleges in Oxford;
2. that there would be comparatively little danger in their going to a Catholic College there;
3. 'the former of these is the actual state of the case';
4. that when he had thought of the Oratorians going to Oxford, it was with a view of meeting this actually existing danger; and
5. if that danger ceased, he 'should not feel any special reason for our going there'.

Newman alleged that Ullathorne had told him that it was not unlikely that the danger *will increase*, i.e. that Catholic youths will be *prohibited* from going to Oxford. Newman expressed surprise that the bishop was apparently still contemplating 'the idea of a Catholic University in England', although he himself had thought it 'not feasible'. He added that: 'Before this great design, the notion of Catholic youth, being at any footing whatever at Oxford shrinks into nothing.'[204]

Ullathorne responded by giving Newman a detailed account of 'what exactly was in my mind at our interview, though I may then have failed in giving it complete expression'. He had 'received a caution from Propaganda about the education of Catholics at Oxford, and had pledged to 'do nothing without its authority'. Also, he felt he could not 'commit the policy of the Church in a matter which concerns not only several Dioceses but several provinces'. In view of the fact that the matter was before the Holy See, he had no right to take any action at present. Hence, he would 'sanction no ecclesiastical connection with Oxford Education until authorised to do so'. The question of a Catholic university was 'in the air'. Ullathorne admitted that he was in an embarrassing position, but would be 'quite willing' if Newman wished, 'to write to Propaganda and ask for direction on the ground of the present offer of land' to Newman.[205] In thanking Ullathorne for his 'most candid and instructive letter', Newman assured him that the Oratorians have 'no intention at present to do more than accept his offer of the Oxford Mission, and with a view to the *future* foundation of an Oratory' for which 'we buy ground'. Their activities would be confined to pastoral duties, and no ties would be made with the University of Oxford or its Colleges; their first step would be to build a church. It was considered judicious to decline Ullathorne's kind offer of writing to Propaganda.[206] The letter received Ullathorne's approval and he read it to the meeting of the English bishops on 13 December, and also gave the substance of it to Barnabo on 4 January 1865.[207]

In one of his customary 'Memoranda', Newman recorded: 'We have to decide today (7 October 1864) about purchasing the land at Oxford.' He summarized the various stages involved in this negotiation, adding that his 'real and one reason for thinking of an Oratory at all' was the chance of attracting novices to the Birmingham Oratory. If that was not likely, the matter was ended as far as he was concerned. He also wished 'to take care of the young Catholics who go to the Protestant Colleges'.[208]

However, as Newman was to tell Hope-Scott, 'there has been no end of hitches about the ground'. The original vendor died suddenly and the family wishes to sell the land immediately'; so Newman 'at once sent Fathers St John and Caswall to Oxford. They have bought the whole in my name for £8,000! I pay at Christmas. Am I, after all to end my days in prison?'[209] Newman also advised Ullathorne of the decision he had had to make quickly, and asked for his agreement to

appeal for financial contributions.[210] The bishop agreed to provide for
the Oxford Mission until July 1865.[211] In a further letter he remarked
that Newman's courage in buying 'so large a block of land in Oxford,
and at so considerable a cost . . . calls for congratulation; and I wish to
give your undertaking all the approval and encouragement I can'.[212]
This exchange of letters closed with Newman stating that the Oxford
Oratory 'will grow out of the Oxford Mission', unlike the Oratories in
Birmingham and London which existed *before* secular missions were
undertaken, so the question could not arise whether or not the Birmingham and London Oratory buildings were Oratory property. He
considered it prudent to place on record 'that what belongs to the
Oxford Mission is the £700 of the Jesuits and the value of St
Clement's property, and on the other hand what belongs to the
Oratory is the (St Giles's) Church and its site'.[213]

In November 1864 Newman called on Wiseman to explain his
Oxford plans but found him decidedly unwell. He listened 'half queru-
lously' to Newman's scheme.[214] More positive opposition came from
Manning which resulted in 'the Oxford scheme being thwarted for the
present – for me probably for good . . . Bellasis told me that, from
what he saw at Rome, he felt that Manning was more set against my
going to Oxford, than merely against Catholic youths going there'.[215]
Meanwhile, Manning had written to Propaganda stating that Wiseman
had 'declared himself entirely opposed to any contact between the
faithful in England and the heretical structure of the country'.[216]
Newman, hearing of the hierarchy's entirely negative attitude,
reflected:

> The same dreadful jealousy of the laity, which has ruined things in
> Dublin, is now at the bottom of this unwillingness to let our youths go to
> Oxford . . . Propaganda and our leading Bishops fear the natural influence
> of the laity.[217]

Earlier, Newman had said to Hope-Scott 'Unless the Catholic gentry
make themselves heard at Rome, a small active clique will carry the
day.'[218] A week later – 28 November 1864 – he told Hope-Scott:

> At present I am simply off the rails. I do not doubt that the sudden meeting
> of the Bishops has been ordered apropos of my going to Oxford. If I
> understand our bishop, the notion is to forbid young Catholics to go to
> Oxford, and to set up a University elsewhere.

He thought he would 'keep two acres – enough for an Oratory and College. The rest I must sell – as I can't afford to keep it'.[219] Another of his intimate friends, T. W. Allies, had written on 10 December to Newman to warn him that he suspected that the bishops' meeting had been 'called expressly to prevent your going to Oxford, and that the Bishop's giving you the mission at Oxford was its immediate momentum'.[220] Newman confided to Pusey that the bishops were meeting that day, and exactly what the outcome would be 'is quite uncertain'; only if things 'were left just as they are', should he found an oratory in Oxford. But as the bishops' decision would have to go to Rome ... 'it is doubtful whether any plan will be brought into execution'.[221] Newman's stressful thoughts about the likelihood of his opening an oratory in Oxford were revealed in a letter to Sir Frederic Rogers, with whom he had shared many of his innermost thoughts: 'I want light upon this Oxford plan – I live in a hole, and light would be welcome from any quarter.' He asserted that 'a small, stirring, violent, influential party are for *prohibiting* any Catholic going to Oxford at all. I don't think they have much chance of success – but still they may so trouble the waters as to deprive *our* own work there of any chance of telling'.[222]

Newman agreed with William Monsell:

We are certainly under a tyranny; one or two persons, such as Manning seem to do everything. It is clear that our Bishop was not in the secret. He offered me the Mission of Oxford, before I dreamed of such a thing; he brought me forward ... But now where am I? with a property of £8,000 or £9,000 on my hand ... I have been left in the lurch many times – by the Cardinal in the Achilli matter – in my Dublin rectorship – in my Dublin church – in my translation of the Scripture; and now I am left in the lurch again. I am selling, I hope I have sold, the land.

Newman's *crie de coeur* echoes throughout this long and impassioned letter.[223]

With Newman's encouragement, a memorial from the laity was taken to Propaganda and, although this did not deflect the decision taken, it indicated to Rome that the English laity considered that their voices should be heard on the important matter of access to higher education. It seems that Newman had been critical of the wording of the memorial, and Monsell noted that 'every thing that gives the memorial the form of a petition' had been left out.[224]

Meanwhile, Pusey had been acting on behalf of Newman in selling the land to the University of Oxford, and Newman had accepted an offer of £9,000 (to include all expenses) for the site he had bought the previous year. Astutely, he had made a small gain on the transaction and, as he told Ullathorne: 'I believe your Lordship considers the arrangement for the Oratory to take the Oxford Mission as at an end. I certainly so consider myself.'[225]

Newman assured the family, from whose late father he had originally bought the Oxford site, that he intended to use the money from the University's purchase of the land exclusively for 'Catholic purposes in Oxford', as would have been the wish of their father. He intended to buy land in Oxford 'for an Oratory Church or other ecclesiastical purpose'.[226]

Cardinal Wiseman had died on 18 February 1865, after a long debilitating illness. Newman noted: 'The Cardinal has done a great work and has gone to his reward. Alas! that his opening act has been to extinguish a hope of a great future and an opening for a wide field of religious action.'[227] To Dr Russell, Newman was more open in his comments:

> The Cardinal has done a great work – and I think has finished it. It is not often this can be said of a man. Personally, I have not much to thank him for, since I was a Catholic. He always meant kindly, but his impulses, kind as they were, were evanescent, and he was naturally influenced by those who got around him and occupied his ear ... I have not seen him above 6 or 7 times in the last 13 years.

He noted, with approval, that Wiseman's funeral had been a great public event in London.[228] In May 1865, Manning was appointed by Pius IX to succeed Wiseman as Archbishop of Westminster.

During August 1865, Ullathorne again approached Newman about an Oxford Mission, as he told Ambrose St John: 'He asked me if I still thought of Oxford. I said absolutely no. I added, I had bought some other land, but for the chances of the future, not as connected with myself. He said he had heard so.'[229] This new site was, in fact, opposite Christ Church – which displeased Ullathorne as being too near to the University – but this did not prevent him from putting the matter to Newman again, in the following year. While acknowledging the bishop's 'great kindness and confidence in them', Newman felt that certain clarifications and assurances, including a guarantee from Cardinal Barnabo, were necessary before commitments at Oxford could be undertaken.[230] In reply, Ullathorne referred to the earlier decision of the bishops regarding the education of Catholics at the University: 'they hold it their duty to discourage Protestant university education for Catholics'. This decision was approved by the Holy See; what future steps might be taken he could not say, but the whole matter might have to be reconsidered if 'the practice of sending Catholics to the University' became more prevalent.[231] Manning's reaction was, however, adamantine – he warned Talbot of the likely outcome: 'The English national spirit is spreading among Catholics, and we shall have dangers.'[232]

Propaganda's approval was now sought for the establishment of an oratory in Oxford under the supervision of Birmingham Oratory; by the end of 1866, Ullathorne had obtained Rome's permission on the understanding that the new Oratory should remain united to that of Birmingham during Newman's lifetime and for three years thereafter.[233] Newman's acceptance was cautious and conditional for, as he told Ullathorne, he had already experienced problems with Propaganda when he was in Dublin.[234]

With Ullathorne's backing, Newman now issued a formal circular asking for contributions to set up the Oxford Oratory. Objectors to the scheme were also active, and as a result Newman received a letter from Cardinal Barnabo, the Prefect of Propaganda, accusing him of disobedience because, contrary to Rome's instructions, he was preparing youths for Oxford, and demanded that this should cease.[235] Newman had already encountered such accusations, based on misrepresentations, he had founded the Oratory School. He assured the Cardinal Prefect that he would always give the Sacred Congregation his ready and careful obedience, although he felt he should point out that hitherto he 'had heard of nothing, absolutely nothing, that had been sent to this country either by the Sacred Congregation or by the Holy Father, whether as precept or as admonition, on the subject of Catholics going to Oxford'. Such matters seemed to be left to the 'prudent discretion' of parish priests and confessors.[236] Fr Ambrose St John – as noted earlier – had made a visit to Rome on behalf of Newman and the Oratory School in order to clarify matters and his representations had been successful. But in the case of the Oxford plans, Ullathorne had already told Newman that Manning and Grant, supported in Rome by Talbot, were opposed to his going to Oxford.[237]

In spite of all these discouragements, Newman persisted in the 'Oxford plan', although he confided to Bishop David Moriarty of Kerry: 'There is a knot of men, who wished me kept from the place

[Oxford] at any price [though] they give other reasons ... If I had a pulpit in Oxford, it would be a great blow to them.' But his bishop and 'a number of (other) persons are determined I should go to Oxford'.[238] Among his supporters was Bishop Thomas Brown of Newport who, in 1859, had delated Newman to Rome for his essay: *On Consulting the Faithful in Matters of Doctrine*, but now wished Newman 'every success' at Oxford, adding that: 'As Catholic parents are resolved to send their sons to Oxford I never could understand on what principle those youths were to be refused such means of preservation as Religion could provide.'[239]

But Newman's hopes were to be shattered when Ullathorne revealed that the letter sent by Propaganda giving permission for an oratory in Oxford contained a 'secret instruction'; that he should 'blandly and suavely' (*blande suaviterque*) recall Newman if he showed signs of intending to reside in Oxford. (This 'secret instruction' had been omitted from the copy of the Propaganda letter sent to Newman.) In Newman's Memorandum of the meeting which took place between the bishop and himself, Newman noted that Manning intended 'to read to the bishops in Low Week a letter from Rome against Catholics going to Oxford or some such subject'; he (Ullathorne) also said that 'I could not take the Oxford Mission, unless the secret instruction was simply cancelled'.[240] Newman was devastated and wrote bitterly to Wilberforce, Coleridge and to Russell.[241] He also drafted a Memorandum in which he itemized the 'correspondence and conversations' relating to the Oxford scheme.[242]

It appeared that Newman was, in fact, 'under a cloud' at Rome because of the delation of his article: *On Consulting the Faithful in Matters of Doctrine*. Ambrose St John, during his discussions on the Oratory School, discovered that Barnabo had never been sent a letter which Newman had written to Wiseman in January 1860, which fully explained the passage under review. Ambrose St John obtained a copy of Newman's letter and presented it to the Cardinal Prefect. As a result, the unfortunate suspicions about Newman's doctrinal soundness, and ecclesiastical disobedience, were dismissed. But the restriction on his residence in Oxford remained, not because his faith was thought to be unsound, but because his presence there would be likely to attract young Catholics.[243] It seemed that Newman had, in fact, noted in a Memorandum dated 21 April 1867 that he had 'consistently told the Bishop and others two things': that his 'going to Oxford would *attract* young men there', that it would 'much hamper' him if

Catholic young men were *not* at the University, and so he had been 'very reluctant to go to Oxford', and given his 'consent with difficulty'.[244] Clearly, he fully realized that his presence in Oxford would, as his detractors claimed, act as a spur to young men to go to the University there.

Only a few days earlier, Newman had been presented with an 'Address' signed by about 200 prominent laymen supporting him, probably with expectations of an Oxford education for their sons.[245] It is said that this initiative 'caused Manning some alarm in case it might influence Propaganda's decision on the Oxford question, and 'he wrote to Mgr Talbot with the object of stiffening its back'.[246]

In August 1867, Newman reported Ullathorne's conversation with him 'on the subject of the Oxford matter . . . He said abruptly and with a grave face, looking straight at me, "I find at Rome they consider the Oxford question at an end"'.[247] This position was confirmed when Propaganda instructed the English hierarchy 'to issue pastorals explaining that those who frequented the non-Catholic universities incurred most grievous danger to faith and morals and that it was well nigh impossible to envisage circumstances in which Catholics could attend without sin'.[248] On Hope-Scott's advice, Newman circulated subscribers to the projected Oxford Oratory offering to refund their contributions, and emphasizing that the 'sole ground' of the restriction barring him from taking up residence in Oxford was the 'apprehension' that this would attract Catholic youths there.[249]

Three days later Newman requested permission from Ullathorne 'to withdraw from my engagement to undertake the Mission of Oxford'.[250] Ullathorne replied that he 'was not at all surprised' at Newman's decision. 'were I in the same position I should do the same'. He added that it was his 'complete conviction that you have been shamefully misrepresented in Rome, and that by countrymen of our own'.[251] So, for the time being, ended the opportunity of founding an Oxford Oratory and of giving Catholics access to higher education. Newman was to refer later to this unhappy period as only one of various instances 'of what may be called Nihilism in the Catholic Body, and in its rulers. They forbid, but they do not direct or create'.[252] His profound disillusionment is evident in a letter to his friend Fr Henry Coleridge in which he mentioned that 'after so many rebuffs' he felt no call to go on with the Oxford undertaking. He would wait to be asked by Propaganda before becoming involved in any other schemes.[253]

Ullathorne's own pastoral had gone as far as to state that the universities were 'essentially anti-Catholic and that there could be no communication between light and darkness'.[254]

During the next year, and in a discursive letter to Pusey, Newman referred to the 'late question about Oxford' and the Pope's personal *wish* that going to Oxford should be prohibited. Although 'he *showed* his wish', he was, Newman stated, 'quite nervous about the result of the English Episcopal meetings', as Ambrose St John had reported. It seemed that 'the Pope never acted without the local hierarchy – then, *when* the bishops had *decided*, the Pope came out with a tremendously strong Rescript'. This insight indicated to Newman that

> Local bishops are the proper channels of communication between the English people, or a portion of them, and Rome. It is their duty to soften difficulties, not to increase them. I cannot deny that Archbishop Manning has done everything in his power to increase them, not to soften them.[255]

The Jesuit Provincial advised Newman on 22 February 1871 that Ullathorne was going 'to entrust to our charge once more the Oxford Mission', provided it could be undertaken immediately and that they 'were ready to pledge ourselves not to open a College there without the sanction of the Holy See or his own approval'. Newman responded: 'Nothing can be more natural than that the Society, which so lately has had the Mission of Oxford, and for so long, should resume it.'[256]

Notes
1. McGrath, 1951, p. 1.
2. McGrath, 1951, p. 5.
3. Meenan, 1987, p. 2.
4. McGrath, 1951, p. 43.
5. Norman, 1985, pp. 292–3.
6. Chadwick, 1972, p. 280.
7. McGrath, 1951, p. 63.
8. McGrath, 1951, p. 64.
9. Newman, 1956, p. 280.
10. Owen Chadwick, 1972, pp. 453–4.
11. Cf McGrath, 1951, pp. 80–2.
12. Ward, 1913, p. 309.

13. LDXV.283–84; LDXXXI.34, Supplement, 3 February 1853.
14. LDXIV.257, footnote.
15. LDXIV.257, Archbishop Cullen, 16 April 1851.
16. LDXIV.267, Archbishop Cullen, 28 April 1851.
17. LDXIV.262, 20 April 1851.
18. LDXIV.305.
19. Newman, 1956, p. 282; LDXIV.313, footnote.
20. LDXIV.315, 23 July 1851.
21. LDXIV.320, footnote.
22. LDXIV.331, footnote.
23. Newman, 1956, p. 281.
24. LDXIV.357, Dr Cullen, 16 September 1851.
25. LDXIV.364, footnote, from Dr Cullen, 20 September 1851.
26. LDXV.71, Robert Ornsby, 18 April 1852.
27. Culler, 1965, p. 137; LDXIV364–5, Archbishop Cullen, 22 September 1851.
28. Culler, 1965, p. 138.
29. Cf Culler, 1965, p. 139.
30. Ibid.
31. Culler, 1965, p. 140.
32. LDXV.29, footnote, from Dr Cullen, 8 February 1852.
33. LDXIV.382, 11 October 1851.
34. LDXIV.389, 14 October 1851.
35. McGrath, 1951, p. 107.
36. Newman, 1956, p. 283; LDXIV.393.
37. McGrath, 1951, p. 123.
38. LDXIV.343, footnote.
39. Culler, 1965, p. 142.
40. LDXV.66–7, 14 April 1852.
41. Cf McGrath, 1951, p. 153, footnote.
42. LDXV.83, 11 May 1852.
43. LDXV.98, 8 June 1852.
44. Newman, 1956, p. 304.
45. Culler, 1965, p. 154.
46. Cf Culler, 1965, p. 154.
47. LDXV.182, Sister Mary Poole, 22 October 1852.
48. Dessain, 1980, p. 102.
49. McGrath, 1951, p. 135.
50. Newman, 1987, p. 3.
51. Cf Chadwick, 1990, p. 57.
52. Cf McGrath, 1951, pp. 163–4.
53. Cf Coulson, 1970, p. 87.
54. Newman, 1987, *Discourse* V, p. 137.
55. Newman, 1987, *Discourse* V, p. 138.
56. Roy Jenkins, 1990, p. 147.
57. Cf Vargish, 1970, pp. 129–31.
58. Tristram, 1952, p. 209.

59. Culler, 1965, p. 168.
60. LDXVII.179, Bishop Thomas Grant, 7 March 1856.
61. McGrath, 1951, p. 186.
62. Newman, 1956, p. 320.
63. LDXVII.178, 7 March 1856.
64. McGrath, 1951, p. viii.
65. Chadwick, 1990, p. 52.
66. Lash, 1990, p. 195.
67. LDXV.225, Henry Wilberforce, 20 December 1852.
68. Vargish, 1970, pp. 148–9.
69. Vargish, 1970, p. 154.
70. Newman, 1987, p. 12.
71. Culler, 1965, p. 189.
72. McGrath, 1951, p. 275.
73. Newman, 1956, p. 285.
74. Newman, 1956, p. 290.
75. LDXVII.441, 9 November 1856.
76. Redmond, 1990, p. 83.
77. LDXV.471, Dr Taylor, 23 October 1853.
78. LDXV.507, 24 December 1853.
79. Newman, 1956, p. 305.
80. LDXV.514, 28 December 1853.
81. Newman, 1956, p. 312.
82. LDXVI.6, 2 Janauary 1854.
83. Newman, 1956, p. 315.
84. LDXVI.31, from Cardinal Wiseman, 20 January 1854; Newman, 1956, p. 315.
85. Newman, 1956, p. 316.
86. LDXVI.44, R. Stanton, 14 February 1854; XVI.55, James Hope-Scott, 24 February 1854; XVI.66, Mrs Wm. Froude, 2 March 1854; XVI.73, The Earl of Shrewsbury, 8 March 1854.
87. Cf McGrath, p. 250
88. LDXVI.99-100, Dessain, footnote.
89. Newman, 1956, p. 319.
90. LDXVI.76, J.L. Paterson, 9 March 1854.
91. Newman, 1956, p. 323.
92. McGrath, 1951, p. 200.
93. Newman, 1956, p. 320.
94. Newman, 1956, p. 322.
95. LDXVI.99, James Hope-Scott, 7 April 1854.
96. LDXVI.112, footnote.
97. LDXVI.126, Archbishop Cullen, 11 May 1854.
98. LDXVI.127, footnote.
99. LDXVI.557–61, Appendix 2, 29 April 1854.
100. LDXVI.166–7, 18 June 1854.
101. LDXVI.273, 6 October 1854.
102. McGrath, 1951, p. 325.

103. LDXVI.273–4, Archbishop of Tuam, 8 October 1854.
104. LDXVI.8 October 1854.
105. LDXVI.339, from Archbishop Cullen, 20 December 1854.
106. Wiseman, LDXVI.146, 5 June 1854; Ullathorne, LDXVI.146, 5 June 1854, *et seq.*
107. LDXVIII.xv, Dessain.
108. LDXVI.286, 3 November 1854.
109. LDXVI.321, Archbishop Cullen, 8 December 1854.
110. LDXI.252, Henry Wilberforce, 24 September 1846.
111. LDXII.221, Ambrose Phillips de Lisle, 15 June 1848.
112. LDXVI.447, footnote.
113. LDXVII.229, J. H. Pollen, 30 April 1856.
114. LDXIX.4, 2 January 1859.
115. LDXIX.20, 18 January 1859.
116. LDXXI.50, 12 February 1864.
117. LDXXI.157, 16 July 1864.
118. LDXXVI.161, 7 September 1872.
119. LDXII.213–4, Miss M. R. Giberne, 6 June 1848.
120. Heimann, 1995, p. 26.
121. Meenan, 1987, p. 5.
122. Culler, 1965, p. 159.
123. LDXVI.535, 31 August 1855.
124. LDXVIII.187, 26 November 1857.
125. Cf Ker, 1990, p. 417.
126. LDXVII.216, 14 April 1856.
127. LDXVII.20 June 1856; LDXVII.280–5, Memorandum, 19 June 1856.
128. LDXVII.301, J.S. Flanagan, 29 June 1856.
129. LDXVII.510–511, 28 January 1857.
130. LDXVIII.30, 7 Mary 1857.
131. Murray, 1980, p. 456, Decree Book, Appendix 6.
132. LDXVIII.359, 28 May 1858.
133. LDXVIII.359, footnote.
134. LDXVIII.xiv.
135. LDXVIII.359, footnote.
136. LDXVIII.415–6.
137. LDXVIII.419, 20 July 1858.
138. LDXVIII.420, 21 July 1858.
139. LDXVIII.426, Robert Ornsby, 26 July 1858.
140. LDXIX.153, footnote.
141. LDXVIII.526, 29 December 1858.
142. LDXIX.216, 26 September 1859, footnote.
143. LDXIX.216, Dr Hayden, 25 September 1859.
144. LDXXIX.216, footnote.
145. Gilley, 1990, p. 291.
146. LDXVIII.228, 12 January 1858.
147. Newman, 1956, pp. 392–430.
148. LDXIX.253, 15 December 1859.

149. Rigney, 1995, pp. 325–6.
150. LDXXIV.46, 4 March 1868.
151. LDXXVII.48, Archbishop of Cashel, 11 April 1874.
152. LDXVII.142, 18 October 1874.
153. McGrath, 1951, p. 494.
154. LDXXX.145, 7 November 1882.
155. LDXXX.317, 20 February 1884.
156. LDXXX.317, 29 February 1884.
157. Cf Sencourt, 1948, p. 160.
158. McGrath, 1951, p. 508.
159. Coulson, 1978, p. 235.
160. Culler, 1965, p. 298.
161. Newman, 1987, preface, p. 9.
162. Ward, 1913, p. 452.
163. Dessain, 1980, p. 110.
164. Ker, 1990, p. 464.
165. LDXVIII.16–17, 17 April 1857.
166. LDXVIII.17, footnote, 30 April 1857.
167. LDXVIII.240, 28 January 1858.
168. LDXVIII.241, 31 January 1858.
169. Hill, 2000, pp. 116–7.
170. LDXVIII.527, footnote, 29 November 1858.
171. LDXVIII.527, 4 December 1858.
172. LDXVIII.527, footnote.
173. LDXVIII.312, 5 April 1858.
174. LDXVIII.319, 13 April 1858.
175. Murray, 1980, p. 462; LDXVIII.325, footnote.
176. LDXVIII.339, 29 April 1858.
177. LDXIX.120, footnote.
178. LDXIX.423, footnote.
179. LDXIX.462, 19 February 1861.
180. LDXIX.462, footnote.
181. LDXX.87–8, 24 December 1861.
182. Trevor, 1996, p. 188.
183. Cf Trevor, 1996, pp. 188–9.
184. Trevor, 1996, p. 190.
185. Murray, 1980, Decree Book, p. 464.
186. Murray, 1980, Decree Book, p. 465.
187. LDXX.141.
188. LDXX.145, January/February 1862.
189. LDXX.201, 17 May 1862.
190. LDXXIII.111, 28 March 1867.
191. LDXXIII.114–5, 30 March 1867.
192. LDXXIII.xiv.
193. Chadwick, 1990, p. 50.
194. Dessain, 1980, p. 110.
195. LDXXI.166, 24 July 1864.

196. LDXXI.167, 25 July 1864.
197. LDXXI.166, footnote.
198. Tristram, 1956, p. 15.
199. LDXXI.206, Memorandum, 31 March 1867.
200. LDXXI.211, 29 August 1864.
201. LDXXI.198, Robert Monteith, 18 August 1864; LDXXI.200, Thomas Gainsford, 20 August 1864; LDXXI.203, James Hope-Scott, 21 August 1864.
202. LDXXI.225–6, William Monsell, 15 September 1864.
203. LDXXI.231–2, Memorandum, 21 September 1864.
204. DXXI.234, 23 September 1864.
205. LDXXI.237–8, 26 September 1864.
206. LDXXI.239, 26 September 1864.
207. LDXXI.240, footnote.
208. LDXXI.251, Memorandum, 7 October 1864.
209. LDXXI.273, 25 October 1864.
210. LDXXI.273, 25 October 1864.
211. LDXXI.274, 25 October 1864.
212. LDXXI.277, 27 October 1864.
213. LDXXI.278–9, 28 October 1864.
214. LDXXI.286, Ambrose St John, 5 November 1864.
215. Newman, 1956, p. 261.
216. LDXXI.308, 8 October 1864.
217. LDXXI.327, T. W. Allies, 30 November 1864.
218. LDXXI.309, 23 November 1864.
219. LDXXI.321, 28 November 1864.
220. LDXXI.340, footnote.
221. LDXXI.341, 13 December 1864.
222. LDXXI.351, 20 December 1864.
223. LDXXI.383–6, 12 January 1865.
224. LDXXI.404, footnote.
225. LDXXI.412–3, 10 February 1865.
226. LDXXI.430, G. B. Smith, 19 March 1865.
227. LDXXI.424, E. S. Ffoulkes, 1 March 1865.
228. LDXXI.425–6, 2 March 1865.
229. LDXXII.37, Ambrose St John, 27 August 1865.
230. LDXXII.221–4, 23 April 1866.
231. LDXXII.224, footnote.
232. Butler, 1926, 2, p. 14.
233. LDXXIII.xiii.
234. LDXXIII.1 January 1867.
235. LDXXIII.91, 11 March 1867.
236. LDXXIII.93–4, 21 March 1867.
237. LDXXIII.120, 2 April 1867.
238. LDXXIII.124–5, 4 April 1867.
239. LDXXIII.47, footnote.
240. LDXXIII.154–5, Memorandum, 14 April 1867.

241. LDXXIII.164–5; LDXXIII.190; LDXXIII.188–9.
242. LDXXIII.192–3, Memorandum, 26 April 1867.
243. LDXXIII.xv.
244. LDXXIII.180, Memorandum.
245. LDXXIII.145, 12 April 1867.
246. Ward, 1913, II, pp. 144–5.
247. LDXXIII.281, James Hope-Scott, 2 August 1867.
248. LDXXIII.xv.
249. LDXXIII.298–9, 15 August 1867.
250. LDXXIII.312, 18 August 1867.
251. LDXXIII.312, footnote.
252. LDXXX.143, Lord Braye, 2 November 1882.
253. LDXXIII.326, 30 August 1867.
254. LDXXIII.xvi.
255. LDXXXIV.78, 24 Mary 1868.
256. LDXXV.290, Robert Whitty, SJ, 22 February 1871.

Chapter 6

The Challenge of Controversy

Newman relished argument, his polemical skills were honed at Oriel College where 'he learned much through academic duels and more by intellectual osmosis'.[1] The challenge of controversy fired his intellect and emotions, and he set about it with enthusiasm. In his writing and publishing he needed a stimulus, without which, he confessed, he could write 'neither with spirit nor with point'.[2] Through most of his adult life Newman was engaged in controversial issues. As Butler puts it, 'for all his gentle and retiring nature, Newman was fated to be the storm centre'.[3]

In the face of the 'storm of obloquy' that resulted from *Tract 90*, Newman had stood his ground and, according to McGrath, his 'resolute bearing' in later controversial encounters revealed a 'steely courage that is all the more remarkable in an avowedly sensitive nature'.[4] Newman was fully aware that his polemical skills were highly developed and largely influenced what he chose to write about. He told W. G. Ward, who had enquired whether, as rumoured, he was writing a book on the doctrine of papal infallibility: 'I am a controversialist not a theologian.'[5]

Involvement in controversy often brought Newman great personal distress, as with the Achilli case, but he bore this suffering with patience, especially when his reputation was assailed on all sides. Only his private correspondence and his journal reveal the depth of his feelings and disappointments. While, however, this 'remotely intellectual and almost introspective' figure may to some 'have seemed altogether too subtle and refined, even old-maidish' for the tough job of 'militant apologetics',[6] any such assessments of Newman were soon shown to be superficial. He entered the arena

and achieved a reputation for his devastating satirical wit and rhetorical skills. As Chadwick observed: as an Anglican, Newman had
'slaughtered the Roman Catholic Church with scorn and satire. As a
new Roman Catholic he slaughtered the Church of England with scorn
and satire, he whipped Achilli and trampled upon ... Kingsley'.[7]

An historic occasion for the resurgent Catholic Church in England
occurred when the first Provincial Synod of Westminster was held in
July 1852, at Oscott. At the opening of the second session, Newman
delivered a sermon which was later published as *The Second Spring*.
This sermon celebrated the re-establishment of the Catholic hierarchy
and the growth of the Catholic Church with what Ker describes as 'an
exuberant, even (to modern ears) embarrassing triumphalism'.[8] Some
other writers have been less inhibited in their praise of Newman's
rhetoric. Gwynn said that the sermon 'expressed most vividly the feelings of all those present, in one of the most memorable discourses
ever written ... The eloquence and music of his style rose superbly as
he described the ending of that winter and the return of spring' for
English Catholics.[9] For Norman, some of Newman's *Second Spring*
was 'rhetorical embellishment, the justifiable exultation of those who
had crossed to Rome, and landed more safely upon her shores than
they could have expected; it was the relief of ancient families whose
recusancy was at last no longer the whispered tradition of the rural
English catacombs'.[10]

Chadwick says that while *Second Spring* expressed 'the euphoria
which was felt in all the Churches', it was Newman's most eloquent
(though far from his best) sermon.[11] Gilley, however, has serious
reservations. While Newman's 'evocation of the present perfectly
captured the mood of the moment among the Oscott Fathers', Gilley
describes the sermon as 'the bane of English Catholic historiography
in its dim and dismal view of the vigorous if hidden Catholic life in
England in the previous three centuries'.[12] This irritation is understandable, for Newman's rhetoric tended at times to lose touch with
historical facts. For example, he alluded mournfully to the days when
Catholicism 'was not a body ... but a mere handful of individuals,
who might be counted like the pebbles and detritus of the great deluge
... a set of poor Irishmen, coming and going at harvest time, or a
colony of them lodged in a miserable quarter of the vast metropolis.
There, perhaps, an elderly person, seen walking in the streets, grave
and solitary, and strange, though noble in bearing, and said to be of
good family, and a "Roman Catholic"'.[13] Newman appeared to have

overlooked – or even ignored for the sake of his rhetoric – that Catholics in the early nineteenth century, as noted in the Prologue, were a coherent body of some size whose members practised their faith in a 'quiet style... in order to respect Protestant sensibilities'. Unfortunately, as Norman suggests, this secretive behaviour had 'something of a reverse effect' and led to suspicions of Catholicism.[14] The heightened emotional atmosphere generated by Newman's oratory overpowered both the preacher and his audience: 'When he came out from the Synod, they crowded upon him, giving full flow to the ardent outpourings of their gratitude.'[15]

Newman had preached this sermon shortly after he had been notified of the adverse verdict in the Achilli trial, because he had not been able, in the time available, to collect all the evidence necessary to prove his charges as we will later discuss. On hearing of the verdict, Wiseman had expressed 'amazement' and invited Newman to preach at the Synod. At the close of the Synod, Newman wrote to Henry Wilberforce: 'We ended the Synod yesterday in great triumph, joy and charity.'[16] The only other references in his *Letters and Diaries* to the Synod and to his sermon are three one-line diary notes recording his attendance and 'preached before the Synod'.[17]

In Birmingham, during 1851, Newman had delivered 'a set of lectures in which I made charges against Dr Achilli, a Dominican friar, who had become a convert to the Protestant faith, which involved me in an action for libel'.[18] These lectures were published as *Lectures on the Present Position of Catholics in England*. As Newman later told R. W. Church, he had 'ever considered' it as his 'best written book'.[19] Newman had heard Achilli was to visit Birmingham during a lecture tour organized by the 'respectable but fanatical' Evangelical Alliance.[20] This 'former Dominican friar had become a popular hero in London by exposing the scandals of the Roman Inquisition. He himself had already been exposed by Cardinal Wiseman in the *Dublin Review* as a person notorious in his own country for the crimes of rape and adultery'.[21] This article, which appeared in July 1850, was reprinted as a pamphlet. In the fifth lecture of his series, *The Logical Inconsistency of the Protestant View*, Newman inserted a denunciation of Achilli, in the belief that 'Wiseman had all the Italian documents necessary to prove what the Dublin Review asserted.'[22] Thus he declared with confidence that Achilli was 'not to be believed', as he behaviour over a period of twenty years clearly showed.[23]

Unfortunately for Newman, a rumour circulated that Achilli,

supported by the Evangelical Alliance, was going 'to prosecute me for what I said of him in Lecture 5, though I only repeated the Cardinal's words, which he let pass'.[24]

Newman wrote also to Dr Charles Russell of Maynooth asking him if he knew a Dominican priest of the same name, who is 'just come from Rome' and who may have some information about Achilli.[25]

Three days later Newman sent a Memorandum of the Achilli case to Edward Badeley: 'From the enclosed, I fear I shall be proceeded against. It will take the Catholic body utterly by surprise, and I trust I shall have their whole energy to get me evidence.'[26] Newman also asked Mgr Talbot in Rome for documents and other assistance in this 'most anxious matter'.[27] He was assured of help by these correspondents.[28] On 27 October 1851, Newman recorded in his diary, 'legal notice serviced on me by Achilli's lawyers'.[29] He approached Talbot again, asking him to send at once an attested copy of Achilli's confession, which he had mentioned in conversation.[30] He also requested Wiseman to provide the documents on which he had based his accusations in the *Dublin Review* of July 1850. The Cardinal promised to do so. Fathers John Gordon and Nicholas Darnell were sent to Italy to seek information about Achilli but their search was unsuccessful because they had not been given adequate instructions and introductions by the Cardinal. 'He has been in a daydream, now he is awakened, and everyone is horribly frightened and very busy, when two good months or rather three have been lost.'[31] Wiseman was, of course, immersed in church affairs and 'overwhelmed with public activities of every kind since the hierarchy was announced',[32] so it is not surprising that Newman's demands failed to have his exclusive attention. The vital documents had been mislaid and were discovered too late, as was the evidence from Rome, to be of effective use. 'Newman was crippled because he could not yet produce evidence to counter Achilli.'[33] He told James Hope that 'Our great difficulty is this, that *at present we have no one good piece of evidence in our hands* – we cannot get any thing, people are so dilatory. I believe there is good evidence, but I have nothing to show the lawyers.'[34] Sister Maria Giberne, who was a sister-in-law of the Revd Walter Mayers, Newman's old schoolmaster and friend and who became a Catholic in 1845, undertook, at Newman's request, a search for Italian witnesses of Achilli's scandalous behaviour. Eventually she located some and brought them to England and, as McGrath puts it, 'shepherded them during the trial'[35] Many, however, 'could not be traced or would not come'.[36] Newman pleaded for time to collect evidence but his plea was rejected and the trial fixed for February 1852,[37] on the serious charge of criminal libel. Meanwhile a national appeal had been opened by Wiseman to meet the costs of the trial. Donations flooded in to such an extent (nearly £13,000) that after disbursements, a sizeable surplus resulted, which Newman was to apply in building the University Church in Dublin.

After a 'series of portentous court hearings before the very anti-Catholic Chief Justice, Lord Campbell ... on the 24th June a verdict was given against Newman'.[38] Newman's lawyers sought a re-trial but this was refused, and on 31 January 1853, he was sentenced by Judge Sir John Taylor Coleridge to a fine of £100 and imprisonment until paid. Furthermore, he had to endure the public humiliation of a 'misjudged lecture' from Coleridge to the effect 'that he had deteriorated in character since he became a Roman Catholic'.[39] As Norman notes, 'Even *The Times* judged the court hearings prejudicial ... Newman had to endure a terrible sequence of events [from Achilli's continued lies] and his reputation sank to its lowest level in Protestant society.'[40] But despite his experiences, Newman felt able to reassure his friends: 'Of course the said fine was paid there and then and we walked off in triumph amid the hurrahs of 200 paddies.'[41] He told Mrs William Froude that Coleridge 'had committed a great mistake and impertinence in what he said ... his speech was full of mistakes and inconsistencies ... But I really think he was performing a duty'.[42]

The date of the trial remained long in Newman's mind, as may be seen from a letter to Mother Margaret Mary Hallahan on 31 January 1866: 'This day is the anniversary of my being had up for sentence in the Queen's Bench, before Judge Coleridge.'[43]

The Evangelical Alliance withdrew their sponsorship of Achilli and he went to New York and joined the Swedenborgian Church. So ended this sordid episode, but until the later years of the nineteenth century, 'The lectures of ex-priests or allegedly ex-priests were apparently a fashionable past-time for the Victorians, for as many as twenty such persons were plying their trade throughout England.'[44]

Shortly after the Oratory School was founded, Newman was entailed in another controversy. This arose from an article that he had written in the July 1859 issue of the *Rambler*. This Catholic journal had been launched by John Moores Capes, a Balliol convert, in 1848, with the approval of his Vicar Apostolic, Ullathorne. When Capes was planning the journal he asked Newman for his views and possible assistance. Newman thought: 'such a magazine as you propose is very much wanted', although he could 'not contribute at present because of earlier commitments'. Furthermore, he would like Wiseman 'to give his formal approval of the project before I promised to assist'.[45] This letter was followed by another the next day, in which Newman told Capes to be prepared for 'anxiety arising from the work being written by *converts* only or principally'. There was also the problem of distribution which, Newman recalled, was 'almost fatal to the Tracts' and took 'some years to overcome'.[46]

Its contributors, for the most part, were well-educated lay converts who tended to have outspoken views across a wide range of topics, including freedom to criticize the acts of the English Catholic bishops.[47] This independent editorial policy became even more pronounced when an Oriel convert, Richard Simpson, was appointed assistant editor in 1854. The *Rambler's* 'latitudinarian spirit manifested by Simpson' caused Ullathorne to write to Newman in 1856 expressing his concern.[48] In 1858, Sir John Acton – 'Döllinger's brilliant pupil[49] – became part-proprietor of the *Rambler*, and Simpson was made editor. The journal continued its policy of free discussion of fields, including theology, to the increasing annoyance of the Catholic hierarchy. According to Ward, the readers of the *Rambler* included 'English country gentry and clergy ... descendants of the persecuted Roman Catholics long excluded from the universities and from public life, or High Church convert clergymen, few of whom were sensitive to intellectual interests' and who 'in their piety and religious instincts were startled at the manner adopted by the *Rambler*'.[50] Although the journal's circulation was only about 800, 'its influence was out of all proportion'.[51]

Matters came to a head when the January and February 1859 issues of the journal contained criticisms of the hostile attitude taken by the Catholic hierarchy to a Royal Commission on elementary education. It was suspected by the bishops that co-operation with the government would lead to interference with the methods of religious teaching in Catholic schools.[52] This unfavourable comment on the Catholic hierarchy's reaction was anonymous. It had, however, been contributed by one of the Catholic Inspectors of Schools who was the leading lay authority on Catholic education, Scott Nasmyth Stokes.

Ullathorne, on behalf of Wiseman and the other bishops, told Newman that it was their unanimous opinion that 'something must be done'[53] about the *Rambler*, and that 'nothing short of Mr Simpson's retiring from the editorship will satisfy'.[54]

Newman at once wrote to Simpson expressing his concern that the 'Bishops are determined to act very promptly and severely, on, he believed, instructions from Rome, about the *Rambler*. He warned that they might openly censure the journal, and even forbid the clergy to read it'.[55] Simpson replied that he would be willing to place the 'whole of the *Rambler*' in Newman's hands. In turn, Newman reported to Ullathorne: 'I did not hesitate to recommend at once the course to which your letters directed me, viz. his ceasing to be Editor'.[56] Newman was glad to console Simpson with the news that Ullathorne was 'so much edified and please' by the way in which he had responded to the concerns expressed over the *Rambler* by the hierarchy.[57] Now there arose the problem of finding a new editor who would be acceptable to the bishops and also to the owners of the journal.

Newman accepted, although reluctantly, Acton's invitation 'to be editor . . . for a while'.[58] This decision was approved by Wiseman and Ullathorne. Newman issued an 'Advertisement' with the May issue of the *Rambler* stating that its editorial aims were 'to combine devotion to the Church with discrimination and candour in the treatment of her opponents; for the refinement, enlargement and elevation of the intellect of the educated classes, etc.'. Coverage would be 'a manly investigation of public interest under a deep sense of the prerogatives of ecclesiastical authority'.[59] Publication would be bi-monthly to allow extended discussion of topics. In Coulson's words, 'his short term policy was to take it out of the front line of controversy'.[60]

Newman's editorship was to be brief and turbulent, for in his very first issue he offended Wiseman and the rest of the Catholic hierarchy by defending Stokes, whose article on education had already annoyed them. While apologizing for the earlier criticisms of the bishops, Newman suggested that 'their Lordships really desire to know the opinions of the laity on subjects in which the laity are especially concerned'.[61] This opinion further incensed the bishops; Ullathorne called on Newman and 'expressed a wish that I should give up the *Rambler* after the July number'.[62] As Dessain remarks, the result was that Newman stopped the Tracts for the Times at 'a word from his Anglican bishop. He resigned the *Rambler* at Ullathorne's wish'.[63] Newman's Memorandum regarding Ullathorne's visit gives insight into the bishop's views: 'Our Laity were a peaceful set, the Church was *peace*. They had a deep faith they did not like to hear that any one doubted.' Newman responded that he saw one side only, the bishop another – 'that the bishop, etc., did not see the state of the laity (etc) in Ireland – how unsettled, yet how docile'. To which Ullathorne 'said something like, "Who are the Laity?" I answered that the Church would look foolish without them – *not* those words'.[64] Some years earlier, Newman had referred to Ullathorne's 'horror of laymen' and remarked that he himself was 'sure that they may be in this day the strength of the Church'.[65] In Ullathorne's opinion, according to Gilley, 'the Church teaching, the *ecclesia docens*, meant the clergy; and this *ecclesia docens* was not the laity, who were merely the passive *ecclesia docta,* the Church taught'.[66]

Newman reflected sadly to Wilberforce: 'All through my life I have been plucked ... it made me feel that my occupation was gone when the Bishop [Ullathorne] put his extinguisher on the *Rambler*.'[67]

Newman's final edition of the *Rambler*, in July 1859, added coals to the fire that he had already set alight when he developed the theme of asking the opinions of the laity in an essay entitled *On Consulting the Faithful in Matters of Doctrine*. In this essay he stressed the significance of the united testimony of the faithful, the *consensus fidelium* – which involves both clergy and laity. 'This had been very fully done in the case of the definition of the Immaculate Conception, 1854'.[68] Dessain comments:

> Newman laid great stress on the consent of the faithful ... [which] was more than a witness to the truth ... The Church was a Communion, with a common conscience, that all of its members, and was not to be looked on as a mere juridical entity, ruled by officers. Bishops, priests and laity formed one body, and there must be consultation and trust, for the laity was an essential part of the Church.

This teaching was to be incorporated in the Conciliar Decree on the Church at the Second Vatican Council. Although Newman's original declaration was resented by English Catholic theologians and authorities, 'no-one was in a position to dispute Newman's facts'.[69]

Some misunderstandings arose, however, over Newman's use of the term 'consulting'. Objections were raised, for example, by Dr John Gillow of Ushaw Seminary, to whom Newman explained,

> Doubtless had the passage been in Latin and formally dogmatic, 'consult' was not the word to have used. But in popular English it seems to me neither inaccurate nor dangerous. To the unlearned reader, the idea conveyed by 'consulting' is not necessarily that of asking an opinion. For

instance, we speak of consulting a barometer about the weather. The barometer does not give us an opinion, but ascertains for us a fact ... I had not a dream of understanding the word, as used in the Rambler, in the sense of *asking an opinion*.[70]

Gillow accepted Newman's explanation, 'It is most gratifying that there is not a shadow of difference between us on any point of principle.'[71] However, the matter was not to rest with this exchange of personal letters. On 3 October 1859, Bishop Brown of Newport complained to the Congregation of Propaganda at Rome about a 'most unfortunate essay published in July last in the *Rambler*'.[72] In his delation to Propaganda, the bishop wrote disapprovingly of 'a great proportion of the converted clergy' who 'join in considerable numbers the Oratory of Dr Newman in Birmingham, or that of Dr Faber in London, neither of which have I believe more than one of the original Catholics among them, so that there is a great danger of certain Protestant motives and feelings being fostered'.[73] This 'very grave matter'[74] was referred to by Cardinal Barnabo, Prefect of Propaganda, who asked Ullathorne – who was on a visit to Rome – for an explanation of Newman's article. On his return to England, Ullathorne saw Newman and sought an explanation. Newman was prepared to give this and drafted a letter to Wiseman, asking for specific details of the passages on which Propaganda sought elucidation. This letter was shown to Ullathorne and then sent to Rome via Wiseman.[75] A schedule of the statements in the *Rambler* requiring explanation was presented to Wiseman by Propaganda but this was never sent on to Newman. This omission resulted in a serious misunderstanding in Rome about Newman's behaviour and, as Dessain says, 'it was concluded and thought for years that Newman had refused to comply'.[76] As Trevor puts it, 'At Propaganda Newman continued to be regarded as a writer of heretical articles who did not trouble to defend himself and who was responsible for all the views printed in the *Rambler*.'[77] Since Newman had kept silence and had heard nothing more from Rome he thought 'the whole matter was hushed up', as he told one of his trusted friends, Miss E. Bowles.[78] It was not until 1867, when Ambrose St John showed Barnabo a copy of Newman's letter to Wiseman that this unfortunate matter was cleared up and Newman's reputation was restored.[79]

The passages in the *Rambler* article requiring elucidation were later pointed out to Newman and, according to Butler, 'he wrote a theological explanation which was accepted as satisfactory'.[80] Speculations about the reasons why this lamentable misconception arose have been various. For Butler, 'the thing was but a piece of unfortunate bungling, for which Wiseman must take the principal blame, but neither Manning nor Talbot can be acquitted of a share in the responsibility'.[81] 'Wiseman's negligence' is explained by Gilley on the grounds that 'he was suffering from the onset of diabetes, and was preoccupied with the Errington affair' – a controversy over his likely successor at Westminster – 'as well as by his legendary inefficiency'. But neither could Manning be absolved. He was said to be 'open to the charge of finding it convenient to leave Newman under suspicion'.[82]

After July 1859 when Newman had relinquished the editorship of the *Rambler*, Acton and Simpson resumed editorial responsibilities. They tended to ignore his advice to 'keep off theology proper and to avoid conflicts with the ecclesiastical authorities and all irritation of average Catholic opinion'.[83] Eventually, complaints from Rome in May 1862, led to the English bishops condemning the *Rambler* and its successor *Home and Foreign Review*, a quarterly which had just been launched. Newman expressed his gratitude to his bishop for the 'clear and direct way' he had stated his objections and with which he 'concurred with all his heart'.[84] Ullathorne acknowledged Newman's support very affably, and sent a copy of his letter to Wiseman. This was shown to Manning who 'read it with great thankfulness: not that I doubted what he [Newman] would say, but I feared that he would not say it. He has a sort of sensitiveness about standing by his friends even when in the wrong which is very honourable to his generosity'.[85]

In a letter dated 1 January 1863, Ullathorne referred again to Newman's letter supporting the action he had taken on the *Rambler* and *Home and Foreign Review*. As promised, Ullathorne had sent a copy of the letter to Talbot and asked him 'to show it to the Pope in confirmation of what I had previously said to His Holiness'. Talbot confirmed that he had done as Ullathorne requested, adding that 'it would remove the remainder of whatever cloud might have been hanging about'.[86] The *Home and Foreign Review* ceased publication after only eight issues.

Newman recorded in his journal that the reason why he had not written from 1859 to 1864 was his 'failure with the *Rambler*'. He thought that he had 'got into a scrape, and it became one to be silent. So they thought in Rome, if Mgr Talbot is to be their spokesman'.[87]

Newman's silence was broken by an unexpected controversy with Charles Kingsley, Regius Professor of Modern History at Cambridge, the rector of Eversley, and a popular novelist. Kingsley's unprovoked attack was unpleasant and, in Chadwick's view, it attempted to capitalize on 'Newman's low reputation. For part of public opinion Newman was one, who had been a secret Roman Catholic while he was an Anglican priest and therefore was associated with underhand behaviour'.[88]

The conflict arose from a review in the January 1864 issue of *Macmillan's Magazine* of some volumes of a history of England by James Arthur Froude, a younger brother of Hurrell, and known for his anti-Catholic feelings.[89] A copy of the review, which appeared under the initials 'CK' was sent, anonymously, to Newman (the sender was later identified as William Pope when he wrote to Newman) ,[90] who protested to the publishers that he had been accused of teaching that truth for its own sake need not, and on the whole ought not to be, a virtue with the Roman clergy. This serious allegation was unsupported by any evidence from his writings. Newman emphasized that he was not seeking reparation, but merely wished to draw the attention of the publishers to a 'grave and gratuitous slander'.[91] To Newman's amazement, Kingsley wrote acknowledging authorship of the review, and stating that his 'words were just' and 'expressly referred to one of Newman's sermons on "Subjects of the Day", published in 1844'. He offered to retract publicly his accusation if he had misunderstood Newman's meaning.[92] Newman responded that the sermon in question was given, and published, when he was an Anglican and vicar of St Mary's, Oxford, and no statement, such as that made in the review, occurred in that sermon.[93]

In a pleasant exchange of letters with Macmillans, Newman conceded that if he 'were in active controversy with the Anglican body, or any portion of it', as he 'had been before now', he should 'consider untrue assertions about me to be in a certain rule of the game, as times go, though God forbid that I should indulge them in the case of another. I have never been very sensitive of such attacks; rarely taken notice of them'. But sometimes he was sent examples of such attacks and 'sometimes they are such as I am bound to answer'.[94] Thereupon, Kingsley sent Newman a draft of the apology he had submitted to his publishers, adding that this was 'the only course fit for a gentleman'.[95] Newman referred the 'apology' to his lawyer friend, Edward Badeley, who considered it 'totally inadequate'.[96] It contained the words: 'No man knows the use of words better than Dr Newman. No man, therefore, has a better right to define what he does, or does not, mean by them.'[97] In a letter to Kingsley, Newman declared that the main fault of the proposed apology was that it 'would lead the general reader' to believe that he 'had been confronted with definite extracts from his works' to support the allegations made in Kingsley's criticism of him.[98] Newman also wrote again to Macmillans about the review, 'which I considered a great affront to myself, and a worse insult to the Catholic priesthood'. He pointed out that as Kingsley's draft apology ignored his principal objections, he had no hesitation in rejecting it.[99]

As he had earlier intimated to the publishers, Newman then arranged to publish the correspondence, preceded by a long extract from Kingsley's review and with the addition of *Reflections* which, with devastating satire, commented on Kingsley's letters.[100] This pamphlet, *Mr Kingsley and Dr Newman: A Correspondence on the Question whether Dr Newman teaches that Truth is not Virtue*, appeared on 12 February 1864.[101] It caused a sensation and aroused much previously latent sympathy for Newman among English Catholics, including many of the clergy as well as laity. Among well-known journalists who supported Newman was Richard Holt Hutton, editor of the *Spectator* and a former Unitarian who had become an Anglican. He wrote an article, *Father Newman's Sarcasm* (20 February 1864), in which he referred to Newman as 'not only one of the greatest of English writers, but, perhaps, the very greatest master of delicate and polished sarcasm in the English language ... Mr Kingsley is a choice though, perhaps too helpless a victim for the full exercise of Father Newman's powers'.[102]

Kingsley was stung by this and 'proceeded to make his case a great deal worse'[103] by publishing, on 20 March, *What then does Dr Newman mean?* This 'proved to be both violent and unscientific in its numerous charges'[104] and according to Maisie Ward was a 'complicated tissue woven out of half truths and entire falsehoods'.[105] Oddie's view is that Kingsley's accusation was not a 'careless mistake' but, on the contrary, 'the result of a long and deeply-felt distaste for the Catholic religion and for Newman personally'.[106]

Newman had been reflecting on the grave but unsubstantiated charges made by a prominent public figure against him and the Catholic priesthood, and he began to recognize the need to develop a well-argued defence of his life and activities. A decade or so later, he wrote that Kingsley had been 'accidentally the instrument in the good Providence of God, by whom I had an opportunity given me which otherwise I should not have had, of vindicating my character and conduct in my *Apologia*'.[107] At the time he had confided to Church that 'it had always been on my mind that some day I should be called on to defend my honesty while in the Church of England'. He had been publicly challenged by Kingsley – 'a furious fellow' – so he must speak, 'unless I speak strongly, men won't believe me in earnest'.[108] He told Copeland,

I am writing my answer to Kingsley's pamphlet, and this is what I think. The whole strength of what he says, *as directed rhetorically* to the popular mind, lies in the antecedent prejudice that I *was a Papist while I was an Anglican*. Mr K. *implies this*. The only way I can destroy this, is to give my history, and the history of my mind, from 1822 or earlier, down to 1845.[109]

After Easter, Newman started to assemble some of his relevant papers, and he also asked his old Anglican friends, such as Church, Keble, Rogers, and Copeland and also his sister Jemima, to lend him letters, which they gladly did. Chadwick notes that

Without intending to write this book, he prepared to write it for three or four years ... when his entire life was challenged, he hardly needed to think what to say. Almost all the material lay at his fingertips.[110] This was also the view of an earlier writer on Newman, who said that there already lay in Newman's mind a series of long-standing, though dormant, unrelated, thoughts and attitudes which were capable potentially of combining for action, let the right stimulus occur.[111]

Newman thanked Richard Hutton for an article in the *Spectator,* 26 March, *Roman Casuistry and Protestant Prejudice*, in which Kingsley's pamphlet *What, then, does Dr Newman mean?*, was dismissed as 'aggravating the original injustice a hundredfold'. He assured Hutton that 'It is impossible not to feel that you have uttered on the whole what I should say of myself, and to see that you have done me a great service in doing so, as bearing external testimony.'[112]

Newman got down quickly to writing the *Apologia pro Vita Sua.* Sencourt says that 'He wrote with a concentration of effort, passion and genius kindred to that with which he had written at Littlemore nineteen and twenty years before.'[113] He worked long hours, 'sometimes at my

work for 16 hours running'.[114] He informed Sir John Acton that 'I am
writing from morning till night, and against time, which is not pleasant.'[115] By mid-June the *Apologia* was written and, as he told Canon J.
Walker, an old friend and parish priest of Scarborough who he
had met at Ushaw in 1846, 'At length I am a free man ... I have had a
terrible time of it, not only from the extreme stress of my work, but from
my great anxiety, and also for the special trial it has been to my
feelings.'[116]

The *Apologia* first appeared in weekly parts on the seven Thursdays
from 21 April to 1 June 1864, with the title *Apologia pro Vita Sua
being a reply to a pamphlet entitled 'What then does Dr Newman
mean?'*[117]

Dr Charles Russell wrote appreciatively of the 'immense impression
the Parts of the *Apologia* were making'. In thanking him for his
encouragement, Newman also recalled the 'real benefits which you
did me in my anxieties 20 years ago' which showed his 'great sympathy for others'.[118] The Prioress of Stone Convent, Sister Mary Imelda
Poole, also wrote saying that the *Apologia* was arousing 'intense interest among the converts in the community'. Newman told her that at
times he was at the point of despair when writing it. 'At other times,
the feeling was, as I expressed it to those around me, as if I were
ploughing in very stiff clay. It was moving on at the rate of a mile an
hour, when I had to write and print and correct a hundred miles by the
next day's post.'[119] To another correspondent Newman admitted:

> I have said to myself , that, if any one of name did make a formal attack
> on me, I would accept the challenge – but I never fancied that I should
> meet with more than that casual pelting, as if from idle boys who shie
> stones, which had so long been going on – But, sure enough, on came Mr
> K's pamphlet ...[120]

The Liberal MP, John Duke Coleridge – who was to become an
admirer and a close friend – wrote thanking Newman 'with all my
heart for the writing and publishing of your *Apologia*'. In acknowledgement, Newman told him that he had taken Kingsley's views as
'representing large classes of men who habitually thought as he spoke;
and I found the effect of this pamphlet as authenticating a floating
tradition, the tradition of thirty years'. Kingsley was 're-kindling slanders'. He had stirred up latent bigotry 'without an effort'.[121]

In May 1865, Newman brought out a second definitive edition of the *Apologia* which omitted the first two polemical sections against Kingsley.[122] Maisie Ward describes the omitted passages as 'journalism, and out of place when the book had taken its permanent form',[123] and Chadwick judges that 'some epigrams against Kingsley were more cheap than worthy'.[124] Newman also inserted a short preface and re-titled the volume simply as *History of my Religious Opinions*. In 1873, the original title was restored with an additional subtitle, *Being a History of Religious Opinions*. As Chadwick points out, the contents of the *Apologia* were 'somewhat changed in successive editions with a view to meeting important critics'.[125] Certain Catholic critics, for example, had regarded some of Newman's remarks about the Church of England offensive, and he modified them.[126] But he told another ecclesiastical critic, 'I have altered only with the purpose of expressing my own meaning more exactly'.[127]

Kingsley was in France while the *Apologia* was appearing and on returning he sent Macmillans an 'ultimatum on the Newman question which could be shown, privately, to any and every one you like'. It was an unrepentant endorsement of what he had written earlier, remarkable only for its bitter animosity and invective. He declared:

> I cannot be weak enough to put myself a second time, by any fresh act of courtesy, into the power of one who, like a treacherous ape, lifts up to you meek and suppliant eyes, till he thinks he has you within his reach, and then springs, gibbering and biting, at your face.[128]

But when, just over ten years later, Newman heard of Kingsley's 'so premature death', he wrote that he was 'shocked' and added that 'I never from the first felt any anger towards him. As I said in the first pages of the *Apologia*, it is very difficult to be angry with a man one has not seen.'[129]

In the early part of 1875, a woman novelist – Geraldine Fitzgerald – had informed Newman, in the course of a letter about her problems with publishers, that she had once met Kingsley in Chester, and he had expressed no feelings of resentment against Newman. Newman assured her that he also had none against Kingsley, who 'lately had softened in his opinions – especially, to the surprise of his theological friends, he stood up for the Athanasian Creed'.[130]

In his journal Newman noted that 1864 had been 'marvellously blest, for which I have regained, or rather gained, the favour of Protestants, I have received the approbation, in formal addresses, of a good part of

the English clerical body ... Then again it has pleased Protestants, and
of all parties, as much or more'.[131] In Chadwick's judgement,
Newman's *Apologia* did more than clear himself of the charge that he
did not care for truth; it 'persuaded Protestants that the Roman
Catholic Church cared for truth'.[132] Once more, Newman became a
well-known and respected figure to whom 'men and women of all religions and none turned to for guidance'.[133] Non-Catholics appreciated
the fairness and historical accuracy with which Newman discussed his
Anglican days, and his obvious respect and warm feelings for the
Church of England were reflected in the *Apologia*. Coulson states that
the work made clear that Newman's move to Rome 'did not imply a
wholesale repudiation of the tradition in which he had been formed but
rather its affirmation in what Newman came to regard as its legitimate
setting'.[134] This fits in with what he had written to Canon E. Estcourt a
few years earlier when he had declared that 'Catholics did not make us
Catholics; Oxford made us Catholics.'[135] His generous references to
the Church of his early life warmed Anglican hearts; they had not
expected a Roman convert to acknowledge publicly and with affection
the influence of the Church of England in his spiritual odyssey.[136] As
Norman points out, Manning and fellow Ultramontanes bristled at
Newman's references to Anglicanism as 'capable of authentic spirituality'[137] and Newman himself was aware that, for some years, he was
regarded with suspicion by the Roman authorities as well as by sections
of the Catholic community in England.[138] While Ullathorne voiced the
general approbation of Catholics, Butler notes that these feelings were
not shared by 'the Manning group, whose antagonism to Newman had
by this date become definite and pronounced'. They were 'little
pleased' by the prestige which the *Apologia* brought to him.[139] In a
letter to Hope-Scott, Newman revealed his awareness of certain hostile
attitudes towards him:

> As to my writing more, speaking in confidence I do not know how to do
> it. One cannot speak ten words without ten objections being made to each
> ... I never can be sure that great lies may not be told about me at Rome.

There had indeed been some rumours that he had been about to leave
the Church. Mgr Talbot 'put it about that I had subscribed to
Garibaldi'. He knew well enough 'how the movement against me in
Rome began, in 1855', and he alluded to the correspondence between
London Oratory and Propaganda against him.[140]

The *Apologia* is not readily classifiable. Griffin describes it as 'in part a chronicle of Newman's own perplexities'.[141] It has also been popularly referred to as Newman's spiritual autobiography, although he did not describe it so himself.[142] It is, as Oddie states, 'notably deficient in the usual biographical details' to qualify as an autobiography, but in Ker's opinion, it is essentially an autobiography, 'an austerely intellectual work', as its subtitle indicates. He agrees that it is often called a 'spiritual' autobiography, but points out that 'in the strictly narrow sense of the word it is very far from being a spiritual work like St Augustine's Confessions, with which it often compared'.[143] Earlier, the same writer described the *Apologia* as 'an intellectual – rather, theological – autobiography'.[144] In a preface to an edition of the *Apologia*, Ker states that it 'stands clearly within a recognizable genre' and was influenced by the English Protestant autobiographical traditions of conversion originated by Bunyan and followed by the Evangelical Thomas Scott.[145] Gilley, however, considers a central portion of the *Apologia* (parts III–VI) 'hardly critical autobiography'; rather, it is the 'spiritual romance of a soul in its loves and hates, and though the facts as Newman reported them were coloured and occasionally distorted by his imagination, the work convinced not so much by its truthfulness as by its obvious allegiance to the spirit of truth, a burning sincerity'.[146]

Chadwick expresses a similar view when he writes that Newman 'must convince the public of his sincerity because it was his sincerity which was challenged, and the book is manifestly true'.[147] This evaluation seems to uphold the comment of an earlier writer, namely that although the title *Apologia* suggests 'consciously intended distortion', after 'examination of his private letters and diaries, and his published works, and the comments of contemporary friends and enemies, we come away convinced that the picture is substantially true. Of course it is shaded a little ... The admirable thing is that under the circumstances Newman deviated so little from the truth'.[148] In a reflective view of Newman's text, a modern writer, A. N. Wilson, states that,

> As a religious treatise, the *Apologia* must be one of the most paradoxical documents in the history of the world ... It describes how Newman came to an unequivocal faith in the Roman Catholic religion ... Yet as every page in the *Apologia* makes clear, Newman was guided by something more mysterious than argument.[149]

Newman himself said that the *Apologia* was not a history of the Oxford Movement but of himself: 'it is an egotistical matter from beginning to end. It is to prove that I did not act *dishonourably*'.[150]

While immersed in the Kingsley controversy, Newman had been seized with 'a very vivid apprehension of immediately impending death, apparently derived from a medical opinion'.[151] After the *Apologia* had been published, and on a sudden inspiration, he started writing, on 17 January 1865, what was to be his longest and most successful poem: *The Dream of Gerontius*, which was completed the following month. As he told a close friend: 'I wrote on till it was finished, on small bits of paper. And I could no more write with any thing else by willing it, than I could fly.'[152] Apparently, when Newman had completed the poem, he put it to one side and it was only when he was asked to contribute to the journal *Month*, founded by Fanny Margaret Taylor in 1864 for 'educated readers', that he unearthed it and sent it for publication. After a year the journal was taken over by the Jesuits and edited by Newman's friend Fr Henry Coleridge, and *The Dream of Gerontius* appeared under his editorship during April and May 1865.

With poetic intensity and religious fervour, *The Dream of Gerontius* described the passage of the faithful Christian soul from this world to its eternal destiny. 'It pierces, indeed, beyond the veil, but in strict accordance or analogy with what every Catholic holds to be there . . . [it is] at once an allegory and an act of faith'.[153]

The 'other-worldliness' of *The Dream* attracted immediate attention (Newman had once belonged to a study group in Oxford, which was set up in 1829 in line with the popular vogue for prophetical speculation about millennial expectations).[154] In 1868, *Hymns Ancient and Modern* included the anthem 'Praise to the Holiest in the height' from the 'Fifth Choir of Angelicals' in *The Dream*. The poem was widely read – even the ill-fated General Gordon had an annotated copy with him at Khartoum in the 1880s.[155]

The Bishop of Newport, now one of Newman's admirers, wrote a warm personal letter saying that he had been moved to tears when reading Newman's poem to the Benedictine nuns of Colwich Priory in Staffordshire. Newman thanked the bishop: 'It is a great gratification to me to receive your Lordship's approbation on any thing which I have written.'[156] The irony of this observation is apparent to those who recall Newman's earlier problems with this prelate. Newman sent Mother Mary Hallahan three copies of *The Dream of Gerontius*, mentioning that he was recovering from illness and wrote with diffi-culty.[157] In his opinion, Newman told Lady Chatterton, Catholics are 'not unpoetical – but English Catholics are for the most part poor and uneducated – and have neither the money nor the taste to provide themselves with books of poetry'. He believed that *Gerontius* sold not for its versification but because it dealt with a *religious* subject, 'which appeals strongly to the feelings of every one'.[158]

In April 1885, Mrs Mary Murphy of Dublin sent Newman a copy of the small edition of *The Dream of Gerontius*, which her late brother Frank Power, a *Times* correspondent at Khartoum, had been given by General Gordon, soon after he had arrived there. There was 'pencil marking through the book done by General Gordon himself'. As requested, Newman returned the book 'with heartfelt thanks'.[159] This annotated copy of *Gerontius* seems to have been presented by Laurence Dillon to Manchester Free Library in September 1888.[160] In a letter date 19 May 1885, to his old friend Frederic Rogers (ennobled as Baron Blachford in 1871), Newman ranged widely over political events, and then closed with a reference to Gordon: 'What struck me so much in his use of *The Dream* was that in St Paul's words he "died daily" – he was always on his death bed, fulfilling the common advice that we should ever pass the day, as if it was to be our last.'[161]

But it was not until Elgar set Newman's poem to music in his Orato-rio, first performed in 1900, that it achieved national recognition. Gilley has commented that to modern sensibilities the 'frank Christian eschatology' of the words of the oratorio 'must sound even more odd than most sacred music to secular sensibilities'.[162]

In September 1865, Pusey sent Newman a copy of a book that he had written whose extended title suggested a peace-offering: *The Church of England a Portion of Christ's One Holy Catholic Church and a Means of Restoring Visible Unity, an Eirenicon, in a letter addressed to the author of the Christian Year*. It was thus ostensibly addressed to John Keble. This publication resulted from a controversy between Manning and Pusey. The former had published the *Workings of the Holy Spirit in the Church of England, a Letter to the Rev. E. B. Pusey* at the end of 1864. In friendly terms it acknowledges the 'great religious wave and outpouring of grace' being experienced by individ-ual members of the Christian community, irrespective of their affilia-tions, but nevertheless maintains, as Butler puts it, that 'the Church of England is in no part of the Church Catholic and in the strictest sense no Church at all'.[163] Pusey had attacked what he alleged were extravagances in the Catholic doctrine and devotion relating to the Blessed Virgin Mary, and also to the infallibility of the Pope (even though the doctrine of papal infallibility was not defined as such until 1870). Pusey's plea for peace and unity between the Churches was, however, curiously designed, for, as Chadwick notes, he 'spent most of the time telling the world what were the main obstacles to unity, which were the errors of the Church of Rome, and therefore his olive branch looked, as Newman said, as though it were 'discharged from a catapult'.[164]

Newman was reluctant to become involved in this controversy, and told Pusey that he felt he had no 'imperative duty to remark on anything you said in your book. I dare say there is a great deal on which I should agree'.[165] This detached view was soon to be discarded for a rigorous response, presumably provoked by reading the book in detail. Newman then wrote,

> It is true, too true, that your book disappointed me. It does seem to me that Irenicon [sic] is a misnomer; and that it is calculated to make most Catholics very angry – and that is because they will consider it rhetorical and unfair ... An Irenicon smoothes difficulties; I am sure people will think that you increase them.

People were saying that Pusey's book was an *attack* on Rome, as the *Guardian* had observed, in his references to 'the cultus of the BVM'.[166]

Newman had told Keble:

> I really marvel that he [Pusey] should have dreamed of calling it an Irenicon – it is said 'If he ask (for) bread, will he give him a stone? or if he ask (for) fish will he give him a serpent? or if he ask (for) an egg, will he give him a scorpion?' I grieve to use such an illustration – But so it is – Pusey's book looks far more like an *argumentum ad hominem* ... Certain, I am, that as an Irenicon, it can only raise a smile – and I wish that were all it would raise.[167]

To these intense feelings, Keble responded with typical gentleness when he wrote that Newman was 'too kind to me, but hardly kind enough to Pusey', and argued that Pusey was 'just amplifying and carrying out the idea in Number 90 (Tract 90), on which his whole book is grounded'.[168] Newman replied that he may be quite sure that 'he would not write to Pusey as freely as I have written to you ... I wish an Irenicon as much as you or any one else, but Pusey's book is a great disappointment ...'[169]

In reply, Pusey avowed that he had 'no intention of attacking anything'. He wished 'the official teaching of the Church [of England] alone to be of obligation and the popular manifestations of devotion to the BVM to be disowned'.[170] Newman commented on this that 'If I am led to publish any thing (of which I have no present intention) I should treat the book simply as an Irenicon [sic], as you wish.'[171]

Newman wrote, on 19 November 1865, to the editor of *The Weekly Register* about an 'admirable review' of 'Dr Pusey's recent work which had appeared' in that journal. This 'asserted by implication' that the 'Church of England is, in God's hands, the great Bulwark against infidelity in this land', and that this was 'originally enunciated by Dr Newman'. He declared that he had written more in his lifetime than he could remember, but ... 'I neither know where I have made this particular statement, nor can I conceive I ever made it ... Certainly it does not express my real judgement concerning the Church of England. Nor have I any reason to think that Dr Pusey ascribed it to me'. Newman pointed out that what he had said in the *Apologia* was: 'Doubtless the National Church has hitherto been a serviceable breakwater against doctrinal errors more fundamental than its own.' Newman explained that the words 'serviceable' and 'break-water' 'both convey the idea of something accidental and *de facto*; whereas bulwark is an essential part of the thing defended'. He added that the reference to 'against doctrinal errors more fundamental than its own' implied 'that, which it happens to serve Catholic truth in one respect, nevertheless in another it has doctrinal errors, and those fundamental'.[172]

Fr H. J. Coleridge, SJ invited Newman's views on a proposal to 'get up a set of Essays ... on a subject *raised* by the Eirenicon, without attacking Dr Pusey where it can be helped'.[173] Although Newman thought the proposal to be 'very seasonable', he 'would not write even indirectly against Pusey anonymously'. At the same time, he agreed that Pusey's work 'is calculated to raise indignation – especially when considered as Irenicon', although he 'verily believed' that Pusey meant it as such. He thought that a 'large body in the Anglican church are growing towards us', so nothing should be done which might 'throw back' that movement.[174]

Over the next few weeks several letters were exchanged, culminating in one in which Newman told Pusey that he intended to 'publish a

Letter on your Irenicon. I wish to accept it as such and shall write in
that spirit'. He wished to correct any misapprehensions that may have
arisen about Pusey's book.[175] Newman also advised Keble of his intention , adding that Pusey's book 'has made people very angry'.[176]
Pusey responded at once 'as you said of me, "I am safe in your
hands"'.[177]

Newman told Pusey, on 19 January 1866, that he had asked Riving-
tons, the publishers, to send him copies of the proofs of his rejoinder
to the Irenicon. He also mentioned that he had written to Keble to say
that he hoped that he had not written anything 'which would pain him
or you'.[178]

Despite illness Newman completed *A Letter to the Rev. E. B. Pusey
DD on his recent Eirenicon* on 8 December 1865, the feast of the
Immaculate Conception of the BVM, and it was published on 31
January 1866. It sold 2,000 copies in a fortnight. Newman limited
discussion to Catholic 'belief and devotion to Our Lady, and appealed
to the witness of the primitive Church'. He also insisted that 'the undeniable devotional extravagances cited by Pusey should be disowned by
Roman Catholics'.[179] Keble and Pusey welcomed the *Letter*, and the
latter wrote that he hoped it would 'be a harbinger of good'.[180] In
thanking Pusey for his kindness, Newman affirmed his sincere intention in writing the *Letter* was to confront the 'extreme statements about
the Blessed Virgin' which were said to be held by Catholics. This
could not be done 'without bringing out my whole mind – if I had not,
my co-religionists would have said it was unfair ... It was not good
writing at all, if I did not carry them with me'. So, he stated, he had to
say, 'however temperately, that there were things in your Volume
which I agreed with them in feeling I could not accept'.[181]

The Times gave it a one-page sympathetic review, written by R. W.
Church, later Dean of St Paul's. Various 'old Catholic' clergymen
gave it their approval but the ultramontanes were 'fiercely indig-
nant'.[182] Manning was warned by Talbot 'to stand firm as the advocate
of Roman views in England against Newman and the Old Catholics
who rally round him in opposition to you and Rome ... To be Roman
is to an Englishman an effort. Dr Newman is more English than the
English. His spirit must be crushed'.

Manning, now Archbishop-elect after the death of Wiseman in
February 1865, assured Talbot that his views of Newman were correct
and that there was 'much danger of an English Catholicism of which
Newman was the highest type. It is the old Anglican, patristic, liter-

ary, Oxford tone transplanted into the Church ... In one word, it is worldly Catholicism, and it will have the worldly on its side, and will deceive many'.[183]

Thomas Allies wrote to Newman complaining of Pusey's 'untruthfulness' which he found 'so revolting'. Newman responded charitably,

> As to Pusey, it is harsh to call any mistakes of his untruthfulness. I think they arise from the same slovenly habit which some people would recognize in his dress, his beard, etc. He never answers letters, I believe, which do not lie in the line of the direct work which he has on hand. And so, in composing a book, he takes uncommon pains about some points ... but he will combine with this extreme carelessness in respect to other statements ... He goes into print with the same heedless readiness and decisiveness with which he would say words in conversation.[184]

In similar vein Newman wrote to Fr H. J. Coleridge, 'It must be recollected that your object is to convince those who respect and love Dr Pusey, that he has written hastily and rashly and gone beyond measure.'[185]

On 12 February, Ullathorne wrote thanking Newman for his 'most beautiful Reply to Dr Pusey's *Irenicon*', but added that 'some priests were uneasy about Newman's exposition of original sin'.[186] Newman immediately replied, 'corrections are being sent to the printers by tonight's post'.[187] Ullathorne sent a copy of this letter to Manning to reassure him of Newman's orthodoxy and wish to clarify what he had written. In general, according to Butler, 'theological opinion among the English Catholics ran with Newman, the counter-current being limited to the group of Manning's inner circle. At Rome, too, the sympathy seems to have been with him'.[188]

Gladstone – who was to become, in 1874, the focus of another of Newman's reluctant challenges – wrote to 'claim a common interest' with Newman and others who were seeking for 'a new reconciliation of Christianity and mankind'.[189] Bishop Brown of Newport once again wrote appreciatively to Newman, this time about the *Letter to Pusey*.[190] Newman acknowledged his approval with 'great gratification'.[191] Bishop William Clifford, always a staunch friend, wrote to *The Tablet* in defence of Newman's arguments. His support caused Newman to write: 'No one can do more than his best, I tried to do my best; and having done so, felt myself willing to submit myself to whatever just criticism came to be for not doing better.' It was a 'great relief and encouragement to have a Bishop and Theologian's public support in the matter'.[192] Another prelate and friend, Bishop Moriarty, was 'stirred to congratulate' Newman by 'some adverse and ignorant criticisms which astounded me'. In thanking his esteemed friend, Newman stated that he 'had intended to pursue the other topics Dr Pusey introduces into his Volume – but I found myself so fatigued when I came to the end of it, that I easily acquiesced in the belief that I had said enough for the moment, and so I think I have'.[193]

Newman's own assessment of the reception given by Catholics to his *Letter to Pusey* is contained in a personal letter in which he thanked Pusey for his 'sympathy about the attacks he had suffered'. He assured Pusey that *The Times'* review was very satisfying, and that 'my own bishop, Dr Clifford and most of the other bishops are with me'. He had received letters from the 'most important centres of theology and of education through the country, taking part with me'.[194]

However, as noted, Newman also experienced unfriendly and even hostile reactions to his *Letter to Pusey*, some of which were from Catholic sources, such as *The Tablet*. This influential journal dedicated several pages to a highly critical review of Newman's publication. This prompted him to write, with marked courtesy, to the editor, pointing out that his declared preference for 'English habits of devotion to foreign' had been misinterpreted and so may have been found 'unpleasing to many excellent and devoted Catholics'. He suggested that others, like himself, were 'as zealous in their own way of devotion as they are in theirs'.[195]

In view of the opposition he had encountered, mostly from the Ultramontanes, Newman decided not to write on other matters, namely, 'the development of Revelation and papal infallibility',[196] which Pusey had raised in his *Eirenicon*. He refuted a press report alleging that he had been 'prevented by superior authority from publishing a second letter to Dr Pusey on the subject of Papal Infallibility, or on any other subject whatever'.[197]

As the first reactions to Pusey's *Eirenicon* and Newman's rebuttal seemed to be settling down, Newman told Fr H. J. Coleridge, editor of the *Month*, that he should continue 'to write as controversialist' in his journal, in view of Pusey's influence on his followers. 'Of course, I take a different view of Pusey from what you do – but for argument's sake I will allow that, as you say, he shuffles desperately – also, I take the very ground that you do, viz. that his word is taken as law by numbers, when it should not be.' But, Newman warned, mere abuse of Pusey 'will neither convert him nor any of his followers'.[198]

Newman admitted:

> I am no biblical scholar, but I know there are great difficulties as regards the text and history of the Old Testament. They have never troubled me – since I have been a Catholic, for this reason, because the Church had been so very silent about the inspiration and definite authority and use of Holy Scripture – and because my faith is formed by what *she* has been guided to declare, not what I may have reasoned out from the sacred text.

But he declared that he should 'never be surprised if the received popular views of Scripture would, as time goes on, undergo some modification, as they *have* done since the time of Galileo'. He emphasized that Catholics are not *pledged* to 'those popular views' (which were being put forward by the Anglican Bishop Colenso and others), 'and, while we look for some determination of the Church to guide us, and we wait patiently for it'.[199]

Newman had been aware of the furore aroused in the 1860s by the publication of *Essays and Reviews*. This controversial collection of essays by six prominent Anglican clerics and a notable layman (the *Septem contra Christum*) represented Broad Church or liberal views in Victorian Anglicanism. Natural rather than miraculous or supernatural explanations of long-held beliefs were promoted. Biblical narratives should be subject to rigorous historical and critical evaluation, bearing in mind, for example, scientific discoveries. Such radical opinions were condemned by the Anglican bishops and by almost 11,000 clergy, although Dean Arthur Stanley suggested that Church should be prepared to discuss the Scriptures in relation to the field of modern knowledge.

At that particular time, Newman argued that the issues raised by the Essayists were less critical for Catholics than for other Christians, because 'Catholics had sufficient base of faith in an infallible Church and did not depend on Scripture alone'.[200] He amplified this point in a letter to a High Church clergyman:

> The religion of England depends, humanly speaking, on belief in 'the Bible and the Whole Bible'... Now the plenary inspiration of Scripture is peculiarly a Protestant questions; not a Catholic. We indeed devoutly receive the whole Bible as the Word of God, but we receive it on the authority of the Church and the Church has defined very little as to the aspects under which it comes from God, and the limits of the inspiration.[201]

It was not until the First Vatican Council's closer definition of the notion of inspiration that Newman considered that a belief in biblical inspiration was likely to cause Catholics any particular difficulties.[202] That he was aware of the problem of biblical criticism may be seen from one of his later letters:

> It is clear that we shall have to discuss the question whether certain passages of the Old Testament are or are not mythical. It is one of the gravest of questions, and we cannot spend too much time in preparing for it.[203]

In 1861 Newman began the task of writing what became known later as *The Inspiration of Scripture*, with the resonant opening statement:

> No doubt, I think, can be raised as to the fact, that, in all the ages of the Church, from the earliest to the present, it has been the universal belief of Catholics that the Holy Scripture is divinely inspired. It has been the belief of Fathers, the belief of the schools, the belief of clergy and people.[204]

Newman proceeded to state that the Church 'has pronounced Scripture to be divine, sacred, authoritative; and it is the Church again, which by a divine light decides what is Scripture and what is not ...'[205] According to Ker, Newman's original drafts on biblical inspiration 'never came to anything' because the 'ecclesiastical climate of the time was not favourable to any original initiatives'.[206] It was not until the last decade of his life that Newman published the article (after taking note of criticism of the drafts), in February 1884.

Newman recognized the highly sensitive nature of the task he had taken on, and so he consulted Archbishop Errington and Bishop Clifford during the time he was writing the article. However, despite his careful approach a Maynooth professor of theology attacked what he had written, though there was no long-standing disagreement. While engrossed in writing the article, Newman commented that he wished that Scripture should be read 'as a book given us by God, inspired, a guide – and a comfort'.[207] His approach to biblical studies was to influence the deliberations of the Second Vatican Council.

In his private journal Newman made a short entry on 30 November 1868, which seems to indicate that he had been reflecting on the many vicissitudes of his life: 'I think the fact arises from the feeling in the public mind that for many, for 20 years, I have been unfairly dealt with. It is a generous feeling desirous of making amends.' The Press had, at last, been giving him 'great considerateness', the new edition of *Parochial Sermons* was selling well, markedly 'among Dissenters', and the Professor of Poetry at Oxford, Sir F. Doyle, 'is paying me the extraordinary compliment of giving a Public Lecture on my *Dream of Gerontius* ... the Pope has directed that I should be asked to go to Rome to take part in preparing matters for the Council', which had caused 'the Catholic Papers who have not hitherto spoken well of me, to say that it has been a special invitation, the first and hitherto only one made to any priest in England, Scotland or Ireland, etc.'.[208] Ullathorne, in fact, had passed to Newman, on 13 October 1868, a letter from the Prefect of the Congregation of the Council asking whether Newman would agree to act as a consultor to one of the commissions that was preparing the business of the First Vatican Council. In this letter the Prefect explained that the Pope was summoning to Rome ecclesiastics who were distinguished for their knowledge of theology and for the holiness of their lives. Ullathorne informed Newman that 'the English bishops had been requested by the Holy See to nominate a theologian but had not been able to meet conveniently for this purpose'. The papal invitation to Newman was, he added, 'a totally distinct thing', and he would be required to go to Rome before the end of the year.[209]

In a Memorandum dated 14 October 1868, Newman set down the pros and cons of the papal invitation; he might be able 'to do some good in the role of consultor; it might benefit our Oratory in being both a sign of favour, and if he returned a Bishop *in partibus*'. On the other hand, the indirect papal approach 'was to *sound* me', and this 'while delicate towards myself, also leaves it open to pay me a compliment, even though it were *wished* that I should decline it'. Also, Newman noted, the appointment of consultor would mean that 'I should be submerged in a number of consultors, and perhaps have to consider subjects quite beyond my knowledge and foreign to my experience, is scarcely more than a compliment'.

After this careful weighing up, Newman considered that 'little or no good, and much harm, would come of accepting it'. Concerns about his health, life expectancy, disruption to his work, problems of working among strangers (as in Dublin), and of undertaking tasks 'foreign' to his talents – 'because I have never succeeded with boards or committees, and also because I cannot speak any language but my own', were among the reasons which led him to conclude that he 'should, by accepting this invitations, lose my independence and gain nothing'.[210]

On 15 November 1868 Newman confided to Pusey that he 'was not going to Rome'; he had 'begged off – and as far as I can see, rightly. I am not a theologian, and should only have been wasting my time in matters which I did not understand'. He alluded to papal infallibility, to which he was 'ever more than inclined', but 'as a matter of expedience, I wish nothing done at the Council about it'.[211]

In the elections of July 1874, Gladstone's government suffered defeat. Gladstone attributed it largely to the Irish hierarchy's opposition led by Cullen, now a cardinal, to his Irish University Bill. This proposed integrating the Catholic University in Ireland into a nondenominational system of higher education. The concept of 'mixed education' had already been rejected by the Irish bishops, as was discussed earlier in Chapter 5.

In a very long letter to Robert Ornsby, Professor of Greek and Latin Literature at the CUI, Newman, however, perceived Gladstone's political reverse as a 'great catastrophe in Ireland, and no one is more to be pitied that Cardinal Cullen ... it seems quite a mistake of the papers to say that he has got a triumph, that the Church has shown her power and the Pope has proved that he is somebody'. For nearly thirty years the Church had protested against mixed education, so 'how then could the Cardinal quietly submit to a Bill which provided that university teachers should belong to any religion, or none? Impossible – He was obliged to repudiate such an arrangement'. However, Newman asserted, had Cullen 'confined himself to the question of principle, all would have been right – but he asked for endowment, and that, after the Irish Establishment (Church of Ireland) had been disendowed ... and in a Pastoral reminded his people of the coming General Election'. Newman considered that by 'these political acts', Cullen had 'put himself in the wrong. He has alienated all parties from him and both Disraeli and Gladstone have in their separate ways declared that they will do nothing for him. What makes it still worse is that he himself cannot possibly listen to the agitation for Home Rule ... he has barked, when he has no teeth to bite with'. Newman's penetrating analysis of the Irish higher education system and its political significance was clearly based on his personal experiences in Dublin over a period of seven years or so.[212] To another confidant, Newman confessed:

It is not Gladstone's fault – he has done all he could – but he might as soon be expected by eloquence or skill to change the course of a railway train, as to change the direction or slacken the speed of the movements which are bringing in a new world.

Although he did not defend Cullen's request *for money*, he supposed it was 'pressed upon him' by the difficulties experienced in funding the CUI. Newman added that Cullen '*would* not have the support of the educated laity, and threw himself upon the peasantry . . . and, it is hard, that they should have been expected to pay for an institution' from which they were excluded.[213]

As a result of losing the election, Gladstone was forced to resign and, freed from prime-ministerial responsibilities and leadership of the Liberal Party, and without the need to cultivate the Irish vote, he felt free to comment publicly and adversely on the influence of Catholicism on political life.

In an article, *Ritualism*, in the 1874 issue of the *Contemporary Review*, Gladstone commented on the Public Worship Regulation Bill, which aimed to suppress the growth of ritualism in the Church of England, and declared that attempts to 'Romanise' the Church of England were 'utterly hopeless' for several reasons. Among these was that any one becoming a Catholic renounced his moral and mental freedom and 'placed his civil loyalty and duty at the mercy of another'.[214] As Chadwick puts it, the decree that defined the doctrine of papal infallibility having been issued in 1870, had been misunderstood and misrepresented by many, including Gladstone, as meaning that a Catholic 'would not be likely to be a loyal citizen of Great Britain'.[215] Gladstone also made several misleading references to the *Syllabus of Errors*, issued in Rome on 8 December 1864, as an appendix to the encyclical *Quanta Cura*.

Ambrose Phillips de Lisle alerted Newman, on 3 November, that Gladstone was about to follow up his article in the *Contemporary Review* with an extended pamphlet. Newman thanked Phillips for this information, adding that he thought Gladstone 'is misled in his interpretation' of the wording of the ecclesiastical acts of 1870. 'Theological language, like legal, is scientific, and cannot be understood without the knowledge of long precedent and tradition, nor without the comments of theologians.'[216] A few days later, Gladstone's pamphlet: *The Vatican Decrees in their bearing on Civil Allegiance: a Political Expostulation* was duly published, and sold almost 150,000 copies within a few weeks.

Gladstone made what Norman describes as an 'extraordinary

outburst' which was a 'classic of antiCatholicism'.[217] According to
Sencourt, not only was his 'language intemperate' but 'his ideas were
inexact'.[218] He confused, for instance, the hostility of the Irish bishops
towards the Irish University Bill and the definition of papal infallibility and its powers. Griffin says, however, that Gladstone's *Expostulation* represents 'the last major complaint of English Protestants against
Roman Catholics – that they were subject to a foreign power and
therefore suspect in their loyalty to the English nation'.[219] Such public
distortions attracted vigorous responses from several prominent
Catholics, including Manning and, most notably, Newman, who was
pressed by his friends, including the Duke of Norfolk, to respond.[220]

During November 1874, Newman was absorbed in writing a refutation of Gladstone's unwarranted attack on the loyalty of English
Catholics. 'Initially he experienced problems in tackling Gladstone's
parenthetic, sweeping declamation', he told Lord Emly – the former
William Monsell, who had recently been raised to the peerage –

> For five or six weeks I have been hard at it for perhaps 5 or 6 hours a day,
> and have produced nothing. I have written quires, but not please myself
> and begun again. Gladstone is so rambling and slovenly, it is so difficult
> to follow him with any logical exactness. I can't get a plan. Today I have
> begun on a new arrangement of matter... and at present I am satisfied with
> it – but my great fear is that in two or three days I shall see it won't do.[221]

These difficulties had also been recorded by Newman in a diary note:
'In these weeks attempted in vain to write on Gladstone's Parenthesis
in the *Contemporary*.'[222] He confided to R. W. Church, his trusted
friend of many years: 'I never thought I should be writing against
Gladstone ... but he is unfair and untrue as he is cruel.'[223] On 27
December 1874, Newman felt able to tell W. J. Copeland: 'My task is
nearly finished – You know I am writing on Gladstone's pamphlet. I
could not help doing so.'[224]

Newman obtained the agreement of the Duke of Norfolk, a close
friend, former pupil of the Oratory School, and the leading Catholic
layman that, in order to avoid addressing Gladstone directly, his reply
should take the form of a Letter.[225] The Duke willingly gave his
consent to this proposal: 'It will of course be a very great happiness to
me to have one of your works in the form of a letter to myself.'[226]

Lord Emly had supported Gladstone's Irish University Bill of 1873,
and Newman recalled this when writing to him again. 'I am very bold
– and cannot be surprised if I made some people very angry. But if I

am to write, I will have my say.' In a postscript he added: 'Don't be angry with me for what I say of Gladstone's University Bill.'[227] Of course, Lord Emly assured Newman that he would not be in the least angry, although he maintained that the proposed legislation would have worked well. Later, on reading the *Letter to the Duke of Norfolk*, Emly told Newman: 'You make out a better case for the Irish bishops, in the university bill, than they make out for themselves.'[228] Another regular correspondent, Mrs Henry Wilberforce, was told by Newman:

> I could not help answering Mr Gladstone; so many friends and strangers asked me – and I felt something was due to my own character – for *could* I allow that I was instrumental in bringing a number of people into the Church in which they lost their mental and moral freedom and were bad subjects of the State?[229]

In his seventy-fourth year – and with eloquence and fervour – Newman dissected Gladstone's 'rambling' accusations and subjected them to scathing commentaries. He dismissed out of hand that Catholics had changed their faith and 'repudiated ancient history', and 'appealed to the practice of the early Church in regard to obedience to the State'.[230] He rejected the unfounded assertion of divided loyalties, declaring that sovereignty, whether of the State or Church, necessarily had limitations and that, in the end, the individual conscience was supreme. This particular point had, in fact, been forcibly stressed by Newman in a letter to the editor of *The Times* some three years earlier: 'No Pope can make evil good. No Pope has any power over those eternal moral principles which God has printed on our hearts and consciences.'[231] In Ker's words: 'At the heart of the *Letter to the Duke of Norfolk* is the celebrated treatment of the sovereignty of conscience.'[232]

Newman was aware of the far-ranging nature of Gladstone's allegations; 'He has touched on so many subjects that it requires a volume to answer them.'[233] In a letter to Bishop William Clifford, he also observed: 'The questions which Mr Gladstone opens in his Pamphlet are so many and so large, that of course what I myself have written only goes a certain way in answering him.'[234]

In 1878, Newman and Gladstone were again in touch with one another, but this time the reason was congenial and arose from a speech made by Gladstone after the opening of the hall and library of Keble College, Oxford, During his oration, Gladstone referred to the Oxford Movement, Keble and Pusey, and he then said: 'But there is a

name which, as an academical name, is greater than either of those –
I mean the name of Dr Newman.' He declared that when the history
of Oxford is written, the 'extraordinary, the unexampled career of that
distinguished man in the University' would have to be recorded.
Newman wrote to Gladstone to tell him of 'the gratification, as well as
surprise' with which he had read of the reference to him in Gladstone's speech. While he could not 'think of appropriating myself all
that you say of me', he hoped 'now that I am so near my end' that
what had been said of him would 'not be found inconsistent with my
profession and preaching'.[235] Gladstone's reply was as gracefully
phrased as his speech: 'Your note supplies one of the instances rather
rare in life – I have received thanks, where I rather felt myself to owe
apology.' What he had said at Keble was 'meant for a piece of history
faithfully rendered', and he had felt it 'important to state the case
fully, when there are so many inclined or tempted to misunder-
stand'.[236]

The *Letter to the Duke of Norfolk* was published on 14 January
1875, and Gladstone wrote at once, thanking Newman for the 'genial
and gentle manner' in which he had treated him.[237] In thanking Gladstone for his 'forbearing and generous letter', Newman assured him
that it had been 'a great grief to have to write against one' whose
career he had always followed with 'loyal interest and admiration'.[238]
Among Catholics, the *Letter* received immediate acclaim. Newman
told Lord Blachford, 'I certainly had my reward ... from the old
Catholics, from bishops, Jesuits, Dominicans, and various clergy,
who have with one voice concurred in what I have written.'[239] In a
pastoral letter, on 14 October 1875, Cardinal Cullen had referred to
Gladstone's *Expostulation* which had been 'admirably answered by the
venerable Dr Newman, for many years the great and pious rector of
the Catholic University, whom Ireland will ever revere'.[240]

Cullen's enthusiastic and open support was particularly valuable,
for he was a notable theologian and held in high regard in Rome.
Newman acknowledged with 'gratification and thankfulness' his
endorsement of *The Letter*, adding that he was 'much touched by our
reference to my connexion in years past with the Catholic University'
[241] Cullen's reply was warm and appreciative of Newman's 'powerful
logic and eloquence' in refuting Gladstone's charges. He assured
Newman that 'Our people and clergy are not forgetful of the services
you rendered us, and that they continually speak of you with feelings
of gratitude and respect.'[242]

Such widespread public support was reassuring to Newman because some complaints had been made about certain passages in the *Letter*, over which Ullathorne had been asked to remonstrate with Newman. He refused to do so and Manning's support for Newman is also evident from his correspondence with Rome.[243] The doctrinal soundness of Newman's pamphlet was finally agreed by Rome. As Fr Henry Tristram observes,

> It was Newman who, of all that distinguished statesman's (Gladstone's) Catholic opponents, made by far the most effective defence of the encyclical *Quanta Cura*, the *Syllabus*, and the Vatican definition (of papal infallibility) in his *Letter to the Duke of Norfolk*.[244]

Dr Charles Russell praised the *Letter to the Duke of Norfolk*, while also noting that there are 'a few things which will be criticised, no doubt; and one or two in which I should not myself fully agree, but as a whole it is admirable'.[245] In thanking him, Newman allowed his imagination to soar:

> I am like a man who has gone up in a balloon, and has a chance of all sorts of adventures, from gas escapes, from currents of air, from intanglements in forests, from the wide sea, and does not feel himself safe till he gets back to his fireside. At present I am descending, I am in the most critical point of my expedition. All I can say is that I have acted for the best, and have done my best, and must now leave the success of it to a higher power.[246]

In his public reply to the *Letter to the Duke of Norfolk*, Gladstone wrote *Vaticanism, an Answer to Replies and Reproofs*, to which *The Times* of 25 February 1875 devoted its third leader, concluding that Gladstone's pamphlets had been 'directed with such curious and seemingly uncalled for energy against the present policy of Rome'.[247] However, Gladstone, in *Vaticanism*, had also spoken of Newman's eminence and of the great affection in which he was held, and Newman, in thanking him for sending a copy of the pamphlet, expressed his appreciation of the 'extreme kindness of the language which you use concerning me'. At the same time, he wished Gladstone to know that from the time – nearly thirty years ago – when he became a Catholic, he 'had never had a moment's misgiving in my conviction that the Roman Catholic Church comes from God, and that the Anglican is external to it, or again in my sense of the duty which

lay upon me to act on that conviction'.[248] Newman dealt with the few
criticisms made by Gladstone in a postscript to the *Letter to the Duke
of Norfolk*, which was published in early March and included in subsequent editions. He explained to Bishop David Moriarty that he felt
obliged to amplify some of the remarks he had made in the *Letter*
because Gladstone had been 'very tender to me, and, where he might
attack me, omits to do so. I don't think I need say much – but a few
remarks are necessary, because I think he mistakes what I have said
sometimes'.[249]

About six years after the controversy which brought about the
Letter, Newman received from Gladstone – who was again Prime
Minister – a letter with documents alleging that some Irish Catholic
priests were giving sermons that, if they were laymen, might well be
considered to be seditious. Gladstone asked Newman to make representations to Rome so that the Pope should direct these priests 'to
fulfil the elementary duties of citizenship'.[250] Newman replied, 'I
think you overrate the Pope's power in political and social matters. It
is absolute in questions of theology but not so in practical matters ...
local power and influence is often more than a match for Roman
right.'[251]

In a further letter to Gladstone, Newman commented that it 'seemed
very doubtful what the Pope could do at a moment. He is a good and
firm friend to the civil power on the whole and on the long run; he
educates a people in obedience, and keeps things straight'. But in any
emergency 'when people are mad', he doubted what the Pope could
do. 'A Garibaldi at a crisis is stronger than a Pope.' Over the last fifty
years, Pope Leo had had 'no encouragement' to participate in events
in Ireland, so it was unlikely that he could now do so 'with good
effect.'[252]

The last public controversy in which Newman took part occurred in
1885, when he was in his eighty-fifth year. This arose from an article
in the *Contemporary Review* of May 1885 written by A. M. Fairbairn,
Principal elect of the Airedale (Congregationalist) Theological
College, Bradford, in which Newman was accused of 'philosophical
scepticism in removing the proofs of religion from the sphere of
reason into that of conscience and imagination'.[253] This assertion
mirrored an earlier one made by James Fitzjames Stephen who, in *St
James Gazette*, had declared that Newman had said that Catholicism
was the only possible alternative to atheism. Newman declined to
write a rejoinder: 'My brain works too slowly and hand too feebly to

allow of my interfering.' Earlier he had discussed Stephen's arguments and told him: 'It is no good our disputing, it is like a battle
between a dog and a fish – we are in different elements.'[254]

In Fairbairn's case, Newman felt that he should rebut the serious
charge made against him. He set to work on an article, *The Development of Religious Error*, which was published in the October issue of
the *Contemporary Review*. 'it was his last explanation of the relations
between reason and faith, and the final clarification of his teaching'.[255]
Fairbairn responded with another article, to which Newman drafted a
reply, on which he sought Lord Blachford's opinion.[256] On Blanch-
ford's advice, Newman decided that it was not becoming to continue
the controversy, but he circulated his reply privately, sending a copy
to Fairbairn, who courteously acknowledged it.

Newman admitted to Richard Holt Hutton – who had contributed to
the March 1886 edition of the *Contemporary Review* an article in
which he expressed his admiration for Newman's qualities and
'profound convictions' – that he had written 'some pages' on Fairbairn's allegations, but that when he was about to send them to the
editor of the journal he had said to himself: 'Is this not after all *infra
dig* to descend into a public arena, like a gladiator at your age?' The
advice of his 'Protestant friends – who saw more of the world than I
do' was that it 'would be a mistake to publish anything more'; so he
intended to 'send to Dr Fairbairn what I have written telling him it
was not to be published'.[257]

In a letter dated 11 March 1886, Fairbairn thanked Newman 'very
cordially' for his paper, and would 'weigh carefully its varied criticisms and elucidations and ... gladly recognize its fair and judicial
tone even where unable to admit the correctness of its views or the
relevance of its arguments'.[258] In a letter to Wilfrid Ward, Newman
said he had received a 'civil answer from Principal Fairbairn, which
was a great satisfaction to me'.[259] When Newman reprinted privately
The Development of Religious Error (see his letter to Lord Blachford
LDXXX.116–17), he added a lengthy postscript which detailed 'how
strangely Principal Fairbairn had misrepresented' his writings.[260]
Newman felt it was important to record formally the controversy
which had arisen as the result of serious misrepresentations about his
writings, and which had been published. If these were left unchal-
lenged, he felt that people, at a later date, might conceivably be
confused.

Newman wrote, on 17 November 1865, to Pusey:

As to the Infallibility of the Pope, I see nothing against it, or to dread in it – for I am confident that it *must* be so limited practically that it will leave things as they are... Even if the Pope's infallibility were defined, it is impossible that there would not be the most careful conditions determining what is *ex cathedra* – and it would add very little to the present received belief.[261]

In the postscript to a letter to Pusey in September 1869, Newman wrote: 'The *one* question which is occupying people's minds is "Will the Pope's Infallibility be determined?" All questions sink before that.'[262]

Two years earlier, Newman had written to Wilberforce deploring the extreme views expressed by some Ultramontane laymen like W. G. Ward. He added that he 'had never taken any great interest in the question of the limits and seat of infallibility'. He had become a Catholic because he recognized that the Church in 'substantial likeness or in actual descent' could rightly claim apostolic descent. The 'great principle' of *securus judicat orbis terrarum* had guided his faith.

I see arguments here, arguments there – I incline on way today, another tomorrow – on the whole I more than incline in one direction – but I do not dogmatise – and I detest any dogmatism when the Church has not clearly spoken.[263]

To Peter Le Page Renouf, a renowned oriental scholar and theologian, Newman wrote, about a year later:

I hold the Pope's Infallibility, not as a dogma, but as a theological opinion; that is, not as a certainty, but as a probability . . . To my mind the balance of probabilities is still in favour of it. There are vast difficulties, taking facts as they are, in the way of denying it... Anyhow, the doctrine of Papal Infallibility must be fenced round and limited by conditions.[264]

Newman's concerns about the dangers of misunderstandings about papal infallibility arising from extravagant claims being made by some over-enthusiastic promoters are also reflected in a letter to Mrs William Froude: 'I have ever held the Pope's Infallibility as an opinion, I am not therefore likely to feel any personal anxiety as to the result of this Council.' He was still, however, 'strongly opposed to its definition' because there seemed no necessity for it: 'there is no heresy to put down', and it is 'dangerous to go beyond the rule of tradition in such a matter ... I am against this definition, because it opens up a long controversy'.[265]

Newman assured another lady enquirer: 'I believe in the infallibility of the Pope myself – that is, as an opinion. I think there are very strong reasons for holding it – but I quite recognize the right of others not to hold it.' If a Council should so determine it as an act of faith, he would 'formally *believe as certain* what I now believe in my own private judgement *as an opinion*'.[266]

He told another earnest correspondent that he had 'long held the infallibility of the Pope' but had never attempted to bring anyone into the Church by means of it. Although he 'held the Pope's Infallibility as most likely, and as having the suffrages of most people in this day, I cannot defend it in a set argument'.[267]

In a forthright letter to Bishop Moriarty, Newman asserted that he 'fears of some unknown definition [of papal infallibility], when every thing is at rest is secretly distressing numbers. What heresy calls for a decision? What have we done that we can't leave alone? Hitherto definitions *de fide* were grave necessities, not devotional outpourings'.[268] The bishop replied from Rome on 3 February that Newman's letter 'comforted him in the anxiety he felt for the Church'.[269]

Throughout their many contacts over twenty years or so, Moriarty had always been ready to reassure and support Newman. 'of all the Irish bishops', he had been the only one who condescended to visit Newman socially when the Catholic University of Ireland was being developed. Tristram records that Moriarty was also the only member of the Irish hierarchy who 'rose to the height of Newman's splendid conception of what a Catholic University should be, and loyally cooperated towards its realization'.[270]

Newman also relieved his anxious feelings to Ullathorne – who was at Rome – in what he was to describe as 'one of the most passionate and confidential letters that I ever wrote'. In it he referred to 'an insolent and aggressive faction' – some Ultramontanists – who were propagating what seemed to be an extreme view of papal infallibility.[271] Although Newman's explosive letter was regarded by him as confidential it was shown to several bishops in Rome; copies were taken and distributed. Newspapers featured extracts including Newman's reference to an 'aggressive insolent faction'. Ullathorne wrote reassuringly to Newman that for his part, he had 'quietly, and in private maintained that a calm and moderate definition should not be opposed, *provided* it was duly balanced by strengthening the authority of the

Episcopate, provided also it was duly limited so as to save us from enthusiastic and fanatical interpretations. And I have insisted on the importance of reviving the old canon in the Sexto against laymen leading in the theological writing and publishing'. He closed his long personal letter by observing, with characteristic caution: 'whatever mischief is doing outside by our own newspapers... moderation will be the upshot of the Council.'[272] Now that his letter was virtually public property and to avoid inaccurate versions of it appearing, Newman sent a copy of it to the *Standard*, where it was published and widely reproduced.[273]

Newman thanked Ullathorne for his 'very tranquilising' letter and commented: 'You have said to me all that need be said. And we must have a little more faith than we have – and rest in quiet confidence that all must turn out well.'[274]

On 14 March, Newman wrote urgently to his bishop to assure him that: 'A passage in today's *Standard* has neither directly nor indirectly come from this House.' The passage in question stated:

> Newman had written to his bishop at Rome, stigmatizing the promoters of Papal Infallibility as an insolent, aggressive faction, praying that God may avert this threatened peril from the Church, and affirming his conviction that, if He does not see fit to do so, it is because He has chosen to delay the Church's ultimate triumph for centuries.[275]

Newman also wrote to the editor of the *Standard* 'disavowing' what had been imputed to him. 'While he deeply deplored the policy, the spirit, the measures of various persons, lay and ecclesiastical, he had neither intention nor wish to deny; just the contrary.'[276] Newman's letter to Ullathorne had been circulated rather freely without Ullathorne's knowledge or concurrence.[277] Newman's uninhibited reference to an 'insolent, aggressive faction' was, of course, in a highly confidential and unguarded letter to his bishop, and it was certainly not intended for general reading. When the phrasing was brought to his attention, he checked the draft of his letter to Ullathorne and discovered that he had actually used the rather inflammatory words quoted by the *Standard*. So he wrote again to the editor, explaining that his rough draft had been difficult to decipher, but that he appeared to have used the phrasing quoted. In clarification, he stated:

> I neither meant that great body of bishops who are said to be in favour of the definition of the doctrine nor any ecclesiastical order of society exter-

nal to the Council. As to the Jesuits, I wish distinctly to state that I have all along separated them in my mind as a body from the movement which I so much deplore. What I meant by a faction, as the letter itself shows, was a collection of persons drawn together from various ranks and conditions in the Church.[278]

Newman's apology and explanation was received gracefully by the editor: 'No other course could have been expected from a person of Dr Newman's elevated and honourable sentiments'.[279] In Ullathorne's letter to Newman, mentioned earlier, it seems apparent that he was quite aware of the problems caused by 'the zealots' at the Vatican Council.

Newman wrote to his many friends, explaining how his unguarded letter to his bishop had landed him in 'somewhat of a mess' when it had 'got out and was shown in Rome'.[280] Resignedly, he told the Jesuit Provincial, Fr Alfred Weld:

The truth is that it is my vocation to knock and be knocked. It has been such now a good forty years – and I have taken it as my Cross. I might easily have had a far heavier one, and do not want it changed.[281]

Meanwhile, Newman informed Coleridge that

The great charge which I bring against the immediate authors of this movement, is that they have not given us time. [The last part of this sentence was written in capital letters.] The beginning and end of my thoughts about this Council is 'You are going too fast'.[282]

Newman had written a similar letter to Fr Robert Whitty, SJ the day before.

The proceedings of the Vatican Council - the first since the Council of Trent in the sixteenth century – dragged on through the heat of the Italian summer of 1870, causing Newman to write to Ullathorne: 'I trust the account in the Papers is true, that the Pope intends to have mercy on the assembled Fathers from St Peter and St Paul to the middle of October.'[283]

On 18 July 1870, at the last public session of Vatican I, the definition of papal infallibility was solemnly declared. Voting was not, however, unanimous; two bishops voted against it, and more than eighty 'had already departed after a compromise was refused by the Pope himself ... the definition restricted infallibility to faith and morals, and could not even be held to infallibalise the Syllabus of Errors'.[284]

The actual text of the decree allayed Newman's fears: 'I am pleased at its moderation ... the terms used are vague and comprehensive; and personally I have no difficulty in admitting it.'[285] To Ambrose St John, he wrote: 'I have ever since a Catholic held the Pope's Infallibility as a matter of opinion, I see nothing in the definition which necessarily contradicts Scripture, Tradition or History.'[286] Earlier, Newman had told James Hope-Scott that he thought that Manning had thrown his lot in with the middle party holding the Pope 'to be inerrable in matters *de fide*', which was '*very far short*' of what his own extreme position had been. W. G. Ward had also modified his earlier theory of infallibility and had admitted that in his original writings 'he had extended it too far'.[287] As Ker puts it: 'The Ultramontanes had not achieved all they wanted at the Council. But their victory was fairly complete throughout the Church and the repercussions were various.'[288]

Over the next two or three years, Newman's correspondence included many letters on the newly defined doctrine of papal infallibility, and he repeatedly reassured those who wrote anxiously to him about the nature and extend of the dogma. He told Lady Chatterton:

> For three centuries we have *practically* been under the operation of that dogma which so oppresses you – and, depend upon it, the Church will not go on very differently during the next three hundred years, as far as the addition of dogmas is concerned.

He had held the Pope's infallibility since he became a Catholic because he had thought it 'very difficult to deny it historically, in spite of the difficulties against it'.[289] He agreed with another correspondent that: 'the wording of the Dogma has nothing very difficult in it', although he felt it to be 'a new and most serious precedent in the Church that a dogma *de fide* should be passed without *definite and urgent cause*'.[290] Newman counselled a troubled enquirer 'to be of good heart' and 'beware of desperate steps ... Councils generally have been attended by much strife and incipient schism. By times things get right – *securus judicat orbis terrarum* – that is the rule'.[291]

To his close friend and fellow Oratorian, Ambrose St John, Newman expressed fears that: 'The tyrant majority is still aiming at enlarging the *province* of Infallibility. I can only say if all this takes

place, we shall in matter of fact be under a new dispensation.'[292]
Newman informed the wife of a prominent Liverpool Catholic:

> I detest many things historically connected with the Pope as much as you
> can – but what I feel is this, that a Universal Church cannot, by the laws
> of human society, be held together without a head ... If then it was in the
> designs of Providence to establish a spiritual Kingdom or universal
> Empire, or was in His designs to have a Pope, unless all was to be carried
> on by miracle.[293]

Newman's pastoral care was reflected in the advice given to another
lady who was troubled in her faith:

> Don't set yourself against the doctrine. Very little was passed, much less
> than its advocates wished – they are disappointed. Nothing is defined as to
> *what acts* are *ex cathedra*, nor to what things infallibility extends. Some
> people believe the degree lessens the Pope's *actual* power.[294]

One of Newman's notable and, as it happened, tragic, correspondents
was Georges Darboy, Archbishop of Paris, to whom he wrote:

> The doctrine of Infallibility has now been more than sufficiently promul-
> gated. Personally I never had a shadow of doubt that the very essence of
> religion is protected from error, for a revelation that could stultify itself
> would be no revelation at all.[295]

(On 24 May 1871, Archbishop Darboy was one of the hostages shot
by the Commune in Paris.)

In response to Bishop Moriarty's request that he might offer some
help to Dr Von Döllinger, the renowned German priest-scholar who
had experienced problems with Rome over papal infallibility, Newman
told him that he attempted to help Döllinger indirectly but he 'did not
expect with any good effect. My position ever had been so different
from D's. I never should have been a Catholic, but for the doctrine of
doctrinal development, and have ever held the Pope's infallibility in
rebus fidei, though I never held it as a motivum for being a Catholic, as
some have; but D sees in it nothing but the establishment of the *unum
sanctam*; the *mirari vos*, and a thousand other strong enunciations'.
There was the 'dreadful prospect' that enforcement of the dogma could
result in either a 'large body of merely nominal Catholics' or to 'widespread outward adherence and secret infidelity'.[296]

The problems which are likely to arise from the dogma of papal infallibility were seen by Newman as being 'questions for the theological school – and theologians will as time goes on, settle the force of the wording of the dogma, just as the courts of law solve the meaning and bearing of Acts of Parliament', he assured Sir William Henry Cope.[297] The following year, 1872, Newman declared to Mr Alfred Plummer, who was acting as an intermediary in discussions with Dr Döllinger, that: 'for these 25 years ... he had spoken *in behalf* of the Pope's infallibility', and he listed these occasions: in 1850 at the Birmingham Corn Exchange; in 1852 at the Rotunda in Dublin; in 1856 in a new Preface 'to the new edition of my *Church of the Fathers*; and in 1868 in passages from his *Dublin Lectures* which was in a collection of passages on the dogma in an Italian translation'. He commented: 'This is quite consistent, in my way of viewing it, in being most energetic against the *definition*. Many things are true which are not points of faith, and I thought the definition of this doctrine *most inexpedient.*'[298]

The editor of the *Guardian* received from Newman a strong and detailed protest against erroneous statements about his reactions to the dogma of papal infallibility which were in a letter from Mr J. M. Capes, published on 11 September 1872. With devastating irony, Newman remarked: 'I thank him for having put into print, what doubtless has often been said behind my back; I do not thank him for the odious words which he has made the vehicle of it.' He continued that he could 'say much from what I have written, upon this nasty view of me' but he would limit himself 'to his Discourse on University Education, delivered in Dublin in 1852, in which he had appealed to the 'ample testimony of history to bear me out'. Also, he cited later writings which clearly set out his views and ended by firmly stating: 'I underwent then no change of mind as regards the truth of the doctrine of the Pope's Infallibility in consequence of the Council.'[299]

Newman brusquely told a journalist: 'Allow me to say you really have not got hold of what we mean by the Pope's Infallibility, and what we hold by the idea, not what you hold by it, must be the starting point of any fruitful controversy.'[300]

In response to an invitation from Bishop Moriarty to write a text on papal infallibility, Newman declined the 'great compliment in wishing me to undertake so difficult a subject ... The Pope's Infallibility is a question of *fact*, and a thesis for *historians* – not a pure revealed doctrine – and to prove it within the compass of a pamphlet or a Letter such as that which I wrote on the Immaculate Conception, is, I hold, an impossibility ... There is no historical question about the Blessed Virgin ... but half a hundred can be brought forward by an adversary in behalf of the fallibility of Popes, and have to be answered'.[301]

Newman told Isy Froude, the eldest daughter of William Froude who became a Catholic in 1859, that the word 'infallibility' was not 'ascribed to the *Church* in any authoritative document till the Vatican Council ... yet the Church acted *as* infallible and was accepted as infallible from the first. What was the case with the Church was the case with the Pope. The most *real* expression of the doctrine is, not that he is infallible but that his decisions are 'irreformabilia' and true.[302]

As noted earlier, obedience to authority had, as Dessain observes, always marked Newman's life both as an Anglican and a Roman Catholic: 'He stopped the *Tracts* at a word from his Anglican bishop. He resigned the *Rambler* at Ullathorne's wish ... he twice dropped the plan of founding the Oratory at Oxford ... at the request of higher authority.'[303] Wilfrid Ward notes that Newman 'very soon treated the dogma Infallibility as of obligation, and urged on all his friends the duty of submission'.[304]

Newman can be seen to have entered fully, if sometimes reluctantly, into controversial debate over issues which he deemed important for the good name of Catholics and of Catholicism itself during the Victorian era. As he told one of his friends, Edward Bellasis, 'I think best when I write. I cannot in the same way think while I speak. Some men are brilliant in conversation, others in public speaking – others find their minds act best, when they have a pen in their hands.'[305] Newman's sword was his pen, which he used with expert effectiveness.

It is perhaps quixotic to observe that Newman used quill pens until the end of his life.[306]

Notes
  1. Chadwick, 1990, p. 14.
  2. Newman, 1956, p. 273.
  3. Butler, 1926, p. 307.
  4. McGrath, 1951, p. 219.
  5. LDXXII.157, 18 February 1866.

6. Nicholls and Ker, 1991, pp. 4–5.
7. Chadwick, 1990, p. 63.
8. Ker, 1990, p. 382.
9. Gwynn, 1946, pp. 240–1.
10. Norman, 1985, p. 10.
11. Chadwick, 1990, p. 2.
12. Gilley, 1990, p. 272.
13. Newman, 1874, pp. 172–3.
14. Norman, 1985, p. 10.
15. Butler, 1926, p. 197.
16. LDXV.128, 18 July 1852.
17. LDXV.126.
18. Newman, 1956, p. 13.
19. LDXXVI.115, 16 June 1872.
20. Trevor, 1996, p. 134.
21. Culler, 1965, p. 135.
22. Chadwick, 1971, p. 307.
23. Newman, 1851, p. 209.
24. LDXIV.338, J. S. Northcote, 28 August 1851.
25. LDXXXI.23, Supplement, 31 August 1851.
26. LDXIV.340, 31 August 1851.
27. LDXIV.344, 1 September 1851.
28. LDXIV.345; 352, 8 September 1851.
29. LDXIV.408.
30. LDXIV.408, 27 October 1851.
31. LDXIV.428, J. J. Gordon, 19 November 1851.
32. Gwynn, 1946, p. 237.
33. LDXIV.430, Dessain, footnote.
34. LDXIV.434, 25 November 1851.
35. McGrath, 1951, p. 208.
36. McGrath, 1951, p. 236.
37. LDXIV.iv.
38. Jenkins, 1990, p. 146.
39. Chadwick, 1971, p. 308.
40. Norman, 1985, p. 328.
41. LDXV.278, F. S. Bowles, 31 January 1853.
42. LDXV.308, 23 February 1853.
43. LDXXII.145, 31 January 1866.
44. Griffin, 1993, p. 63.
45. LDXI.205, 13 July 1846.
46. LDXI.207–8, 14 July 1846.
47. Butler, 1926, p. 309.
48. Butler, 1926, p. 310.
49. Dessain, 1980, p. 111.
50. Ward, 1913, p. 475.
51. Coulson, 1970, p. 102.
52. Cf Dessain, 1980, p. 111.

53. LDXIX.xiii, Dessain, 1969.
54. LDXIX.41, 16 February 1859.
55. LDXIX.42-3, 16 February 1859.
56. LDXIX.45, 19 February 1859.
57. LDXIX.46, 22 February 1859.
58. LDXIX.85, James Burns, 21 March 1859.
59. LDXIX.88-9, Lady Day 1859.
60. Coulson, 1970, p. 104.
61. LDXIX.xiv, Dessain.
62. LDXIX.142, Robert Ornsby, 24 May 1859.
63. Dessain, 1980, p. 119.
64. LDXIX.140-1, 22 May 1859.
65. LDXIV.252, J.M. Capes, 10 April 1851.
66. Gilley, 1990, p. 303.
67. LDXIX.181, 20 July 1859.
68. Butler, 1926, p. 315.
69. Dessain, 1980, pp. 115-16.
70. LDXIX.134-5, 16 May 1859.
71. LDXIX.144, from Dr John Gillow, 18 May 1859.
72. LDXIX.175, Dessain, footnote.
73. LDXIX.240, from Bishop Brown, 3 October 1859.
74. LDXIX.241, Dessain, footnote.
75. LDXIX.289-90, 19 January 1860.
76. LDXIX.xiv, Dessain, 1969.
77. Trevor, 1996, p. 183.
78. LDXX.446, 19 May 1863.
79. XIX.290, footnote.
80. Butler, 1926, p. 321.
81. Ibid.
82. Gilley, 1990, p. 307.
83. Butler, 1926, p. 473; LDXIX, 24 October 1859.
84. LDXX.324, 24 October 1862.
85. LDXX.325.
86. LDXX.382.
87. Newman, 1956, p. 272.
88. Chadwick, 1996, p. 163.
89. Barry, 1905, p. 125.
90. LDXXI.62, 27 February 1864.
91. LDXX.571-2, 30 December 1863.
92. LDXXI.10, from Charles Kingsley, 6 January 1864.
93. LDXXI.11, 7 January 1864.
94. LDXXI.12-16, 8 January 1864.
95. LDXXI.19, from Charles Kingsley, 14 January 1864.
96. LDXXI.19, Dessain, footnote.
97. LDXXI.18.
98. LDXXI.20, 17 January 1864.
99. LDXXI.26, 22 January 1864.

100. LDXXI.37–9, Edward Badeley, 5 February 1964.
101. LDXXI.47, diary note.
102. LDXXI.1, Dessain, footnote.
103. Maisie Ward, 1991, p. viii.
104. LDXXI.xiii, Dessain, footnote.
105. Maisie Ward, 1991, p. viii.
106. Oddie, 1993, p. xix.
107. LDXXVII.219, 13 February 1875.
108. LDXXI.100, 23 April 1864.
109. LDXXI.90–1, 31 March 1864.
110. Chadwick, 1990, p. 61.
111. Houghton, 1945, p. 7.
112. LDXXI.89–90, 27 March 1864.
113. Sencourt, 1948, p. 189.
114. LDXXI.109, Diary, 9 May 1864.
115. LDXXI.94, 15 April 1864.
116. LDXXI.116, 16 June 1864.
117. LDXXI.95.
118. LDXXI.130, 24 June 1864.
119. LDXXI.132, 25 June 1864.
120. LDXXI.134, Charlotte Wood, 25 June 1864.
121. LDXXI.259, 12 October 1864.
122. LDXXI.468, W. J. Copeland, 16 May 1865; LDXXI.xiv, Dessain.
123. Ward, 1976, p. ix.
124. Chadwick, 1972, p. 415.
125. Ibid.
126. LDXXI.221–2, Bishop D. Moriarty, 8 September 1864.
127. LDXXI.447–8, Dr Charles Russell, 19 April 1865.
128. LDXXI.120, footnote.
129. LDXXVII.29, Sir W. Cope, 13 February 1875.
130. LDXXVII.206–7, 27 January 1875.
131. Newman, 1956, p. 60.
132. Chadwick, 1972, p. 416.
133. Dessain, 1980, p. 163.
134. Coulson, 1970, p. 55.
135. LDXIX.352, 2 June 1860.
136. Chadwick, 1972, p. 414.
137. Norman, 1986, p. 100.
138. Chadwick, 1996, p. 163.
139. Butler, 1926, p. 332.
140. LDXXI.144–5, 6 July 1864.
141. Griffin, 1993, p. 103.
142. Griffin, 1993, p. 97.
143. Ker, 1996, p. 186.
144. Ker, 1988, p. 548.
145. Ker, 1994, p. xxv.
146. Gilley, 1990, p. 330.

147. Chadwick, 1972, p. 413.
148. Houghton, 1945, pp. 96-7.
149. Wilson, 1990, p. 137.
150. LDXXI.97, W. J. Copeland, 19 April 1864.
151. Ward, 1913, II, p. 76.
152. LDXXII.72, T. W. Allies, 11 October 1865.
153. Barry, 1905, pp. 210-11.
154. Jay, 1991, p. 220.
155. Ward, 1913, II, p. 76.
156. LDXXII.39, 28 August 1865.
157. LDXXII.126, Mother Margaret Hallahan, 14 January 1866.
158. LDXXV.208, 18 September 1870.
159. LDXXXI.51, 7 April 1885.
160. DXXXI.264, footnote 6.
161. LDXXXI.67, 19 May 1885.
162. Gilley, 1990, p. 341.
163. Butler, 1926, p. 354.
164. Chadwick, 1990, p. 62.
165. LDXXII.44, 5 September 1865.
166. LDXXII.89-91, 31 October 1865.
167. LDXXII.68-9, 8 October 1865.
168. LDXXII.91, footnote.
169. LDXXII.91, 1 November 1865.
170. LDXXII.93, Dessain, footnote.
171. LDXXIII.93, 3 November 1865.
172. LDXXII.105.
173. LDXXII.109, footnote.
174. LDXXII.110, 24 October 1865.
175. LDXXII.119, 8 December 1865.
176. LDXXII.118, 8 December 1865.
177. LDXXII.199, Dessain, footnote.
178. LDXXII.133.
179. LDXXII.xxiv.
180. LDXXII.137, footnote.
181. LDXXII.137, E. B. Pusey, 22 January 1866.
182. Trevor, 1996, p. 210.
183. Butler, 1926, pp. 358-9.
184. LDXXII.158, 19 February 1866.
185. LDXXII.211, 13 April 1866.
186. LDXXII.154, Dessain, footnote.
187. LDXXII.154, 13 February 1866.
188. Butler, 1926, p. 368.
189. LDXXII.162, footnote.
190. LDXXII.163, footnote.
191. LDXXII.163, 22 February 1866.
192. LDXXII.182, 17 March 1866.
193. LDXXII.187, 23 March 1866.

194. LDXXII.201, 2 April 1866.
195. LDXXII.173, 5 March 1866.
196. LDXXII.xiv, Dessain.
197. LDXXII.186, Editor of the *Guardian*, 23 March 1866.
198. LDXXII.306, 24 October 1866.
199. LDXX.360–2, William Wilberforce, 4 December 1862.
200. Holmes, 1979, p. vii.
201. LDXIX.488, Malcolm Maccoll, 24 March 1861.
202. Cf. Holmes, 1979, p. vii.
203. LDXXVI.66, Canon H. P. Liddon, 18 April 1872.
204. Holmes, 1979, p. 72.
205. Holmes, 1979, p. 73.
206. Ker, 1990, p. 735.
207 LDXXX.201, Lord Emly, 9 April 1883.
208. Newman, 1956, p. 266.
209. LDXXV.161, footnote.
210. LDXXIV.161, Memorandum, 14 October 1868.
211. LDXXIV.171, 15 November 1868.
212. LDXXVI.279–80, 23 March 1873.
213. LDXXVI.282, Canon H. P. Liddon, 27 March 1873.
214. LDXXVII.xiii.
215. Chadwick, 1990, p. 62.
216. LDXXVII.152, 6 November 1874.
217. Norman, 1985, p. 310.
218. Sencourt, 1948, p. 233.
219. Griffin, 1993, p. 163.
220. LDXXVII.158, 15 November 1874.
221. LDXXVII.159, 23 November 1874.
222. LDXXVII.129, 7 October 1874.
223. LDXXVII.170, 10 December 1874.
224. LDXXVII.177, 27 December 1874.
225. LDXXVII.177, 19 December 1874.
226. LDXXVII, footnote.
227. LDXXVII.179, 31 December 1874.
228. LDXXVII.180, footnote.
229. LDXXVII.186, 9 January 1875.
230. LDXXVII.xv
231. LDXXVII.9 September 1872.
232. Ker, 1988, p. 688.
233. LDXXVII.162, P. Girard, 30 November 1874.
234. LDXXVII.185, 9 January 1875.
235. LDXXVIII.351, 26 April 1878.
236. LDXXVIII, footnote, 28 April 1878.
237. LDXXVII.192, from W. E. Gladstone, 15 June 1875.
238. LDXXVII.193, 16 January 1875.
239. LDXXVII.211-13, 5 February 1875.
240. LDXXVII.220, Dessain, footnote.

241. LDXXVII.220, 14 February 1875.
242. LDXXVII.221, 19 February 1875.
243. LDXXVII, Appendix I, pp. 401–10.
244. Newman, 1956, p. 16.
245. LDXXVII.199, footnote.
246. LDXXVII.199, 19 January 1875.
247. LDXXVII.234, footnote.
248. LDXXVII.236, 26 February 1875.
249. LDXXVII.237, 26 July 1875.
250. LDXXX.36, 17 December 1881.
251. LDXXX.36-7, 23 December 1881.
252. LDXXX.45, 2 January 1882.
253. Ker, 1990, p. 742.
254. LDXXIX.337, W. S. Lilly, 17 February 1881.
255. LDXXXI.xiii, Introductory Note.
256. LDXXI.113, 4 February 1886; 114, 6 February 1886; 116–17, 16
     February 1886.
257. LDXXXI.122, 1 March 1886.
258. LDXXXI.125, footnote.
259. LDXXXI.131, 5 April 1886.
260. LDXXXI.299–302.
261. LDXXII.103–4.
262. LDXXIV.332, 12 September 1869.
263. LDXXIII.275, Henry Wilberforce, 21 July 1867.
264. LDXXIV.91-2, 21 June 1868.
265. LDXXIV.377, 21 November 1869.
266. LDXXIV.324–5, Mrs Helbert, 30 August 1869.
267. LDXXIV.389, J. F. Secombe, 14 December 1869.
268. LDXXV.16–17, 28 January 1870.
269. LDXXV.17, footnote.
270. Tristram, Henry, 1933, p. 159.
271. LDXXV.19, 28 January 1870.
272. LDXXV.27, 4 February 1870.
273. LDXXV.xvi.
274. LDXXV.27, 9 February 1870.
275. LDXXV.53, 14 March 1870.
276. LDXXV.54, 15 March 1870.
277. LDXXV.54, footnote.
278. LDXXV.61, 22 March 1870.
279. LDXXV.61, footnote.
280. LDXXV.81, A. P. L. Phillips, 7 April 1870.
281. LDXXV.119, 2 May 1870.
282. LDXXV.98–9, 13 April 1870.
283. LDXXV.138, 6 June 1870.
284. Gilley, 1990, p. 369.
285. LDXXV.154, Ambrose Phillips de Lisle, 24 July 1870.
286. LDXXV.168, 27 July 1870.

287. LDXXV.9, 16 January 1870; Ward, 1913, II, p. 235.
288. Ker, 1990, p. 662.
289. LDXXV.174, 6 August 1870.
290. LDXXV.174, W. J. O'Neill Daunt, 7 August 1870.
291. LDXXV.185, Emile Perceval, 15 August 1870.
292. LDXXV.192, 21 August 1870.
293. LDXXV.203, Anna Whitty, 9 September 1870.
294. LDXXV.216, Mrs Wilson, 20 October 1870.
295. LDXXV.259, 'late 1870'.
296. LDXXV.315, 11 April 1871.
297. LDXXV.447, 10 December 1871.
298. LDXXVI.139, 19 July 1872.
299. LDXXVI.166, 12 September 1872.
300. LDXXVI.169, R. F. Littledale, 15 September 1872.
301. LDXXVI.198, 5 November 1872.
302. LDXXVII.286, 24 April 1875.
303. Dessain, 1980, p. 118.
304. Ward, 1913, II, p. 373.
305. LDXXV.300, 12 March 1871.
306. LDXXVII.110, footnote.

Chapter 7

'Champion of the Laity'

According to Owen Chadwick, in the first half of his life Newman 'wound up the Church of England to its Catholic heritage. In the second half of his life he wound down the Church of Rome – that is, he sought to persuade its leaders not to push their Catholicity into fanaticism, or superstition, or irrationality, or rigid hierarchy; and therefore to keep their minds open to the old principle of primitive Catholic faith, and from that broader base to listen to the discoveries of the age'.[1] Chadwick's model provides a valuable approach to summing up Newman's life and activities.

To 'wind up' has, of course, several connotations; Chadwick seems to use this phrase to draw attention to Newman's belief that, in his Anglican days, he had the mission of saving the Church of England from the perils which he perceived to be threatening it.[2] This sense of personal responsibility led to the foundation of the Oxford Movement, and to the first of the 'Tracts for the Times', *The Ministerial Commission* (1833), a vigorous call to the clergy of the Church of England to recognize that their spiritual authority was based on their apostolic descent. Newman openly challenged the clergy, who were diversified in their observances, ranging from High Church to Low Church and Evangelicals, to realize that they had a Catholic heritage. In this self-imposed task of 'winding up' the Church of England Newman was to work closely with several of his Oxford contemporaries, especially Pusey, Froude and Keble. Newman's influence was considerable and pervasive. He wrote most of the Tracts and gave a series of lectures and sermons by means of which he acquired a reputation for stirring up discussion on religion in the University.[3] But even in the midst of his many activities, Newman experienced doubts about the essential nature of the Church of England. To an intimate friend he confided as early as 1836 that 'my heart is with Rome'.[4] His anxieties persisted, as his correspondence witnesses, [5] eventually leading to his secession from the Church of England. In the process of 'winding up' the Church of England, Newman had argued that a form of Catholicism existed that was not Roman. This view resulted in the Anglo-Catholic revival in the Church of England.[6] After Newman had become a Catholic, the Oxford Movement was to enter a second phase of its existence in parochial activities in the industrial cities and towns. Anglo-Catholics 'adopted the language and ritual practices of Roman Catholicism without the structure of doctrinal authority'.[7]

In the matter of 'winding down' the Church of Rome, Newman also made significant contributions, and these can be summarized under the topics of his persistent emphasis on the need for an educated, well-instructed laity; the cultivation of an identifiable type of English Catholicism in harmony with the traditions of the 'old' Catholics; the importance of intellectual excellence in higher education in which spiritual values were recognized; the foundation of a distinctive English style of Oratorianism; and his remarkable capacity for combining spiritual and intellectual stimulation through his sermons and treatises and by his contributions to controversial issues.

Chadwick relates his assertion that Newman 'wound down the Church of Rome', to Newman's influence on the emergence of the Catholic Church from relative obscurity in English national life to a respected place in society. As Dessain states,

> He wanted Roman Catholics to come out of the ghetto and take their place in the world, to adapt themselves, to enlarge their minds in the confidence that truth could never contradict truth, and to be guided like responsible men by their enlightened consciences.[8]

It is, perhaps, paradoxical that a scholarly cleric who had spent many years in comparative obscurity – he had held no office in the Church until he was made Cardinal in his seventy-ninth year – should urge Catholics to 'come out of the ghetto' and to take part in national life. He himself was a peripheral figure in the Church for many years after becoming a Catholic virtually half-way through his long life. Yet through his extensive writings and range of influential friends and contacts he was able to affect profoundly the regeneration of Catholicism in the nineteenth century. One of his favourite sayings was that 'life is for action'; by force of circumstances he was often drawn into controversy and conflict but these fairly frequent disputes, although personally stressful, had a catalytic effect. They spurred this solitary, introspective figure to defend, for example, the supremacy of conscience. In his prime he had left the privileged and protective environment of the Established Church, after recognizing that, as he wrote in the *Apologia*: 'down had come the *Via Media* as a definite theory or scheme'.[9]

As a stranger he had entered the portals of Catholicism, where Ultramontanism – the conventional doctrinal approach – contrasted sharply with the Erastianism of the Church of England. After the emancipation of Catholics in 1829, various parties seemed to emerge: these have been typified as 'old Catholics', the 'new Catholics', and the 'English Catholics'. Newman kept clear of these movements or cliques, although they, individually, sought to attract his support. He was wary of identifying himself, for example, with the 'old Catholics' because of their tendency towards closely linking political and religious doctrines as, indeed, he had already perceived in the underlying Erastianism of the Church of England. Moreover, he held steadfastly to his views that:

> For the last fifty years, since 1827, there has been a formidable movement among us towards assigning in the national life political or civil motives for social and personal duties and thereby withdrawing matters of conduct from the jurisdiction of religion. Men are to be made virtuous, and to do good works, to become good members of society, good husbands and fathers, on purely secular motives. We are having a wedge thrust into us, which tends to be destructive of religion altogether ...[10]

In his private journal an entry of 22 February 1865 records that Newman felt that he had 'got hardened against the opposition made to me, and have not the soreness at any ill treatment on the part of certain influential Catholics – and this simply from the natural effect of time'.[11]

Unlike Manning, Newman seldom hastened to intervene in political or social problems; he 'regarded the spiritual nature of men as being in much greater immediate hazard than their material situation'.[12] At the same time he did not fail to show compassion for the poor and needy, as his concern about providing educational facilities for the village children of Littlemore and for those of the working-class families of Birmingham clearly showed.

In advocating that Catholics should contribute positively to political and social policies, Newman maintained that they should show that the adherents of English Catholicism were willing and able to contribute to the development of national policies in the areas of health, education, social welfare, etc. Newman insisted that the laity had to equip themselves to undertake their roles as well-instructed Catholics and also as loyal citizens, whose opinions would be recognized as informed, constructive and objective. In his early years as an Oratorian, Newman had deplored that so few Catholics could 'write well' when putting forward their religious beliefs.[13]

The Jesuit Provincial, Fr Peter Gallwey, wrote to Newman in February 1865 asking for his opinion on the prospects for a Catholic periodical. Newman suggested that his enquirer – who saw 'so many more persons' – would be better able than most to answer that question. 'In such matters supply must go before and create the demand.' He added that the Jesuits had many 'able and learned men in the English and Irish provinces', who would be 'capable of creating the supply'. Newman preferred to 'speak of the need of such a publication', and he felt that, as with 'secular power, rank and wealth are great human means of promoting Catholicism, so especially in this democratic age is intellect'.[14] This correspondence coincided with the appearance of the *Month* – for 'educated readers' – launched by Fanny Taylor in 1864, and taken over by the Jesuits in 1865, under the editorship of Fr Henry Coleridge, one of Newman's long-standing friends. In 1880, the *Downside Review* – an academic journal – was founded by Gasquet; while Wiseman and O'Connell had founded *The Dublin Review* as early as 1836.

Although Newman left the Church of England, he always had an affectionate regard for the Church in which he had spent the first half of his life. He viewed the Established Church as 'a great power in English society for good – for religion and against the growth of infidelity'. He declared that 'to weaken the establishment was to damage a bulwark of religion, while Roman Catholics had as yet no adequate force to supply in its place'.[15]

Ker has observed that Newman, for 'all his new-found energy and excitement' when he founded the Oratory, 'was careful, unlike some converts, to advise against direct attacks on the Church of England'. He considered that 'the Catholic Church at that time was too weak to take its place as the guardian of revealed Christianity in the country at large'. This role was being filled by the Church of England as the 'only bulwark against infidelity'.[16]

In the *Apologia*, Newman wrote:

The Church of England has been the instrument of Providence in conferring great benefits on me . . . and I have received so much good from the
Anglican establishment itself, can I have the heart or want of charity,
considering that it does for so many others, what it has done for me, to
wish to see it overthrown? I have no such wish while it is what it is, and
while we are so small a body.[17]

These attitudes are reflected in his correspondence with J. M. Capes
'Who at *this moment* would any how not adopt Roman Catholicism,
but go the other way were the Establishment destroyed?'.[18] In a
further letter to Capes, Newman emphasized,

I don't look on the Church of England as important, in contrast to *Dissent*,
but as a bulwark against Infidelity, which Dissent cannot be. Were the
Church of E. to fall, Methodism might remain a while – I can't tell, for I
don't know – but, surely, on the whole, the various denominations exist
under the shadow of the Establishment, out of which they sprung, and, did
it go, would go too . . . Infidelity would take the possession of the bulk of
the men and women.[19]

Newman had written, in November 1865, to the editor of the *Weekly
Register* to correct a misleading reference to his stated views on the
Church of England. Nearly twenty years later, this matter again
emerged, when the *Standard*, in a leading article, stated: 'The Church
of England, says Newman, is the only barrier left in Christendom
capable of correcting it (infidelity).' One of Newman's correspondents
sent a copy of Newman's letter of 19 November 1865, and it was
printed again in the *Weekly Register*.[20] Newman made a Memorandum, dated 7 January 1883, in which he stated:

'The Anglican Church is a bulwark of Catholic truth.' No, I did not say
this in the first sentence of my *'Difficulties'* [*Certain Difficulties felt by
Anglicans in Catholic Teaching*] – but the only *political* bulwark of the
dogmatic principle. In the *Apologia* I was speaking of 'Catholic truth', and
I called it, not a bulwark but a breakwater. I denied that the Church was
more [than] a great wall as regards Catholic Truth, a 'serviceable breakwater' against errors more fundamental than its own. On the other hand,
enumerating the fair side of Angl. (Anglicanism) I certainly say that its
Church is a bulwark, but what kind of bulwark – 'A *political* bulwark of
the (dogmatic) principle'.[21]

An interesting contribution to the subject of the terminology used to describe the Church of England's significant role occurred when the son of Augustus Welby Pugin, the renowned Victorian architect, sent Newman a republished copy of his father's pamphlet of 1850, *Church and State; or Christian Liberty*, in which he wrote of the Church of England as 'a great *breakwater* between the raging waves of infidelity and Catholic truth in this land'. Newman responded that it 'was a great satisfaction to see that he (A. W. Pugin) had used the word *breakwater* of the Church of England before me, as showing by the coincidence between us that the term was a natural and suitable description of its relation to the Catholic Church'.[22]

About three years after he had written the Memorandum concerning the perceived role of the Anglican Church, Newman acknowledged receipt of a pamphlet opposing disestablishment of the Church of England, which was being advocated by the radical wing of the Liberal Party at the General Election in November 1885. In thanking his correspondent, Newman described the pamphlet as 'bold and powerful, with certain grave drawbacks'. While he agreed with its main principles he 'grieved for Gladstone with a tenderness' which he 'did not recognise' in the pamphlet. He was clearly concerned about the statesman's reappearance on the 'public stage', after his earlier declared intention of 'retiring from political life or at least from all conflicts'. Newman must have had in mind the occasion when he felt it necessary to rebut Gladstone's groundless allegations against Catholics which resulted in his writing the *Letter to the Duke of Norfolk*. In his letter to the present correspondent, Newman, in his advanced old age, also felt it desirable to state, adamantly:

> As to the Church of England, I have no wishes just now for its destruction [referring to disestablishment]. I should rejoice to fancy the possibility of its reconciling itself to that Holy Catholic Church, whose boast it is that it concedes nothing; but I should not wish to purchase even the power and popularity of the Anglican Church at the price of surrendering one jot or tittle of Catholic Roman teaching. The Bishop of Durham with you speaks of the Disestablishment of the Ch of E as a great national sin: No – that sin was committed three centuries ago, when the state sent the true Church right about and installed the Anglican in her place.[23]

Almost thirty years earlier, Newman had told Ambrose Phillips de Lisle – a zealous convert to Catholicism and close collaborator of Pugin and the 16th Earl of Shrewsbury: 'You must not suppose I am one of those who wish the Church of England overthrown, though I cannot regard it, as a *Catholic*, in any 'corporate capacity'. I quite agree with you that we may contemplate the English *Nation* as a body. The words are 'teach all nations' not 'teach all Churches'.[24]

Towards the end of his life, Newman told another correspondent that as a boy he had 'learned those great and burning truths' from evangelical teaching. 'The Holy Roman Church has added to the simple evangelicism [sic] of my first teachers, but it has obscured, enfeebled, nothing of it.'[25] Accordingly, as Sheridan Gilley puts it, Newman 'died as he had lived, a Catholic, but an Evangelical as well'.[26]

Newman had been reflecting deeply on the 'subject of grace, regeneration, etc.', and on 13 January 1825 there is an entry in his private journal noting that 'before many months of his clerical life were over', he had 'taken the first step in giving up the evangelical form of Christianity; however, for a long time while certain shreds and tatters of that doctrine hung about his preaching, nor did he for a whole ten years altogether sever himself from those great religious societies and their meetings, which then as now were the rallying ground and the strength of the Evangelical body'.[27] During this period of re-alignment, Newman was a curate at St Clements, Oxford, and he concluded 'that Calvinism was not a key to the phenomena of human nature, as they occur in the world. And, in truth, much as he owed to the evangelical teaching, so it was, he never had been a genuine evangelical'.[28]

He never repudiated the fifteen University sermons he preached as an Anglican. In 1853 he wrote, 'I stand by my [Oxford] University Discourses . . . and am almost a zealot for their substantial truth',[29] and in 1872 he issued a third edition of these sermons. Newman thus claimed that a convert like himself 'had the advantage of both knowing Catholic doctrine and having Protestant experience'. But he admitted that this meant that he was 'too often looked at with suspicion by the Protestant because he had become a Catholic and by the Catholic because he had been a Protestant'.[30]

This third edition of his University Discourses was dedicated to Richard Church, Dean of St Paul's, whose friendship had been 'resumed after a period of 15 years in June 1865, when Newman was in London for Manning's consecration and stayed with Frederic Rogers, and there found Church to welcome him'.[31] In an elegant and moving dedication, Newman recalled 'how, in the February of 1841 you suffered me day after day to open my anxieties and plans', and had responded with warm and generous friendship.[32] After this historic meeting, Church and Rogers presented Newman with a violin to mark 'their renewed friendship ... To him the violin proved to be an undiluted joy'; it was in constant use until 1883, 'and then he in turn passed it on to Church's daughter, Mary'.[33]

An Anglican cleric, who had been a member of Oriel before Newman's time, wrote to tell him 'how much his parochial sermons had helped in pastoral work in London ... For I have preached in simple words very many of your parochial sermons'. Newman thanked him warmly and commented: 'There is very little in them which I should not say now, altering some forms of expression.' He prized them not only for the associations they bring, but 'because they are still a sort of bond between me and those dear Oxford friends, the loss of whom was the greatest trial of my change of religion'.[34]

Almost throughout his life, both as an Anglican and then a Catholic, Newman was the target of unfriendly, even hostile comment; in addition, suspicions abounded. Rumours that he was going to return to Anglicanism often circulated. Almost everything he wrote was subject to searching scrutiny; he was delated to Rome, accused of heretical beliefs, etc. To some degree Newman's life was spent on a battlefield, although he was a highly skilled campaigner who relished the challenge of controversial issues.

In June 1861, J. Spencer Northcote, President of Oscott, showed Newman a report which made serious allegations concerning his religious convictions. Newman told the Oscott president that the report was but 'one of the thousand and one pieces of gossip which have been put about concerning me for nearly 30 years, and will be put about to the end – for it is the chronic state of my reputation'.[35] In a rough draft of this letter, Newman noted: 'It is marvellous what things people will say. Never since I have been a Catholic, have I had one doubt of the truth of Catholicism: never one moment have not thanked almighty God for making me one.'[36]

A year later Newman was again involved in repudiating statements about himself and his religious life, including the possibility of his leaving the Catholic Church. Various journals such as the *Globe*, the *Morning Advertiser*, and the *Record* had picked up rumours and had avidly reported that he was about to leave the Oratorians and return to the Church of England. To the editors of these papers, Newman wrote stating that he 'had not had one moment's wavering of trust in the

Catholic Church ever since I was received into her fold'. He confirmed his complete allegiance to the Pope and to the 'creed in all its articles', adding in characteristic style, that it would be superfluous to reiterate all this, 'except that Protestants are always on the look-out for some loophole or evasion in a Catholic's statement of fact'.[37] To the editors of the *Morning Advertiser* and the *Record*, he replied similarly.[38] In closing his letter to the editor of the *Globe* Newman had observed, perhaps unguardedly: 'I should be a consummate fool (to use a mild term) if in my old age I left "the land flowing with milk and honey" for the city of confusion and the house of bondage.' This caused *Aris's Birmingham Gazette* to publish a stinging article accusing Newman of insulting 'a body to which he himself once belonged, and to express in the most abusive words he could use, his hatred towards the clergy and laity of the Church of England'.[39] Newman wrote expressing his regrets that his letter to the *Globe* should have caused offence, but he was concerned to stop an erroneous report about himself in that paper. His references to Protestantism were strictly related to himself; he had said that he 'would be a fool to return to Protestantism'. He asserted; 'So I should; but I did not say, nor did I mean to say (what I should be quite as great a fool for saying) that the criticism, which would rightly attach to me, if I went back, was actually due to those who remained faithful to their existing religious convictions.'[40]

Newman disliked ostentation and public display. He wished Catholicism in England to grow quietly, avoiding devotional excesses, and preferring 'English habits of belief and devotion'.[41]

Towards the end of his life Newman was approached by an aspiring convert, who was advised:

> The soul is like the body; - different medicines suit different persons. I think there is just a chance of one or other of my Sermons [*Parochial and Plain Sermons*], if you read this and that, being useful to you. So I shall ask you to accept a copy from me.

He reminded his enquirer that before becoming a Catholic, he 'must gain the gift of faith first'.[42] In just under two years, this earnest enquirer was received into the Church.[43]

Newman himself told Mrs Froude that,

> There is a marked contrast in Catholicity between the views presented to us by doctrine and devotion respectively. Doctrines never change, devotions

vary with each individual. Catholics allow each other, accordingly, the greatest licence, and are, if I may so speak, other *liberals*, as regards devotions, whereas they are most sensitive about doctrine.[44]

A few years later he revealed to another correspondent

> As an Englishman I do not like a Roman religion – and I have much to say, not, God forbid, against the Roman Catholic, but against the Roman Catholic Church. I have no great sympathy with Italian religion, as such – but I do not account myself the worse Catholic for this.[45]

Although he found Faber's Italianate-style devotions and writings personally unappealing, Newman was prepared to tolerate them. He wrote to one correspondent that, 'As to Fr Faber's book [*Growth in Holiness*], I suppose it is a perfect magazine of valuable thoughts – but it must not make you scrupulous. What suits one person, does not another.'[46] Soon after meeting Faber, Newman noted in his diary that 'he is much more poetical in the largest sense of the word than the Oratorians'.[47]

Like the 'old' Catholics, Newman disliked the exaggerated pious practices and emotionalism associated with Ultramontanism. His journal shows clearly that he was not devoid of emotion, but it also discloses that he felt uneasy about excessive dependence on emotional appeals and satisfactions in religion. He counselled Faber,

> The *end* of the Oratory of Brothers is doubtless to *save the soul*. If anyone or any Oratory can arrive at this end by no means or by any other means (allowable), let him do it. One can't prescribe one's own means to others. If you can attain the end directly and immediately, by all means do it and use no means.[48]

Maisie Ward states:

> Newman's genius found its scope in a unique vocation – at once spiritual and intellectual – of drawing the world nearer to God not by prayer but by thought . . . he lived and moved more among the early Fathers than among his living friends close as they were to him.[49]

This blending of the spiritual and intellectual was developed by Newman in *The Idea of a University*. He saw the need for religion to have a recognized place in a university, without which it could not rightfully claim academic eminence. Hence, spiritual growth and intellectual excellence were essential constituents of higher education.

Closely associated with his stimulating views on higher education was Newman's persistent advocacy of the role of the laity on the Catholic Church. He wanted Catholics to be better educated so that they could become accepted into English society at large. At the same time, he urged that the distinctive role of the laity should be readily acknowledged by the clergy. In a series of lectures in Birmingham during 1851, which were published as *The Present Position of Catholics in England*, Newman not only attempted to dismiss popular myths about Catholicism, but also stressed that the laity should accept their responsibilities to become better informed about their faith so that they could give enquirers reliable knowledge about its beliefs and practices. He told his listeners:

> I want a laity, not arrogant, not rash in speech, not disputatious, but men who know their religion ... I want an intelligent, well-informed laity ... I wish to enlarge your knowledge, to cultivate your reason, to get an insight into the relation of truth to truth, to learn to view things as they are, to understand how faith and reason stand to each other.[50]

Newman developed the concept of the *consensus fidelium* – 'the consensus of the faithful, the common mind of ordinary worshippers'.[51] He wanted an end to the submissive passivity of the laity, such as he had discovered during his stressful years in Ireland. There the laity 'were treated like good little boys - were told to shut their eyes and open their mouths, and take what we give them – and this they do not relish'.[52] He held that the opinions of the laity on matters of special concern to them should be listened to by the English Catholic hierarchy. On this issue, Newman was forthright in his correspondence: 'As far as I can see, there are ecclesiastics all over Europe, whose policy is to keep the laity at arms-length; and hence the laity have become discouraged and become infidel, and two parties exist, both ultras in opposite directions.'

He added that he had left Ireland 'with the distressing fear, that in that Catholic country, in like manner, there was to be an antagonism, as time went on, between the hierarchy and the educated classes'. As regards the Catholic University of Ireland, he counselled his correspondent to endeavour to develop the University as 'a middle station at which clergy and laity can meet, so as to learn to understand and to yield to each other'. This common ground would enable both parties to 'act in union upon an age, which is running headlong into

infidelity'.[53] Newman's wise guidance was gratefully received and
influenced the representations made by students of the CUI to the
governing body. It resulted in various reforms, including laymen to be
opted to the Episcopal Board.[54] Although Newman was not directly
involved in these reforms – which he had always advocated when he
was rector of the CUI – his influence in these matters was still significant, although covert, and had led to the more enlightened policies
now adopted.

   A few years earlier, Newman alerted James Hope-Scott, his trusted
friend, that he had heard from Fr Weld, the Jesuit Provincial, that
Manning was 'going to set up a House of higher studies ... near
Reading' for which 'he has got large sums of money'. He stressed that
'this concerns both you and me, for your influence as a layman cannot
be overlooked, and I wish to act with you'.[55] Hope-Scott's reply
crossed Newman's letter in the post; he informed Newman that 'the
Jesuits have been asked to establish a kind of College, to carry young
men over what may be called the university period of their lives'. Fr
Weld had spoken to him about the project and had said he would
consult Newman. Fr Weld, Hope-Scott assured Newman, 'feels the
necessity of giving a more hearty English tone to the system of
management, and has Anglican converts in the Society who would be
likely to support his views. Such a scheme would 'open up something
like a University to your elder boys, without the objections raised to
Oxford and Cambridge'. Hope-Scott thought that this proposal could
be a 'great shield' between Newman and 'most of your present
assailants'. As far as the Jesuits were concerned, 'There is no religious body which loves and admires you more than the SJ.'[56] Further
exploration of this topic seemed halted and at the Low Week 1868
meeting of the English hierarchy, a resolution was passed that some
steps should be taken to provide higher education for Catholic youths,
from eighteen to twenty-two years old, especially those in the higher
echelons of society. The notion of an English Catholic university was
dismissed and the bishops recommended that alternatives should be
considered by a commission.

   Eventually, in autumn 1871, Manning and two other bishops
convened a conference to implement the proposals of the bishops'
conference; a sub-committee was set up, which included Northcote,
President of Oscott College, who was well known to Newman. On 17
February 1872, Northcote sent Newman a copy of the questionnaire
on higher education for young Catholic laymen and invited his views.

Newman replied: 'For youths between 18 and 22 I know of no system of Liberal Education except University Education; and for that as regards English Catholics there is at present, not merely deficient provision, but no provision at all.' As regards examinations, Newman held that these 'hold but a subordinate part', as he had maintained in *The Idea of a University*, Discourse VI: 'Residence without Examination comes nearer to the idea of a University Education than examinations without residence.'[57]

Northcote thanked Newman but expressed disappointment that he had avoided answering a question for proposals to meet the difficulty of providing higher educational facilities for young Catholic men. This prompted Newman to say:

> What is the good of consulting how to supply a need, before there is a general agreement what the need is. There must be a common basis of sentiment to secure a common action. I cannot answer questions about University Education, till I know in what sense the words are used. One must have something to aim at, in order to take aim.[58]

Newman's mind was obviously reflecting on the difficulties he had experienced throughout the seven years he dedicated to developing the Catholic University in Ireland. He felt that no real progress with the present proposal would be likely if its aims and objectives were not agreed upon by all concerned in its foundation and development.

On 6 August 1872, Northcote sent Newman a copy of his report on higher education; Newman felt that it 'would be sure to do great good'. In a long letter, Newman recounted his disappointing experiences in Dublin with the setting up of the CUI and his realization that the 'English bishops, clergy and laity would have nothing to say in its support'. Later, when he was asked by his bishop 'to undertake the business of Oxford ... my unwilling compliance was gained without any idea or wish on my part of establishing a College there'. At no time had he seen his way 'to recommend or to further any plan for the admission of Catholic youth to a Protestant University'. He declared that he had 'never taken an initiative in the suggestions or (much less) actively advocated the step, of a Catholic College or Hall in Oxford'. He was aware that 'the cultivation of the intellect' involves a risk to faith, but 'where it is absolutely excluded, there is no cultivation'. He drew attention to 'two main instruments of infidelity just now: physical science and history'. The former 'is used against Scripture; and the latter against dogma'. As a result of the Vatican Council, Newman asserted: 'Now we are new born children, and we are going to war without strength and without arms. We do not know what exactly we hold – what we may grant, what we must maintain.' Newman's 'candid' letter was intended to indicate that he felt it 'scarcely possible' for him to answer the 'main question', i.e. of providing proposals for the higher education of Catholic youths.[59]

In a letter to Lord Howard of Glossop, Newman commented:

> We are driving into a corner just now, and have to act, when no mode of action is even bearable. It is a choice of great difficulties ... Certainly, the more I think of it, the less am I satisfied with the proposal of establishing a Catholic College in our Universities; and I suppose the idea of a Catholic University, pure and simple, is altogether out of the question.

He thought that the bishops ought to repeal their decision which meant that young Catholics were 'virtually prohibited from going to the existing colleges'. Also, the Jesuits' Mission at Oxford should be strengthened.[60]

More than a decade later, Newman informed an academic – who, unknown to him at the time, held a post at the 'College in Kensington' – that 'twenty years ago I was desirous that Catholic youths should be allowed to continue at the Protestant Colleges, the Bishop of Birmingham wishing, as he said, an Oratory to be established in Oxford. Now the peril of infidelity is so great that I dare not undertake the responsibility of recommending it'. He speculated whether 'the Jesuits might be willing and able to be involved in some way'.[61]

To Manning's dismay, the sub-committee of the bishops' conference favoured a Catholic College at Oxford (which Newman had not advocated), but their proposal was rejected, and the activities of the sub-committee then ceased.

When Newman was invited to serve on the Senate of the Catholic University College at Kensington he told Manning,

> I feel an insurmountable difficulty ... I could not without a great inconsistency take part in an Institution, which formally and 'especially' recognises the London University, a body which has been the beginning, and source, and symbol of all the Liberalism existing in the educated classes for the last 40 years.[62]

Some months earlier, Newman had warned one of his close friends, a member of the subcommittee set up by the Catholic hierarchy to consider the state of Catholic higher education, that

> The Archbishop [Manning] is not contemplating a real University education for young Catholics; but wishes to do just as much as will stop the present clamour, and take off the edge of the evident injustice of forbidding Oxford and substituting nothing for it.

Newman did not favour the establishment of a Catholic University or College at Oxford, because his experiences in Ireland in 1851–8, and in England over 1864–7 had caused him to lose faith in church authorities. He 'dreaded a minute and jealous supervision on the part of authority which will hamper every act of the heads of the University'.[63] In a further letter, Newman advised that

> On the whole, perhaps delay is the best thing for us – though we may suffer through it for a whole generation. We may do a bad thing now; we may do a good thing years hence. Great changes are taking place in Rome ... There is no reason why both [clergy and laity] should not be well educated for their respective duties in life.

But he confessed that he was 'inclined to think that the Archbishop considers only an ignorant laity to be manageable'.[64]

Manning's concept of a university was that of an institution providing technical and scientific training. This was far removed from Newman's idea of a university. When invited to preach at the formal inauguration of the Catholic University College, Newman again stated that he had difficulty in accepting because he recollected that the original prospectus 'recognised the London University' as the institution which would set examinations and award degrees. Also, he was 'not unmindful of the important fact that the English bishops, who thought residence at Oxford and Cambridge dangerous to Catholic Youth, are tolerant of the course of studies pursued at the London University'. He could not preach 'without being at liberty ... to speak against any such recognition'. He declined the invitation.[65]

The Kensington venture only lasted about eight years, due to lack of support from Catholic parents and problems with the rectorship. The rector was forced to resign and the college 'ceased to be a work of the English hierarchy'.[66] In its brief and undistinguished existence, the Kensington college had also suffered from the competitive ambitions of the Jesuits, who had plans to open their own college of higher studies at Richmond. Administrative incompetence, and the sharply-worded criticisms of Newman and other distinguished Catholics also hastened its end.[67]

In the early 1880s, some influential English Catholics had, with the agreement of the hierarchy, reopened the proposal that Catholics should be able to finish their education at Oxford. Because of advanced age and infirmity, Newman could not travel to Rome but he willingly authorized Lord Braye and others to represent his supporting views in an audience with Pope Leo XIII. These representations were doubtless influential in the withdrawal, some ten years later, of the ban by the Holy See on Catholics attending the national universities.[68]

Before the second Vatican Council (1962–65), a clear distinction existed between the teaching Church – the *ecclesia docens* (i.e. the clergy) and the taught Church – the *ecclesia docta* (i.e. the laity). As Coulson points out, however, Newman's concept of theology 'implies an active and educated laity'.[69] An educated laity would be able to make a valuable contribution to the 'healthy functioning of the Church'.[70] In his essay, *On Consulting the Faithful in Matters of Doctrine*, Newman emphasized the significance of the combined testimony of clergy and laity, namely, of the *consensus fidelium*. He told Mathew Arnold, the poet son of Dr Arnold, the well-known headmaster of Rugby School, that 'he could not follow your thinking that by "the Church" ought to be meant "the laity", any more than the word is equivalent to "the clergy"'. He reinforced his argument: 'I think the people the *matter*, and the hierarchy the *form*, and that both together make up the Church.'[71]

As Sullivan points out:

> Far from wishing to divide the Roman Catholic Church between its official teachers and the rest of the Church, Newman was concerned to show that the infallible teaching of the Church resides in the whole community of faith and not exclusively with its official teachers. He is not saying that the infallible party in the Church consults the fallible part in order to reach an infallible decision.[72]

Newman's use of the term 'consult' in this matter gave rise to misunderstanding until he clarified precisely what he meant by it.

On 25 April 1867 Talbot, an inveterate critic of Newman over many years, wrote to Manning warning him that the laity, influenced by Newman's article in the *Rambler*, 'are beginning to show the cloven hoof ... Newman is the most dangerous man in England'. Talbot then added his own idiosyncratic definition to the role of the laity as, 'to hunt, to shoot, to entertain. These matters they understood, but to meddle with ecclesiastical matters they have no right at all'.[73] Manning was annoyed but treated Talbot's intemperate comments with distinct reserve for he had no wish to cause open conflict among the bishops on the issue in question.[74]

Newman himself was intent on fostering intellectual life within the Catholic Church but, as he told Henry Wilberforce, he deplored the extreme views of (Ultramontane) laymen like W. G. Ward which 'unsettle the minds of I can't tell how many Catholics. He is free to have his own opinion, but when he makes it part of the faith' he is 'making a Church within a Church, as an Evangelical preacher, deciding that the Gospel is preached here, and is not preached there ... such behaviour destroys our very argument with the Anglicans', by striking at the heart of doctrinal uniformity.[75] Newman feared that the Catholic Church was in danger of some kind of Novationism – a third-century schism in the Roman Christian Church which was characterized by narrow exclusiveness. At the same time, he states that he 'detested any dogmatism when the Church *has* not clearly spoken. And if I am told "The Church has spoken", then I ask where? and if, instead of having any plain thing shown me, I am put off with a string of arguments, or some strong words of the Pope himself, I consider this a sophistical evasion'. He comforts himself 'with the principle that: *Lex dubia non obligat* – What is not taught universally, what is not believed universally, has no claim on me and, if it be true after all and divine my faith in it is included in the *implicate fides* I have had in the Church'.[76] In correspondence with W. G. Ward, Newman said that he considered theological differences between them as unimportant in themselves, whereas Ward made 'great moment' of them. They both shared the same faith and he, Newman, remained in the 'same temper of forbearance and sobriety which I have wished to cultivate'.[77] A few days earlier, Newman had told Ward, 'now that my own time is drawing to an end, the new generation will not forget the spirit of the old maxim, in which I have ever wished to speak and act myself: *In necessaries unitas, in dubiis, libertas, in omnibus charitas* [sic] [Freely translated as: *Unity in matters that are vital; freedom where there is doubt, and in all things let there be charity (love)*].[78] Sheridan Gilley writes that Newman's impact on Roman Catholic theology has been enormous: he was the 'Church of England's great gift to Catholic theology, being the development and fulfilment of his theological work as an Anglican. His insistence on the continuities of his own life declares that a convert is someone who discovers he is wrong, but also in some profound sense that he is already right'.[79] Dessain has observed that

> Since the new era in Newman studies it has been recognised that he was no abstract thinker or solitary, but always a pastor. From the time of his Anglican ordination, all his activity had some apostolic purpose. Doctrine was there not for speculation but to be lived.[80]

Newman was accustomed to being misrepresented and misunderstood. As he informed one of his correspondents,

> Some Catholic papers delight in putting in gossip about me. It is a great thing to set up a puppet in order to knock it down. There is just as much truth in saying that I ever dreamed of writing on Faith or Rationalism, as in saying that any person in authority ever dreamed of hindering me; and that is, no truth at all.[81]

As Owen Chadwick notes,

> While he [Newman] was a Protestant, tutors and heads and bishops poured over his words to decide whether they were unfitting for a loyal English clergyman. While he was a Roman Catholic censors at Rome poured over his words to decide whether they were heretical, or offensive to pious ears, or impudent, or merely unfitting for a loyal priest. His mental processes were all his own, and he did not care if he startled.[82]

Among achievements which were to have a lasting effect on English Catholicism was Newman's introduction into England of Oratorian values and a lifestyle based on a specifically modified version of the Rule of St Philip Neri. The Oratory appealed to him mainly because of its suitability for himself and the group of Oxford converts who had gathered about him; 'it was adapted to the habits of educated men, and seemed most likely to allow of a free development of their combined talents in their priestly work for Roman Catholicism in England'.[83] Community life was closely modelled on that of an Oxford College; unlike a religious Order, no vows were taken and very few rules were imposed. Behaviour was influenced, however, by acceptance of the need to build a common bond of *carita* [sic] or supernatural charity. This was the vocation which Newman chose in 1847, and to which he remained faithful until his death in 1890. In his journal, Newman recorded that despite 'great trials ... incidental to a new foundation', the Birmingham Oratory and, later, the London Oratory 'were successful'.[84] The Oratorian way of life enabled Newman and his associates to apply themselves as missioners and preachers in industrial Birmingham and also the fashionable district of Brompton in London. Catholicism was made more acceptable by these well-educated Englishmen to whom the Pope had given the specific task of serving the spiritual needs of the educated upper classes in England. They did not, however, confine themselves to this stratum of society.

Notes

1. Chadwick, 1990, p. 58.
2. Newman, 1956, p. 120.
3. Cf. Maisie Ward, 1948, p. 255.
4. LDV.303–5, H. J. Rose, 23 May 1836.
5. LDVII.244–6, Mrs John Mozley, 25 February 1840.
6. Cf. Trevor, 1996, p. 47.
7. Norman, 1985, p. 28.
8. Dessain, 1980, p. 168.
9. Newman, 1993, p. 176.
10 .LDXXVIII.363–4, Canon T. Longman, 298 May 1878.
11. Newman, 1956, p. 260.
12. Newman, 1985, p. 317.
13. LDXIII.6, J. M. Capes, 3 January 1849.
14. LDXXI.422–3, 26 February 1865.
15. Ward, 1913, p. 258.
16. Ker, 1991, p. 363.
17. Newman, 1993, p. 304.
18. LDXIV.165, 12 December 1850.
19. LDXIV.172–4, 24 December 1850.
20. LDXXX.174, footnote.
21. LDXXX.174, Memorandum, 7 January 1883.
22. LDXVII.217, E. W. Pugin, 10 February 1875.
23. LDXXXI.104, R. Bosworth-Smith, 22 December 1885.
24. LDXVIII.71, 1 July 1857.
25. LDXXXI.189, G. T. Edwards, 24 February 1887.
26. Gilley, 1990, p. 421.
27. Newman, 1956, p. 78.
28. Newman, 1956, p. 79.
29. LDXV.381, E. H. Thompson, 12 June 1853.

30. LDXX.543, D. R. Brownlow, 25 October 1863.
31. Tristram, 1933, p. 188.
32. Tillman, 1997, pp. v–vi.
33. Tristram, 1933, p. 189.
34. LDXX.449, Charles Robins, 20 May 1863.
35. LDXIX.521, 29 June 1861.
36. LDXIX.521, footnote.
37. LDXX.215, Editor of *Globe*, 28 June 1862.
38. LDXX.216–17, 29 June 1862.
39. LDXX.219, footnote.
40. LDXX.219, 3 July 1862.
41. Dessain, 1980, p. 135.
42. LDXXXI.141, J. Crawford Bredin, 21 May 1886.
43. LDXXXI.141, footnote.
44. LDXVI.341, 2 January 1855.
45. LDXX.471, Lady Chatterton, 16 June 1863.
46. LDXVI.436–7, Catherine Bathurst, 6 April 1855.
47. LDXII.137, 25 December 1847.
48. LDXIV.247, 6 April 1851.
49. Maisie Ward, 1948, p. 228.
50. Newman, 1851, p. 390.
51. Chadwick, 1990, p. 41.
52. Newman, 1956, p. 328.
53. LDXXVI.394, George Fottrell, 10 December 1873.
54. LDXXVI, footnote, p. 393.
55. LDXXIII.343, 25 September 1867.
56. LDXXIII.344, footnote.
57. LDXXVI.25, 23 February 1872.
58. LDXXVI.33, 27 February 1872.
59. LDXXVI.58, 7 April 1872.
60. LDXXVI.75–7, 27 April 1872.
61. LDXXX.320, St George J. Mivart, 9 March 1884.
62. LDXXVI.390, 24 November 1873.
63. LDXXVI.60–2, J. Spencer Northcote, 9 April 1872.
64. LDXXVI.65–6, J. Spencer Northcote, 17 April 1872.
65. LDXVII.253, Mgr Capel, 23 March 1875.
66. LDXVII, footnote.
67. Newsome, 1993, pp. 324–5.
68. Cf Ward, 1913, II, p. 147.
69. Coulson, 1970, p. 179.
70. Coulson, 1970, p. 181.
71. LDXXVIII.6, 3 January 1876.
72. Sullivan, 1993, p. 54.
73. Ward, 1913, II, p. 147.
74. Cf Trevor, 1996, p. 216.
75. LDXXIII.274, 21 July 1867.
76. LDXXIII.275, 21 July 1867.

77. LDXXIII.216, 9 May 1867.
78. LDXXIII.197, 30 April 1867.
79. Gilley, 1997, pp. 8–9.
80. Dessain, 1980, p. 181.
81. LDXXIV.381, Malcolm Mascoll, 29 November 1869.
82. Chadwick, 1990, p. 13.
83. Murray, 1980, p. 127.
84. Newman, 1956, p. 257.

Chapter Eight

Newman – The Later Years

Fr Henry Tristram has commented that Newman's contemporaries 'often wondered, and expressed their wonder, that so great a man should be content in so small a sphere, and sought to explain what seemed to them to be a mystery by saying that he was a disappointed and sour man'. But Tristram asserts that there was 'no mystery': Newman had 'chosen his vocation', in which he persevered to the end of his life. 'His external influence', exercised from the Birmingham Oratory, was undoubtedly great and widespread'. He 'seldom left for any appreciable time, the community, of which he was perpetual superior', and which 'lay at the very core of his being'.[1]

From his *nidulo* or nest – an Oratorian's private room – Newman conducted a remarkable correspondence with prelates, politicians, old Anglican friends, and many others. Dessain says that Newman's letters bring us into touch with him more than any of his works: 'It becomes possible to know him also like a living friend, and in spite of his reserve, they reveal his natural, energetic, humorous and practical character.'[2] He regarded the writing of letters as an important part of his pastoral duties. It was, as Ward observes, 'a means of exerting personal influence on the large numbers who sought his advice and judgement . . . he devoted immense labour to his letters'.[3] Newman's writing style won the admiration of *The Times* (10 April 1869) which classed him, with De Quincey and Macaulay, as 'the three greatest masters of English style in the generation which is just closing'. In acknowledging this graceful tribute, Newman said that he had to take great pains with everything he wrote and that Cicero, because of 'his clearness', was the 'only master of style' who had influenced him.[4]

A student at Maynooth had once asked Newman for advice on the writing and delivery of sermons, and also on models of good English writing. With regard to the former, Newman advised him 'to concentrate on one well-defined subject, not several, and to sacrifice every thought, however good and clever, which does not tend to bring out your one point, and to aim earnestly and supremely to bring that one point to the minds of your hearers'. Concerning the latter, Newman observed that 'one great difficulty recommending particular authors and models of English arises from the Literature of England being Protestant and sometimes worse' (he quoted examples). He felt that everyone should 'form his style for himself', and he offered 'a few general rules': 1) a writer 'should be in earnest', i.e. not write for the sake of it or for more eloquence, but to express his thoughts 'accurately, forcibly and in few words'. This may entail writing sentences 'over and over again'. He should seek 'to be understood', using words which are most likely to convey his message clearly. 'He who is ambitious will never write well - humility, which is a great Christian virtue, has a place in literary composition.' Newman's counselling closed with the admonition that 'He who tries to say simply and exactly what he feels or thinks, what religion demands, what Faith teaches, what the gospel promises, will be eloquent without intending it, and will write better English than if he made a study of English literature.'[5] He frequently rewrote chapters of books and re-drafted letters; all this, he says, 'took me a great deal of time and tried me very much'.[6]

Newman would present the same ideas differently to different correspondents, as we see in his *Letters and Diaries*. To intimate friends he frequently displayed a quiet sense of humour; on occasion, his satiric wit enlivened exchanges on controversial issues. From his vast correspondence 'it has become possible to know him almost like a living friend, and in spite of his reserve, they reveal his natural, energetic, humorous and poetic character'.[7]

In thanking Bishop Ilsley for remembering his eightieth birthday, Newman responded in typical style:

A long life is like a long ladder, which sways and jumps dangerously under the feet of the man who mounts, the higher he goes, and, if any one who needs prayers for perseverance, it is a man of 80.[8]

Among Newman's many correspondents was Fr Gerard Manley Hopkins, the Jesuit priest and poet, who had been received into the

Church by Newman in 1866. He had proposed writing a commentary on the *Grammar of Assent*, but Newman adamantly refused him permission, stating,

> I could not but consider it at once onerous and unnecessary. The book has succeeded in twelve years far more than I expected ... Of course those who only read so much of it as they can while cutting open the leaves, will make great mistakes about it.[9]

Newman's association with Gerard Manley Hopkins was long-standing. On 28 August 1866 Hopkins wrote to Newman 'with great hesitation' to say that he was 'anxious to become a Catholic'.[10] Newman entered a diary note for 27 September 1866: 'Mr Hopkins called about this time.'[11] Hopkins' parents were shattered by the news of their son's intended conversion, and they strongly urged him to wait until he had graduated. Hopkins declared that a delay of 'more than half a year' was 'impossible' and he proposed to visit Newman as quickly as possible. Newman assented; and on Sunday, 21 October 1866, he recorded: 'Mr Hopkins came from Oxford and was received [into the Church].'[12]

In the summer of 1867, Hopkins took a double First, and came to the Oratory to be a master at the School on 13 September 1867. Newman had written earlier to say that he thought 'it good that a recent convert should pass some time in a religious house, to get into Catholic ways'.[13] Later, Newman was to assure Hopkins: 'I think you would get on with us, and that we should like you.'[14] However, Hopkins found that teaching and the life at the Oratory was not congenial and he decided to leave the Oratory School in the spring of 1868.

A few months later Hopkins decided to become a Jesuit and, in congratulating him, Newman mentioned that he had 'dreamed of your having a vocation for us' but he had realized otherwise 'from the moment you came to us. Don't call "the Jesuit discipline hard", it will bring you to heaven'.[15] Hopkins was ordained a priest on 23 September 1877, at St Beuno's College, North Wales, and Newman sent him congratulations.[16]

In 1884 Hopkins, who had just been appointed Professor of Greek at the new Royal University of Ireland, wrote to tell Newman of his new responsibilities.[17] For five years this gifted Jesuit priest worked assiduously at his academic duties and also wrote some of his most powerful poetry. He died prematurely, from typhoid fever, on 8 June 1889, at the age of forty-five years.

With reference to the *Grammar of Assent*, for which Newman had, as noted, declined Hopkins' offer of writing a commentary, this treatise, although published in 1870, had been germinating in Newman's mind for twenty years. According to Dessain, Newman 'wanted to find the answer to a crucial problem; he wished to justify men's right to be certain, and especially their right to certitude in matters of religion'.[18] He felt the need to extend discussions on the philosophy of religion, which had been outlined in the Oxford University Sermons.

Dr Charles Meynell, Professor of Philosophy at Oscott, had regularly corresponded with Newman over his various writings. Newman told him in January 1860 that he was thinking of writing a new work, which would be on 'the popular, practical, and personal evidence of Christianity', and that 'its object would be to show that a given individual, high or low, has as much right (has as real rational grounds) to be certain, as a learned theologian who knows the scientific evidence'.[19] Newman disclosed that 'a dear Protestant friend' had asked him to write such a book; the friend was, in fact, William Froude, the distinguished scientist and the younger brother of Hurrell Froude, who had been Newman's closest friend at Oxford.

To another old friend, Newman wrote on 1 August 1868:

> I have my own subject, one I have wished to do all my life . . . I have the same fidget about it, as a horseman might feel about a certain five feet stone wall which he passes by means of a gate every day of his life, yet is resolved he must and will some day clear – and at last he breaks his neck in attempting. It is on 'Assent, Certitude, and Proof'. I have no right to look to having time to do anything – but if I have, it must be this.[20]

In his private journal, Newman revealed that the *Grammar of Assent* was 'nearly the only exception' to his many other writings in having been written 'without a *call*'. The writing of such a treatise 'had been on my conscience for years, that it would not do to quit the world without doing it. Rightly or wrongly I had ever thought it a duty . . . I had tried to do it again and again and failed, and though at length I did it, I did it after all with great difficulty'.[21] In a letter to Miss Mary Holmes, who had known Newman since his Tractarian times, he confided that he had 'given away near 100 copies of *A Grammar of Assent*' which, he admitted, 'was a difficult book'.[22]

Newman told the Oratorian hymn-writer, Fr Edward Caswall, that, essentially, the *Grammar of Assent* had a two-fold objective: 'The first part shows that you can believe what you cannot understand. In the second part that you can believe what you cannot absolutely prove.'[23] This elegantly phrased thesis was the inspiration which led Newman to undertake the laborious task, which involved numerous drafts and lengthy correspondence, as a letter to Robert Ornsby shows: 'I always say that book writing is like child birth ... I suppose I have written this small book over ten or fifteen times.'[24]

The title of Newman's *An Essay in aid of a Grammar of Assent* required a short explanation: 'Grammar' was derived from an obscure meaning of 'elementary principles of knowledge' and a second meaning, 'book or treatise on these principles of knowledge'. 'Assent' refers to the 'firm acceptance of the truth of a proposition', which must be full consent, nor conditional or partial. By 1833 this term had become an intrinsic element of Newman's philosophical vocabulary. Victorians would have readily grasped the meanings of the terms used in the title.[25]

The *Grammar of Assent* has been described as a 'seminal work in the philosophy of religion', although 'its primary purpose is apologetic, and its standpoint personal'.[26] It is structured in two parts: 'Assent and Apprehension' and 'Assent and Inference'. Part I focuses on 'the importance and value of doctrinal statements in religion'; theology is defended 'because there can be no sound Christianity without it'. Newman declared that theology 'merely holds a truth in the intellect, whereas faith gives a real assent to a concrete reality, which is appropriated by the imagination and the heart'. Conscience is seen as 'the connecting principle between the creature and his Creator'.[27] Newman consistently championed the role of conscience in spiritual development. In Part II Newman deals with the basic problem of certitude, particularly in matters of religion. This crucial concern had long occupied his mind, and he 'felt a kind of obligation ... to show how right and reasonable it was' to have certitude especially in religious beliefs. He was concerned with countering rationalism, and aimed to explain 'how faith, whether in the sphere of religion or of ordinary life, was a reasonable act, even when not based on strictly scientific demonstration'.[28] He had in mind two distinct classes of people:

1. the educated high-minded Victorian agnostics and rationalists;

2. he vast majority of mankind, who believed the truths which they
were quite incapable of either explaining satisfactorily or defending
logically.[29]

With these disparate categories of people in mind, Newman wrote –
for the educated and for the unlearned – a defence of Christian faith.
Dessain has stressed that the *Grammar...* 'is not a treatise on the
theory of knowledge, a manual of epistemology. It is, as Aldous
Huxley realised, rather a book of psychology'.[30]

During his fevered writing of the *Grammar*, Newman regularly
sought Charles Meynell's views and guidance and, as the proofs eventually arrived, Newman sent them to Meynell for his criticism. On 24
July 1869, the young professor of philosophy told Newman that the
Grammar 'systematizes many random thoughts which I have had, and
gives the account and reason of those incompatibilities'.[31] Newman
encouraged Meynell:

> Pray bring out always what you have to say. I am quite conscious that
> metaphysics is a subject on which one cannot hope to agree with those
> with whom in other matters one agrees most heartily, from its extreme
> subtlety – but I am also deeply conscious of my own ignorance on the
> whole matter, and it sometimes amazes me that I have ventured to write on
> a subject which is even accidentally connected with it.[32]

As their correspondence progressed, it is evident that, between the
two clerics, a degree of informality and mutual trust developed which
bridged the twenty-six years' gap in their ages. This relaxation can be
seen, for instance, when Meynell's proofreading spotted occasional
errors, which Newman gratefully noted: 'Many thanks again for your
notice. I had found out my blunder on reading the proof again, and set
it right. It is astonishing how difficult it is not to make mistakes.'[33] On
17 November 1869, Newman told Meynell:

> I quite agree with you that the deepest men say that we can never be
> certain of any thing – and it has been my object therefore in good part of
> my volume to prove that there is such a thing as *unconditional* assent. I
> have defined certitude, a conviction of what is *true*. When a conviction of
> what is not true is considered as if it was a conviction of what is true, I
> have called it a false certitude.

He added that Meynell would be 'sadly disappointed in my "illative
sense" – which is a great word for a common thing'.[34]

Towards the end of 1869 Meynell's onerous task was almost over, and he 'felt quite sorry I am coming to the end'. He acknowledged that he had 'learnt a great deal' from Newman, and when he reflected on his role as a critic, he 'was amazed' at himself.[35] With the publication of the *Grammar*, their pleasant and productive partnership had achieved success; Newman thanked his collaborator for the 'long and lasting task which you have so valiantly performed on my behalf. All I can say is, whatever be the amount of trouble you have had from your charitable undertaking, my amount of gain from it has been greater'. He wished to present 'some keepsake in token of my gratitude' to Meynell, who asked only for a copy of the *Grammar*. Newman also gave him a silver chalice, inscribed with his thanks.[36]

Newman entered in his private journal on 30 October 1870:

> Since I published my *Essay on Assent* last March, I have meant to make a Memorandum on the subject of it. It is the upshot of a very long desire and effort – I don't know the worth of it, but I am happier to have at length done with it and got it off my hands. Authors (or at least I) can as little foretell what their books will be before they are written, as fathers can foretell whether their children will be boys or girls, dark or fair, gentle or fiery, clever or stupid. The book itself I have in mind at writing this twenty years – and now that it is written I do not quite recognise it for what it is meant to be, though I suppose it is such.[37]

Some readers of the *Grammar* confessed to problems in tackling it. Fr Thomas Harper, SJ wrote that he had 'considerable difficulties about the logical and philosophical scaffolding' of the *Grammar*.[38] Newman was always aware of his philosophical limitations and, in a letter – some seven years later – to Fr Robert Whitty, SJ, he admitted:

> If anyone is obliged to say 'I speak under correction' it is I, for I am no theologian, and am too old, ever have been, to become one. All I can say is, I have no suspicion, and do not anticipate that I shall be found in substance to disagree with St Thomas.[39]

To a London journalist who asked his views of the Affirmation Bill (which had been rejected in the House of Commons, by only three votes, on 30 May 1833) Newman replied:

> I neither approve nor disapprove. I express no opinion upon it; and that first because I do not commonly enter upon political questions, and next, because, looking at the Bill on its own merits, I think nothing is lost to

Religion by its passing and nothing is gained by its being rejected.[40]

Responding to a law student who feared a tide of atheism would result from the passing of the Affirmation Bill, Newman reassured him that he 'had ever anticipated a great battle between good and evil', but over the centuries the Church had survived. 'so I think it will be now. We shall have a bad time of it, but "be still and see the salvation of God"'.[41]

Even as late as his eighty-fifth year, Newman had to state firmly his reasons for becoming a Catholic. A letter to Margaret Ellen James reads:

> Cardinal Newman is sure that Miss James' letter did not reach him, or that he has answered it. The notion that he became Catholic in order to get rid of doubts is utterly unfounded. He became a Catholic because our Lord set up a Church in the beginning as the Ark of Salvation and the Oracle of Truth. And the Roman was it. So he has said in all he has written. Look to his *Apologia*, his *Sermons to Mixed Congregations*, the postscript to his *Letter to the Duke of Norfolk*, or to his *Development of Christian Doctrine*. He has never had a doubt since he became a Catholic. He became a Catholic because he was certain the Catholic was the true faith. Miss James must excuse his bad writing but he writes with an effort and with difficulty. [42]

To another enquirer Newman wrote that he 'joined the Catholic Church for *its own* sake and that no one can have ready my *Essay* on the Development of Christian Doctrine without seeing this'.[43] A few months later, Newman again stated firmly the reasons which caused him to become a Catholic:

> I left the Anglican Church because I could not believe it was a portion of that Catholic Body which the apostles founded and to which the promises are made. I felt that I could not be saved, if I remained where I was. In my *Apologia* I think I have brought this out; and that the present improved state of the Anglican Church would have been a temptation adverse to that conviction, I do not of course deny – but from first to last I have had the clear conviction, independent of all such accidents, that the Church of England is a Parliamentary Church.[44]

To a Free Church minister, Newman reflected: 'What a mystery it is that in this day that there should be so much which draws religious minds together, and so much which separates them from each other.'

While members of the various Christian communities felt 'such tenderness for each other', the differences which divided them were never greater or stronger.[45]

An earnest enquirer after salvation was told by Newman that

> The only reason for becoming a Catholic, is that the Roman Communion is the only true Church, the Ark of Salvation. This does not mean that no one else is saved who is not within the Church, but that there is no other Communion or Polity which has the promises, and that those who are saved, though not in the One Church, are saved, not by virtue of 'the Law or Sect which they profess', as the 39 *Articles* say, but because they do not know better, and earnestly desire to know the truth.[46]

Dr Charles Russell, President of Maynooth College, whose influence on Newman's conversion has been noted, had had a fall from his horse in January 1877, and two and a half years later, at sixty-seven years of age, had felt obliged to resign his post. Newman had written to him expressing his sadness that 'a mere accident should have suddenly cut you short in the midst of your work and closed a career of usefulness'.[47] A few months later Newman, on hearing of Russell's death on 26 February 1880, wrote to his nephew, Fr Matthew Russell, SJ: 'I have just heard of dear Dr Russell's death to whom I owe so much.'[48] During the following year, Fr Russell advised Newman that he was preparing a short memoir of his uncle and asked permission to use correspondence which had taken place between the two notable clerics. Newman sent him copies of Russell's 'three last letters', commenting that

> Dr Russell was never a correspondent of mine – though every now and then letters passed between us. His letters were generally to the effect that he was coming to England, or passing near Birmingham on a certain day, and could I give him a night's lodging? which I was very glad to do. On these occasions we conversed for long hours – this superseded correspondence.[49]

On 15 November 1872, Newman wrote a 'Memorandum on Future Biography' [50] in which he specified how he wanted his papers dealt with. These large collections, which Newman hoped to 'put into shape and chronological order' should be used 'only in defence, i.e. if enemies make misstatements or imply motives . . . I don't wish my life written . . . In the *Apologia* I have virtually written my life up to 1845 – and there is little of nothing to say since'.

A few years later, Newman issued another instruction regarding his papers.[51] 'I don't want a panegyric written of me, which would be sickening, but a real fair downright account of me according to the best ability and judgement of the writer.' Such a memoir should be in two parts dealing specifically with his Anglican years and then his life as a Catholic. In an additional note, dated 22 October 1876, Newman expressed a wish that 'all statements which reflect on others to be withheld from publication, unless and until reflections are published in any quarter against me ... But such publication is not to be determined on hastily, or without real necessity'.

Some forty years after their original publication, Newman edited his two-volume *Via Media*. The first volume, *Lectures on the Prophetical Office of the Church*, had been first published in 1837. In a letter to the publishers, Newman intimated that the edited first volume – which included an extended new Preface – was 'now nearly ready – the second part not yet begun'.[52] However, the second volume was occupying Newman's attention and he told an old friend, the architect of the University Church in Dublin, 'I am full of business, racing with time, not knowing how long it will be or at least having no confidence how long I can do the head work.'[53] Both volumes were published during the second half of 1877 and were well received among Catholics.

In 1877 the publishers Rivington proposed to publish a selection from Newman's *Parochial and Plain Sermons* which, as seen in Chapter 2, first appeared in 1834 and covered sermons preached to congregations at Oxford and Littlemore over the years 1835–41. Newman told Fr Henry Coleridge that he had 'made it a condition that only sermons should be selected' which would 'stand a Catholic censorship'. He intended to 'publish them as from myself and not from Copeland [his former Anglican curate] as editor', and 'I mean to pluck all of those selected which have any thing un-catholic in them.' He added, in parenthesis, 'Perhaps you will say "Then they will *all* be plucked".'[54]

Newman received a reassuring reply from Fr Coleridge on 13 April: 'I should think that your own judgement would be most amply sufficient, and more than sufficient, to all Catholics, especially if you said simply that you were not *aware* of anything, which as a Catholic, you should alter.'[55] So the new edition – with the recommended author's statement – emerged in 1878, the year before Newman was created a cardinal. It was the first of his Anglican writings to be re-published in his Catholic days.

Tristram comments that although Copeland retained his 'unfailing affection for Newman himself' as the years went by he 'became more and more hostile to the Catholic Church'. He appears to have been embittered by the 'intransigent attitude' taken by Rome on the issue of 'corporate reunion', and this led him to instruct that after his death (which occurred in 1885), the many letters which he had received from Newman should not fall into Catholic hands.[56]

On 18 December 1877 Newman wrote to tell Ullathorne – 'one of the first' – that his old College, Trinity, 'where I was an undergraduate from the age of 16 to 21', had offered him an honorary fellowship. It was, he emphasized, 'a mark of extreme kindness from men I have never seen, and it is the only instance of their exercising their power since it was given to them'. To see Trinity again – 'the one and only seat of my affections at Oxford – is a prospect almost too much for me to bear'.[57] Ullathorne congratulated Newman and remarked that, as he viewed it, the Fellows 'do themselves the most honour in linking your name anew to Trinity College'. Dean Church thought the news 'one of the most delightful announcements' he had heard for a long time, adding, perhaps wryly, 'and to think that Oriel should have missed doing it first'.[58] Among many of his friends to whom he told his exciting news was Lord Emly. To him Newman confided that his 'affections have ever been with my first College, though I have more and more intimately personal Oriel friends. There was too much pain at Oriel, to allow of its remembrances being sweet and dear – hence I rejoice that it is Trinity, not Oriel, that has reclaimed me'.[59]

S. W. Wayte, President of Trinity College, Oxford, suggested that Newman should spend a few days in college, from 26 February, to which invitation Newman gladly responded.[60] Newman re-visited his old college for the first time since he had left it in February 1846, and was given a great welcome, dined in hall, and made a short speech. He also called on Pusey, and visited Oriel and Keble Colleges. On returning to the Oratory, Newman wrote thanking the President of Trinity and expressed his sincere hope 'that Trinity College and all who belong to it may grow and abound in the best of gifts and be endowed with the choicest of blessings'.[61] In gratitude for the 'gracious compliment' paid to him by making him 'once more a Member of a College dear to me from Undergraduate memories', Newman dedicated the new edition of *An Essay on the Development of Christian Doctrine*, on which had had been working recently, to the President of Trinity.

Over the period 1874–81, Newman had his portrait painted by three talented artists, although he was not, at first, always a willing sitter.

Lady Coleridge, the wife of Newman's faithful friend Lord Coleridge, the son of Sir John Taylor Coleridge – who had sentenced Newman at the Achilli trial and also publicly humiliated him by remarking that his character had 'deteriorated since becoming a Roman Catholic' [62] – shared her husband's admiration for Newman and wished to draw a portrait of him. Lord Coleridge wrote to Newman on 25 May 1874, asking if he had 'ever seen or heard of any' of his wife's drawings which their mutual friends 'Church and Blachford would tell you that they are not common things'. Her portraits had been 'thought successful', and, 'from a photograph', she had started on a portrait of Newman. It would be a 'very great favour' if he 'could let her finish it from you'.[63]

Through R. W. Church, a mutual friend, Newman was asked if he would sit for Lady Coleridge so that she could complete her drawing of him. Newman replied that 'in common gratitude' he could not decline her invitation, and recalled with gratitude her husband's kindness when, 'from the time of his father's speech over me', and 'so many gave me up, he took me up and continued over many years to show true friendship'.[64] A month later, Newman wrote thanking Lord Coleridge for the gift of some 'beautiful books', and added, 'I shall be quite ready to attend the summons of Lady Coleridge, whenever she sends for me.'[65] In February 1875, Newman told Mrs F. J. Watt, whom he had known from childhood, that he had just returned from a visit to London to Lord Coleridge 'who is having my likeness taken in chalk by his wife, who is a genius in drawing'.[66] Lord Coleridge's father died on 11 February 1876, and Newman's second visit for a sitting had to be postponed until 4 May.[67] The final sitting took place in June 1876.

On May 17 1877 Newman wrote to Lord Coleridge thanking him and his wife for a 'wonderfully kind an beautiful present' – one of the three portraits Lady Coleridge had made of him.[68]

Ker has described this portrait as a 'mysteriously evocative drawing (which) strikingly conveys the kind of impression his expression and manner made on strangers who met him for the first time'.[69] Later, Newman presented this portrait to the community of the Birmingham Oratory.

Sadly, not long after Lady Coleridge had completed her dedicated artistic task, she died suddenly. Newman wrote a moving letter of condolence to her deeply grieving husband: 'She was so good to me, and the words passed between us gave me so easily and naturally to see glimpses of her beautiful mind.'[70]

Following Newman's acceptance of Trinity College's conferment of an honorary Fellowship, Professor James Bryce, a Fellow of Oriel, wrote to Newman on 15 March 1878, that he had 'been commissioned by some friends, both members of the Oriel Common Room and others', to invite him to sit for a portrait by the celebrated portrait artist Walter William Ouless, which would be presented to Oriel College.[71] R. W. Church, Dean of St Paul's, had already mentioned this proposal to Newman, whose response had been guarded: 'I don't like to be made an artistic subject: and Mr Ouless' saying that he will come down here for nothing is as if he paid me for a sitting.'[72] However, Newman's marked reluctance was overcome when he realized that Oriel Common Room was involved, and he accepted with pleasure the invitation,[73] although he had earlier confided to Church that he felt that the Oriel honours 'have a grave significancy in them. To use sacred words, they are anointing for burial ...'[74] The sittings went ahead and Ouless painted two portraits – one for the Brompton Oratory and the other for Oriel.

It appears that Newman's disinclination to take up readily offers of having his portrait painted originated from an unfortunate experience in the 1860s when, as he told Lord Blachford, only after considerable pressure did he eventually agree to a portrait being made by a local artist, William Thomas Roden, although he 'had no wish at all to be put into a collection together with a set of liberal party men or town [Birmingham] celebrities with whom I have nothing in common ... (Further) a few weeks ago the eventual painting was in a pawn-broker's shop, as the artist could not get paid for it', and it was 'lately bought as a speculation to be shown in principal towns'.[75] In a foot-note dated 1 August 1874, the painting was stated to be now in the possession of the Birmingham Art Gallery.[76] To an 'unknown corre-spondent' Newman explained that the painter's projection of him had been influenced by 'some passage of my *Apologia*, in which I speak of my sorrow at my loss of my Oxford friends', and so he was repre-sented as mourning for them.[77]

In 1881, the Duke of Norfolk wrote to tell Newman that many of his friends wished to 'obtain a good picture of you that we could present to some public gallery in London', and that John Everett (later, Sir John) had agreed to paint his portrait.[78] By return, Newman wrote 'with much gratitude' accepting 'this kindness and honour'.[79] He told Miss M. R. Giberne (Sister Pia): 'I am to be painted by Millais, which is a great compliment.'[80] While the portrait sittings were under way, Newman stayed at Brompton Oratory, although the Duke had offered him accommodation at his London residence, and a carriage to take him to Millais's studio. Everything went well: the Fathers of the London Oratory were happy to have Newman with them; the artist and his sitter enjoyed themselves; and the result was a portrait which, accomplished in a 'few short sittings', was regarded by Millais as 'the best he has done' – and the one he wishes to go down to posterity by'.[81] This portrait now hangs in the National Portrait Gallery in London.

A different artistic genre was evident in the caricature of Newman by Leslie Ward, better known as 'Spy', that appeared in the January 1877 issue of *Vanity Fair*. John Rouse Bloxam, who had held various Oxford University posts and fully sympathized with the Tractarians, presented Newman with the 'Spy' caricature. He acknowledge this to be 'very clever and good'.[82] This witty depiction of Newman has retained its popular appeal.

Anne Mozley, sister of James Mozley, and sister-in-law of Harriet and Jemima Newman, had edited her brother's essays and correspondence in 1885. This caused Newman to invite her to edit a selection of letters from his Anglican years. She accepted this onerous task, which was completed before Newman's death. The resultant volumes were published shortly before her own death on 27 June 1891 in her eighty-second year. Newman had supplied her with letters and other research material, stipulating that he should never see her work, which was to be published only after his death. The resultant two volumes: *Letters and Correspondence of John Henry Newman during his Life in the English Church*, have been said 'in spite of its omissions, errors and silences, (to) give the substantially true account for which he had hoped'.[83]

Pope Pius IX died on 7 February 1878 after a reign of thirty-two years, and was succeeded by Leo XIII who, according to Ker, when he was 'nuncio in Brussels, had been familiar with the Oxford Movement, and he had met Dominic Barberi ... immediately after Barberi had received Newman into the Church. After being elected Pope, he is supposed to have said that the policy of his pontificate would be revealed by the name of the first Cardinal he created'.[84]

But the path to the cardinalate was to be far from smooth for

Newman; indeed, it was more a traumatic experience than a joyful
journey and typified the many occasions during Newman's long and
eventful life when he seemed almost destined to be the focus of
controversy and conflict. Misinterpretations of his written words and
utterances often led to misunderstandings of his intentions and desires;
at times even deliberate distortions were perpetrated. Perhaps the
subtlety with which he expressed his thoughts and aspirations may
have sometimes given rise to misconceptions and to a lack of appreciation of his intentions. Further, his fearless pursuit of topics such as
academic excellence and his zest for controversy, while winning
admirers, had also irritated those who seemed to resent his pervasive
influence in the deliberations of the Church.

   Some brief account, based principally on contemporary correspondence over this period, should shed light on this rather fraught episode
in Newman's life, when his bishop and influential Catholic laity
rallied to support him.

   When Newman[85] heard of the intended promotion, he had feared
that this might entail his compulsory residence in Rome, as was then
customary for cardinals who were not diocesan bishops. Through
Ullathorne he had, therefore, petitioned to be allowed to spend his last
few years in the Oratory which he had founded in Birmingham over
thirty years ago. This request accompanied his grateful acceptance of
the honour and was sent by Ullathorne, with a covering letter, to
Manning for transmission to Rome.[86] Manning's letter was entrusted,
in 1878, to Cardinal Howard, a descendant of the twelfth Duke of
Norfolk and Protector of the English College, whose travelling time to
Rome extended over several weeks. Hence, the Duke of Norfolk, in
an audience with Leo XIII in early December – and before Cardinal
Howard had reached Rome – intimated that Catholic laymen wished
for Newman to be made a cardinal, particularly because of his
estimable work and also for his dedicated writing on behalf of the
Church.

   Meanwhile, Manning, however, appears to have forwarded only
part of the correspondence received from Ullathorne, causing the
determined Birmingham prelate to write to him again, explicitly
stating that the 'only real reason' for Newman's apparent hesitation
lay in his reluctance to leave his Oratory at his advanced age.
Ullathorne's explanatory letter was intended to correct any misinter-
pretation of Newman's letter which 'by itself *could* be read as declining the proffered dignity though by no means as an unconditional

refusal'.[87] In spite of Ullathorne's second letter, Manning, before leaving London, allowed it to be said that Newman had been offered the cardinalate and refused it. This misleading report was quickly picked up and disseminated by the media, including *The Times* and the *Tablet*, the latter journal being owned by Bishop Herbert Vaughan of Salford. In the meantime, Manning had written from Paris, to the Duke of Norfolk advising him that Newman 'had declined the offer' of being created a cardinal.[88] On 22 February the Duke responded, stating strongly that he gathered 'that Father Newman did not mean the Pope to interpret his letter in the way in which it has been interpreted by the papers. But the Pope may think the interpretation of the papers the right one, *if it not be contradicted*, and he may abide by that interpretation'. He added that he thought the Pope 'ought to know that Father Newman did not mean in his letter what the papers said he did'. He closed this 'confidential' letter: 'As I was the one who asked you to bring this matter before the Pope and as I spoke to him myself of it, may I ask you to lay before him my heartfelt thanks for his condescension in vouchsafing to consider it.'[89] The following day, the Duke wrote again to Manning:

> It seems now to be getting generally known that the answer sent to Rome was not a distinct refusal and I fear that it will be said that the offer was made in such a way that it could not be accepted ... Who, I wonder, told you that Fr Newman had declined. The public report may have come from the same source.[90]

On 25 February Manning wrote from Rome to the Duke: 'This is the first moment that I have doubted the plain meaning of Dr Newman's letter to Cardinal Nina.' He enclosed a copy of Newman's letter of 5 February in which he told Manning:

> I could not be so ungracious whether to the Holy Father or to the friends at home, who have interested themselves in this matter, as to decline what was so kindly proposed, provided that it did not involve unfaithfulness to St Philip.[91]

Manning explained that he 'understood this note as saying that he had declined it ... and he had 'never doubted of this meaning until your letter came'. He promised that he would 'do all in my power to clear what has been misunderstood'.[92] Later the same day, Manning wrote to the Duke saying that Cardinal Howard and he had been to Cardinal

Nina and to the Pope, and had explained 'the letter of Dr Newman which had been understood as declining on account of the reasons stated'. The Holy Father had authorized him 'to say that Dr Newman need not change his way of life nor leave the Oratory nor even come to Rome; and that a letter in this sense will be sent to him'.[93] A similar letter was also sent on the same day to Ullathorne, who was asked to 'kindly make this known to Dr Newman'.[94]

At Ullathorne's recommendation, Newman wrote formally to Manning to express his appreciation of the Pope's 'condescending goodness' in permitting him to 'keep place within the walls of my Oratory in Birmingham'.[95] Newman appears to have been worried about rumours which were still circulating because he had not yet had official notification from Rome, so he wrote again to Manning the following day:

> Wishing to guard against all possible mistake ... As soon as the Holy Father condescends to make it known to me that he intends to confer on me the high dignity of Cardinal, I shall write to Rome to signify my obedience and glad acceptance of the honour, without delay.[96]

On 8 March, Manning wrote to Newman, assuring him that an official letter from Rome would be sent to him, and that the Pope gave 'full permission' for him 'to continue to reside at your Oratory'.[97] In a further letter on the same day, Manning told Newman: 'I have not a second time failed to understand your intention.' He had 'fully believed' that Newman had, for the reasons he had given in earlier correspondence, declined the Pope's offer. However, as a result of correspondence with the Duke of Norfolk, he had acted quickly: 'I write this because if I misunderstood your intention it was by an error which I repaired the instant I knew it.'[98] This letter appears to be the first direct information that Newman received of Manning's handling of his original response to the papal invitation.

Doubtless, the persistent efforts of the Duke of Norfolk, the Marquis of Ripon, Lord Petre and other members of the Catholic Union played a crucial role in influencing the Holy See's decision to confer a cardinalate on Newman. Dessain comments:

> At any rate the idea was taken up by the Duke of Norfolk and some of the English laity, who approached Leo XIII. Newman was made a Cardinal, but only after what, now the correspondence has come to light, seems definitely to have been a last-minute manoeuvre of Manning's to prevent it.[99]

Gilley believes that: 'Manning stands convicted of extraordinary clumsy misreading of confidential documents in order to deprive Newman of his honour.'[100]

This tortuous matter was at last settled, as Newman happily told his loyal friend, the Duke of Norfolk; he also expressed his warm feelings of gratitude to Ullathorne: 'And it is only the crown of the kindness and affectionateness of so many. And especially of yourself, for whom I shall always give thanks and pray as one of my benefactors.'[101]

However, Newman himself emphatically, and perhaps diplomatically, contradicted 'any ideas that may be afloat as to my dissatisfaction with any step taken by Cardinal Manning'.[102]

On 12 March 1879, Newman wrote to the Duke of Norfolk:

Never had a man such good friends ... I wish it all swept out of every one's mind and my own – and shall be sorry if it is not so. I wish it known that I am quite satisfied, and am very grateful to him (Manning) for the trouble he has taken in my matters.[103]

The Duke wrote to Manning on receiving Newman's letter, thanking him for 'managing this matter of Father Newman with such great success'.[104]

In 1879, and at the end of his private journal, Newman merely added a note: 'Since writing the above, I have been made a Cardinal.'[105]

During this time of jubilation, Newman recalled that for years he had been regarded with suspicion, and had been 'under a cloud' as a result of misconceptions over, for example, his essay: *On Consulting the Faithful in Matters of Doctrine*, which had been cleared as the result of Fr Ambrose St John's visit to Rome. In a letter to Anne Mozley, Newman stated that if he had refused 'the offer of a Cardinal's Hat ... it would have created a suspicion that it was true that I was but a half and half Catholic, who dared not commit himself to a close union with the Church of Rome, and who wished to be independent'.[106] To Dean Church, he wrote in similar vein: 'All the stories which have gone on about me being half a Catholic, a liberal Catholic, under a cloud, not to be trusted, are now at an end.'[107]

While thanking Fr John Thomas Walford, SJ for the congratulations sent to him from the Beaumont Jesuit community, Newman also referred to the problem which might have arisen if he had declined the cardinalate. It might be 'taken by Protestants, nay by some Catholics as a proof that at heart I am not an out and out Son of the Church . . . I have suffered so much from the obstinacy of all sorts of people to believe that I am a good Catholic that this wonderful opportunity . . . must not be lost except for very grave reasons'.[108]

Replying to a letter from Pusey, in which he had evidently assumed and approved that Newman had declined his promotion, Newman told him:

> We are looking at things from different points of view. Here have I for thirty years been told by men of all colours of belief that I am not a good Catholic. It has given me immense trouble, much mortification, and great loss of time.

It had been used, Newman asserted, 'as an argument to keep men back from joining the Church; men have said "Just you see – how his own people do not trust him – the Pope snubs him"'. If the Pope was willing to offer him a cardinalate 'how can I not supplement his act by giving my assent to it?'[109] Pusey explained that he would not have written as he had but he was under a misapprehension as a result of widespread rumours.

From Rome, on 15 March 1879, Manning sent to Newman, 'with great joy', a letter from Cardinal Nina, Secretary of State, which was the official offer of the Cardinalate,[110] to which Newman via Manning formally accepted 'with deep gratitude'.[111] Newman duly informed his bishop of the formal letter from the Vatican.[112] Manning confirmed that he was sending Newman's formal acceptance to Rome and also mentioned that it now seemed certain that the Consistory would not be taking place before the middle of May. He offered Newman help, if he wished to attend, in making the necessary preparations for this event, including travel and accommodation, etc. Newman responded that he would be 'very glad' to take up Manning's offer, and declared: 'I certainly wish to come now', but added that for many years he had been 'unable to stand the night air'.[113] In a further letter to Newman, Manning, at Cardinal Nina's request, advised him that the Rector of the English College in Rome hoped that he would 'make his home here when you come'.[114] Newman also heard from Mgr Woodlock who had succeeded him as Rector of the Catholic University of Ireland, and had just been appointed Bishop of Ardagh. He spoke of the 'honour conferred on the CUI in the person of its first Rector and well-nigh Founder'.[115]

Old and frail, at last Newman set out for Rome, reaching it on 24 April and, three days later, was 'received with marked affection by Leo XIII'.[116] Despite a heavy cold – 'I have seldom had so bad a one ... The Holy Father has been abundantly kind, inquiring after me every day', Newman wrote to W. S. Lilly, the secretary of the Catholic Union.[117]

On 12 May Newman, although not fully recovered, was well enough to attend the various ceremonies of his cardinalate and to respond formally in his 'biglietto' speech. In this he spoke of the spirit of liberalism in religion: 'the tendency to regard one religion as good as another and to encourage each one to think as he felt inclined'.[118] This long-held conviction appeared in his *Essay on the Development of Christian Doctrine* many years earlier.

The motto chosen by Newman when he received the cardinal's hat in 1879 was: *Cor ad cor loquitur ('*Heart speaketh unto heart*').* Harrold reflects: 'All of John Henry Newman's work was addressed to his readers' hearts.'[119]

A more recent biographer has observed that there 'was an uncanny anticipation of the idea which formed its pregnant expression in Newman's choosing St Francis de Sales' words, *cor ad cor loquitur*, for his coat of arms as Cardinal of the Roman Catholic Church'.[120]

Before leaving Rome, Newman wrote to the Duke of Norfolk thanking him and the members of the Catholic Union for the 'singularly kind and opportune Address, of 20th February 1879, they sent me', and which had 'cheered and encouraged' him.[121] Newman could not have, openly and earlier, acknowledged the valuable and instrumental support of the Duke and the Catholic Union, until the Pope's formal announcement had been made of his cardinalate. But he was fully aware of the role played by these leading laymen throughout these delicate negotiations. He had championed the cause of the laity in the Church; they had responded with warmth and vigour. As Ullathorne was to tell Newman, the Pope 'wished to do an act pleasing to the Catholics of England, and to England itself, and that pleasure had been given in full measure'.[122]

In January 1888, Lord Selborne gave the Pope a message from Newman, and on hearing of him, His Holiness's face lit up as he said:

My Cardinal! It was not easy, it was not easy. They said he was too liberal, but I had determined to honour the Church in honouring Newman. I always had a cult for him. I am proud that I was able to honour such a man.[123]

Owen Chadwick writes that the Pope had overcome opposition in the
curia and the reluctance of Manning to make Newman a cardinal, and
that 'Educated Protestant England was glad and accepted it as an
honour justly conferred upon a great Englishman. This was no small
tribute to the change of attitude wrought by Newman. He was the first
Englishman to win non-Catholic applause for becoming a cardinal.'[124]

Among the many who sent Newman congratulations on his elevation
to the Sacred College was Cardinal Manning on behalf of the English
hierarchy. In this letter he recorded that Newman's 'name had been
bound up with the Catholic Church in England for the last thirty
years, and we have regarded you with so true a friendship and veneration for your many virtues, your sacerdotal example, and your signal
services to the Catholic Faith ...'[125] Manning preceded this formal note
with a personal letter proposing that the 'Catholic laity' should be
invited to a reception in London in Newman's honour.[126] Newman,
writing from Rome, thanked Manning for his congratulations but
regretted that he was not well enough to travel to London at the
present time.[127] Manning's formal letter of congratulations was also
acknowledged by Newman, on his way back from Rome, in a letter
written from Leghorn. He asked to be excused the delay in replying
formally, due to illness, and expressed his gratitude for the message
from Cardinal Manning and the episcopate. It was, he wrote, 'a great
satisfaction to be told in so formal an address, that even when there
was not such a bias in my favour, equally as when there was, I have
through so many years, and under such varying circumstances, and by
such men, been so tenderly and considerately regarded'.[128]

Throughout the many celebratory occasion, including a series of
receptions in London, as guest of the Duke of Norfolk, a reception by
two hundred clergy, Vespers and Benediction at the London Oratory,
and a ceremonial visit to Trinity College, Oxford, Newman tried to
complete a revision of the *Select Treatises of St Athanasius in controversy with the Arians*. He confided to his intimate friend, R. W.
Church, Dean of St Paul's:

> I wonder when I shall get a little quiet; or at least a little leisure to finish
> my revision of the *Athanasius*. This Cardinalate, I grieve to say, has
> spoiled the revision, and I shall not live for another ... of all my volumes
> I wished *Athanasius* to be least imperfect, and it will be most so.[129]

In 1881 the edition was published but Newman's disappointment with
it was apparent from a letter he sent to Lord Blachford (the former

Frederic Rogers): 'having been at it since October 1878', the end result was 'not so good a work as it was in the Oxford edition ... The only thing which I can think of in its favour is that the text is easier to read than overgrown ad calcem notes in small type...'[130]

In excusing an invitation for his portrait to be painted, Newman mentioned that:

> My time is not my own, as if I were young ... I have no certainty when the supply of time will cease, and life end. You may recollect the histories of St Bede and St Anselm. They were each finishing a great work, and they had to run a race with time. Anselm was 76 – but Bede was only 62. I alas, alas, am 86.

He said that he was 'labouring to carry two volumes of St Athanasius through the press'. This will take 'at least half a year, so he suggested that the artist might write again later, 'if I am then alive'.[131]

During the latter part of 1886, despite increasing physical frailty and failing eyesight but with his mind alert and interested in keeping in touch with his wide – but sadly diminished – circle of friends, Newman had increasingly resorted to dictating his correspondence. In one of his last letters, dated 7 January 1887, which he wrote entirely by hand, Newman said he was comforted that, 'in this day of religious indifference and unbelief' there was a 'silent and secret process going on in the hearts of many' which, 'in due time, might bring Christians all over the world together'.[132]

In Chapter 1, the early influence of the Revd Walter Mayers on the teenage Newman's religious beliefs and, in particular, his introduction to Calvinism were noted. The effects of this evangelical teaching proved to be indelible, as he was to record in his private journal.[133] These dramatic influences on Newman's intellectual and spiritual progression wee also chronicled by him in the *Apologia*.[134]

When Newman learned of the sudden death of his revered teacher on 22 February 1828, he had been shocked, and he confessed that: 'I must ever think of one to whom I am so much indebted' with gratitude for 'the affection he always showed me, the anxious pains he took to be of service to me, the earnestness with which he sees to pray for me, and the readiness he ever manifested to assist me in any object I had in view, and again of his deep and spiritual views of religion, his singleness of mind and (purpose), and great generosity'. To this moving tribute Newman added – in words which echoed those he was to choose for his own epitaph:

For this world is but a shadow and a dream – but we think we see things and
we see them not – they not exist, they die on all sides, things dearest and
most beloved. But in heaven we shall all meet and it will be *no* dream.[135]

Over fifty years later, Newman was to tell Thomas Mozley, who had
written his reminiscences of Oriel and the Oxford Movement, which
he, Newman, had found 'full of mistakes and personally unacceptable', that 'I never dreamed of being "converted" and had no lasting
religious thoughts till I knew Mr Mayers'.[136]

The early and lasting influence of evangelicalism was also admitted
by Newman to another correspondent, to whom he confirmed his
'simple love and adhesion to the Catholic Roman Church, and then
alluded to 'those great and burning truths, which I learned when a boy
from evangelical teaching'. These were 'impressed upon my heart
with fresh and ever increasing force by the Holy Roman Church',
which had 'added to the simple evangelicism my first teachers'.[137]

Ullathorne had been Newman's bishop for many years, during which
time they had worked closely together in Birmingham and had developed a deep understanding and friendship. In June 1886 Newman
joined 'with all my heart' in the Address of congratulation from the
Birmingham diocesan clergy to Bishop Ullathorne on the fortieth year
of his episcopate. Newman told the Provost of the Birmingham
Chapter that 'he recollected the day of his consecration well', and that
he was introduced to 'that holy woman, Mother Margaret Hallahan'.[138]

On his last visit to Newman at the Birmingham Oratory, on 18
August 1886, Ullathorne found the Cardinal 'much wasted, but very
cheerful'. They had 'a long and cheery talk'. As the bishop was about
to leave, Newman, 'in low and humble accents' asked for the 'great
favour' of his blessing, for which he knelt submissively. Ullathorne
was profoundly moved: 'I felt annihilated in his presence: there is a
Saint in that Man!'[139]

Newman expressed movingly his debt to Ullathorne, who had
always supported him, particularly in times of stress, such as the
problems associated with the conferment of his cardinalate. He wrote
to his bishop:

How good God has been in giving me such kind friends! It has been so all
through my life. They have spared my mistakes, overlooked my defeats,
and found excuses for my faults. God reward you, my dear Lord, for your
tenderness towards me, very conscious as I am of my great failings. You
have ever been indulgent towards me; and now you show me an act of

considerate charity, as great as you can, by placing my name at the beginning of the last work of your long life of service and sacrifice. It is a token of sympathy which, now in my extreme age, encourages me with the prospect of the awful journey which lies before me.[140]

(The work referred to in Newman's letter was *Christian Patience*, which was dedicated to him.)

Following a partial paralysis, Ullathorne retired in 1887 and died on 21 March 1889. So ended what might be described as a lustrous spiritual partnership of two Englishmen, near neighbours in the industrial city of Birmingham, who were utterly dedicated to the pastoral care of people of all ages and classes. Ullathorne's sturdy Yorkshire character differed in many ways from Newman's scholarly introspective nature. Newman's loyalty to his bishop was always evident, while Ullathorne's respect and fraternal affection for Newman transmuted a formal ecclesiastical relationship into a rare and lasting friendship.

In the autumn of 1888 Newman suffered a fall, resulting in shock and difficulty in eating, but he rallied quickly and by early November his doctors announced that no further bulletins would be issued. Gladstone, who was staying in Edgbaston, enquired about the possibility of visiting Newman; he was assured by Fr Neville that the 'Cardinal will be very glad indeed to see you and you need not fear that he will be wishing you gone'.[141]

During the last decade of Newman's life, Fr William Neville had been 'his inseparable companion, almost his shadow, and acted as his secretary'.[142] On 2 April 1851, Newman had received Neville and others into the Church. A week later, Neville came to the Birmingham Oratory, where he lived until his death in 1905. He became Newman's literary executor; like Newman, he was a graduate of Trinity, for which Newman always had fond memories.

Newman dictated a letter to Cardinal Manning, on 29 September 1889, congratulating him on settlement of the London Dockers' strike. Manning replied very cordially.[143] In November 1889, Newman himself 'went out in the snow to act as a peacemaker' in a strike of Catholic women workers at Cadbury's chocolate works in Birmingham, who were obliged to attend daily Bible instruction. Mr George Cadbury and his brother met Newman and 'were charmed by the loving Christian spirit with which he entered into the question'. The matter was settled amicably.[144]

A senior Roman cardinal enquired about Newman's knowledge of

Fr Dominic Barberi, the Passionist priest who, in 1845 received Newman into the Church. On 2 October 1889, Newman responded:

> Certainly Fr Dominic of the Mother of God was a most striking missioner and preacher and had a great part in my own conversion and in that of others. His very look had a holy aspect which when his figure was into sight in my circle most singularly affected me, and his remarkable *bonhomie* in the midst of his sanctity was in itself a real and holy preaching. No wonder, then, I became his convert and penitent. He was a great lover of England.[145]

On Christmas Day 1889, Newman said Mass for what was to be the last time. He 'was attempting to learn more or less by heart from a missal for the partially blind'.[146]

Aware of his increasing frailty, Newman wrote on 23 March 1890, to the Dominican Mother Provincial at Stone Convent, which both he and Ullathorne had visited over the years:

> Don't be pained that I do not write to you and yours. Strange to say I have no time. I pray for you all with all my heart, however badly. I have so many necessary letters to write about, so many papers, so many anxieties, so many prayers to accomplish, especially prayers in the Mass, so many ailments, though, thank God, not painful, for me to attend to, so many duties from the kind urgency of the medical men, and so on, that you would feel for me if you knew them.

He closed by saying that he wished he could visit 'the dear Archbishop's grave'.[147] (Archbishop Ullathorne's body was, as he had wished, entombed in St Joseph's Chapel in St Dominic's, Stone.)

Dr Bartholomew Woodlock, Archbishop of Ardagh and Newman's successor at the CUI, who had kept in touch with him over the years, called to see him in April 1890. They discussed the 'present state' of the university.[148]

On 20 July 1890 Newman, seated in the recreation room of the Oratory, received an Address from the Catholic Truth Society. 'He looked particularly well, and spoke in low but clear tones', in expressing his gratitude 'for this sign of your affection'.[149]

Grace Mozley, the only child of Newman's sister Harriett, had married in 1864 and emigrated with her husband to Australia. Now, as Mrs William Longford, she called, as arranged, on Newman on 9 August 1890. He had not seen her since 1843, when she was four years old. His sister 'had broken off relations with him as he became more Catholic'.[150] Grace wrote a long account of her visit, mentioning the Cardinal's kindness, and that, as she left, he gave her his blessing, 'as he does to all visitors'. On behalf of Newman, Fr Neville presented her with 'a small volume nicely bound of the Cardinal's earlier poems with his and my initials in his own hand'.[151]

On the next day, Sunday 10 August 1890, Newman was taken ill and died of pneumonia during the evening of the following day.[152] His passing was mourned by the great and the humble alike; most of those who mourned him 'were younger by more than half a lifetime ... Within the year his intellectual legacy was provoking controversy...'[153] Throughout his long life Newman had been a vigorous controversialist and a gifted writer. On his death, the issues to which he had applied his redoubtable energy and powerful intellect over many years were still largely unresolved. Newman's pervasive influence had been felt first in the Church of England and, later, in the Church of Rome. His talents and energies were directed by his deep personal spirituality and dedication to what he perceived to be his vocation in life. Undoubtedly, he affected the ways in which Catholicism developed in the Victorian era, but his influence has extended far beyond that period and is active in Christian thought and behaviour today.

The epitaph chose by Newman for his memorial tablet in the cloister wall of the Birmingham Oratory has a haunting elegiac beauty, which reflects the essence of his spiritual odyssey: *Ex umbris et imaginibus in veritatem* – 'Out of shadows and images into truth.'

From far and wide came expressive tributes to Newman; newspapers at many levels and of diverse interests, including 'those of the Jewish community, the sporting fraternities, the local papers of the unimportant towns, filled their columns'[154] with accounts of his distinguished contributions to Christian religious life and regeneration over the many years of his intellectual and pastoral activities. *The Times* of 12 August 1890 wrote of Newman; 'Whether Rome canonizes him or not he will be canonized in the thoughts of pious people of many creeds in England.'[155] In the course of an eloquent panegyric given by Manning in a crowded London Oratory, he declared: 'No living man has so changed the thought of England. His withdrawal closes a chapter which stands alone in the religious life of the century.'[156] 'Thousands of people lined the roads'[157] as the funeral cortege travelled the five miles or so to Rednal, where under the Lickey Hills in Worcestershire,

Newman, in 1854, 'had bought a 3-4 acre plot of land, on which to build an Oratorian rural retreat and also a small cemetery'.[158] In this peaceful setting, his body was buried, as Wilfrid Ward noted, 'in accordance with the instructions he had left, in the grave of his beloved friend Ambrose St John'.[159]

Notes

1. Tristram, 1933, pp. 214–15.
2. Dessain, 1980, p. 164.
3. Ward, 1913, p. 314.
4. LDXXIV.241–2, John Hayes, 13 April 1869.
5. LDXXIV.44, 2 March 1868.
6. LDXXIV.391, Edward Bellasis, 15 December 1869.
7. Dessain, 1980, p. 164.
8. LDXXIX.340, 23 February 1881.
9. LDXXX.191, 27 February 1883.
10. LDXXII.288, footnote.
11. LDXXII.294, footnote.
12. LDXXII.302, footnote.
13. LDXXII.327, 16 December 1866.
14. LDXXIII.67, 22 February 1867.
15. LDXXIV.73, 14 Mary 1868.
16. LDXXVIII.269, 13 November 1877.
17. LDXXX.317, 20 February 1884.
18. Dessain, 1980, p. 148.
19. LDXIX.294, Dr Charles Meynell, 23 January 1860.
20. LDXXIV.112, Edward Bellasis, 1 August 1868.
21. Newman, 1956, pp. 272–3.
22. LDXXV.132, 22 May 1870.
23. Dessain, 1980, p. 148.
24. LDXXIV.389, 14 December 1869.
25. Griffin, 1993, p. 127.
26. Newman, 1992, p. 12.
27. Dessain, 1980, pp. 148–9.
28. LDXXIV.xiii.
29. Dessain, 1980, pp. 151–2.
30. Dessain, 1980, p. 153.
31. LDXXIV.293, 25 July 1869.
32. LDXXIV.297, 27 July 1869.
33. LDXXIV.345, 3 October 1869.
34. LDXXIV.375, 17 November 1869.
35. LDXXIV.384, 18 November 1870.

36. LDXXV.39, 23 February 1870.
37. Newman, 1956, p. 269.
38. LDXXV.118, footnote.
39. LDXXVIII.430-1, Fr Robert Whitty, 20 December 1878.
40. LDXXX.216, F. W. Chesson, 8 May 1883.
41. LDXXX.220, Michael Frost, 17 May 1883.
42. LDXXXI.71, 30 May 1885.
43. LDXXX.373, Joseph Whitaker, 23 June 1884.
44. LDXXX.403, Shirley Day, 27 September 1884.
45. LDXXVI.187, David Brown, 24 October 1872.
46. LDXXVI.364, Miss Rowe, 16 September 1873.
47. LDXXIX.177, 19 September 1879.
48. LDXXIX.242, Matthew Russell SJ, 26 February 1880.
49. LDXXX.19, 6 November 1881.
50. LDXVI.200.
51. LDXXVIII.92, 24 July 1876.
52. LDXXVIII.221, B. M. Pickering, 9 July 1877.
53. LDXXVIII.234, John Hungerford Pollen, 23 August 1877.
54. LDXXVIII.191, 10 April 1877.
55. LDXXVIII, p. 139, footnote.
56. Tristram, 1933, p. 89.
57. LDXXVIII.283, 18 December 1877.
58. LDXXVIII.284, footnote.
59. LDXXVIII.289, 26 December 1877.
60. LDXXVIII.309, 2 February 1878.
61. LDXXVIII.322, 1 March 1878.
62. Chadwick, 1971, part I, p. 308.
63. LDXXVII.69, footnote 2.
64. LDXXVII.71, R. W. Church, 3 June 1874.
65. LDXXVII.87, Lord Coleridge, 3 July 1874.
66. LDXXVII.228, 21 February 1875.
67. LDXXVII.22, footnote.
68. LDXXVIII.198.
69. Ker, 1988, p. 697.
70. LDXXVIII.310, 7 February 1878.
71. LDXXVIII.329, 16 March 1878.
72. LDXXVIII.321, 1 March 1878.
73. LDXXVIII.323, 3 March 1878; LDXXVIII.329, 16 March 1878.
74. LDXXVIII.307, 23 January 1878.
75. LDXXVIII.178, Lord Blachford, 10 March 1877.
76. LDXXVII.98, footnote 3.
77. LDXXVII.199, 20 January 1878.
78. LDXXIX.6 April 1881, from Duke of Norfolk, footnote.
79. LDXXIX.361, 8 April 1881, Duke of Norfolk.
80. LDXXIX.371, 4 May 1881.
81. LDXXIX.398, 21 July 1881.
82. LDXXVIII.259, 25 October 1877, J. R. Bloxam.

83. LDXXXI.xiv.
84. Ker, 1990, p. 715.
85. LDXXIX.xiii.
86. LDXXIX.xiv.
87. Ibid.
88. LDXXIX.23, 10 February 1879.
89. LDXXIX.46–7, footnote, 22 February 1879.
90. LDXXIX.47, footnote, 23 February 1879.
91. LDXXIX.22, 5 February 1879.
92. LDXXIX.47–8, 25 February 1879.
93. LDXXIX.48, Duke of Norfolk, 25 February 1879.
94. LDXXIX.48, Ullathorne, 25 February 1879.
95. LDXXIX.57, Manning, 4 March 1879.
96. LDXXIX.60, Manning, 5 March 1879.
97. LDXXIX.60, 8 March 1879.
98. LDXXIX.61, 8 March 1879.
99. Dessain, 1980, p. 165.
100. Gilley, 1990, p. 397.
101. LDXXIX.51, Ullathorne, 1 March 1879.
102. LDXXIX.76, W. S. Lilly, 12 March 1879.
103. LDXXIX.77, 12 March 1879.
104. LDXXIX.77, from Duke of Norfolk.
105. Newman, 1956, p. 275.
106. LDXXIX.50, 1 March 1879.
107. LDXXIX.72, 11 March 1879.
108. LDXXIX.52, 1 March 1879.
109. LDXXIX.55–6, 2 March 1879.
110. LDXXIX.84, from Cardinal Nina.
111. LDXXIX.85, Cardinal Nina, 20 March 1879.
112. LDXXIX.88, Ullathorne, 22 March 1879.
113. LDXXIX.92, 28 March 1879.
114. LDXXIX, footnote, 12 April 1879.
115. LDXXIX.104, footnote.
116. LDXXIX.xv.
117. LDXXIX.124, W. S. Lilly, 10 May 1879.
118. Sencourt, 1948, p. 277.
119. Harrold, 1945, p. 376.
120. Jaki, 2000, p. 49.
121. LDXXIX.130, 25 May 1879.
122. LDXXIX.148, 2 July 1879.
123. LDXXIX, Appendix I, p. 426.
124. Chadwick, 1972, p. 420.
125. LDXXIX.137, 19 May 1879.
126. LDXXIX.127, footnote.
127. LDXXIX.127, 19 May 1879.
128. LDXXIX.137, 5 June 1879.
129. LDXXIX.173, 29 August 1879.

130. LDXXIX.334, 28 January 1881.
131. LDXXIX.194, Emmeline Deane, 3 March 1887.
132. LDXXIX.181, William Knight, 7 January 1887.
133. Newman, 1956, p. 29.
134. Newman, 1993, pp. 89–91.
135. LDII.57, Richard Greaves, 27 February 1828.
136. LDXXX.94, 9 June 1882.
137. LDXXXI.189, George T. Edwards, 24 February 1887.
138. LDXXXI.145, J. Spencer Northcote, 2 June 1886.
139. Butler, 1926, p. 284.
140. LDXXXI.159–60, 1 September 1886.
141. LDXXXI.277, footnote.
142. Tristram, 1933, pp. 241–2.
143. LDXXXI.276.
144. LDXXXI.277–8, footnote.
145. LDXXXI.276, Cardinal Parocchi, 2 October 1889.
146. LDXXXI.283, footnote.
147. LDXXXI.285.
148. LDXXXI.286, footnote.
149. LDXXXI.289, footnote.
150. LDXXXI.299, footnote (1).
151. LDXXXI.299, footnote (2)
152. LDXXXI.299, footnote (3).
153. Gilley, 1990, p. 422.
154. Sugg, Joyce (1996), p. 298.
155. Johnson, H. J. T., *The English Catholics 1850–1950*, (ed), G. A. Beck, Burns, Oates, 1950, p. 262.
156. Sencourt, R., 1948, p. 262.
157. Trevor, Meriol, 1962, p. 646.
158. LDXVI.227, Miss Giberne, 18 August 1854; LDXVI.207, 28 July 1854, note; Murray, Placid, 1980, p. 461.
159. Ward, Wilfrid, 1913, vol. II, p. 537.

Chapter Nine

Sainthood

Newman's Views on Sainthood

Sainthood was a subject on which Newman had, as usual, well-argued opinions reflecting his wide reading and willingness to challenge some conventional views. To one of his 'special friends' – Henry Wilberforce – who had asked Newman whether he believed that, according to a *Life of the Saints*, St Rose 'when 3 months old, had practised mortification upon her finger'. In reply, Newman 'confessed' that he 'did not think it antecedently impossible, nor in a saint unlikely'. However, he could 'not be sure that it did not happen' and 'the chance of its happening' is one of 'a number of sacred facts which belong to a saint'. Newman concluded with the cryptic comments: 'A Saint is a peculiar being.'[1]

During 1850 Newman exchanged a number of letters with Miss A. Munro, in one of which he emphasized that he had 'no tendency to be a saint – it is a sad thing to say.

Saints are not literary men, they do not love the classics, they do not write, they do not write Tales. I may be well enough in my way, but it is not the "high line". People ought to feel this, most people do. But those who are at a distance have fee-fa-fum notions about one. It is enough for me to black the saints' shoes – if St Philip uses blacking, in heaven'.[2]

In an introductory note to Newman's *Oratory Papers No.7, Lent 1853*, Dom Placid Murray, referring to Newman's *Fragment of the Life of Saint Philip Neri* that follows, states that it should be judged 'not so much as a piece of original research, but as an interpretation' – Newman's own view of St Philip's life and character.[3] Newman himself stated that there are 'two ways in which the life and actions of a Saint may be viewed piecemeal and as a whole'. The latter approach to 'considering the Saints and their doings' is not only valuable in itself but has added value in viewing them as 'living and breathing men, as persons and invested with personal attributes and a character of their own, and peculiarities of habit and feeling and opinion such as belong to him and not another'. He wanted to possess a 'living view' of St Philip, whom he had never seen but wished 'to be as though I had seen him'. The resultant 'Fragment' (of over 5,000 words) reflects fully Newman's approach to writing about the saints.[4] Doubtless, he recalled the problems associated with Faber's *Lives of the Saints* (see Chapter 4) when, following Ullathorne's instruction, publication had been suspended because they were considered to be 'unsuited to England, and unacceptable (offensive) to Protestants'. Publication was resumed in early 1849.[5]

In a letter dated 9 April 1854, to J. Spencer Northcote, Newman admitted that it is 'very disgraceful not to engage to write a life of St Philip'. Although he wanted to 'see a life of St Philip written which is *not* devotional, but historical, he felt that he 'might not be able to undertake such a task for 10 years to come'.[6] Newman's distinction between the devotional and the historical treatment of the lives of the saints is more fully discussed in Volume II of *Historical Sketches*. He reflects that reading the life of St Augustine or St Basil left him 'wandering in a labyrinth', of which he 'cannot find the centre or heart, and am but conducted out of doors again when I do my best to penetrate within'. With appealing candour, he comments: 'This seems to me, to tell the truth, a sort of pantheistic treatment of the Saints . . . They do not manifest a Saint, they mince him with spiritual lessons.'[7] He was, of course, aware that 'numerous imperfections are likely to attach to a work which is made up, in so great a measure as this is, of personal opinions and views, of minute historical details, and of translations'. Newman closes this spirited Introduction by admitting that he was 'getting far more argumentative than I thought to be when I began; so I lay my pen down, and retire into myself'.[8]

The Cult of Saints

The cult of saints in public worship of the early Christian Church originated with the honouring of those who had suffered martyrdom for their faith, such as St Stephen. With the sanction of local bishops, the veneration of these heroic Christian witnesses developed into distinctive cults associated with their lives. It was not until later in the history of the early Church that the status of saint was extended to those who were not martyred but who openly confessed their adherence to a Christian way of life; these holy persons became known as confessor saints. A further progression of potential candidates occurred when those Christians who through their lives had shown what was termed 'heroic virtue' and had died 'holy deaths' were regarded as worthy candidates for sainthood.

Donald Attwater, in his 'Introduction' to a revised edition of *Butler's Lives of the Saints* observed:

> It has been suggested ... that in the case of holy people held in honour during the first thousand years of the Church's history either for their virtues or for their violent death in the cause of Christ, it is by no means easy to determine which among them should be recognised as saints and as entitled to the prefix often attached to their names in historical records.

He considered that: 'So far as such servants of God have a claim to the honour of saintship, they own the privilege to what is called an "equipollent" (i.e. virtual) canonisation.' Some names 'in the Roman Martyrology' may conceivably have appeared 'due to the strange blunders of medieval copyists, others representing nothing more than prehistoric sagas which have been embellished and transformed by a Christian colouring'.[9]

By the tenth century, the local and relatively informal regulation of nominating saints had developed into the more centralized authority exercised by the Holy See. Under Gregory IX (1227–41) this discipline became enforced by Canon Law. Under the Second Vatican Council (1962–5) a new compilation of existing church laws was undertaken.

The process of canonization is noted to have two stages: beatification, 'which allows veneration of the blessed, (while) canonisation requires it'. This final stage 'usually requires two miracles', one of these is at the beatification level, the other at the canonization stage. These miracles are 'to attest the heroic virtue of the saint'.[10] The bishop of the diocese appoints a 'postulator of the cause', whose duty is to promote the cause and to ensure that the candidate's life and reputation for sanctity or heroic virtue, including all writings, are strictly evaluated. Any miracles that may be attributable to the person being studied are also subject to intense scrutiny by theologians and other specialists who have to be satisfied that there is no conventional, scientific explanation for the specific cure or other occurrence. Newman's own view of miracles has been given, in his Anglican days, in a letter to his close friend J. S. Bowden about a publishing proposal: *Saints of the British Isles*, 'I think they (miracles) may be treated as matters of fact, credible according to their evidence.'[11]

'Ecclesiastical Miracles'

The nature of miracles had attracted Newman's attention in the 1860s, when he responded vigorously to Kingsley's unprovoked attack on his personal probity and was stirred to write, in 1864, and at phenomenal speed, the *Apologia pro Vita Sua*, as seen in Chapters 2 and 6. In the following year a second edition appeared, entitled *History of My Religious Opinions*, in which polemical references to Kingsley were removed and additional appendices were introduced, among which was one headed *Ecclesiastical Miracles*.[12] Newman declared that: 'Catholics believe that miracles happen in any age of the Church, though not for the same purposes, in the same number, or with the same evidence, as in Apostolic times', when these 'were wrought in evidence of their divine mission', and in a country in which 'faith and prayer abound they will be more likely to occur, than where faith and prayer are not'.[13] Newman also commented that 'although faith and prayer obtain miracles ... it is often very difficult to distinguish between a providence and a miracle ... providential mercies are what are sometimes called "*grazie*" or "favours"'.[14]

Newman then referred to earlier proposals he had made in 1826 when he 'proposed three questions about a professed miraculous occurrence:

1. Is it antecedently *probable*?
2. Is it in its *nature* certainly miraculous?
3. Has it sufficient *evidence*?

He then proceeded to apply these 'general principles' to a detailed examination of the specific charges brought by Kingsley concerning miraculous phenomena associated with St Walburga.[15]

Opening of Newman's Cause

Newman's cause was opened in Birmingham in 1958 and he was declared 'Venerable' by Pope John Paul II in 1991; this title is noted to be derived from the Latin *venerabilis/venerari*: 'to regard with religious awe' and 'is given to the Servants of God after the state of their heroic virtue or martyrdom has been proved and a solemn decree to that effect has been signed by the Pope'.[16]

Father Paul Chavasse, Provost of the Birmingham Oratory, of which he has been a member since 1980, was elected Postulator-General of the Oratorian Confederation in 2000 and has assiduously cultivated Newman's cause for canonization. As noted, this involves an exacting examination and assessment of the life, writings and reputation as well as any reported miraculous occurrences which may be thought to be attributable to the intervention of the Venerable John Henry Newman. Only after such rigorous assessments by medical experts and learned theologians, may it be decided that there is no contemporary scientific explanation, in some cases, for the reported phenomena. Father Chavasse was reported, in October 2006, to have said that he and his fellow Oratorians were 'quietly confident. The Pope is extraordinarily keen on Cardinal Newman so I am sure he would be happy if the work by the Archdiocese of Boston was upheld by the Congregation for the Causes of Saints'.[17] (The Archdiocese of Boston was involved because of the alleged complete recovery of a disabled man in Boston, Massachusetts.)

With special insight, Father Chavasse has commented on Newman's 'truly extraordinary' influence as a preacher in both Anglican and Catholic pulpits, which made him 'that sure guide for Christian men and women in their efforts to lead holier and more prayerful lives'. Throughout the long years of his ministry, Newman was always conscious of his pastoral duties as a preacher, and to which he dedicated himself zealously. His pastoral sermons have become 'established as one of the great classics of Christian spirituality'.[18]

In the early 1930s, Father Henry Tristram, a distinguished member of the Birmingham Oratory, produced an absorbing collection of the many dedications with which Newman prefaced his numerous publications. In expressive language, he acknowledged the friends who had inspired his life and supported him in the various vicissitudes of his life. Such luminous personalities included Keble, Pusey, Bowden, Copeland and Ullathorne. Fr Tristram's sensitive narrative on these dedications shows that Newman held deeply felt loyalties and affection for his friends and these elements of his character were particularly influential throughout his life.[19]

Father Drew Morgan, Provost of the Pittsburgh Oratory, has drawn attention to Peter Jennings' account of the historic pronouncement which was made by another prominent Birmingham Oratorian, Father Gregory Winterton, at the closure of the centenary celebrations of Newman's birth: that 'their founder's influence was now worldwide', and they were 'completely confident that in God's good time he will be canonized and made a Doctor of the Church, to give the Church's authority to his already great and increasing spiritual influence'.[20] Father Drew Morgan briefly examines the nature of the office of Doctor of the Church and discusses whether Newman fulfils the established *Norms and Criteria* of this historic process. He quotes recent evidence from the writings and addresses of Cardinal Ratzinger (now Pope Benedict XVI) and Pope John Paul II, 'that indicate an affirmative, positive response to Newman's fulfilment of the *Norms and Criteria*'.[21] In conclusion, Fr Morgan asserts that while advocating it, 'Newman's ecclesial doctorate will not be without its challenges', although there is 'no evidence of obstacles regarding his holiness or eminent learning'; but the existing 'restrictive view of the role of this eminent office' may well call for a more expansive approach.[22] Fr Morgan has also emphasized that although we are 'fortunate that Newman like Therese, wrote an autobiography ... it is his *Letters and Diaries* that inform us of the true man ... where we really find him in the long suffering, the confusion, the frustration and the abandonment to Divine Providence, the trust in prayer, the perseverance in charity, the dedication to his mission in God'.[23]

Progression to Beatification

During his historic visit to Britain in May 1982, Pope John Paul II emphasized his long-held and dedicated interest in Cardinal Newman, who had contributed so much to the resurgence of Catholicism in Victorian England and whose influence is also evident across the world today. As noted, Newman's cause had been promoted from the late 1950s and, in 1991, John Paul II had declared him to be *Venerable* – the first step towards canonization.

Interest in Newman's cause has been further advanced because Pope Benedict XVI is known to have first encountered Newman's writings when he was a seminarian. This enlightening introduction has developed into a lifelong commitment.

The second step towards canonization – beatification – entails rigorous evaluation of Newman's life and works, including his remarkable literary and pastoral output of letters, sermons and many other influential writings, such as the *Apologia pro Vita Sua*. In addition to this exacting assessment, the process of beatification is particularly demanding and involves the presentation of incontrovertible evidence that a miraculous event has taken place which may be regarded as attributable to the intervention of the Venerable Cardinal Newman. Such evidence is subject to the strictest scrutiny to ensure that no established scientific explanation could account for the specific healing experienced by the person involved. This systematic investigation by medical experts and Vatican theologians is conducted by the Congregation for the Causes of Saints.

As briefly mentioned earlier, from the United States of America came reports, in 2006, of the alleged miraculous cure of a severely disabled man who had prayed to Cardinal Newman. For some years, the identify of this person was not revealed, although in October 2005, Fr Paul Chavasse had indicated that he was a sixty-year-old permanent deacon in the Archdiocese of Boston.[24] Cardinal Sean O'Malley, Archbishop of Boston, had set up a tribunal to investigate this reported miraculous event and, in 2006, the subject was revealed to be Jack Sullivan from Marshfield, Massachusetts, a deacon of the Archdiocese who had suffered a crippling spinal condition which had prevented him from walking. This severe disablement had caused him to put aside his studies for the diaconate. However, he prayed earnestly to Cardinal Newman that he might be cured of his serious condition, which had not been relieved from an earlier operation. In April 2001 he suddenly experienced a 'return to full health and mobility . . . and the doctors who treated him . . . have no explanation for his cure'.[25] He was able to resume his diaconal studies and no scientific explanation could be given for his remarkable and total recovery.

Fr Paul Chavasse, as postulator, had participated in the final session of the Boston Archdiocesan tribunal and confirmed that he had heard earlier of the deacon's case: with enthusiasm, he declared: 'At last we have a miraculous cure.'[26] The findings of the Boston tribunal, including medical records and sworn testimonies, were carried to Rome by Dr Andrea Ambrosi, the Roman Postulator of the Cause. These comprehensive data were submitted for consideration by the

Congregation for the Causes of Saints. Following a favourable decision and final approval by the Pope, Newman's beatification would be formally approved and he would be given the title of *Blessed*. His cause could then proceed to the final stage of sainthood, for which another attributable miracle would be required.

In April 2008, the Vatican's Congregation for the Cause of Saints made a formal application to the British Ministry of Justice for the exhumation of Cardinal Newman's body from the small cemetery in Rednal, Worcestershire, so that his remains might be entombed in a marble sarcophagus within his memorial church of the Birmingham Oratory. Fr Paul Chavasse has commented that:

> One of the centuries-old procedures surrounding the creation of new saints by the Catholic Church concerns their earthly remains. These have to be identified, preserved and, if necessary, placed in a new setting which befits the individual's new status in the Church.[27]

After several months of negotiation, the Ministry of Justice finally recognized Newman's growing influence in the Catholic Church as well as in religious thought and behaviour in general. On the 118th anniversary of Newman's death, a licence was granted for the exhumation to take place. Peter Jennings, press secretary for the Oratory, has emphasized that the order for exhumation 'had come from the Vatican'. He admitted, however, that 'some people don't want his body moved at all'.[28] Responding to some critical views of the planned exhumation, Fr Paul Chavasse stated that he 'believed the Cardinal would have accepted the will of the Vatican that his body be moved elsewhere ... (he) would have been the first to insist on obeying a request of the Holy See, and the last to insist that his own personal wishes be regarded as immutable'.[29] During the process of Newman's exhumation, the 'normal procedure' includes the 'retrieval of relics', such as fragments of bone taken for veneration. These age-old rituals were said to be 'a sure sign that his beatification is inevitable'.[30]

On Thursday, 2 October 2008, Feast of the Guardian Angels, the grave of the Venerable John Henry Newman was 'excavated with the utmost care'. In a statement issued on Saturday, 4 October 2008, on behalf of the Fathers of the Birmingham Oratory, it was stated:

> During the excavation, the brass inscription plate which had been on the wooden coffin in which Cardinal Newman had rested was recovered from his grave. The Latin inscription on the plate was: *Eminent (issimus) et*

Reverend (issimus) Joannes Henricus Newman, Cardinalis Diaconus S Georgii in Velabro, Obiit die Xi August MDCCXC, RIP. English translation: 'The Most Eminent and Most Reverend John Henry Newman, Cardinal Deacon of St George in Velabro, Died 11 August 1890. RIP.' Brass, wooden and cloth artefacts were found. However, there were no remains of the body of John Henry Newman. The medical and health professionals, who were in attendance at the exhumation, considered that burial in a wooden coffin in a very damp site makes this total decomposition of the body very unsurprising.

Following what some may have believed to be Roman tradition, there appeared to be expectations that Newman had been buried in a lead-lined coffin but exhumation had proved otherwise.[31]

Fr Paul Chavasse had, as indicated earlier, planned that Newman's body might be placed in a marble sarcophagus within the Birmingham Oratory. However, the distinctly limited findings of the exhumation necessitated new arrangements for the veneration of his remains. These included locks of Cardinal Newman's hair (some of which were already in the possession of the Fathers of the Oratory), a small cross and clothing found in the grave and some wood from the Cardinal's original oak coffin. These were placed in a glass-sided casket in the Upper Cloister Hall at the Birmingham Oratory on Friday 31 October and Saturday 1 November 2008. Over this period of dedicated prayer, a series of special Masses were celebrated in the Oratory Church. Fr Chavasse has stressed that the lack of 'substantial physical remains does nothing to diminish our deep reverence for Cardinal Newman'... or 'affect the progress of his cause in Rome'.[32]

On Sunday, 2 November 2008 (the transferred feast of All Saints), the Fathers of the Birmingham Oratory arranged for the celebration of a Solemn High Mass, in Latin, in their church, which was offered by His Grace, the Archbishop of Birmingham, Most Revd Vincent Nichols in the presence of over thirty bishops and priests in the sanctuary, and also hundreds of laity in the crowded church. The sermon was preached by the Very Revd Paul Chavasse, Provost of the Birmingham Oratory and the Postulator of the Newman Cause. During this Mass, the remains of the Venerable John Henry Newman were ceremoniously placed in the Chapel of St Charles Borromeo, a friend of St Phillip Neri, where they will rest while the processes of the beatification of Cardinal Newman continues in Rome.

Over the next few months, the Congregation for the Cause of Saints, set up in Rome by Pope Benedict XVI, continued its detailed scrutiny and evaluation of the medical evidence, in particular, which had been presented by the Procurator. After some media speculation, the Roman panel announced, in early July 2009, that the healing of American deacon Jack Sullivan from a severe debility of the spine in 2001 occurred as a result of widespread intercessions to Newman. Their positive findings were presented to the Holy Father, who signed the formal declaration conferring the title of 'Blessed' on Cardinal Newman. Following beatification, the final stage of sainthood would require a further physical miracle, directly attributable to prayers to Blessed John Henry Newman, and not medically explicable.

Pope Leo XIII

Notes

1. LDXIII.3–4, 1 January 1849.
2. LDXIII.419, 11 February 1850.
3. Murray, Placid (1980), p. 255.
4. Ibid., pp. 256–9.
5. Ibid., pp. 257–8; LDXII.316, 3 October 1848.
6. LDXVI.100–1.
7. Newman, (1857), p. 229.
8. Ibid., p. 231.
9. Attwater, Donald, 'Introduction' to *Butler's Life of the Saints*, 2nd edition, 1956, p. xi.
10. Hardon, John A., SJ, *Modern Catholic Dictionary*, Robert Hale, London, 1981, p. 79.
11. LDIX.298–9, 3 April 1843.
12. Newman, (1865), *Ecclesiastical Miracles*, History of My Religious Opinions, pp. 298–309.
13. Ibid., p. 298.
14. Ibid., p. 299.
15. Ibid., pp. 300–9.
16. Hardon, John A., SJ (1981), p. 558.
17. Caldwell, Simon, *Pope Benedict places Newman on 'fast-track' to canonisation*, *Catholic Herald*, 27 October 2006.
18. Chavasse, Paul 'Newman the Preacher', in Philippe Lefebvre and Colin Mason (eds), *John Henry Newman in His Time*, Oxford, Family Publications, 2007, p. 129.
19. Tristram, Henry *Newman and His Friends*, London, The Bodley Head, 1933.
20. Jennings, Peter (ed), Benedict XVI and Cardinal Newman, Oxford, Family Publications, 2007, p. 105.
21. Morgan, Drew 'Newman Doctor of Conscience: Doctor of the Church?', Philippe Lefebvre and Colin Mason (eds), *John Henry Newman in His Time*, Oxford, Family Publications, 2007, p. 244.
22. Ibid., p. 261.
23. Ibid., p. 255.
24. Pisa, Nick and Simon Caldwell, The 'Miracle' that may give Britain its first saint for 35 years', *Daily Mail*, 19 October 2005.
25. Farrell, Christina, 'Deacon breaks silence over Newman miracle', *Catholic Herald*, 4 November 2005.
26. Ibid.
27. Jennings, Peter, 'Cardinal Newman to be exhumed ahead of imminent beatification', *Catholic Herald*, 18 July 2008.
28. Wynne-Jones, Jonathan, 'Delicate question of a Cardinal and the man he was buried with!', *Sunday Telegraph*, 20 July 2008.
29. Caldwell, Simon, 'Gay rights Activist criticizes plan to exhume Newman', *Catholic Herald*, 5 September 2008, p. 12.
30. 'Pontiff speeds up Newman's Cause', *Catholic Herald*, 8 August 2008, p. 5.

31. Jennings, Peter, 'Report of Cardinal Newman's Internment in August 1890 sheds light on Empty Grave in 2008', Press Release, Birmingham Oratory, 4 October 2008.

32. Jennings, Peter, 'Solemn Return of Cardinal Newman's Remains to the Birmingham Oratory', Press Release, Birmingham Oratory, 10 October 2008.

Bibliography

Allen, Louis, *John Henry Newman and the Abbe Jager*, Oxford, Oxford University Press, 1975.

Amherst, W. J., *The History of Catholic Emancipation and the Progress of the Catholic Church in the British Isles – chiefly in England – from 1771 to 1820*, vols 1 and 2, London, Kegan, Paul & Co., 1886.

Bacchus, J. (ed.), *Correspondence of John Henry Newman with John Keble and Others*, London, Longmans Green & Co., 1917.

Barry, William, *Newman*, London, Hodder & Stoughton, 1905.

Beard, Madeleine, *Faith and Fortune*, Leominster, Gracewing, 1992.

Best, Geoffrey, *Mid-Victorian Britain 1851–75*, London, Fontana Press, 1985.

Boekraad, Adrian J. and Henry Tristram, *The Argument from Conscience to the Existence of God*, Louvain, Editions Nauwelaerts, 1961.

Bossy, John, *The English Catholic Community: 1570–1850*, London, Darton, Longman and Todd, 1976.

Bowden, John Edward, *The Life and Letters of Frederick William Faber DD*, London, Thomas Richardson & Son, 1860.

Briggs, Asa, *Victorian People: a Reassessment of Persons and Themes, 1851–67*, Harmondsworth, Penguin Books, 1990.

Butler, Cuthbert, *The Life and Times of Bishop Ullathorne 1806–1889*, vols I & II, London, Burns, Oates & Washbourne, 1926.

Chadwick, Owen, *The Mind of the Oxford Movement*, London, A & C Black, 1960.

—— , *The Victorian Church, Part I, 1829–1859*, London, ICM Press, 1971.

—— , *The Victorian Church, Part II, 1860–1901*, London, ICM Press, 1972.

—— , *Newman*, Oxford, Oxford University Press, 1990.

—— , 'A Consideration of Newman's Apologia pro Vita Sua' in Paul Vais (ed.), *From Oxford to the People, Reconsidering Newman and the Oxford Movement*, Leominster, Gracewing Books, 1996.

Church, R. W., *The Oxford Movement: twelve years 1833–1845*, London, Macmillan & Co., 1891.

Coulson, John, *Newman and the Common Tradition: a Study in the Language of Church and Society*, Oxford, Clarendon Press, 1970.

—— , 'Newman's Idea of an Open University and Its Consequences today' in James D. Bastable (ed.), *Newman and Gladstone Centennial Essays*, Dublin, Veritas Publications, 1978.

Culler, A. Dwight, *The Imperial Intellect: A Study of Newman's Educational Ideal*, New Haven and London, Yale University Press, 1965.

Davies, Horton, *Worship and Theology in England: from Newman to Martineau, 1850–1900*, London, Oxford University Press, 1962.

Dawson, Christopher, *The Spirit of the Oxford Movement and Newman's Place in History*, London, St Austin Press, 2001.

Dessain, Charles Stephen (ed.), *Catholic Sermons of Cardinal Newman*, London, Burns and Oates (see Newman), 1957.

—— , 'Newman's Philosophy and Theology' in David J. De Laura (ed), *Victorian Prose: a Guide to Research*, New York, Modern Languages Association of America, 1973.

—— , *The Mind of Cardinal Newman*, London, The Catholic Truth Society, 1974.

—— , *Newman's Spiritual Themes*, Dublin, Veritas Publications, 1979.

—— , *John Henry Newman*, Oxford, Oxford University Press, 1980.

Duffy, Eamon (ed.), *Challoner and His Church: a Catholic Bishop in Georgian England*, London, Darton, Longman & Todd, 1981.

—— , *The Stripping of the Altars: traditional religion in England c.1400–1580*, London, Yale University Press, 1992.

Dulles, Avery, SJ, 'Newman: the Anatomy of a Conversion', in Ian Ker (ed.) *Newman and Conversion*, Edinburgh, T&T Clark, 1997.

Ffinch, Michael, *Newman: Towards the Second Spring*, London, HarperCollins, 1992.

Gaughan, J. Anthony, *Newman's University Church: a history and guide*, Dublin, Kingdom Books, 1997.

Gilley, Sheridan, *Newman and His Age*, London, Darton, Longman & Todd, 1990.

——, 'The Ecclesiology of the Oxford Movement: a Reconsideration' in Paul Vais (ed.), *From Oxford to the People, Reconsidering Newman and the Oxford Movement*, Leominster, Gracewing Books, 1996.

——, 'Newman and the Convert Mind' in Ian Ker (ed), *Newman and Conversion*, Edinburgh, T & T Clark, 1997.

Golby, J. M. (ed), *Culture and Society in Britain 1850-1890: a source book of contemporary writings*, Oxford, Oxford University Press, 1992.

Grave, S. A., *Conscience in Newman's Thought*, Oxford, Clarendon Press, 1989.

Griffin, John R., *A Historical Commentary on the Major Catholic Works of Cardinal Newman*, New York, Peter Lang, 1993.

Gwynn, Denis, *A Hundred Years of the Catholic Emancipation: 1829–1929*, London, Longmans, Green & Co., 1929.

——, *Father Luigi Gentili and Second Spring (1835-1848)*, Dublin, Clonmore & Reynolds, 1931.

——, *Bishop Challoner*, London, Douglas Organ, 1946.

——, *Lord Shrewsbury, Pugin and the Catholic Revival*, London, Hollis and Carter, 1946.

Harrold, Charles Frederick, *John Henry Newman: an expository and critical study of his mind, thought and art*, London, Longmans, Green & Co., 1945.

Heimann, Mary, *Catholic Devotions in Victorian England*, Oxford, Clarendon Press, 1995.

Hill, Roland, *Lord Acton*, New Haven, Yale University Press, 2000.

Hollis, Christopher, *Newman and the Modern World*, London, Hollis and Carter, 1967.

Holmes, J. Derek, *More Roman than Rome: English Catholics in the Nineteenth Century*, London, Burns and Oates, 1978.

—— (ed.), *The Theological Papers of John Henry Newman on Biblical Inspiration and on Infallibility*, Oxford, Clarendon Press, 1979.

Houghton, Walter, *The Art of Newman's Apologia*, Yale, Yale University Press, 1945.

Hutton, Richard H., *Cardinal Newman*, London, Methuen & Co., 1891.

Jaki, Stanley L., *Anglican Difficulties* (see Newman), 1995.

——, *Newman's Challenge*, Grand Rapids, William B Eerdmans

Publishing Co., 2000.

Jay, Elisabeth, 'Newman's Mid-Victorian Dream' in David Nicholls and Fergus Kerr (eds), *Reason, Rhetoric and Romanticism*, Bristol, Bristol Press, 1991.

Jenkins, Roy, 'Newman and the Idea of a University' in David Brown (ed), *Newman: A Man for Our Time*, London, SPCK, 1990.

Jenkins, Roy, *Gladstone*, London, Macmillan, 1995.

Jennings, Henry J., *Cardinal Newman: the story of his life*, Birmingham, Houghton & Co., 1882.

Jennings, Peter (ed), *Benedict XVI and Cardinal Newman*, Oxford, Family Publications, 2005.

Kenyon, John, *The Popish Plot*, New York, St Martin's Press, 1972.

Ker, Ian, *Newman: a Biography*, Oxford, Oxford University Press, 1990.

—— , (ed), *Newman the Theologian: a reader*, London, Collins Religious Publishing, 1990.

—— , *Newman on being a Christian*, London, HarperCollins, 1991.

—— , *The Achievement of John Henry Newman*, London, Harper-Collins, 1991.

—— , *Healing the Wound of Humanity: the spirituality of John Henry Newman*, London, Darton, Longman and Todd, 1993.

—— , *Preface to Apologia pro Vita Sua*, Harmondsworth (see Newman), 1994.

—— 'What kind of book is the Apologia?', in Paul Vais (ed), *From Oxford to the People, Reconsidering Newman and the Oxford Movement*, Leominster, Gracewing Books, 1996.

—— , (ed), *Newman and Conversion*, Edinburgh, T & T Clark. 1997.

—— , (ed), *The Catholic Revival in English Literature 1845–1961*, Leominster, Gracewing, 2003.

Koenigsberger, H. G., George L. Mosse and G. C. Bowler, *Europe in the Sixteenth Century*, London, Longman, 1989.

Lash, Nicholas, 'A Seat of Wisdom, a Light of the World: considering the University', in Terrence Merrigan (ed), *John Henry Newman: 1801–90*, Leuven, Louvain Studies, vol. 15, nos. 2–3, 1990.

Lash, Nicholas (ed), *John Henry Newman: A Grammar of Assent* (see Newman), 1992.

Lefebvre, Philippe and Colin Mason (eds), *John Henry Newman in His Time*, Oxford, Family Publications, 2007.

Leslie, Shane, *Henry Edward Manning: his life and labours*, London,

Burns, Oates and Washbourne, 1921.

Leys, N. D. R., *Catholics in England, 1529–1829: social history*, London, Longmans, Green & Co., 1961.

McClelland, V. Alan (ed), *By Whose Authority? Newman, Manning and the Magisterium*, Bath, Downside Abbey, 1996.

McGrath, Fergal, *Newman's University: idea and reality*, Dublin, Brown and Nolan, 1951.

McGrath, Francis, *John Henry Newman: universal revelation*, Tunbridge, Burns & Oates, 1997.

McRedmond, Louis, *Thrown among Strangers: John Henry Newman in Ireland*, Dublin, Veritas Publications, 1990.

Martin, Brian, *John Henry Newman: his life and work*, London, Geoffrey Chapman Mowbray, 1990.

Mathew, David, *Catholicism in England 1535-1935: portrait of a minority: its culture and tradition*, London, Longmans, Green & Co., 1936.

Meenan, F. O. C., *Cecilia Street: the Catholic University School of Medicine 1855–1931*, Dublin, Gill and Macmillan, 1987.

Merrigan, Terrence (ed), *John Henry Cardinal Newman 1801–1890*, Leuven, Louvain Studies, vol. 15, no. 2, 1990.

Meynell, Wilfrid, *John Henry Newman: the Founder of Modern Anglicanism and a Cardinal of the Roman Church*, London, Kegan Paul, Trench, Truebner & Co., 1890.

Moore, James (ed), *Religion in Victorian Britain: Vol III, Sources*, Manchester, Manchester University Press, 1992.

Mozley, Anne (ed), *Letters and Correspondence of John Henry Newman during his life in the English Church*, vols. I & II, London, Longmans, Green & Co., 1898.

Murray, Placid, *Newman the Oratorian*, Leominster, Gracewing, 1980.

Nable, Clyde, *Mystery and Religion: Newman's epistemology of religion*, Lanham, University Press of America, 1988.

Nash, Andrew (ed), *Lectures on the Present Position of Catholics in England: addressed to the Brothers of the Oratory*, Leominster, Gracewing/University of Notre Dame Press (see Newman), 2000.

Newman, Bertram, *Cardinal Newman: a biographical and literary study*, London, G. Bell & Sons, 1925.

Newman, John Henry, *Lectures on the Present Position of Catholics in England: Addressed to the Brothers of the Oratory*, London, Burns, Oates & Co., 1851.

—— , *Historical Sketches*, vol. II, Longmans Green, 1857.

—— , *History of My Religious Opinions*, London, Longman, Green, Roberts and Green, 1865.

—— , *Historical Sketches*, vol. 1, London, Longmans Green & Co., 1872.

—— , *Sermons preached on Various Occasions*, London, Burns, Oates & Co., 1874.

—— , *Essays Critical and Historical*, vol. I, London, Pickering & Co., 1881.

—— , *Essays Critical and Historical*, vol. II, London, Longmans, Green & Co., 1885.

—— , *Selection from the Parochial and Plain Sermons*, London, Longmans, Green & Co., 1900.

—— , *Historical Sketches*, vol. III, London, Longmans, Green & Co., 1913.

—— , (ed) Henry Tristram, *Autobiographical Writings*, London, Sheed and Ward, 1956.

—— , (ed) Charles Stephen Dessain, *Catholic Sermons of Cardinal Newman*, London, Burns and Oates, 1957.

—— , *The Idea of a University Defined and Illustrated*, (ed) Martin J. Svaglic, San Francisco, Rinehart Press, 1960.

—— , *The Via Media of the Anglican Church*, vols. I & II, Westminster MD, Christian Classics Inc., 1978.

—— , *The Kingdom Within: discourses addressed to mixed congregations*, Denville, Dimension Books Inc., 1984.

—— , *The Idea of a University Defined and Illustrated*, (ed) Daniel O'Connell, Chicago, Loyola University Press, 1987.

—— , *An Essay on the Development of Christian Doctrine*, (foreword) Ian Ker, Notre Dame, University of Notre Dame Press, 1989.

—— , *Apologia pro Vita Sua*, (ed) Maisie Ward, London, Sheed and Ward, 1991.

—— , *An Essay in Aid of a Grammar of Assent*, (ed) Nicholas Lash, Notre Dame, Notre Dame University Press, 1992.

—— , *Apologia pro Vita Sua*, (ed) William Oddie, London, J. M. Dent, 1993.

—— , *Apologia pro Vita Sua*, (ed) Ian Ker, Harmondsworth, Penguin Books, 1994.

—— , *Selected Sermons*, (ed) Ian Ker, New York, Paulist Press, 1994.

—— , *Certain Difficulties felt by Anglicans in Catholic Teaching*, (intro) Stanley L. Jaki, Fraser, Realview Books, 1995.

——, *Fifteen Sermons preached before the University of Oxford*, (intro) Mary Katherine Tillman, Notre Dame, University of Notre Dame Press, 1997.

Newsome, David, *The Parting of Friends: the Wilberforces and Henry Manning*, Leominster, Gracewing Books, 1993.

——, *The Convert Cardinals: John Henry Newman and Henry Edward Manning*, London, John Murray, 1993.

Nicholls, Aidan, *From Newman to Congar: the idea of doctrinal development from the Victorians to the Second Vatican Council*, Edinburgh, T & T Clark, 1990.

Nicholls, David and Fergus Kerr (eds), *John Henry Newman: Reason, Rhetoric and Romanticism*, Bristol, Bristol Press, 1991.

Nockles, Peter Benedict, 'Oxford Tract 90 and the Bishops' in David Nicholls and Fergus Kerr (eds), *John Henry Newman: Reason, Rhetoric and Romanticism*, Bristol, Bristol Press, 1991.

——, 'An Academic Counter-Revolution: Newman and Tractarian Oxford's Idea of a University, in *History of Universities*, vol. X, Oxford University Press, 1991.

——, 'Newman and Early Tractarian Politics', in V. Alan McClelland (ed), *By Whose Authority? Newman, Manning and the Magisterium*, Bath, Downside Abbey, 1996.

——, *The Oxford Movement in Context: Anglican High Churchmanship 1760–1857*, Cambridge, Cambridge University Press, 1997.

Norman, Edward, *Church and Society in England 1770–1970: a historical study*, Oxford, Clarendon Press, 1976.

——, *The English Catholic Church in the Nineteenth Century*, Oxford, Oxford University Press, 1985.

——, *Roman Catholicism in England from the Elizabethan Settlement to the Second Vatican Council*, Oxford, Oxford University Press, 1986.

——, *The Roman Catholic Church: An Illustrated History*, London, Thames and Hudson, 2007.

Norris, Thomas J., *Only Life gives Life: revelation, theology and Christian living according to Cardinal Newman*, Dublin, The Columba Press, 1996.

O'Brien, Felicity, *Not Peace but a Sword: John Henry Newman*, Slough, St Paul Publications, 1990.

O'Connell, Daniel (ed), *The Idea of a University* (see Newman), 1987.

Oddie, William (ed), *The Idea of a University* (see Newman), 1993.

Parsons, Gerald (ed), *Religion in Victorian Britain, Vol. IV: Interpretations*, Manchester, Manchester University Press, 1992.

—— (ed), *Religion in Victorian Britain, Vol. I: Traditions*, Manchester, Manchester University Press, 1995.

—— (ed), *Religion in Victorian Britain, Vol. II: Controversies*, Manchester, Manchester University Press, 1995.

Pawley, Bernard and Margaret Pawley, *Rome and Canterbury through Four Centuries: a study of the relations between the Church of Rome and the Anglican Churches: 1530–1973*, Oxford, Mowbrays, 1974.

Pawley, Margaret, *Faith and Family: the life and circle of Ambrose Phillips de Lisle*, Norwich, the Canterbury Press, 1993.

Perrott, M. J. L., *Newman's Mariology*, Southampton, St Austin Press, 1997.

Przywara, Erich (ed), *The Heart of Newman*, San Francisco, Ignatius Press, 1971.

Reynolds, E. E., *Three Cardinals: Newman, Wiseman and Manning*, London, Burns, Oates & Washbourne, 1958.

Rigney, William J., 'Bartholomew Woodford and the Catholic University of Ireland 1861–79', unpublished Ph.D. Thesis, University College Dublin, National University of Ireland, August 1995.

Selby, Robin, *The Principle of Reserve in the Writings of John Henry Cardinal Newman*, Oxford, Oxford University Press, 1975.

Sencourt, Robert, *The Life of Newman*, London, Dacre Press, 1948.

Sugg, Joyce (ed), *A Packet of Letters: a selection from the correspondence of John Henry Newman*, Oxford, Clarendon Press, 1983.

—— , *Ever Yours Affly: 'John Henry Newman and His Circle'*, Leominster, Gracewing Books, 1996.

Sullivan, Emmanuel, *Things Old and New: an ecumenical reflection on the theology of John Henry Newman*, Maynooth, St Pauls, 1993.

Svalgic, Martin (ed), *The Idea of a University* (see Newman), 1960.

Tillman, Mary Katherine (ed), *Fifteen Sermons of John Henry Newman preached before the University of Oxford* (see Newman), 1997.

Tillotson, Geoffrey (ed), *Newman Prose and Poetry*, London, Rupert Hart-Davis, 1957.

Trappes-Lomax, Michael, *Pugin: a medieval Victorian*, London, Sheed and Ward, 1932.

— , *Bishop Challoner*, London, Longmans, Green & Co., 1947.

Trevelyan, G. M., *British History in the 19ᵗʰ century and after: 1782–1919*, London, Longmans, Green & Co., 1948.

Trevor, Meriol, *Newman: the pillar of the cloud*, London, Macmillan, 1962.

—— , *Newman: light in winter*, London, Macmillan, 1962.

—— , *Newman's Journey*, London, HarperCollins, 1996.

Trevor-Roper, H. R., *Religion, the Reformation and Social Change*, London, Macmillan, 1967.

—— , *Catholics, Anglicans and Puritans: seventeenth century essays*, London, Secker & Warburg, 1987.

Tristram, Henry, *Newman and His Friends*, London, Bodley Head, 1933.

Tristram, Henry (ed), *John Henry Newman: centenary essays*, London, Burns, Oates and Washbourne, 1945.

—— (ed), *The Idea of a Liberal Education: a selection from the works of Newman*, London, George G. Harrap, 1952.

—— (ed), *Autobiographical Writings of John Henry Newman* (see Newman), 1956.

Turner, Frank M. (ed), *The Idea of a University*, New Haven, Yale University Press, 1996.

Ullathorne, William B., *The Devil is a Jackass*, Leominster, Gracewing, 1995.

Vais, Paul (ed), *From Oxford to the People: reconsidering Newman and the Oxford Movement*, Leominster, Gracewing, 1996.

Vargish, Thomas, *Newman: the Contemplation of Mind*, Oxford, Clarendon Press, 1970.

Walgrave, J. H., *Newman the theologian: the nature of belief and doctrine as exemplified in his life and works*, London, Geoffrey Chapman, 1960.

Walsh, Walter, *The Secret History of the Oxford Movement*, London, Swan, Sonnenschein & Co., 1898.

Ward, Bernard, The *Dawn of the Catholic Revival in England 1781–1803*, London, Longmans, Green & Co., 1909.

Ward, Maisie, *Young Mr Newman*, London, Sheed and Ward, 1948.

Ward, Wilfrid, *William George Ward and the Catholic Revival*, London, Macmillan & Co., 1912.

—— , *The Life of John Henry Cardinal Newman, Vols. I & II*, London, Longmans, Green & Co., 1913.

Watkin, E. I., *Roman Catholicism in England from the Reformation to 1950*, London, Oxford University Press, 1957.

Wilson, A. N., 'Newman the Writer', in David Brown (ed), *Newman: a man for our time*, London, SPCK, 1990.

Withey, Donald, *John Henry Newman: the liturgy and the breviary*, London, Sheed and Ward, 1992.

Wolffe, John, *Religion in Victorian Britain, Vol. V: Culture and Empire*, Manchester, Manchester University Press, 1997.

Index

Achilli, G., 139, 185, 187–9
Acton, Sir John (Lord), 164
Affirmation Bill (see Newman)
Allies, T.W., 164, 173
Anglicanism/Anglo-Catholicism, 24–5
Arianism, 28–9, 30–1

Badeley, Edward (see Kingsley)
Bagot, Bishop Richard, 36,42, 46, 50
Barberi, Fr Dominic, 67–8, 76, 119
Barnabo, Cardinal, 119
Bellasis, Edward Serjeant, 165
Blachford, Lord (see Rogers, Frederic)
Bowden, John W., 23, 47
Bowden, Mrs J.W., 68, 85, 93, 102, 103
Braye, Lord, 250
British Critic, 35–6
British Magazine, 31
Brown, Bishop Thomas Joseph
    admiration of *The Dream of Geron-tius*, 303
    appreciative of *Letter to Pusey*,208
    delation of Newman, 193
    support for Newman's Oxford plan, 175

Calvinistic influence on Protestantism (see Newman)
Campbell, Lord (see Achilli Trial)
Capes, J.M., 115, 189, 239
Caswall, Edward, 116, 260
Catholic University of Ireland (CUI)
    Birmingham Oratory recall Newman, 157
    church architecture, 153
    CUI: success or failure? 160–1
    Cullen's narrow concept of higher education, 138
    medical faculty founded, 155
    Newman's *Discourses* in Dublin, 140
    Newman's model of higher education, 139
    Newman nominated Rector, 137
    Newman relinquished involvement with CUI, 158–9
    Newman's rising concern about Cullen's proposals, 138–9
    Papal brief established CUI, 150
    The Idea of a University, 244
    University Church in Dublin, 152
Chavasse, Fr Paul, 290, 292–4
Church, R.W., 45, 51–3, 63, 242, 267–8
Church of England, 25, 32, 34, 35, 71, 236–41, 391
Coleridge, Henry James, SJ, 265
Coleridge, Lady (see Newman: portraits)
Coleridge, Lord (see Newman: portraits)
Coleridge, Sir John Taylor (see Achilli Trial; Newman: portraits)
consensus fidelium (see Newman)
Copeland, Rev. William John, 26, 79, 265–6
Cullen, Archbishop Paul
    consecrated Archbishop of Armagh, 134
    created Cardinal, 212
    invited Newman to give lectures, 115
    Papal Brief 1854 (CUI), 150

proposed Newman as president of new university, 136

Dalgairns, J.D. (Bernard), 75, 80, 83-4, 124-5
Darnell, Nicholas, 165, 167
Darwin, Charles: *On the Origin of Species* (1859), 83, 85
Disraeli, Benjamin, 233
Döllinger, Dr Johann Joseph Ignaz von, 190
Donatists, 33-4
Dublin Review, 33

ecclesia docens, 250
ecclesia docta, 250
Elgar, Sir Edward (see *The Dream of Gerontius*),
Emly, Caron (see Monsell, William)
English Catholicism and class distinctions
  'Old' and 'New' Catholics, 240, 241, 307
Erastianism
  and Gorham case, 111
  and Irish Church, 36
  and Oxford Movement, 35
Escourt, Canon E., 200
Essays and Reviews, 209
Evangelical Alliance (see Achilli)

Faber, Frederick W.
  community of 'Wilfridians', 94
  death, 124-5
  Growth in Holiness, 244
  head of London Oratory, 117
  Lives of the Saints, 99
  move to Cotton Hall, 95
  Newman's anxieties over Cotton, 97
  problems with Newman (see Oratorianism)
  Newman corrected Faber's misconceptions 108
Fairbairn, A.M., 260
Froude, Hurrell, 22, 25, 36
  Remains, 37

Galileo (see *Essays and Reviews*)
Gentili, Fr Luigi, 73, 78
Gerontius, Dream of (see Newman)
Giberne, Maria R., 109
Gillow, Dr John, 192-3

Gladstone, William Ewart
  enforced resignation, 213
  furore over *Vatican Decrees*, 214
  Newman's refutation, 214
Golightly, C.P., 38, 45
Gordon, General (see *Dream of Gerontius*)
'Gordon Riots', 112
Gorham, Rev. George, 111

Hallahan, Mother Margaret Mary, 43, 202
Hampden, Renn Dickson, 26
Hawkins, Edward, 18, 27, 41, 66
Hope-Scott, James, 79, 166, 171, 246
Hopkins, Gerard Manley, SJ, 161, 258
Hutton, Richard Holt, 114

Inglis, Sir Robert, 18, 133
Irish Church and Tracts, 24
Irish Church Temporalities Act, 20-1

Jager, Abbé Jean Nicholas, 30
Jenkins, Roy, 143
Jesuits
  Fr Peter Gallwey, 238
Johnson, Manuel, 78-9, 141

Keble, John, 29, 53, 72
Kingsley, Charles, 186, 195-7

Leo XIII
  Accession, 269
  'cult for Newman', 270
Littlemore (see Newman)
Lockhart, William, 78

Macmillan's Magazine (see Kingsley)
Manning, Cardinal Henry Edward, 51, 88, 172, 207-8, 246, 248, 270-1
Marriott, Charles, 66
Martyrs' Memorial, Oxford (see Golightly)
Mayers, Rev. Walter, 3, 9, 277
Maynooth Grant, 133
Meynell, Dr Charles, 261-2
Millais, Sir John Everett (see Newman: portraits)
Monsell, William, Baron Emly, 266
The Month, 202
Morgan, Mgr Drew, 291
Mozley, Anne, 66, 269

Murray, Dom Placid, OSB, 106

Neville, Fr William, 279, 281
Newman, John Henry
  Achilli, charges against, 187
  advised Wiseman of intention to found
    English oratory, 87
  'Apostolicals', 25
  as a stylist, 227, 256
  assumed responsibilities of head of
    family, 6
  banking crisis, 1–2
  birth and early years, 1–2
  Bishop Bagot, 36, 42, 46–7
  Canonisation, process of, 290–5
  Charles Russell, influence of, 67–70
  concern about children's education,
    143–4
  confirmed at Oscott, 74
  conscience, supremacy of, 50
  consensus fidelium, 245, 250
  cor ad cor loquitur, 275
  Cotton Hall handed over to Birming-
    ham diocese, 109
  created Cardinal by Leo XIII, 269–76
  death and burial, 281–2
  death of Newman's father, 5–6
  decline of family lifestyle, 1–2
  declined term 'Newmanites', 24
  dedicated celibacy, 16, 18
  disappointed over Lenten preaching in
    London, 102
  disappointing examination results, 3
  dislike of ostentation and public
    display, 243
  'doctrines never change: devotions
    vary', 243
  Early Fathers of the Church, influence
    of, 25, 31–2
  early schooling at Ealing, 2
  emphasized role of educated laity,
    145–6
  ex umbris et imaginibus in veritatem,
    281
  failure of papal proposal to make
    Newman a bishop, 149
  family circle, 2
  father's lack of business skills, 2
  feared antagonism between Irish
    hierarchy and educated classes,
    245
  founded Oratory School, 163

  Froude's *Remains* (see Froude)
  influence of Walter Mayers and
    Calvinism, 2, 3, 8
  in necessariis unitas, in dubiis liber-
    tas, in omnibus charitas, 251
  Irish higher education (see CUI)
  Kingsley controversy, 195–9
  "Lead, Kindly Light", 10
  lex dubia non obligate, 251
  'Liberalism', views on, 17
  Littlemore, 40–3
  long-held devotion to Our Lady, 93
  made Doctor of Divinity by Pope,
    115
  multi-faceted character, 16
  'Noetics', influence of, 63
  Novationism, fear of, 251
  never lost affection for Anglican
    Church, 113
  oratorian novitiate in Rome, 87
  ordained Anglican minister, 5
  Oriel, influence of, 28
  Oriel tutorship, problems of, 27
  Oxford intellectualism: *genius loci*, 18
  Oxford Mission proposals, 169
  Oxford Movement (see separate entry)
  polemical skills, 185
  portraits painted, 267–8
  principle of reserve or 'economy', 29
  private audience with Pope, 83
  Propaganda vetoes Newman's Oxford
    residence, 176
  raised to priesthood, 86
  recalled from Dublin by Oratory (see
    CUI)
  received into Roman Catholic Church,
    67–8
  resignation from St Mary's, Oxford,
    50
  resignation of Oriel Fellowship, 63,
    65
  retraction of charges against Roman
    Catholicism, 50
  returned to England with Ambrose St
    John, 94
  Sainthood, views of, 286–7
  secured Birmingham premises, 103–4
  secured Oriel Fellowship, 4
  securus judicat orbis terrarium, 33
  spiritual crises and 'three great
    illnesses', 7–10
  study at Rome, 82

sudden death of sister Mary, 6
target of rumours about his return to Anglicanism, 242
Temporalities Act (see Irish Temporalities Act)
Transubstantiation, doctrine of, 29
Trinity scholarship, 2
trying time at Maryvale, 80
'under a cloud' at Rome, 176
via media, 112
viewed Church of England as 'bulwark', 238
vocational commitments, 11
Newman: publications and sermons
An Essay on the Development of Christian Doctrine, 52, 75, 108, 266
Apologia pro Vita Sua, 21, 32, 34, 199, 201
Autobiographical Writings, 7
Certain Difficulties felt by Anglicans in Catholic Teaching, 43–4, 110–12
'Christ upon the Waters', 116
Development of Christian Error, 219
Discourses addressed to Mixed Congregations, 85,108
Essay in aid of a Grammar of Assent, 258
Essay on Justification, 35
Fifteen Sermons preached before the University of Oxford between 1826 and1843, 49, 241
Lead, Kindly Light, 10–1
Lectures on the Doctrine of Justification, 35
Lectures on the Present Position of Catholics in England, 30, 113–14, 245
Lectures on the Prophetical Office of the Church, 265
Letter to the Duke of Norfolk, 216
Letter to the Rev. E.B. Pusey, 206
Letter to the Rev. J.H. Jelf, 45
On Consulting the Faithful in Matters of Doctrine, 192
On the Inspiration of Scripture, 210
Parochial and Plain Sermons, 265
'Parting of Friends', 52
Remarks on the Oratorian Vocation, 84, 121, 252
Select Treatises of St Athanasius in controversy with the Arians, 28

Sermons on Various Occasions (including 'The Second Spring'), 186
The Arians of the Fourth Century, 28–9
'The Dream of Gerontius', 202
The Idea of a University (Discourses), 140
The Tamworth Reading Room, 43
Tracts for the Times (Tract XC), 45–8
'The Second Spring', 186
Noetics (see Newman)
Norfolk, Henry Fitzalan-Howard, 15th Duke of, 214, 268, 270–1, 272, 276
Northcote, Very Rev. J. Spencer, 69, 113, 242

Oakley, Frederick, 39
O'Connell, Daniel, 17, 33, 133
Oratorianism
    Alcester Street Oratory, 102
    'Brothers of the Oratory', 114
    Edgbaston Oratory founded, 116
    foundation of first English Oratory, 93
    London Oratory becomes independent, 118
    London Oratory opened, 107, 117
    move to Birmingham, 98
    Newman's problems with Faber, 94–5
    Our Rule is our Vocation, 84, 121–2, 252
    problems with Faber and London Oratory, 117–120
Oriel College, Oxford, 27, 63, 64, 107, 268
Ornsby, Robert, 212
Oscott College (see Newman)
Ouless, Walter William (see Newman: portraits)

Palmer, William, 22
Papal infallibility, 204, 214, 220–1
Peel, Sir Robert, 17–8, 133, 135, 143
Phillips (de Lisle), Ambrose, 81, 213, 240
'Pillar of Cloud' (see Newman)
Pius IX, death of, 269
Pollen, John Hungerford, 153
Pugin, Augustus Welby, 81
Pusey, Edward Bouverie, 24, 48, 64, 73

Queen's College, Ireland, 133, 139
The Rambler (Home and Foreign Review), 190–4

Relief, Act 1793, 132
Reserve, Principle of (see Newman)
Roden, William Thomas (see Newman: portraits)
Rogers, Frederic (Baron Blachford), 24, 37, 42
Royal University of Ireland, foundation of, 160
Russell, Charles, influence of (see Newman)

St John, Rev. Ambrose, 67, 74, 76, 85, 119, 140, 167
Shrewsbury, John Talbot, 16th Earl of, 80, 95, 97, 108, 117
Simpson, Richard, 190
Spencer, Hon. and Rev. George, 39–40
'Spy' caricature (see Newman: portraits)
Stanton, Richard, 68,82, 94

Talbot, Mgr George, 112, 169, 200, 206
Temporalities Act (see Irish Church)
The Times, 43
Tractarianism (see Oxford Movement)
Tracey, Gerard, 39
Trent, Council of, 74
Trinity College, Dublin (TCD), 132
Trinity College, Oxford, 18, 247–8
Tristram. Fr Henry, 114, 256, 290–1

Ullathorne, Bishop William Bernard, 79, 108, 115, 170–1, 207, 266, 271
Ultramontanism
  Cullen, 134
  Manning, 51
  Newman's views, 243–4
  Wiseman, 220

Vatican Council
  First: 1869–70, 210
  Second: 1962–65, 250
Via media (see Newman)

Ward, William George, 40, 67, 114
Westmacott, Richard, 54–5
Whately, Archbishop Richard, 19, 64
Wilberforce, Henry, 43, 67, 83
Wilson, A.N., 201
Wiseman, Cardinal Nicholas Patrick Stephen
  Achilli Trial papers mislaid by Wiseman, 188
  Death, 206
  Dublin Review, 33
  informed by Newman of English Oratory, 87
  insights into Newman, 75
  invited Newman to Oscott, 75
  Newman's view of Wiseman, 80
  Rambler article, 54, 58
  wanted Newman to open Oratory in London 106
Woodlock, Bishop Bartholomew, 160–1, 280

Lightning Source UK Ltd.
Milton Keynes UK
19 July 2010

157202UK00001B/6/P